AN INTRODUCTION TO EDUCATIONAL ADMINISTRATION
Social, Legal, and Ethical Perspectives

AN INTRODUCTION TO EDUCATIONAL ADMINISTRATION
Social, Legal, and Ethical Perspectives

Emil J. Haller
Kenneth A. Strike
Cornell University

Longman
New York & London

Executive Editor: Raymond T. O'Connell
Developmental Editor: Naomi Silverman
Production Editor: Halley Gatenby
Cover Design: Steven August Krastin
Text Art: J & R Services, Inc.
Production Supervisor: Judith Stern
Compositor: Pine Tree Composition, Inc.

An Introduction to Educational Administration

Longman Inc.
95 Church Street
White Plains, N.Y. 10601

Associated companies:
Longman Group Ltd., London
Longman Cheshire Pty., Melbourne
Longman Paul Pty., Auckland
Copp Clark Pitman, Toronto
Pitman Publishing Inc., Boston

Library of Congress Cataloging-in-Publication Data

Haller, Emil J.
  An introduction to educational administration.

  Bibliography: p.
  Includes index.
  1. School management and organization—
United States. 2. Academic freedom—United
States. 3. Education and state—United States.
4. School management and organization—Law and
legislation—United States. I. Strike, Kenneth
A. II. Title.
LB2805.H26 1986   371.2′00973   85–18071
ISBN 0–582–28441–4

86 87 88 89   9 8 7 6 5 4 3 2 1

To Evelyn, who has enriched my life and profoundly shaped for the better the lives and characters of our children.

E. J. H.

And To Merle Strike, whose quiet integrity remains my foremost example of decent human living.

K. A. S.

Contents

Conclusion   325

Bibliography   331

Author Index   343

Subject Index   345

Preface

This is an unusual textbook for an introductory educational administration course. It departs from the traditional textbook in two very different ways. First, it employs a case study approach. Although several excellent books of cases are currently available, this volume goes considerably beyond a simple collection of administrative incidents. It *uses* cases: they provide a view of reality that shapes and directs the intellectual content of the book. The ideas developed in each chapter are related to the particular case that introduces the chapter, providing both a realistic and a paradigmatic illustration of a common administrative situation. This approach requires the student not only to learn a set of abstractions but also to use them to analyze and solve a real set of problems.

Second, the book involves a significant change in the usual curriculum. Like many educational administration texts, it includes relevant material from the various social sciences. However, it adds to this material discussions of the ethical and legal concepts that apply to the cases and issues discussed. Indeed, these concepts are not only a considerable part of the text; they are used to organize the issues with which we deal. The organization of material tends to reflect our sense of the relevant distinctions to be drawn between the ethical and legal issues more than a breakdown of the social science topics. Thus the standard fare of educational administration courses is reorganized herein and is subservient to a set of problems formulated first and foremost as moral and legal issues.

Our approach offers some considerable advantages over what is commonly done in introductory texts in educational administration. We see the major advantages to be the following.

First, the case study approach makes the material both more relevant to the student and more likely to be applied by the student. Educational administration students are highly oriented to the practice of their profession and are skeptical of research of dubious application. The issues we discuss are real. We are not reluctant to ask the student to think hard about some difficult and abstract ideas. But we tie these ideas to problems that everyone will recognize as real problems. Moreover, by tying the concepts to cases, we hope to teach the student to see specific problems as instances of these concepts. Often, we suspect, students learn to talk about abstract concepts but not to apply them. They learn neither the habit of thinking with them nor the ability to see problems as instances of them. Our use of cases will help the student to see the world through the concepts we teach.

We have given emphasis to a set of ethical and legal issues because of our view of what educational administration is and what educational administrators do. Educational administrators are not just technicians who apply a set of specialized techniques to the solution of technical problems. They are people who must find ways to implement some of the most fundamental ideas of our society. And they are people who must interact with other people to resolve conflicts of principle and personality in ways that are both effective and fair. It follows that educational administration is a moral as well as a technical business. The administrator needs to understand the ideals he or she is attempting to implement and needs to understand what counts as fair treatment of others.

The usual training of educational administrators seems, however, to see them primarily as technicians. For example, many programs take great pains to develop budgeting skills, a facility for motivating subordinates, a capacity to diagnose problems in organizational communication, and competence in research and evaluation techniques. Of course, mastering these technical matters is important. But such training lacks a serious attempt to teach the point of these matters—their links to such basic ideals as intellectual freedom, equality of opportunity, and due process. An education that provides the administrator with technical skills but fails to communicate anything of how ideals of liberty, equality, and fairness apply to administering educational institutions seems sadly incomplete.

Indeed, we believe that many educational administrators fail because they lack the ability to apply such concepts to their work. They fail because they are perceived as not understanding the values their institutions serve or because they are seen as devious or unfair in dealing with students, teachers, or parents. Of course, merely understanding ethical concepts will probably not make the administrator a better person. We do not see ourselves reforming administrative personnel. But understanding will allow men and women of goodwill to articulate their basic concerns and to govern their actions by appropriate ethical standards. And it will help them to be sensitive to how their fellow human beings should be treated. If they have inappropriate ideals or treat others badly, it will not be for lack of understanding.

Organizing technical and social science considerations in a larger moral and legal context has the considerable virtue of allowing them to be studied in their natural habitat. It allows the student to see them against the background of the ideals and standards they should serve. Thus students should get a more complete and whole view of their role and should gain a sense of the point and the limits of the skills they learn. Many professionals show the limits of overly narrow training. Physicians can come to treat people as malfunctioning machines, and lawyers can see justice as little more than a complex chess game requiring adroit courtroom moves. Educational administrators, in turn, are often accused of viewing students as statistics, faculty as sources of resistance and inertia, and parents as bearers of complaints. In these instances, the administrator has ceased to be an educator and has become a husbander of dollars and a manipulator of persons. We are not so naive as to believe that one text will cure all the ills to which the species *Homo administratus* is prone. We do, however, believe that we can get students off on the right foot by beginning their professional education in a way that locates the technology and science of administration in its larger moral and legal setting.

We are grateful to Sidney Doan and Berni Oltz, who typed, proofread, retyped, and reproofread our often illegible manuscripts; who were understanding of lost bibliographic entries, misplaced text, last-second changes, and unreasonable deadlines; and who were both competent and cheerful through it all. The book would not have been possible without their dedication.

We also wish to thank our students, on whom we tested our cases and our arguments, and our colleagues, including those at the University of British Columbia, who read and commented on portions of the manuscript.

Finally, we should note that there is a compelling rationale for the ordering of our names on the cover—*H* precedes *S* in the alphabet. We have contributed equally to this work, except for the errors, which should be ascribed to my coauthor.

AN INTRODUCTION TO EDUCATIONAL ADMINISTRATION
Social, Legal, and Ethical Perspectives

Introduction:
Administrative Problems

The Nature of Administrative Problems

Educational administrators are, above all, problem solvers. It is rare that the administrator gets the opportunity to develop a new program from the ground up. Usually the administrator inherits a program together with its budget, its staff, its clientele, and its problems. In these situations some problems are likely to be long-term ones. The program has a certain weakness, the budget is too small, or the staff needs improvement. Here the administrator needs to move the organization in a profitable direction over a reasonable period of time.

These chronic and endemic difficulties are not the only kind to face practitioners. Other problems require immediate attention. Something has gone wrong, someone has done or not done something, someone is angry, someone is demanding. Here the administrator must act and act quickly. Indeed, the "fire fighting" that these immediate problems require often precludes giving sufficient attention to long-term issues. However, three features are shared by almost every problem, regardless of its duration.

Problems Occur in a Concrete Set of Circumstances   A problem is more than a question to which one does not know the answer. It is, rather, a clash between someone's expectations, desires, ideals, or principles and current circumstances. Practical problems do not arise simply from a lack of understanding. We have a problem when something is wrong or when something can be made better. We may need to understand something in order to solve a problem, but the simple failure to understand is not in itself a problem. Further, people living in the same set of concrete circumstances can have different problems because they have different expectations or values. Concrete circumstances are necessary for problems, but they do not become problematic unless they are at odds with what we want them to be or with what we believe they ought to be. Circumstances are problematic when they conflict with our values.

An important corollary of this point is that the same objective set of circumstances presents different problems to different participants. A single event may present different and inconsistent problems. Perhaps an example will help to illustrate this. Recently, in a little rural community, a small group of fifth- and sixth-grade pupils was discovered smoking marijuana behind their school—an event that triggered considerable discussion and alarm in the town. Note that the "objective facts" were the same for all parties—eleven-year-old children were using drugs. However, these same facts triggered various conceptions of what the problem was. For some people the problem was the lack of a drug education program in the elementary grades. For others, it was educators' relative indifference to the circulation of "soft" drugs. For still others the issue was teachers' failure to supervise their charges adequately. Undoubtedly there were other conceptions of "the problem" in the community. The important point to note, however, is that as a result of these differing conceptions, the school superintendent was presented with several problems, not one. As a consequence, *any* action he took in response to this event was likely to be seen as inadequate by substantial numbers of people. For example, if he implemented a new drug education program, that would surely be judged an inadequate response by people who thought teachers were failing to keep track of the whereabouts of their children. This, then, is one reason administrators often find themselves in trouble: They are seldom presented with a problem. Rather, a single event generates several problems.

Problems Call for Action   Saint Francis is credited with the prayer, "Lord, grant me the serenity to accept the things I cannot change, to change the things I can, and the wisdom to know the difference." No doubt there are problems about which nothing can be done and others that will take care of themselves without human intervention. Nevertheless, problems are circumstances that are somehow deficient and about which something needs doing. A problem is a situation that calls for action. An obvious implication of this point is that the kind of knowledge educational administrators need is knowledge about what to do.

Knowledge capable of guiding action has some special requirements that distinguish it from theoretical knowledge. Practical knowledge must inform an administrator about the consequences of actions that the administrator can perform. Educational practice is aided little by theories exploring relationships among variables that cannot be manipulated; yet much research in administration is concerned with just such variables. Literally thousands of studies concern the effect of teachers' values on various things, but no one really knows how values are changed. Also, knowledge about the consequences of a course of action is insufficient as a guide to action. Knowledge about what to do also involves knowledge about what actions are permissible or right. Generally, two kinds of knowledge are relevant if the administrator is to know what is right or permissible: knowing what is legal and knowing what is moral. We thus suggest that three kinds of knowledge are important for the administrator in dealing with problems: One must know the consequences of one's actions, one must know whether one's proposed actions are legal, and one must know whether one's proposed actions are moral.

Problems Can Be Thought About   The kind of knowledge required for thinking about problems differs from theoretical knowledge. However, it does not follow that practical matters cannot be thought about in systematic or fruitful ways. Indeed, the central purpose of this book is to help the administrator to think about problems.

Of course, this is a cliché. No one is likely to disapprove of thinking, and every book on every topic will want to claim the virtue of helping people to think better about that topic. The important abilities are recognizing what is meant by "thinking better" and knowing how it is done. Our approach is a function of two ideas.

First, being able to think about an event depends primarily on possessing a set of concepts capable of illuminating it. Being able to think about something is not just knowing some procedure or being open to new ideas; it is a matter of having ideas that can be used. To think about the problems of educational administration, one needs a set of concepts that are useful for doing so. If we are right in what we have said about the kinds of knowledge that are important to the solution of administrative problems, the concepts one will need are to be found in the social and behavioral sciences, law and ethics. To think about administrative problems, one needs to know, for example, about leadership, due process, and individual rights. Such concepts are the tools of thought. Accordingly, one of the purposes of this volume is to introduce appropriate concepts from the behavioral and social sciences, law and ethics.

The second idea is that in order to employ a concept effectively to think about a problem, one must learn to see the problem in terms of the concept. The study of educational administration is rather infamous for its minimal effect on the behavior of administrators. Jean Hills, for example, a respected scholar in educational administration, has written a rather plaintive account of how little use he found his social science theories when he left academic life to serve as a school principal (Hills, 1975). One possible cause of this difficulty is that students of administration may not learn to see the routine phenomena with which they deal in terms of the concepts they have learned. It is one thing to know what federal courts have had to say about due process. It is quite another to be able to see placing an anonymous letter of complaint into a teacher's file as a violation of due process. To think about real problems, one needs to be able to see real events in terms of concepts that are useful for thinking about them.

To assist the student to see the world in terms of useful concepts, we link the concepts we wish to teach in this volume to a set of cases. These are what a lawyer might call hard cases: cases in which the evidence is conflicting and the decision is difficult. Reasonable people will be able to disagree about them. They are, however, useful devices to allow the student to grasp both the application and the difficulties of a range of points.

In presenting these concepts and in analyzing these cases, we do not assume that there is always a right or a best answer. Some answers are, however, more reasonable than others, and some courses of action are more defensible than others. We believe that the student of educational administration who considers the ideas and the cases we present will be a more thoughtful and, therefore, a better administrator.

Ways of Thinking about Administrative Problems

We have claimed that three kinds of knowledge are particularly important to thinking about educational administration. The first has to do with knowing the consequences of our actions, the second is legal knowledge, and the third is ethical knowledge. We need to characterize briefly each of these sorts of knowledge.

Knowing the Consequences of Our Actions   The prevailing orthodoxy concerning knowledge about the consequences of actions treats such information as scientific knowledge—a matter for the behavioral and social sciences. To have it is to be in the possession of social or behavioral theories whose predictions have been confirmed by empirical evidence. These theories are also the basis of our ability to forecast the consequences of our actions. Thus if we wish to know the consequences of our behavior, we should turn to disciplines such as psychology, sociology, and economics.

Is this a defensible view? Though we do not wish to discourage or disparage disciplined scientific inquiry into educational administration, we want to suggest that this view is limited. Its strengths and weaknesses can be expressed in three points.

First, theories and concepts of social and behavioral science disciplines provide important ways of seeing educational phenomena. However, few of these theories are well confirmed or provide clear and accurate predictions concerning the consequences of administrative behavior (or any other kind). Further, each discipline provides many competing theories for the same phenomena. In psychology, for example, an act may be viewed from behavioristic, psychoanalytic, and Gestalt perspectives, to name but a few—and each of these has numerous variations. Many of these provide useful insights and important suggestions for action, but the disciplines that generated this multitude of competing theories provide no guidance to a school administrator regarding which is appropriately applied to a particular problem he or she faces. From sociology, the notion of socioeconomic status (SES) is important for understanding many social phenomena. A great deal is claimed concerning SES and how it functions in educational events. Many of those claims are controversial. Yet an administrator who lacked the concept would lack an important tool for observing what goes on. A good deal of interest would escape attention.

Second, the concepts and theories of social and behavioral science disciplines often are not organized as effective guides to action. The first consideration of an academic discipline is to find ways of understanding the world. The questions a discipline asks may be important for advancing such understanding. But the concepts of a discipline need not provide handles for actions, and the questions that occupy disciplinary scholars are not the problems that occupy educational administration. The concept of anomie may be very important for understanding violence in a society. Indeed, it may be important for understanding school violence. But unless knowing about anomie indicates that the administrator can deal with some problem—say, vandalism—by manipulating some variable within his or her power to manipulate, a theory of anomie will be of little value as a guide to action. It will do the administrator little good to know that anomie may be a product of the decline of religious faith or that it may be more pronounced in Protestant countries. Such ideas may be both true and illuminating, but they offer few guides for action.

Third, much of the knowledge that is important to effective administrative practices is not, in any sense, scientific. It is a matter of knowing how something is done in a given organization, what the common practices are, how certain matters are routinely accomplished, how people have agreed to deal with one another, or what the traditions and common understandings are. Some of this information is codified: It appears in a state law, a collective bargaining agreement, or a written school board policy. Most of it is not. For instance, it is important for an administrator to know who needs to be consulted in developing a policy or a program. But knowing who to consult is often a matter of knowing an organization's traditions, the kinds of practices it has evolved, or the character and expectations of individuals in the organization. An approach to working with people may succeed in one organization and not another for no other reason than that the organization's members have evolved different traditions and expectations. Thus for much of what an administrator does and how successfully he or she does it, social science theories are irrelevant.

These comments on the character of social science knowledge are not meant to suggest that it is unimportant in the study of educational administration. The ability to see educational organizations through the concepts of various social science disciplines is important. Nevertheless, our sense of the potential remoteness of social science theory from concrete problems has led us to organize this volume around classes of problems. This has the asset of tying research to a context in which it makes a difference and the liability of obscuring its theoretical organization; this is a positive trade.

Legal Knowledge   An essential component of success as an educational administrator is the ability to work within the framework provided by our legal system. The administrator does not need to be able to deal with legal details; lawyers can handle those. But administrators cannot have lawyers accompany them on their daily rounds. They need a basic sense of what problems and situations generate litigation and what kinds of actions are likely to generate legal difficulties. This requires a grasp of some basic legal concepts and the ability to apply them to real cases.

The avoidance of unnecessary litigation is not the only, or even the most important, reason for knowing something about education law. The law is one way in which a society formulates its principles of justice and fairness and applies them to concrete situations. Thus a study of the law can be a way of discovering the character of some basic moral principles and studying them in concrete applications.

Two sources for the law should be distinguished. One major source is legislative. Laws are passed by legislatures, school boards, or other groups who are empowered to create statutes. The second source is judicial. Judges and courts apply and interpret the law, particularly in areas where the law is expressed in highly abstract and general form, such as the U.S. Constitution. Judges are significant in interpreting what the law is. The constitution says that every citizen is entitled to the equal protection of the law. What counts as equal protection has been, in large part, decided by judges.

Legal reasoning is the process whereby legal abstractions are refined and applied to concrete cases, particularly new or novel ones. It characteristically employs a kind of reasoning by example (Levi, 1948). Judges will seek to govern their decisions by the opinions of judges in prior similar cases. A legal argument appeals to some set of established legal precedents and is usually designed to show that a given case is sufficiently similar to (or different from) a given precedent such that the rule of law expressed in that precedent should (or should not) be applied in the current case. In the process of considering these relevant similarities and differences, judges will be required to formulate a viewpoint that expresses the reasons for their judgment. Their opinions will further refine the legal doctrine employed for considering a certain type of case and will contribute to the basis for thinking about further cases.

Such case law is important to the student of educational administration not only because it is a crucial source of information concerning what the administrator's duties and obligations are but also because it provides one model of a way in which abstract principles, often principles of fairness or justice, are applied to concrete situations. We learn about the meaning and application of the concept of equal protection to the education of minority children from a careful reading of *Brown v. Board of Education of Topeka.*

Ethical Knowledge   This kind of knowledge is difficult to characterize. On the one hand, there is little agreement concerning moral principles and moral reasoning. Indeed, in philosophical circles there is much doubt about whether moral knowledge is possible and whether moral reasoning can be objective (see Ayer, 1935). On the other hand, moral knowledge and the capacity to engage in moral reflection are crucial to the administrator. Perhaps the characteristic that is most to be desired in any individual who has the power to make important decisions concerning other people's lives is that this power be used in an ethical fashion. Administrators are quite rightly expected to act in ways that are not only effective and legal but also principled. It is important for the administrator to be able to judge an action from a moral point of view and to be able to evaluate and construct moral arguments.

Here we assume that it is possible to construct cogent moral arguments and that moral knowledge is possible. We do not mean by this that there is always one right answer to a moral problem, that every issue can be clearly decided, or that reasonable people never disagree. We do, however, believe that some moral arguments can be shown to be better than others. Cogent moral arguments, for example, must meet standards of consistency and impartiality. A person who will not apply standards to himself used to judge the conduct of others is inconsistent. Moreover, there do appear to be some cases where we know something to be wrong. Do we not, for example, know that it is wrong to discriminate against people on account of their race?

It is not possible for us to defend here the claim that objective moral reasoning is possible (see Strike & Soltis, 1985). Perhaps the best defense is the plausibility of the moral arguments we shall construct throughout the text. We can, however, provide a brief characterization of the nature of moral questions and the factors we believe are important in moral judgments.

Moral judgments should be distinguished from value judgments (Strike & Soltis, 1985). Philosophers have often wished to distinguish between judgments about what things are good and judgments about what things are right. The claims that the Mona Lisa is a good painting, that ice cream tastes good, or that Harvard provides a good education are judgments of value, but they are not moral judgments. Usually to say that something is good is to say that it meets some appropriate standard of evaluation. Such standards may be, or may include, moral criteria. When we say that someone is a good person, we often mean that he or she is a moral person. However, typically when we describe some object or event as good, we are not making a moral judgment about it.

Moral judgments, by contrast, concern the rightness of actions. To say that an action is moral is to say that it meets some appropriate standards for rightness or correctness. Actions may be good as well as right. If someone enjoys skiing, that makes it a good thing to do. It does not make it moral or immoral. Being charitable, however, may be both good and right.

One reason for distinguishing moral judgments from value judgments is to make it clear that moral judgments are not mere statements of personal preference or taste. If you claim that olives are good and we say they aren't, we have not said much more than that you like olives and we don't. We expressed our tastes or preferences; we did not really disagree about anything. If, however, we claim that it is OK to be dishonest and you claim that it is not, we have done more than express our personal preference about honesty. We have disagreed about something. A debate about whether one should be honest makes sense in a way that a debate about whether one should like the taste of olives does not.

Often when people disagree about some matter, one will retort, "That's a value judgment." The phrase "that's a value judgment" is a thought stopper. It means that a matter of individual taste or preference is being examined and that further discussion is useless. There is no right or wrong about it. Such an assertion, said in the context of a discussion of liking olives, is reasonable. Said in the context of a discussion of the merits of honesty, it is not. It is important to be clear that, in this sense, moral judgments are not value judgments.

Just as moral judgments are not matters of individual preference, they are not matters of collective preference. To say that some act is moral is to say more than that everyone approves of it or that it has been democratically chosen; it is to say that it is the right thing to do. If morality were merely a matter of collective preference or democratic choice, it would be impossible to hold that societies can behave in immoral ways. Does anyone seriously believe that, if most Germans agreed with Hitler's treatment of Jews, that treatment was moral for Germans? Or since slavery was a democratically chosen practice in some states before the Civil War, that slavery was a moral practice? If morality was a matter of democratic choice, it would be impossible to have an unjust law in a democratic society. Morality is not just what most people approve or agree to.

The final thing to note is that moral questions cannot be settled simply by an appeal to facts (Moore, 1959). We may know, for example, that a given action produces a certain consequence. To know that that action is moral, we must also know that we ought to produce that consequence. Indeed, it is often not sufficient to conclude that an action is right to know that it produces good consequences. There will be cases when the administrator can produce a better result by being devious or unfair. It does not follow that it is right to do so. Generally, no amount of knowledge about the consequences of our actions is sufficient to show that an action is right. There is always a moral residue. To be able to justify the rightness of an action, one must be able to show that it is consistent with moral principles.

How, then, does one justify a moral judgment? This is a most difficult question, on which there is much disagreement. Here we wish to express what we believe to be some very fundamental criteria for evaluating moral judgments. The concepts we shall sketch will be appealed to or presupposed frequently in the text.

We can develop these moral criteria by means of an analysis of a familiar moral idea. Take, for example, the Golden Rule: "Do unto others as you would have others do unto you." What kinds of commitments does this involve? What can be said for it?

The Golden Rule seems primarily a way to affirm that ethical judgments should meet certain standards of formal adequacy. In proposing that how we wish to be treated should be the standard for how we should treat others, it affirms the importance of a particular kind of consistency that can be termed impartiality. It expresses a rule that can be stated as follows: "Any conduct that is considered to be appropriate treatment of person A must also be considered appropriate treatment for person B, when A and B are similarly situated." Persons who are unwilling to apply to themselves, their families, or their groups the same principles that they apply to others behave inconsistently.

Looked at in a slightly different way, the Golden Rule can be seen as expressing the demand that we be willing to generalize or universalize any principle of conduct we apply to others. Philosopher Immanuel Kant (1956) expressed the idea as a rule he called the categorical imperative. The categorical imperative demands that people act so that the rule that describes their behavior could consistently be willed to be a universal rule of human conduct. One should not lie unless one is willing to be lied to. One should not steal unless one is willing to be stolen from. We must be willing to treat our moral principles as moral universals.

The Golden Rule thus expresses some principles for the formal adequacy of moral judgments, consistency, impartiality, and universality.

Other moral ideas are also presupposed by the Golden Rule. It assumes that it matters how people are treated. In doing so, it assumes that human beings are objects of intrinsic worth. That is why how they are treated matters. Therefore, it is wrong to treat other people as though they were merely means to an end. They must be accorded the dignity and respect due to beings who are ends in their own right.

Also implicit in the Golden Rule is a concern for actions that have desirable consequences. If we would do unto others as we would have them do unto us, we must be concerned for how our actions affect the well-being of others. Not only that, we must be concerned to understand how others see the consequences of our actions. We need to be able to assess the desirability of the consequences of our actions from their point of view.

Finally, the Golden Rule requires us to judge our actions according to the kind of principles we have just noted (see Kant, 1956). In doing so, it also presupposes the value of reflecting on our actions. In demanding that we respect such principles as consistency, impartiality, and universality, it implies the value of reason. It indicates that honesty, rationality, truth, and a respect for evidence are important moral values (see Peters, 1970).

These considerations can be summarized by expressing them as four criteria for assessing actions and moral principles. Actions and moral principles can be judged to be adequate by the extent that (1) they exhibit consistency, impartiality, and universality; (2) they exhibit equal respect for the value and dignity of persons; (3) they exhibit a concern for consequences that are, and are seen as, good for people; and (4) they exhibit a respect for reason, evidence, and truth.

The Problems of Educational Administrators

Problems can be grouped in numerous ways. In this book topics are grouped in terms of the moral concepts predominant in their discussion. We have chosen this format in part because of our commitment to the importance of ethical concerns in thinking about educational administration and in part because there is a good deal of isomorphism between the ethical and legal organization of topics.

Intellectual Freedom and Administrative Leadership

Among the most central purposes of educational institutions are the promotion of the growth of knowledge and the growth of the intellectual capacity of individuals. Note first the distinction between these two ideas. To promote the growth of knowledge is to increase the store of knowledge and wisdom human beings have collectively produced. This is not so much concerned with increasing what individuals know but with increasing what is known in general. It is concerned with the research or inquiry functions of educational institutions.

Educational institutions also have a teaching function. They are concerned to promote the knowledge, the wisdom, the understanding, and the intellectual capacity of particular persons. The concern is to distribute what is known.

It is often held that serving these purposes requires certain kinds of freedom for the members of educational institutions. The growth of knowledge, for example, is best promoted by arrangements that permit and encourage extensive criticism and debate. Ideas are tested and refined by being subjected to criticism. Moreover, intellectual progress depends on the freedom to introduce and explore new ideas. The growth of knowledge requires freedom. Intellectual progress requires people to be able to introduce new ideas and to criticize current ones without fear of censorship or sanction. To use a well-honored phrase, educational institutions must be "marketplaces of ideas." Ideas that thrive must do so because they have triumphed in the free market of ideas, not because they are enforced by civil or institutional authority.

A second argument holds that people are or should become responsible moral agents (Strike, 1982b). Ultimately people are to be held morally responsible for their own lives, for their choices, and for their actions. People who are moral agents need the widest possible latitude to act on their choices. It makes no sense to hold people responsible for their decisions and actions unless they can choose and act freely. The value of moral agency entails the value of freedom. Also, if people are to be responsible for their choices, they need the competence and the resources to choose reasonably and wisely. This means that people require an education that develops the capacity to choose between the various options that life presents. It also requires free access to the information, ideas, and discussions that permit informed and competent judgment.

These are arguments commonly employed to justify free institutions. They place particular emphasis on intellectual liberty and the freedom to express and to have access to ideas, and they generate numerous issues with which educators and educational administrators must deal.

They also place constraints on administrative discretion and have implications for administrative leadership. Administrators in a free society may not behave in ways that deny to students and teachers the right to express their own opinions. Moreover, administrators must lead in ways that recognize the moral agency and the value of the opinions of others. What kind of leadership is consistent with the values of intellectual freedom?

Leadership and Academic Freedom   Academic freedom is the view that if teachers and scholars are to promote the growth of knowledge, they require the freedom to teach and conduct inquiry without fear of sanction or reprisals should they express an unpopular or controversial idea. Academic freedom raises numerous issues for the administrator. What specific rights are covered by academic freedom? Is any teacher free to advocate any idea to any student in any manner? If not, what are the proper bounds of academic freedom? Are there occasions when the right to academic freedom must be balanced against the rights or interests of students, of the community, or of parents? What kind of leadership is consistent with the academic freedom of teachers? And just exactly what is leadership?

Conflict Resolution and Censorship   What to teach is surely among the most important questions we face. The decisions of educators about what to teach have come under increasing public scrutiny and are increasingly subjected to challenge. What do the arguments concerning intellectual liberty demand concerning what goes into the curriculum or what comes out of it? Are people who protest some part of the curriculum necessarily engaged in censorship? Do parents have the right to prevent their children from learning material they deem offensive? Do educators have the right to teach whatever a consensus of professional judgment requires? Are there occasions when the free exchange of ideas must be balanced against the rights of parents or the interests of the community? When faced with an issue of censorship, how should an administrator deal with it? What are some of the general features of conflict resolution?

Student Control and Student Rights   Administrators are responsible for student behavior and for providing an environment that is not only safe and orderly but also conducive to learning. But what do the arguments for intellectual freedom have to say about the rights of students? Do students have rights analogous to the teachers' right to academic freedom? Does the fact that students may be immature or that they are novices in most of the subjects they study indicate that their rights should differ from those of other citizens in our society or from teachers? Does freedom promote growth? How may an administrator control the political activity of students? To what extent and in what ways are students entitled to express unpopular ideas? What kind of discipline is effective, and what kind of discipline is fair?

Equal Opportunity and Resource Allocation

Educational institutions perform a distributive function: They are an important component of a set of social institutions that influences who gets what and determines the rules and conditions under which the competition for social benefits takes place. What happens in educational institutions affects an individual's life chances. Schools can affect the skills a person brings to the competition for social goods and can determine an individual's eligibility for further education or for a given occupation.

A major concern for any institution that can affect the life prospects of individuals is that it do so fairly. This is easy to say. Knowing what counts as fairness and how to promote fairness is, however, a formidable task. One way to begin thinking about these issues is to return to two of the basic moral concepts developed earlier: We must treat people as objects of respect and dignity, and people must be treated with impartiality.

Together these ideas imply a third principle, which we call "the equal consideration of interests." The basic idea is that if people are objects of respect, their wants, needs, and interests must be taken seriously. Obviously, people cannot have a right to have every need met and every want fulfilled. But that people are ends, not means, does at least imply that the very fact that a person wants or needs something is a reason why that person should have it. It is not a sufficient reason, but it is a reason. That we must treat people impartially implies that no one is entitled to preferential treatment. Each person's claim must be treated as valid, but no one at the outset has a better claim than anyone else. We must give equal consideration to everyone's interests.

Equal consideration need not imply that everyone is entitled to an equal share of the goods and services a society produces. Our society tends to see equal consideration as requiring fair conditions in the competition for social goods—as equality of opportunity. Individuals are entitled to keep what they earn. The equal consideration of interests requires that the conditions under which people compete be equal. This view is often illustrated by a racetrack. Fairness in a race does not consist in there not being winners or losers. The race should go to the swift. Fairness consists in everyone competing according to the same rules on a track of equal difficulty. Unequal rules or an unequal track violates the notion of equal consideration of interests. Likewise, rules or conditions of competition that favor some over others at the beginning of the competition violate the equal consideration of interests. Assumed in any such inequality is the idea that some people are inherently more entitled to have their needs met and wants satisfied than others.

The idea of fair competition assumes a distinction between relevant and irrelevant grounds for treating people differently. In a race it is permissible to reward people because they run faster. It is not permissible to reward them for anything else. Likewise, in our society it is usually permissible to reward people because they are more productive or more talented. It is not, however, permissible to reward people on the basis of race, sex, or family background.

In our society, schools are part of the racetrack. Schools distribute educational opportunities—the resources on which learning depends. Looking at schools in this way leads us to ask what constitutes relevant and irrelevant criteria according to which these educational resources might be varied. Having developed a satisfactory view of what counts as relevant reasons, we must also ask what kinds of differences in treatment are justified. We may all agree, for example, that it is appropriate to consider ability to profit from instruction as relevant to the distribution of educational resources. But what differences should this ability make? Should high-ability students receive more resources than low-ability students because they can make better use of them or less because they have less need of them? Questions of this sort are the kind we need to answer if we are to understand the idea of equal opportunity.

Desegregation and the Effects of Schooling   Segregation surely has resulted in the distribution of educational resources on the irrelevant criterion of race. Its evil may, however, be more fundamental. Segregation seems rooted in the assumption that the segregated individuals are somehow unworthy to associate with the majority population. Thus it not only results in an unjust distribution of resources but seems to be a direct denial of the principle on which the demand for equal resources is based. Segregation seems rooted in the denial that all individuals are entitled to equal respect and are equally worthy of fair treatment.

The problems administrators now face have not so much to do with the evils of segregation as with the remedies for it. What is to count as a desegregated school system? How can students whose races and cultures have long been separated be taught and learn in a common environment? How can schools be kept from resegregating internally? How can we deal with the stresses that often accompany desegregation? What consequences has desegregation had on the education of all our children?

Resource Allocation and School Effectiveness   The allocation of educational reources is the basic process whereby decisions are made concerning the values the educational system will serve. In a sense, many of the issues we have sketched are concerned with the allocation of such resources. Many issues of equity, for example, concern what characteristics of individuals are relevant or irrelevant to the allocation of resources to them. Various means of program evaluation are among the tools employed to judge how resources should be allocated. Benefit-cost analysis, for example, allows us to judge whether a given program provides a reasonable rate of return on our investment and allows us to compare it with other programs. More generally, various types of evaluations are intended to reveal the consequences of our actions. But what standards shall we use to decide what is to count as a desirable or optimal pattern of results? Suppose we wish to adopt one of two math programs, A and B, where the average results of A were higher than those of B, but they were also more skewed—that is, a few students in A do very poorly. Should we prefer the more equal result or the one with the higher average? How are we to decide how to choose between efforts with considerably different goals? How are we to judge the appropriate balance between English, civics, and vocational education? What counts as a fair and principled way of distributing resources between competing educational views? And what resources make schools effective?

Democracy, Decision Making, and Personnel

One of the most important properties of a decision is that it be legitimately made. But what makes a decision a legitimate one? Decisions are not primarily legitimated by being right. One may object to a decision by arguing that the person who made it was not entitled to do so or that the procedures followed in making it were unfair. These two things are important in understanding the notion of legitimacy. One aspect of a legitimate decision is that it be made by persons who are entitled to make it. A second aspect is that a legitimate decision is made by following a fair procedure.

How do we know who is entitled to make a decision? Perhaps the first thing to be decided is when a group or a society is entitled to make a decision that is binding on its members. Some decisions are not legitimately made by anyone other than the person whom they affect. Individuals, not a group or society, should decide. Deciding what kinds of decisions can be made by a society requires us to have a concept of the public interest. That is, it requires us to be able to identify decisions that have sufficient impact on the public that they can legitimately be made by the society and imposed on its members.

Having identified a class of decisions that can be justifiably termed public decisions, we need to have a view about how they may legitimately be made. Here we can distinguish two basic orientations. The first, democracy, holds that decisions should be made in a way that allows for the participation or representation of the members of the group. Administrators appeal to democratic authority to justify their right to make decisions when, for example, they note that they were appointed by the school board, which was elected by the voters of a given district.

The second basic orientation, professionalism, holds that decisions should be made by people who are competent to make them. Administrators appeal to professionalism when they note that their training and expertise entitle them to make a given decision.

These views of legitimate authority need not be seen as mutually exclusive. Ideally, the administrator will be both an expert and the representative of a democratic process. It is sometimes important, however, to differentiate when which view is appropriate, for this has some bearing on who is entitled to make a decision. Consider, for example, decisions about a biology curriculum. It seems quite appropriate that biologists should define the content of the biology curriculum. They are in a position to know what biology is. They are not, however, experts on whether biology is more important than mathematics or physics. Questions of the value of a piece of the curriculum either should be made democratically or should express the individual choices of students or their parents.

The second aspect of a legitimate decision is that it is made by following fair procedures. The relevant concept is that of due process. The demand for due process is essentially the demand that decisions be reasonable. Put negativel;, decisions should not be arbitrary or capricious. A decision is arbitrary when it is not based on available evidence. Thus one demand of due process is that the procedures for collecting and employing evidence ensure that decisions are warranted by available facts. The right to a hearing and the right to refute negative evidence are instances of such procedures.

The second component of due process is that decisions should not be capricious. A decision is capricious, for example, when it is based on an unknown or unannounced standard or achieved in an untimely or irregular way. Due process seeks to ensure that decisions be made according to standards that are public and general and are applied in an orderly and regular fashion. Consider some issues governed by these concepts.

Democratic Authority and the Professional-Bureaucratic Interface   One of the most popular recent criticisms of public schools argues that a class of professional educators has taken effective control and usurped the rightful place of parents and communities in education (Tucker & Zeigler, 1980). To what extent is this true? To what extent should it be true? To what extent and for what reasons should school boards or legislatures defer to the judgment of professional educators? To what extent should teachers or administrators be free to ignore or overrule the wishes of parents concerning the education of their children? How can we apportion the roles of experts, the general public, parents, and teachers in educational decision making? Are teachers and administrators professionals?

Democratic Authority and Unionization   Unionization has spread throughout teaching. A majority of teachers are represented by a union and have collective bargaining agreements with their school district. Those who are not have nevertheless had their salaries and working conditions influenced by what unions have achieved in other districts. How has unionization affected education? Particularly, how has unionization affected how decisions are made? Is it proper, in a democratic society, for boards of education to bargain matters of educational policy with a union? Is it proper for administrators to share their authority with teachers? Is unionization a threat to democratically governed schools?

Teacher Evaluation and Due Process   Among the most important decisions made concerning educational institutions are those concerned with the selection and retention of staff. The procedures used to judge teachers should be both accurate and fair and should lead to the highest-quality teaching staff consistent with fair and humane treatment of teachers. The major concept important to judging the fairness of a teacher evaluation procedure is that of due process. Teachers are entitled to evaluation procedures that protect them from arbitrary or capricious judgments. But what kinds of procedures are fair and effective? Is it possible to have a procedure that protects the rights of teachers but allows administration the discretion necessary to select and retain a quality staff? Is it possible to have a procedure that allows administration significant discretion but does not allow the violation of teachers' rights? Are there trade-offs to be made between fairness and effectiveness? How should we evaluate teachers?

This set of issues does not, of course, exhaust the range of pertinent concerns for educational administrators. It does, however, provide a sample of topics that are important in themselves and that may serve as a vehicle for introducing a set of ethical, legal, and social science concepts that we believe are central to the understanding and practice of educational administration.

CHAPTER 1

Administrative Authority, Leadership, and Academic Freedom

America the Beautiful

"Look, Sam, I feel as bad about this as you, but there's no point in discussing it further. I know that by not using the damned book I'll cause problems for you. Lord knows I've created enough difficulties for you in the past. But I'm *not* going to adopt the *America the Beautiful* series. The books misrepresent American history and government. If I used them in my social studies classes, I'd be violating my responsibility to teach the truth as my training in history enables me to see it. Don't you see that selecting a curriculum is *not* a democratic process? And it's certainly not an administrator's prerogative. Sure, the people in this town should have a voice in deciding what their kids learn. And I'll admit that you administrators should have your say. But in the end, it's an *academic* matter. If you try to force me to use *America the Beautiful,* you'll be trampling on my academic freedom. I can't let you do that, Sam, and neither will the rest of the faculty. If you push me, I'll file a grievance, something we'd both like to avoid. Think it over."

Sam Cook, the principal of Jefferson High, had thought it over. But no matter how he looked at it, "academic freedom" could not mean that John Milton could teach his classes any way he liked, regardless of the rest of the school's program or the wishes of the community. "I have an obligation to coordinate the program at Jefferson," he thought, "and I have to have the cooperation of my staff to do that. I don't think I can let John get away with this."

Sam reflected on John Milton's history. He certainly had created more than his share of trouble during his years at Jefferson. John was a capable teacher. Most students liked him and seemed to learn from him. The problem was that he had a positive talent as a lightning rod for community hostility.

Though John was not a fiery-eyed radical, he was certainly more liberal than many people in the community. Fundamentally, his problems with parents arose because he was committed to the idea that high school social studies should be devoted to an examination of issues, an examination that required that all sides be considered in free and open discussion. Since his students tended to hold the same beliefs as their parents, John frequently was in the position of arguing for unpopular views. Over the years this had provoked numerous complaints requiring Sam's intervention to smooth ruffled feathers—sometimes a parent's, sometimes John's, usually both. On occasion, however, he did feel that John went too far, and he had had to work out a compromise between the parents and the teacher.

But this case seemed to be different. John had refused to use the text recommended by the Jefferson Curriculum Committee in his civics class. The irony here was profound. It was John who had argued vociferously for including parents on the Curriculum Committee. It was John who said that decisions needed to be more democratic and more sensitive to community ideas. It was John who had lectured Sam on the responsibility of a leader to secure community support. Then, to John's chagrin, these very parents had tipped the committee's vote toward the *America the Beautiful* curriculum. It was a four-year series of textbooks beginning with *Civics: The American Way of Government*, moving through two years of history, *A Free People* and *America's Destiny*, and ending with a sociology and economics book titled *The Way of Free Enterprise*.

John had argued vigorously against the series, saying that the whole curriculum had a conservative bias. Moreover, John had developed for his civics class a good set of documents and materials that he felt constituted a superior teaching tool. His materials engaged students in debates and projects. They did far more than simply describe the structure of the U.S. government.

Sam did not understand John's viewpoint. Certainly the *America the Beautiful* series tilted to the political right. Perhaps also John's style of teaching would be inconsistent with the new series. The parents on the Curriculum Committee had, however, wanted a social studies course that taught patriotism and a positive view of America. That did not seem to Sam to be such a terrible thing. And, as John himself had argued, parents deserve a role in the education of their children.

Now John had refused to go along with the committee's decision. On one hand, Sam did not see how he could allow that. The board had accepted the committee's recommendation and purchased the series. John's refusal to use it seemed nothing more than simple insubordination. The principal could not see that ''academic freedom'' had much to do with choosing high school textbooks. Moreover, each part of the curriculum built on what went before. The civics text was the key. If John did not use it, the other teachers would have to work its contents into their courses. Sam did not believe that John's views should be allowed to make the teaching of his colleagues more difficult. He had to be subservient to the program of the school.

On the other hand, Sam was reluctant simply to demand that John comply with his wishes. Sam prided himself on his ability to get along with his staff. He saw himself as a friendly, approachable administrator, attentive to the needs of his teachers and willing to discuss with them any differences of opinion that might arise. Always in the past, when such differences occurred, Sam had been able to negotiate a settlement of the dispute. This time, however, John was clearly unwilling to negotiate. He had taken a ''hard line,'' and Sam felt himself being pushed into a similar stance. He foresaw an open conflict with the teacher that might array his own faculty against him and force him to fall back on his authority as principal to order John to use the text. Sam feared that doing so would make him seem a despot in the eyes of John and the rest of his staff and would undermine the good working relationship he had established with the teachers at Jefferson. At heart Sam did not think that *ordering* a teacher to do something was either appropriate or desirable.

Finally, the grievance procedures were painful. Cook understood that although they were designed to protect teachers' rights, they exacted a high cost in administrative time and effort. It would be far easier to give in to John. But had John gone too far? "How can I run a school if teachers can teach whatever they want because they have academic freedom? How can I lead if no one has to follow?"

Introduction

What is the nature of a principal's authority? Some observers of these events at Jefferson High would respond to this question by pointing out that teachers are, after all, simply *employees* of the Board of Education. As employees, they are required to comply with the legitimate orders of their supervisor. Teachers, in this sense, are no different than workers in the city's sanitation department or its parks department or persons on an industrial assembly line. All must comply with their supervisors' legitimate demands. As principal of Jefferson, Cook had an obligation to ensure that the board's decisions are followed and the authority to order Milton to use *America the Beautiful.* He should do so. Surely, they might argue, "academic freedom" does not justify an insubordinate teacher's pursuit of his own ideological views.

Unfortunately, the matter is not so simple. Because the rights of teachers and administrators often conflict, especially in the matter of what is to be taught and how, it is critical that school managers have a clear conception of the constraints and ambiguities surrounding the exercise of authority in schools—their own authority as well as that of their faculties. John Milton's relation with his supervisor is, in important respects, the same as a garbage collector's, a park attendant's, and an assembly line worker's with theirs. However, it is different in important respects as well, perhaps most notably in the freedom that Milton has in the conduct of his work.

Administrative Power, Authority, and Leadership

Max Weber and the Idea of Authority

"Power" and "authority" are central conceptions of administrative thought, and the work of Max Weber (1864–1920) stands as the intellectual foundation of many twentieth-century writers on those topics. One of Weber's principal concerns was the question of obedience. Why do some people obey others? In his discussion of this matter, he distinguished between power and authority. *Power,* he wrote, is "the probability that one actor within a social relationship will be in a position to carry out his own will despite resistance" (Weber, 1947, p. 152). Coercion, whether explicit or implicit, is a part of the exercise of power. *Authority,* in contrast, is "the probability that certain specific commands (or all commands) from a given source will be obeyed by a given group of persons" (p. 324). Here, Weber is suggesting that power may be distinguished from authority by the willingness of a person to comply with a request from another. A person has exercised authority over another when the latter willingly complies with the former's order.

A special sort of willingness is involved in formal organizations. As Herbert Simon notes, an authority relation is one in which a subordinate "holds in abeyance his own critical faculties for choosing between alternatives and uses the formal criterion of the receipt of a command or signal as his basis of choice" (Simon, 1957, p. 126). In other words, in an authority relation, a person does not act upon his or her own judgment of the merits of some action but on the judgment of someone else. For example, a teacher may complete a report required by a principal simply because it is "part of the job," even though the teacher believes the report to be a waste of time. Thus a second distinction between power and authority in formal organizations is that the latter involves a preexistent commitment to comply with another's wishes. Notice that this attribute of authority characterizes ordinary employer-employee relations. By accepting a position, an employee recognizes that he or she has incurred the obligation to obey legitimate requests and to comply with specified duties, without independently evaluating their merits. This criterion also serves to distinguish authority from certain forms of influence, particularly persuasion. In the latter case, a person may comply with a request when convinced by the reasons another has given, but the person does not suspend his or her own judgment prior to hearing those reasons. We shall return to this point later.

You will have noticed that the term legitimate appeared several times in the foregoing discussion of authority. Authority, Weber said, is evidenced in compliance with a legitimate order. Authority is legitimated power. But what makes power legitimate? Weber distinguished three bases of legitimate authority: Charismatic, traditional, and legal.

Charismatic authority derives from the exceptional personal qualities of the leader. Individuals may obey someone because of their devotion to and admiration—even worship—of that person. (The religious overtones are deliberate; the word's Greek root, *kharisma,* means "divine gift"—the leader is touched by God.) Charismatic authority is perhaps best exemplified by the founders of some revolutionary religious and political movements (Jesus and Gandhi come to mind) and by the willingness of followers to renounce even their most vital personal and family interests in favor of the leader's interests.

Traditional authority is based not on the quality of the leader's personality but on societal custom and precedent. Obedience is owed a person by virtue of the position that person occupies, a position that is itself venerable. Occupancy of these positions commonly occurs through inheritance (as in the case of a monarch), or through a biological mechanism (as in the case of a parent). Thus obedience is grounded in the traditions and culture of the society itself.

In the case of *legal authority,* obedience is owed to people neither because of their vision and inspiration nor because they occupy a position venerated by tradition. Indeed, obedience is not owed to individuals at all. Rather, it is owed to a set of legal principles or laws. Such principles require that we obey directives issued by the incumbent of a particular office, regardless of who that incumbent might be. Thus we obey a superior on our jobs or a policeman on the corner because of a system of laws that prescribes that under some circumstances these individuals should be obeyed. All modern organizations—factories, government bureaus, public schools—are founded on the basis of legal authority. The idea of legal authority is encapsulated in the idea "the rule of law, not men." Thus a third distinction between power and authority rests on the notion of legitimation. Authority is power legitimated by charisma, tradition, or legal principle.

Blau and Scott add a final criterion to Weber's distinctions between power and authority as it applies to modern organization: "A value orientation must arise that defines the exercise of social control as legitimate, and this orientation can arise only in a group context" (Blau & Scott, 1962, pp. 28-29). The suggestion is that not only must authority be legitimated in one of the three ways already noted, but a norm must arise among subordinates that defines obedience as proper. Thus, for example, it is not sufficient that a principal's authority be legitimated by a set of legal principles external to the school; it is also necessary that the faculty be characterized by a *shared value orientation*—a norm—that defines compliance as "the proper thing to do." The significance of this norm is that the group itself will enforce an individual's compliance, through the informal sanctions that operate in all such groups. In this way authority is made at least partly independent of its roots, whether those roots are in a system of legitimating legal principles, charisma, or tradition.

We can summarize these criteria now by defining authority as it exists in modern organizations, including schools: *Authority exists when an individual willingly disregards his or her own judgment and complies with the legally legitimated orders of another in the context of a group whose norms support such compliance.* This conception leads to the (for some) startling conclusion that *authority ultimately lies with the subordinate, not the supervisor.*

With these ideas in mind, we can begin a consideration of Sam Cook's problem with John Milton. In this situation, has Cook the authority to require Milton to use *America the Beautiful*? The answer would seem to be no. Of the four criteria of authority, only one has been met. Cook's order to use the text is probably a legitimate one: The board is legally empowered to adopt a curriculum for Jefferson High School, and Cook's position as principal makes him an agent of the board. We are unsure, from the facts given, of the extent to which the faculty is characterized by a normative structure supporting compliance. In any case, it is clear that Milton did not suspend his own judgment on matters of curriculum choice prior to Cook's decision. Indeed, his judgment is clear: He believes that his status as a teacher, and the academic freedom this entails, entitles him to decide what is to be taught in his classroom. Finally, he will not willingly accede to his principal's wishes. In short, though Cook may have the power to force *America the Beautiful* on Milton—that is, to coerce him to use it—he does not fully possess the authority to do so.

This analysis suggests that a primary concern of school administrators will often be the expansion of their authority—to secure the willing compliance of teachers, pupils, or parents to administrators' requests. Moreover, this concern may often pertain not to a single individual (e.g., John Milton), nor to a single request (e.g., the specific books at issue), but rather to the extension of administrative authority over an entire group in regard to a whole class of decisions. Thus Cook is properly concerned that his authority to implement the board's curriculum decisions in his school may be severely curtailed if he accedes to Milton's wishes. The latter's refusal may be simply the tip of the iceberg; if the faculty shares Milton's views, Cook's responsibility has outrun his authority. Although he is legally responsible to implement the board's curricular decisions, this analysis suggests that he lacks the authority to do so. How can that authority be secured? Before we turn to that question, we need to examine the matter of administrators' power. If administrators often lack the authority they require, perhaps it is pointless to worry about gaining that authority. The exercise of power may be all that is required.

Administrative Power in Public Schools

"Power tends to corrupt," Lord Acton said, and "absolute power corrupts absolutely." If Sam Cook does not have the authority to secure the implementation of *America the Beautiful,* does he have the power to do so? Recall that power is conceived as the capability to carry out one's will despite resistance. Since Milton is clearly resisting, we need to consider Cook's power to overcome that resistance.

Perhaps the first point to note is that power is a fundamental aspect of administrative life. Certainly there is something faintly noxious about its exercise. In a society with a strong egalitarian ethic, such as ours, the obvious exercise of power is often viewed with suspicion or alarm. If we describe an administrator as using "raw power" or being "power hungry," we are not being complimentary. After all, the greater an administrator's power, the greater a subordinate's impotence, and no one likes to feel impotent. Nevertheless, to get a subordinate to do something that he or she does not wish to do—that is, to exercise power— is the everyday stuff of administrative life. And though a fist of velvet may be preferable to one of iron, it is nonetheless a fist. Since unwillingness to perform organizational tasks is a common enough occurrence, it is doubtful that administrators who refuse to exercise their power at appropriate times can hope to achieve their school's objectives effectively.

Central to a conception of school administrators' power is an understanding of the rewards and penalties available to them. That is, a common method for securing the cooperation of a recalcitrant employee, such as Milton, is to offer an incentive or disincentive for the behavior in question. What sorts of incentives or disincentives are available to school administrators?

Lortie (1975) provides a useful analysis of what teachers find rewarding. He suggests that an occupation's rewards are of three types: extrinsic, ancillary, and intrinsic. *Extrinsic rewards* are the compensations that accrue to individuals by virtue of performing their work role. Money is paradigmatic, but prestige and power are also included. *Ancillary rewards* are qualities of an occupation that are objectively part of a job and may be perceived by some of its practitioners as rewards. For example, lengthy vacation periods, relatively clean work, and daily schedules that accommodate family responsibilities are ancillary rewards of teaching. *Intrinsic rewards* are the attributes of an occupation that make it psychically satisfying. They are the pleasures that people find in the doing of their work. The nature of intrinsic rewards varies from person to person. For teachers, intrinsic rewards are the pleasures that arise from teaching itself and include such things as working with children, the opportunity for self-expression that the occupation provides, and its relative freedom from intense competition (p. 101).

Which of these classes of rewards do teachers find most satisfying? Lortie's analysis demonstrates the overwhelming importance of intrinsic rewards to teachers—rewards that accrue through their work with students in the confines of a classroom. The "joys of teaching," to use Jackson and Belford's (1965) phrase, are found in the classroom, not in the lounge or the front office.

When viewed in administrative perspective, these findings raise an important issue. Which of these rewards are capable of administrative manipulation? Which can be granted or denied? Extrinsic rewards are either set by boards and teachers' organizations through a negotiating process (e.g., salaries), or they are granted to teachers by the public at large (e.g., prestige). Salary is almost entirely beyond a principal's control. Even in the few districts with "merit pay" (a practice strenuously resisted by teachers themselves), the amounts of money available for a discretionary award is a tiny fraction of a teacher's total salary, perhaps as little as a few hundred dollars. Granting or withholding such meager sums is unlikely to serve as a significant incentive. In teaching, annual salary increments come automatically (from a principal's point of view) as a consequence of another year's experience or as an outcome of contract talks. Similarly, ancillary rewards such as vacation days, hours of work, and security (after tenure is awarded) are virtually immutable. Finally, intrinsic rewards, dependent on the quality of pupil-teacher interactions, are beyond the direct control or manipulation of school principals. Lortie's analysis suggests, then, that principals have little to work with by way of important incentives or disincentives to teacher behavior.

All of this is not to say that principals are unimportant to teachers. They are not. They assign teachers to classes and pupils to teachers. And since the quality of the pupil-teacher interaction is of such overriding importance, this power is significant. Principals are important for student discipline—teachers speak approvingly of principals who "back them up" either with pupils or with parents (Lortie, 1975, pp. 196–200). Nevertheless, these resources and potential sources of power are relatively untractable; principals cannot easily provide or withdraw them on the basis of variations in a particular teacher's willingness to cooperate. Thus while Lord Acton may be correct, Sam Cook (and school principals generally) seems to be in no immediate danger of absolute corruption.

The Zone of Acceptance

We have noted that authority involves a willing disregard of personal judgment when complying with legitimate orders. The obvious question, however, is orders about *what*? If we confine our attention to formal organizations, it is immediately obvious that there is likely to be a range of acceptability evident among subordinates. That is, some individuals may suspend their own judgments and willingly comply with virtually all orders from a superior. For others, the range might be considerably narrower. As an extreme example, there are few teachers who would unthinkingly comply with a principal's order to wear their hair in a particular style. On the other hand, almost all would obey a blanket order to refrain from swearing before pupils. This aspect of obedience—the range of acceptability of a superior's decisions and demands—was noted more than forty years ago by Chester Barnard. In a now-classic book, *The Functions of the Executive* (1983), Barnard called attention to the variations among subordinates in the acceptability of decisions made by their superiors, which he termed the "zone of indifference"—that is, the range of commands to which employees would accede unquestioningly. Some years later, Herbert Simon (1957, p. 133) applied the now more commonly used term *zone of acceptance* to Barnard's concept.

Within the zone of acceptance, administrators' requests will be met without difficulty; outside it, requests will be resisted, and an exercise of power may be required to secure compliance. The critical area is the boundary between the two. This boundary will vary among individuals and within the same individual over time. Indeed, the boundary may shift systematically in an entire profession. For example, it is likely that one consequence of the rise in teacher militancy in recent decades has been a substantial shrinking of the zone of acceptance. Unfortunately, there have been few empirical studies of this zone or its shifts. One of the most relevant was carried out by Clear and Seager.

Clear and Seager (1971) administered a questionnaire designed to map the zones of acceptance of a sample of teachers and administrators. Their instrument consisted of sixty-six "situation items" and asked each respondent to consider whether or not a school administrator *should* attempt to influence a teacher's behavior in regard to that situation. Clear and Seager suggest that these sixty-six items could be grouped into three categories (though they did not carry out such a classification). One concerned organizational maintenance activities—the adequacy and accuracy of teachers' reports, meeting deadlines, the care and maintenance of school equipment, and the like. A second set was personal in nature, concerning teachers' dress standards, hair and beard length, and contributions to charitable organizations. The third class concerned core teaching activities—evaluating pupils, teaching the required curriculum, and student discipline. Clear and Seager compared the responses of administrators to those of teachers as to whether or not the former should attempt to influence the behavior of the latter.

Not surprisingly, administrators were more likely to think they should attempt to influence teachers' behavior than were teachers willing to accept such influence; the mean differences for the large majority of items were statistically significant. However, most of these differences were substantively unimportant. That is, both groups were in agreement that administrators should (or should not) attempt to influence a particular behavior; they differed merely in degree. However, when the items were considered in terms of their categories, a somewhat different picture emerged.

The smallest discrepancy concerned personal matters. Administrators did not feel free to influence teachers in these regards, nor were teachers willing to accept such influence. More disagreement concerned organizational maintenance. However, sharpest disagreement was evidenced over core teaching activities. Principals were likely to claim the right to influence classroom activities, while teachers were likely to reject such claims. Polarization was evident concerning the extent to which curriculum guides must be followed, methods of pupil discipline, techniques of pupil evaluation, and teaching methods.

These findings suggest that teachers' zones of acceptance are narrowest, relative to administrators' desire to exert influence, in precisely the matters that are of central educational concern—the teaching and learning processes in classrooms. Indeed, one of the areas of sharpest disagreement was whether or not principals should attempt to influence teachers' adherence to the prescribed curriculum, the subject of the dispute between Milton and Cook. Thus teachers seem willing to grant administrators authority over the "administrivia" of school operations—filing attendance reports, participation in in-service programs, and the care of school equipment—and to deny them authority over the activities most likely to contribute directly to the accomplishment of the school's central purpose, pupil learning.

There is an irony here. Administrators are responsible for the accomplishment of organizational goals; it would seem that legitimate administrative authority must extend to those efforts rationally linked to goal accomplishment. In schools this may not be the case. Lortie (1975) concludes that for school administrators, responsibility may often outrun authority, making a central problem the extension of their authority over classroom events. Of course, it may be argued that principals must work *within* teachers' zones of acceptance, exerting their influence over those matters in which teachers are willing to accept it. In fact, such a view seems to be espoused by Clear and Seager, who write that it "is incumbent upon school administrators to be aware of these zones of acceptance and to operate within them whenever possible" (p. 62). To do otherwise, they suggest, will have the consequence of provoking resistance and hostility. We suspect, however, that this view will be unacceptable to many administrators; their problem is to *overcome* resistance—to expand teachers' zone of acceptance so that it includes core classroom activities—*without* provoking hostility. Cook's problem may be that he has failed in this task. He has failed to exercise leadership.

Administrative Leadership

There are literally thousands of studies of leadership in the literature of educational administration. Despite this voluminous outpouring, a great deal remains unknown, and the relevance to practitioners of much of that literature is unclear.

Leadership has been variously defined (see, for example, Katz & Kahn, 1978, p. 528; Hanson, 1979, p. 234; Lipham, 1964, p. 122). Many of these definitions seem to catch the issue of Cook's problem with Milton and support the view that the former has failed to exercise leadership in his role as principal of Jefferson High School. A common element that runs through these ideas is the notion that an act of leadership has occurred when one or more persons have been induced to behave in new ways intended to achieve some organizational purpose more successfully. Thus, according to these views, if Cook is unable to extend his authority over Jefferson High's curriculum, he will have failed to lead.

Traits and Situations in the Study of Leadership

Two contrasting views have dominated the study of leadership, the oldest often being termed the "trait" or "great man" approach. This view suggests that leaders are distinguished by certain qualities or traits that set them apart from others. This perspective led to a search for the traits that separate leaders from followers. An astonishingly large array of personal attributes has been investigated—height, weight, speech fluency, energy level, intelligence, introversion-extroversion, initiative, self-confidence, and physical attractiveness, to name but a few. Years ago Stogdill (1948) provided a comprehensive review of this research and concluded that the trait approach had yielded little in the way of significant results. There seemed to be few if any personal qualities that were consistently present among leaders. If some studies indicated that extroversion, for example, was positively correlated with leadership, others indicated that the correlation was zero or even negative.

For a period of time in the early 1950s these results led some to conclude that a search for characteristic traits of leaders was a fruitless endeavor (Owens, 1970). More recent reviews, however, have concluded that some traits rather consistently distinguish leaders from followers (House & Baetz, 1979; Stogdill, 1974). However, there are two important caveats to this conclusion. First, though a few traits seem to be rather consistently correlated with holding a leadership position, these correlations are quite low. For example, Stogdill (1974) found that the intelligence-leadership correlation averages about .28, a rather weak relationship. (He also noted that an extreme discrepancy in intelligence between leaders and followers militates against the successful exercise of leadership.) Second, these traits are interesting from our perspective because many of them would seem to be relatively resistant to training. Thus, for example, intelligence, energy level, dominance, and self-confidence are unlikely to be much affected by training programs in educational administration. (From a practitioner's perspective, of course, they do suggest relevant selection criteria.) However, superior knowledge of the tasks to be performed is also an attribute of successful leaders and can arguably be an outcome of instruction.

Partly as a reaction to these inconclusive results, a second approach to the study of leadership came to the fore. The *transactional approach* recognizes that who emerges as a group's leader depends on the nature of the task the group faces as well as on any traits the leader may possess. Leadership is a transactional phenomenon. In a given group faced with a particular task, one individual might come to prominence; faced with a different task, someone else from the group might emerge.

Such a conception is easy to advance. It is quite another matter, however, to specify it in any sort of useful way. Precisely what sorts of situations require what sorts of traits? In a sense, leadership research over the past several decades has had as its focus the attempt to answer this question, to specify the details of the trait-situation interaction. As we shall see, although promising starts have been made, the question remains largely unanswered.

The Ohio State Studies and the LBDQ Tradition

The research program that has had the greatest impact on educational administration emerged from the work of investigators at Ohio State University following World War II. This work led to the development of an instrument to measure leadership, which has seen extensive use in educational and industrial settings, and to a conceptualization of leader behavior as a two-dimensional phenomenon.

As a reaction to the apparently fruitless search for leader traits, the Ohio State reseachers turned their attention to trying to define and measure actual behaviors that could differentiate effective from ineffective leaders. They sought to identify what leaders *do* rather than to identify any common traits they might possess. After considerable work, an instrument was developed, the Leadership Behavior Description Questionnaire (LBDQ; Halpin & Winer, 1952). It consists of a number of short, behaviorally descriptive items, each of which asks respondents to rate an individual on the extent to which that person engages in the behavior described. Sample items include "He treats all staff members as his equals," "He lets staff members know what is expected of them," and "He emphasizes the meeting of deadlines." Most commonly, subordinates rate their superiors (e.g., teachers rate their principals), but the LBDQ has been modified to permit ratings of subordinates by superiors, self-ratings, and ratings by outsiders (e.g., parent ratings of principals).

After hundreds of studies, a picture of leader behavior that seems to vary along two dimensions—initiating structure and consideration—has emerged.

Initiating structure *refers to the leader's behavior in delineating the relationship between himself and the members of his work group, and in endeavoring to establish well-defined patterns of organization, channels of communication, and methods of procedure (Halpin, 1966, p. 86).*

Examples of LBDQ items descriptive of initiating structure are "He makes his attitudes clear to the staff," "He maintains definite standards of performance," and "He sees to it that staff members are working up to capacity." Thus a person who is perceived as emphasizing organizational goal attainment—getting the job done—is scored high on this dimension.

The second dimension of leadership is behavior oriented toward group satisfaction—attention to the needs of individual members and to feelings of trust and support. "*Consideration* refers to behavior indicative of friendship, mutual trust, respect, and warmth in the relationship between the leader and the members of his staff" (Halpin, 1966, p. 86).

An important point to note about this two-dimensional structure is its correspondence to many theoretical analyses of the nature of leadership. For example, Barnard (1938), in discussing whether or not subordinates will cooperate with superiors, said such cooperation would depend on two factors: the extent to which goals are achieved and the extent to which individual needs are met. He labeled these "effectiveness" and "efficiency," respectively. Similarly, the extensive studies of small group interaction processes carried out at Harvard led Bales (Bales & Slater, 1955) to suggest the need for two types of leadership, task and social, which correspond rather closely to the LBDQ results. This correspondence of theoretical and empirical work lends considerable support to the validity of the claim that the behavior of leaders can be parsimoniously described using these two fundamental concepts (Brown, 1967).

Since these two factors seem to be separate dimensions of leader behavior (i.e., they are not opposite ends of a continuum), it was a natural next step to cross-classify the two, thus creating the four "styles" of leadership shown in Table 1.1. School administrators rated above the mean on both initiating structure and consideration are placed in quadrant I, while those below average on both are placed in quadrant III. Mixed styles—individuals characterized as high on one dimension and low on the other—are placed in their respective off-diagonal cells. This scheme has guided a number of studies that have attempted to identify the relative effectiveness of each of these various styles.

Halpin (1966) provides a summary of much of the work done on school administrators' leadership using the LBDQ and its variants. He reached three conclusions: (1) Effective administrators were rated high on both dimensions of leadership (i.e., they fell in quadrant I). (2) Superiors and subordinates tend to emphasize different dimensions. For example, when rating principals, superintendents tended to stress initiating structure, while teachers rating the same principals stressed consideration. (3) There was little relationship between administrators' self-rating and how others describe their behavior. Brown (1967) modified Halpin's first conclusion by suggesting that effective administrators need not be high on both initiating structure and consideration; being very high on one dimension could make up for being low on the other.

What can we learn about Cook's problems at Jefferson High School from the leadership research we have reviewed? Perhaps most important, Cook may be suffering from a confusion that plagues many administrators: He seems to believe that exercising his power and authority decisively as principal of Jefferson

TABLE 1.1
LBDQ LEADERSHIP QUADRANTS

Initiating Structure	Consideration	
	Low	High
High	(IV)	(I)
Low	(III)	(II)

SOURCE: Adapted from W. K. Hoy and C. G. Miskel, 1982, *Educational Administration: Theory, Research, and Practice* (2nd ed.), New York: Random House, p. 223.

may cost him the support, goodwill, and esteem of John Milton and perhaps that of his other faculty as well. He fears that demanding compliance with organizational rules, without negotiating a settlement, will mark him as something of a tyrant. To put this in LDBQ terms, he thinks that initiating structure is the polar opposite of consideration. The more one sets expectations, insists on compliance with rules and policies, coordinates the work flow, or distinguishes carefully between the role of principal and that of teacher, the less likely one is to be seen as friendly and approachable, collegial, congenial, and attentive to teachers' needs. The research initiated by the Ohio State studies suggests that this view is in error—that it is possible to "initiate structure" without losing in consideration.

Studies using the LBDQ have been plagued by the same problem confronting much of educational research—the lack of an independent and defensible criterion of effectiveness. How are we to recognize a "good" principal? Criteria that have been used in LBDQ research include the judgments of outside observers, measures of staff morale, teacher turnover, school climate, various personality traits implicitly judged desirable (e.g., "open-mindedness"), and pupil test scores. In our judgment, studies using the last criterion have produced particularly significant results, and these studies seem to have received less attention than they deserve. For example, Keeler and Andrews (1963), in an early and carefully designed study of Alberta schools, showed that pupil scores on provincewide tests in academic subjects are significantly higher in schools whose principals are rated high on both dimensions of the LBDQ. Further, these results were obtained when the obvious confounding factors—pupil intelligence and socioeconomic status and the training or experience of both principals and teachers—were controlled. Until recently, relatively few studies have indicated that principals' behavior of any sort has a substantial effect on children's learning. The Keeler and Andrews work, therefore, is of special note and badly needs to be replicated.

More recently, researchers working in what may be called the "effective schools tradition" have reached similar conclusions regarding principal leadership and pupil performance. In these studies, typically, the researcher first uses various characteristics of communities, teachers, and pupils to predict the average achievement levels of students in a number of schools. For example, measures of family socioeconomic status, district wealth, staff characteristics, and pupil intelligence are used to estimate mean achievement for a sample of institutions. Then schools that consistently achieve higher and lower levels of pupil learning than what might be expected are selected for intensive study. The researcher seeks to identify characteristics that distinguish effective from ineffective schools. These studies also suggest that the principals of effective schools exercise strong programmatic leadership. For example, Wellisch, MacQueen, Carriere, and Duck (1978) found that such principals hold high expectations for pupil achievement and make those expectations clear to their staffs. Blumberg and Greenfield (1980); Clark, Lotto, and McCarthy (1980); and Lipham (1981) note that effective schools are marked by principals who emphasize instructional goals and performance standards for pupils and who express optimism about pupils' meeting those standards. (See also Brookover, Beady, Flood, Schweitzer, & Wisenbaker, 1979; Brundage, 1980.) Further, it appears that principals who are active and influential in curricular decisions—who ensure that curricula are followed and coordinated—are more likely to have schools with high student achievement (Wellisch et al., 1978). Many of the principal behaviors described in these studies bear a substantial resemblance to the initiating structure dimension of leadership as operationalized by the LBDQ.

Similarly, effective schools seem to be characterized by good human relations between administration and staff and among teachers, and the behavior of principals may be important in establishing such a climate, which is in turn related to pupil learning (Gross & Herriott, 1965; Comer, 1980; Anderson & Walberg, 1974; Edmonds, 1979). Moos (1979), summarizing many of the school climate studies, concluded that pupil achievement is found most often in schools characterized by a warm supportive atmosphere, a stress on academic excellence, and an insistence on orderly pupil behavior. Such research findings imply that the principal behavior labeled "consideration" on the LBDQ is also an aspect of effective schools.

At this point it is worthwhile to note the bearing of some of the leadership and effective schools research on the particular problem of Sam Cook. Cook views his differences with Milton as concerning curricular coordination. He notes that each part of the curriculum builds on previous parts, that a textbook is a key determinant of what is taught and learned, and that if John Milton did not use *America the Beautiful,* other teachers would have to work its content into their courses. Are such matters of serious concern? Are they worth risking a protracted grievance? Is this matter important enough for Cook to exercise his power (since he has not the authority) and threaten or impose whatever sanctions he can muster to force Milton to comply?

These questions cannot be answered solely on the basis of research. The research, however, is not irrelevant, for it suggests that curricular choice, implementation, and coordination are matters over which administrators can exercise considerable control and which in turn seem to be related to pupil achievement. In a recent review of research on the role of the principal in instructional management, Bossart, Dwyer, Rowan, and Lee (1982) singled out curriculum matters as one important area that is subject to administrative manipulation and also affects student learning. Their conclusion imparts added weight to an argument that Cook should intervene and ensure that Milton uses the text adopted by the district. Finally, Lortie (1975) concludes that schoolwide or districtwide curricular decisions are among those over which most teachers are willing to grant considerable authority to administrators. (Though, as Clear and Seager, 1971, noted, teachers have not given up the right to depart from a prescribed curriculum in the day-to-day course of their work.) Thus John Milton's demand for final authority over curricular choice may not be one that his colleagues at Jefferson High School would support.

Before we leave our discussion of the LBDQ research we wish to note a particularly imaginative study that linked principals' leadership behavior with teachers' zones of acceptance. Earlier we called attention to Barnard's notion that organizational members can be characterized by the degree to which they grant administrators authority to make decisions about classroom matters. We also noted that among teachers, withholding authority seemed to be most evident in what we called "core activities"—the processes involved in classroom instruction. Finally, we pointed out that although some people might suggest that school administrators must work within teachers' zones of acceptance, many would reject such advice as being tantamount to an abdication of their legitimate responsibilities. In the case at hand, for example, following that advice would lead Cook to accede to Milton's demand for control over the social studies curriculum in his classroom, since that decision is clearly outside Milton's zone of acceptance. Cook, at least, has doubts about the wisdom of doing so; "it is John Milton's zone of acceptance that needs modification," he might say, "not my administrative responsibilities." But how are such modifications to be obtained? How are principals to *extend* the zone of acceptance of teachers beyond the "administrivia" of completing required reports, caring for equipment, and ordering books to the significant core of teachers' classroom action that bears directly on pupil learning? A study by Kunz and Hoy (1976) is suggestive in this regard.

Kunz and Hoy developed an instrument of thirty items focused on core professional matters. The researchers posed a series of activities over which a principal might make unilateral decisions and then asked ten randomly selected teachers in each of fifty secondary schools to indicate how often they would comply with those decisions, on a scale ranging from "sometimes" to "never." Examples of these items are "the change and modification of existing curricula," "the methods of conducting parent conferences," and "the methods to be used to discipline students in a classroom." In addition, teachers rated their principals on a version of the LBDQ. Kunz and Hoy then asked whether a principal's leadership style might influence the width of teachers' zones of acceptance.

The researchers reasoned that principals who were high or low on both dimensions of the LBDQ would have teachers with the widest and narrowest zones of acceptance, respectively. More interestingly, they also reasoned that in cases where leadership strength was split—high on one dimension and low on the other—consideration would be more influential than initiating structure in widening zones of acceptance. That is, they thought that administrators who were perceived as thoughtful and attentive to the needs of their staff would be more successful at getting teachers to accede to their decisions than would authoritative but relatively unfeeling administrators.

Kunz and Hoy found that, indeed, principals high on both dimensions of the LBDQ had staffs with the widest zones of acceptance, while those low on both had staffs with the narrowest. However, they found that consideration had little to do with increasing the domain of principal authority. Rather, initiating structure was the dominant factor that accounted for teachers' willingness to comply with principals' decisions. Thus while teachers may prefer consideration to initiating structure in their principals (Halpin, 1966), they seem more likely to comply with the wishes of those who are businesslike and task-oriented and provide clear guidelines as to what is expected.

Kunz and Hoy's finding should obviously not be interpreted as a counsel that administrators may safely ignore the personal needs and relationships of their staffs. Attending to those needs and relationships, however, may not help to expand administrative authority over professional matters. The finding also suggests a modification of Brown's (1967) conclusion, noted earlier, that school administrators could make up for weakness in one aspect of leadership by demonstrating particular strength in another. Insofar as compliance with administrative requests is concerned, strength on the consideration dimension of leadership may not make up for weakness on initiating structure.

The Kunz and Hoy study puts Cook's problem in a somewhat different light. If he is concerned that many of his staff might reject any attempt on his part to influence their choice of curricula, the study implies that attempting to expand his authority requires that he deliberately seek opportunities to exercise leadership in that area. John Milton's dissent may provide just such an opportunity. Put another way, success in exercising leadership may increase the probability of future success. This may come about through two mechanisms: First, the successful solution of a problem may increase subordinates' perceptions of the administrator's competence and willingness to confront an issue directly, and second, successfully treating a problem may increase the administrator's actual competence in handling future problems. We learn from our successes as well as our failures. The effective schools research seems to support a similar conclusion: Effective principals provide strong leadership, establish a climate conducive to learning, and monitor the teaching process closely (Bossart et al., 1982).

An interesting sidelight to Kunz and Hoy's work was their finding that few demographic variables (e.g., school size) were related to zones of acceptance. However, three of those investigated were related: sex (women were more accepting of administrative decisions), subject area taught (teachers of nonacademic subjects had wider zones of acceptance), and level of training (teachers with advanced degrees were more accepting). The last finding seems counterintuitive; one might expect that the higher the level of training, the more likely a teacher would be to resist administrative decision making in matters of professional concern. Thus the Kunz and Hoy study, like the work of Keeler and Andrews, needs replication badly.

Before we leave this section, we should mention that the view of leadership as a two-dimensional phenomenon is explicit in other conceptions found in education and industry. Perhaps the best known of all of these is that of Blake and Mouton (1978), who posit "concern for production" and "concern for people" as the underlying structure of leader behavior. Their research instrument and its accompanying schema, the Managerial Grid®, have seen extensive use both in studies of leadership and in executive training. Students interested in further work in the area would do well to review the Blake and Mouton work and its derivatives.

Contingency Approaches to Leadership

The LBDQ, the work of Blake and Mouton, and similar "dimensional views" of leadership have had a considerable impact on current administrative thought. However, in our judgment these views share a serious limitation. Earlier we described the changed conception of leadership—the replacement of a trait perspective with a transactional one. It is clear that today (despite a modest revival of interest in leader traits) the dominant conception is that effective leadership is situation-dependent. That is, whether a particular behavior is effective depends on the particular situation in which it is enacted. But such an assertion is vacuous unless an adequate conception of situations is available as well as an adequate conception of leader behavior. On what does effectiveness in fact depend? While the dimensional perspective is at least a start toward a useful conception of leadership, both the LBDQ and the Managerial Grid® provide no systematic view of the situations in which leadership occurs. At best they provide but half the picture. Several current leadership theories strive to rectify this imbalance. Space limitations prevent a discussion of all of these. Instead we will focus our attention of Fiedler's "contingency model," which incorporates a notable attempt to address the dependent nature of effectiveness. Other theories that explicitly consider trait-situation interaction can be found in House (1971), Reddin (1970), Vroom and Yetton (1973), and Hersey and Blanchard (1977).

Perhaps the dominant theory of leadership today is the one formulated by Fred E. Fiedler. (The basic reference is Fiedler, 1967; additional and more recent formulations may be found in Fiedler & Chemers, 1974; Fiedler, Chemers, & Mahar, 1976; and Fiedler, 1978.) Fiedler's contingency model is an attempt to incorporate motivational aspects of a leader and specific aspects of a situation into a single theory capable of predicting group effectiveness. The theory states that the effectiveness of a group in achieving some task depends on the match between the motivational structure of the leader and the degree to which he or she can control the situation. Each of these aspects—group effectiveness, motivational structure, and situational control—must be examined in some detail.

Perhaps the first thing to note about Fiedler's theory is that *effectiveness* is defined in a much more restricted way than is true for many of the LBDQ studies. For Fiedler, the major criterion of an effective leader is the extent to which the leader's group accomplishes its primary task. For example, in a factory setting, a foreman's effectiveness is to be judged on the basis of the number of units of product a work crew produces. Other aspects of group behavior, such as morale, turnover rates, and personal satisfaction, are not considered by Fiedler as indicators of leader effectiveness. They may contribute to effectiveness, but they are not measures of it. (You will recognize an immediate problem in applying the theory to educational organizations, where generally accepted criteria of productivity are notably scarce.) Ultimately, then, the purpose of the theory is to predict group productivity as a function of leadership.

A second aspect of contingency theory is its focus on the underlying motivation of leaders rather than on their behavior. You will recall that the LBDQ is a device that allows others to describe the way a leader behaves, or at least their perceptions of that behavior. In contrast, Fiedler's approach has been to attempt to define and measure the nature of a leader's motivation, which he terms "style." This distinction between style and behavior is critical to understanding the theory. Style is defined as "the underlying need-structure of the individual which motivates his behavior in various leadership situations. Leadership style thus refers to consistency of goals or needs over different situations" (Fiedler, 1967, p. 36). In contrast, a leader's behavior is viewed as " the particular acts in which a leader engages in the course of directing and coordinating the work of his group members" (p. 36). Thus leadership behavior is seen as a transitory phenomenon that may vary considerably from time to time, while style is a relatively constant aspect of an individual's personality that motivates a variety of behaviors. It is this underlying personality attribute of the leader, interacting with certain characteristics of the situation, that produces a particular behavior. In a sense, this aspect of contingency theory is not unlike the earlier trait approach to leadership.

A leader's motivational structure is operationally defined or measured with a simple self-report device that asks the leader to describe his or her least preferred coworker (LPC) in terms of eighteen bipolar adjectives (e.g., "pleasant–unpleasant," "tense–relaxed"). That is, the leader is asked to recall the one person with whom he or she found it most difficult to work and then to characterize that person on the adjectival scales. A simple sum of the individual items yields a total that is said to distinguish "task-motivated" from "relationship-motivated" leaders. Fiedler (1978) describes task motivation as follows:

An individual who describes the LPC in very negative, rejecting terms (low LPC score, i.e., less than about 57) is considered task motivated. In other words, the completion of the task is of such overriding importance that it completely colors the perception of all personality traits attributed to the LPC. In effect, the individual says, "If I cannot work with you, if you frustrate my need to get the job done, then you can't be any good in other respects. You are . . . unfriendly, unpleasant, tense, distant, etc." (p. 61)

On the other hand:

The relationship-motivated individual who sees his or her LPC in relatively more positive terms (high LPC score, i.e., about 63 or above) says, "Getting a job done is not everything. Therefore, even though I can't work with you, you may still be friendly, relaxed, interesting, etc., in other words, someone with whom I could get along quite well on a personal basis." Thus, the high LPC person looks at the LPC in a more differentiated manner—more interested in the personality of the individual than merely in whether this is or is not someone with whom one can get a job done. (p. 61)

Note the apparent similarity between the notions of task-motivated and relationship-motivated individuals and those of initiating structure and consideration. The concept pairs, however, are conceptually distinct. The former pair refers to an unobserved (and unobservable) psychological state, while the latter pair refers to overt behavior.

The LPC score is the most important variable in the model; it is determinative of leader effectiveness. However, whether a task-motivated or relationship-motivated person is effective in a particular situation is dependent on the degree to which the leader can exercise control over subordinates and tasks. Specifically, task-motivated persons perform best in situations where they have either a great deal of control *or* where they have very little control. Relationship-motivated persons perform best in situations that provide them with moderate control. Group productivity depends on the match between the leader's motivational structure and the degree of control the situation provides.

A leader's control over the situation is determined by three factors: leader-member relations, task structure, and position power, which are seen as differentially important in determining a leader's control. The relation between a leader and group members is most important, while position power is least so.

Leader-member relations refers to the degree to which the leader has the support and the loyalty of group members. If this relationship is good, the leader is said to be able to depend on subordinates. He or she can be sure that they will do their best to comply with requests, even without direct supervision. If, on the other hand, relations are poor, close supervision is required, and the leader "will need to be considerably more circumspect in his dealing with subordinates and continuously on guard to assure that his directions or policies are not subverted" (Fiedler, 1978, p. 62). Leader-member relations have been measured in several ways, most commonly via a rating instrument completed by the leader.

The second most important determinant of situation control is *task structure*. When tasks are well structured, when the leader can provide clear unambiguous directions that ensure goal achievement if followed, the leader has more control than when the route to success is unclear. In Fiedler's scheme, task structure is dependent on four factors: *decision verifiability* (are there clear standards for judging the product or service?), *goal-path multiplicity* (is there one best way of achieving the task?), *goal clarity* (is a complete description of the finished product available?), and *solution specificity* (in problematic situations, is there always one best solution?). If the answer to each of these is yes, the task provides the leader with a situation in which he or she can exercise more control than if the reverse were true.

The last aspect of situation control is *position power*. This refers to "the degree to which leaders are able to reward and punish, to recommend sanctions, or otherwise to enforce compliance by subordinates" (Fiedler, 1978, p. 65). In situations where these conditions obtain, a leader has greater control.

Using these three aspects of situational control, situations can be arranged along a continuum from high to low control. The most common way of doing this is to divide each scale at its midpoint, making two groups for each. This is done in order of their importance: first leader-member relations (good–poor), then task structure (structured–unstructured), and finally position power (strong–weak). This yields eight points, or octants, as shown in Table 1.2. Situations in octant I, describing a circumstance where leader-member relations are good, tasks are structured, and position power is strong, provide the leader with the greatest

TABLE 1.2

OCTANTS OF SITUATIONAL CONTROL

Leader-Member Relations	Good				Poor			
Task Structure	Structured		Unstructured		Structured		Unstructured	
Position Power	Strong	Weak	Strong	Weak	Strong	Weak	Strong	Weak
Octant	I	II	III	IV	V	VI	VII	VIII
Degree of Control	High			Moderate				Low

SOURCE: Adapted from F. E. Fiedler and M. M. Chemers, 1974, *Leadership and Effective Mangement*, Glenview, IL: Scott, Foresman, p. 80.

control. At the other end of the continuum, in octant VIII, relations between superior and subordinates are poor, the task to be accomplished is unstructured, and the superior has little power to discipline recalcitrant group members. Octant VIII situations are least favorable for the exercise of leadership.

The heart of Fiedler's conception is the relationship between a personality attribute of leaders (whether they are task- or relationship-oriented) and the degree of control a situation affords them; it is the interaction of these two that determines group productivity. Fiedler argues that in the low-control situations (octant VIII) with poor leader-member relations, unstructured tasks, and weak position power, the relationship-oriented person (high LPC) becomes anxious and excessively concerned with poor relations with the group. He or she seeks emotional support by becoming nondirective, often refusing to exercise whatever position power is available or to structure the task as adequately as is possible. Group accomplishment is sacrificed. In contrast, the task-oriented person is not motivated by a strong desire for good relations with subordinates. Rather, because achieving the goal is paramount, "he will not hesitate to reprimand or punish or discard them" (Fiedler, 1978, p. 102). While this might lead to further deterioration in leader-member relations, these are assumed to be already so poor that any further decline is relatively unimportant for task accomplishment. The decline is more than offset by whatever improvements can be brought about through improved task structure and the use of position power.

At the other end of the scale, in situations of high control, the task-oriented leader is also more effective. Here, Fiedler's argument goes, the low-LPC leader's primary motivation of task accomplishment is being satisfied with little or no intervention. After all, the leader enjoys mutual trust with subordinates, the task is clearly structured, and power is high. Tasks are accomplished virtually without attention, and the group requires little or no supervision. In such situations, the leader relaxes and may even appear more considerate of subordinates than the relations-oriented counterpart. Any attention devoted to group relations, while redundant, is relatively harmless as far as productivity is concerned. In contrast, the relations-oriented leader, whose primary motivational needs are also being met, turns attention to the task. Attempts to impose further structure, to provide strong leadership, however, are counterproductive, and effectiveness falls. Behavior becomes maladaptive.

In the middle range of control, octants IV and V, high-LPC leaders are more effective. Fiedler suggests that octant IV work groups are usually characterized by tasks that require free expression of opinions and information. (Examples are policy and decision-making committees, research and development teams, and units in which coordination rather than control is required.) These situations require negotiating and conciliatory skills. In octant V, though tasks are structured and power is high, poor relationships dominate. The high-LPC person who attends to personal relationships is likely to succeed in both of these situations, while the task-oriented leader is not (Fiedler, 1978, pp. 101–102).

Fiedler's conceptualization and reasoning regarding the components of his theory is not a model of clarity, as several of his critics have indicated (see, for example, Vecchio, 1977; Schriesheim & Kerr, 1977). However, the theory has provoked literally hundreds of laboratory and field studies, most of which, Fiedler claims, support it (Fiedler, 1978, p. 67). Crehan (1984), however, in a careful metanalysis of a large number of studies in schools, concludes otherwise. Regardless of the eventual outcome of these disputes, Fiedler has provided a notable attempt to specify the situational determinants of leader effectiveness.

We have reviewed some of the more salient ideas concerning administrative leadership and discussed some of their implications for the conflict at Jefferson High School. However, that dispute is not simply one of style, of Cook's capacity and mode of asserting control over the curriculum. It has an important substantive content, for it raises the issue of the place of academic freedom in our schools, of what shall be taught and who is to decide what shall be taught. Put another way, Cook's capacity to lead is constrained not simply by his relative lack of control over organizational rewards, by his leadership style, or by his motivational structure. More important, perhaps, it is constrained by the academic freedom that all teachers enjoy. As we have seen, administrative influence on decisions about what and how to teach are likely to be resisted by teachers, and these matters are central aspects of academic freedom. It is not just university professors who are entitled to academic freedom; academic freedom is a right of public school teachers as well. Thus we need to consider the legal and ethical aspects of that matter if we are to understand fully the events at Jefferson High.

Protecting Academic Freedom: Tenure and the Law

The dispute at Jefferson High School is a dispute about rights—Cook's right to implement the decision about what is to be taught and Milton's right to make and implement that decision himself. These rights must be balanced. But who is to do this balancing? The problem is that in schools, as in all organizations, the power and authority of the parties to a dispute are often not equal. This is especially obvious when one of the persons involved is subordinate to the other, as in the case at hand. To leave the required balancing up to the superior, however, is to run a significant risk that an injustice will be done. Yet that is how we customarily handle these matters in the everyday life of organizations. Alternatively, the dispute may be appealed to the next higher level of authority. The "chain of command" is also a chain of appeal. While such an appeal may mitigate the chance of doing an injustice, it does not eliminate it, for the higher-level administrator is unlikely to be an entirely disinterested party. Hence mechanisms have arisen to protect the rights of subordinates, and this is true of a teacher's right to academic freedom. Thus arguments about academic freedom must be set against the background of the institutions that have been created to protect it.

The primary need in protecting academic freedom is job security. If a teacher or scholar is to be free to "follow the argument where it leads," he or she must have some form of protection against dismissal for the expression of an unpopular idea.

Tenure

The institution that is supposed to provide this security is tenure. Before tenure became widespread in this century, it was not uncommon for a teacher to lose a position, after years of competent service, by expressing views that a school board or an administrator disliked.

The general idea of tenure is this: Upon hiring, a new faculty member is given a contract for a period of a certain duration, during which time the faculty member is considered to be on probation. The probationary period provides a time for the new faculty member to demonstrate competence and for the institution to judge that competence. If, at the end of this period, the individual is judged to meet the institution's standards, the faculty member is granted tenure. Having achieved tenure, the individual has a high level of job security. A tenured instructor can generally be terminated only for cause or financial exigency and only after due process requirements are complied with. (Dismissal for cause is discussed at length in Chapter 8.) Termination for causes such as professional incompetence, moral turpitude, or insubordination are relatively rare in public elementary or secondary education and are almost nonexistent in higher education. Terminations for financial exigency have, in times of declining enrollments and tight budgets, become more common but are still infrequent. The due process requirements for dismissal of a tenured faculty member, and the turmoil, alienation, and litigation that commonly result from such attempts, attach a significant penalty to the administrator bold enough to contemplate such a move.

Still, one may question the effectiveness or the appropriateness of tenure. Administrators who wish to inhibit the expression of an unpopular view have available lesser penalties more easily employed. Moreover, tenure affords no protection to those who lack it. Although there are legal safeguards to protect the academic freedom of the nontenured, they are unlikely to be effective against administrators possessed of even modest guile. Conversely, tenure may protect far more than academic freedom. The high cost of removal for cause can and does lead administrators to tolerate incompetent faculty.

The system of promotion and tenure operates differently in higher education than in elementary and secondary education. In higher education, the probationary period is normally longer—six years as opposed to the more usual three years at the lower levels. In both cases there is substantial local variation.

The most significant difference is the role of peer evaluation. In major universities, tenure judgments are commonly made by the senior colleagues of a nontenured faculty member. The departmental vote decides tenure. Although a dean or president may officially have the power of decision, it is not often exercised. In elementary and secondary education, however, tenure recommendations are normally the direct responsibility of an administrator, characteristically the building principal. Though power to grant tenure resides in the school board (just as in higher education it resides in the board of trustees), the substantive judgment on which the decision rests is the principal's.

Nevertheless, despite the significantly greater administrative presence in the award of tenure to public school teachers, once awarded it provides considerable legal protection to academic freedom. As a tenured member of Jefferson's faculty, John Milton's job security gives him wide latitude in the exercise of that freedom—latitude in deciding what and how he will teach. As we shall see, however, that freedom is not unrestricted. In any case, in addition to his job security, his academic freedom is itself afforded the protection of the law.

Legal Aspects of Academic Freedom and Free Expression

Academic freedom is not a constitutional right, but it is quite similar to the right of free speech, which is protected by the First Amendment to the Constitution. Thus academic freedom does have constitutional protection insofar as it is isomorphic with the right of free speech.

Moreover, judges have characteristically held that academic freedom is an important value to be upheld by the schools of a free society. The remarks of Chief Justice Earl Warren in *Sweezy v. New Hampshire* illustrate this sentiment:

The essentiality of freedom in the community of American universities is almost self-evident. No one should underestimate the vital role in a democracy that is played by those who guide and train our youth. To impose any strait jacket upon the intellectual leaders in our colleges and universities would imperil the future of our Nation. No field of education is so thoroughly comprehended by man that new discoveries cannot yet be made. Particularly is that true in the social sciences, where few, if any, principles are accepted as absolutes. Scholarship cannot flourish in an atmosphere of suspicion and distrust. Teachers and students must always remain free to inquire, to study and to evaluate, to gain new maturity and understanding; otherwise our civilization will stagnate and die. (p. 169)

The Supreme Court has also viewed the free speech of teachers as contributing to the making of educational policy. Justice Marshall writes in *Pickering v. Board of Education:*

More importantly, the question whether a school system requires additional funds is a matter of legitimate public concern on which the judgment of the school administration, including the School Board, cannot, in a society that leaves such questions to popular vote, be taken as conclusive. On such a question free and open debate is vital to informed decision-making by the electorate. Teachers are, as a class, the members of a community most likely to have informed and definite opinions as to how funds allotted to the operation of the schools should be spent. Accordingly, it is essential that they be able to speak out freely on such questions without fear of retaliatory dismissal. (p. 600)

Federal courts, then, have generally brought academic freedom under the umbrella of free speech, affording it the protection of the Constitution. Two general ideas are crucial to understanding how this protection works.

First, courts have consistently held that an individual cannot be required to waive constitutional rights as a condition of employment or be terminated for the exercise of such rights. Justice Marshall notes in *Pickering:*

To the extent that the Illinois Supreme Court's opinion may be read to suggest that teachers may constitutionally be compelled to relinquish the First Amendment rights they would otherwise enjoy as citizens to comment on matters of public interest in connection with the operation of the public schools in which they work, it proceeds on a premise that has been unequivocally rejected in numerous prior decisions of this Court. (p. 598)

Here a teacher's right to academic freedom (or any other right protected by the Constitution) does not depend on whether or not he or she has tenure.

Second, however, whether or not one has tenure has a great deal to do with one's ability to demonstrate in court that a right has been violated. Tenure gives one the right to a hearing and means that dismissal must be for cause (see Chapter 8). It thus shifts the burden of proof from the teacher to the teacher's employer and gives a teacher threatened with dismissal a legal means to investigate whether or not his or her rights have been violated. Probationary teachers have less opportunity to demonstrate a violation of their rights.

Knowing that academic freedom has constitutional protection does not, of course, do much to specify its legal content. We shall try to give a general picture of what this content is by looking at certain key cases that have addressed this matter.

First, it is reasonably clear that both teachers and students have the right to express personal political opinions in the classroom. The case that established this right (*Tinker v. Des Moines*) concerned a group of students who wore black armbands to school to protest the Vietnam war and were suspended for doing so. In the resulting suit, the Supreme Court ruled that (1) teachers and students do not give up their constitutional rights to free speech when they enter a school, (2) wearing a black armband was a form of "symbolic speech," and (3) free speech may be restricted only if it appeared likely to lead to a material and substantial disruption of the educational process. *Tinker* was explicitly extended to teachers in *James v. Board of Education of Central District No. 1* (in which the armband was worn by a teacher). Here the judge ruled that unless a teacher explicitly tries to convince his students that his values and only his values are appropriate, the teacher's right to free expression was protected.

Second, teachers have the right to express their opinions publicly on educational matters, even when those opinions are in direct conflict with their employing board. In the case of *Pickering v. Board of Education,* Pickering, a teacher, wrote a rather insulting letter to the editor containing a number of factual errors. The letter condemned the board for its handling of school funds. Pickering was fired as a result. The Supreme Court, however, held that Pickering's action was constitutionally protected. Writing for the majority, Justice Marshall held that a teacher's right to speak out on issues of educational policy serves to inform the electorate and that neither the factual errors nor the insulting tone of the published letter was sufficient to override his First Amendment rights.

Third, teachers have the right to choose their methods of teaching, even if those methods are controversial, unless the method in question has been explicitly forbidden by school authorities. In *Mailloux v. Kiley,* a teacher, in the course of a lesson on free speech and pornography, had written the word *fuck* on the blackboard and was dismissed as a consequence. The court ordered his reinstatement on the grounds that the word was relevant to the lesson, was not beyond the sophistication of the students, did not have a disturbing effect on them, and no student was compelled to participate in the ensuing discussion. The judge further noted that it is the purpose of academic freedom to protect "a teaching method which is relevant and in the opinion of experts . . . has a serious educational purpose." He concluded that when a teacher employs a controversial method, "the state may suspend or discharge [him] but it may not resort to such drastic sanctions unless the state proves he was put on notice either by regulation or otherwise that he should not use that method." While a choice of teaching method is thus not fully protected by academic freedom, a teacher has considerable latitude in using his or her professional judgment in choosing among methods that are not expressly forbidden.

Perhaps the most difficult question to decide is whether or not John Milton's refusal to implement the *America the Beautiful* curriculum might enjoy some legal protection. Here the issues are complex.

In our judgment, it is likely that a court would require Milton to adopt the curriculum. In a case dealing with a teacher who emphasized sex education in a health course against the wishes of his department, a federal court held that there was no constitutional right to override the decisions of colleagues or superiors on course content (*Clark v. Holmes*). Generally, the power to determine the curriculum resides in the school board or in those to whom they delegate that power. Other things being equal, academic freedom will not permit teachers to subvert the intent of the board.

This is not, however, the end of the matter. The interesting question is not whether Milton is free to ignore the *America the Beautiful* curriculum altogether. It is whether he is free to modify it, supplement it, teach it in a way so as to serve his view of how social studies should be taught. Milton might, for example, wish to omit particularly offensive passages of the book. He might supplement the texts with other material designed to challenge its assumptions. He might use this material in a way not intended by its authors. He might, for example, have students analyze it as an exercise in political indoctrination. How far might the teacher go in molding this curriculum to his purposes?

Here the answer is far from clear. Courts have upheld the dismissal of teachers for refusing to conform to an expected teaching style (*Hetrick v. Martin*). On the other hand, in one of the more noteworthy cases on academic freedom in the high school context, *Parducci v. Rutland,* a federal court upheld the right of Marilyn Parducci to assign a Kurt Vonnegut story against the expressed wishes of her principal. And another court has held that teachers cannot be dismissed because of a disagreement over educational philosophy (*Beebee v. Hazlitt Public Schools*). In both cases the courts pointed to the importance of permitting experimentation.

These cases seem close to the balance point between the demand for administrative and public control over the educational process. In any issue where courts are called upon to balance claims that are in themselves legitimate and important, it is always possible to construct or imagine cases that are close to the balance point and in which the result of litigation is highly unpredictable.

The Institution of Academic Freedom

As the law on academic freedom should illustrate, few rights are absolute. There are always cases where the exercise of a right begins to interfere with the rights of others. As someone has quipped, "Your right to swing your fist ends where my nose begins." When rights conflict, a way must be found to balance them.

Sam Cook's reaction to John Milton's claims to academic freedom can be expressed as a point about balancing rights. The teacher has asserted a right to academic freedom and has said that this right extends to his selection of what and how he shall teach. The principal has not denied that the teacher's right to academic freedom must be balanced against other rights. He expresses these rights in terms of his capacity to lead: "How can I lead if no one has to follow?"

Leadership, however, is not an end in itself. If the principal had to justify his right to lead, he might want to say something like this: "My leadership is important to the successful operation of Jefferson. The purpose of this school is to serve the needs of its pupils and those of the community. How those needs are to be met is ultimately a decision of the citizens of this town and of the state, voiced through their elected representatives. Those representatives, specifically the Board of Education, have appointed me to ensure that their decisions are implemented. I am obligated by my position to use my power, authority, and leadership to see to it that the public's wishes are served. Hence, ultimately my ability to lead will affect how well Jefferson is able to serve its students and its community." The real interests that underlie Cook's concern for leadership are the interests of Jefferson's students and the community Jefferson serves.

Nor is academic freedom valued simply for its own sake. If John Milton is to defend his right to academic freedom successfully, he must be able to explain what its point is. What good is it? Whose interests does it serve? Some ideas about questions like these may help us to understand how the teacher's right to academic freedom can be balanced against the principal's obligation to exercise leadership.

The Rationale and Mores of Academic Freedom

What is the point of academic freedom? Consider these comments by J. S. Mill taken from his essay "On Liberty" (Mill, 1956). Mill is summarizing his arguments for what he calls freedom of opinion and freedom of expression.

> First, if any opinion is compelled to silence, that opinion may, for aught we can certainly know, be true. To deny this is to assume our own infallibility.
>
> Secondly, though the silenced opinion be an error, it may, and very commonly does, contain a portion of truth; and since the general or prevailing opinion on any subject is rarely or never the whole truth, it is only by the

collision of adverse opinions that the remainder of the truth has any chance of being supplied.

Thirdly, even if the received opinion be not only true, but the whole truth; unless it is suffered to be, and actually, is vigorously and earnestly contested, it will by most of those who receive it, be held in the manner of a prejudice, with little comprehension or feeling of its rational grounds. And not only this, but fourthly, the meaning of the doctrine itself will be in danger of being lost or enfeebled, and deprived of its vital effect on the character and conduct: the dogma becoming a mere formal profession, inefficacious for good, but cumbering the ground and preventing the growth of any real and heartfelt conviction from reason or personal experience. (p. 64)

Mill is not arguing for academic freedom. He is arguing for such broad civil liberties as free speech, free press, and freedom of conscience. Academic freedom, while a close kin to such rights, differs from them in being more narrowly applied to educational institutions. Mill's arguments, however, do suggest two points that are crucial to understanding the purpose of academic freedom.

The first point is that freedom is important to the growth of knowledge. Here the focus is on research—on adding to what human beings collectively know. If inquiry is to be possible, ideas must be seen as tentative and subject to modification; criticism and debate must be permitted. The argument is put most persuasively in these remarks from a group of senior scholars from the University of Cape Town and Witwatersrand quoted by Justice Frankfurter in *Sweezy v. New Hampshire:*

In a university knowledge is its own end, not merely a means to an end. A university ceases to be true to its own nature if it becomes the tool of Church or State or any sectional interest. A university is characterized by the spirit of free inquiry, its ideal being the ideal of Socrates—"to follow the argument where it leads." This implies the right to examine, question, modify or reject traditional ideas and beliefs. Dogma and hypothesis are incompatible, and the concept of an immutable doctrine is repugnant to the spirit of a university. The concern of its scholars is not merely to add and revise facts in relation to an acceptable framework, but to be ever examining and modifying the framework itself.

Freedom to reason and freedom for disputation on the basis of observation and experiment are the necessary conditions for the advancement of scientific knowledge. A sense of freedom is also necessary for creative work in the arts which, equally with scientific research, is the concern of the university.

. . . It is the business of a university to provide that atmosphere which is most conducive to speculations, experiment and creation. (pp. 262, 263)

One function of academic freedom, then, is to establish a proper climate for the growth of knowledge by permitting and encouraging an environment where ideas can be questioned, examined, and debated.

A second function of academic freedom is to encourage the growth of individual learners. Note that encouraging the growth of knowledge is not in and of itself sufficient to promote the growth of individual competence among the members of a society. A society may encourage inquiry among researchers while at the same time attempting to confine that knowledge to an elite. Academic freedom, however, may be conceived not just as the right of university researchers but as a right of any teacher or learner. When this right of academic freedom is treated as a right of any learner, the hope is not that something new will be added to the store of human knowledge. No one, after all, expects that Milton and his students will add much to our collective understanding of the political system. Rather, the hope is that by participating in a process of critical and free inquiry, students will acquire the knowledge and skills that are prerequisite to becoming competent, autonomous, and thoughtful persons. A society that values the competence and independence of its members must value intellectual liberty as well.

The National Education Association (NEA, 1984) has expressed such a "learner-oriented" view of academic freedom:

> *The National Education Association believes that academic and professional freedom is essential to the teaching profession. Controversial issues should be a part of instructional programs when judgment of the professional staff deems the issues appropriate to the curriculum and to the maturity level of the student. Academic freedom is the right of the learner and his/her teachers to explore, present, and discuss divergent points of view in the quest for knowledge and truth. (p. 223)*

In short, academic freedom is not simply a right of university professors. In a free society, it is a right belonging to teachers and learners at all levels of the educational system.

The point of academic freedom, then, is to promote growth, both the growth of human knowledge and the growth of the individual learner's competence and independence. Note that these objectives of academic freedom do not merely serve the interests of researchers, teachers, and students; they serve the public interest. In a free democratic society, both knowledge and widespread personal competence must be highly valued. Insofar as academic freedom contributes to such objectives, it serves an important social good.

These two objectives of academic freedom will, of course, be served differently by different kinds of educational institutions. Encouraging free inquiry so as to promote the growth of knowledge will be a concern largely of higher education. Learning, however, is a primary objective for education at any level. When we consider education at any level, we must be interested in establishing an environment to encourage the development of independent and competent people.

What, then, is academic freedom, and what is its scope? A start at a definition can be made by suggesting that *academic freedom is the right to hold and advocate whatever opinions one chooses and to criticize the opinions of others without fear of punishment or reprisal.* A moment's reflection, however, should suggest that this definition is too broad. It would seem to prohibit some very common activities. A student who believes that Lincoln was the first president, or one who holds that the angles of a triangle add up to 125 degrees, may well find that his or her grade in history or geometry is lowered on that account. Likewise, universities are unlikely to hire or promote astrologers, alchemists, or even conventional researchers whose work fails to gain the respect of professional colleagues. Are such activities violations of academic freedom?

Let us ask the question more generally. The activities just described are all cases of evaluation. They involve judgments about the competence or quality of an individual's work. Are such activities precluded by academic freedom? After all, like freedom, evaluation is an important condition of the growth of knowledge and the growth of individual competence. Knowledge cannot expand if every opinion must be regarded as being as good as every other. Individuals do not grow if they receive no criticism on the quality of their performance. The question, then, is how the definition of academic freedom may be modified so as to permit evaluation.

We would suggest that the best way to state the ideals of academic freedom is to make a distinction between the content of an idea and the competence with which it is held. Imagine two students, both of whom believe that the sum of the angles of a triangle need not total 180 degrees. Suppose further that the first simply refuses to accept or cannot understand geometry, while the second student sees and can show that the sum of angles is 180 degrees only of triangles on a plane surface. Although the content of their beliefs may be similar, the first student demonstrates a lack of understanding of geometry and the second a good understanding because of the manner in which these beliefs are achieved. Thus academic freedom precludes making evaluative judgments based on the content of beliefs but permits evaluative judgments based on the competence of their holding. People may not be penalized because they hold unpopular beliefs. They may be penalized because they arrive at them in incompetent ways. With this distinction in mind, Strike (1982b) formulates the core of the concept of academic freedom. "Scholars may not be rewarded, denied rewards or punished on account of the content of the views they express, but may be rewarded, denied awards or punished on account of the competence with which they argue their views" (p. 77).

Recall that John Milton's conflict with Sam Cook was not per se rooted in his advocacy of some idea rejected by Cook. It is focused on the teacher's refusal to teach the prescribed curriculum. Does academic freedom extend to the teacher's right to choose what to teach or how to teach?

Consider an argument to show that it does: What one teaches and how one teaches cannot be separated from the content of one's convictions. John Milton might argue this by making four points. The first is that the *America the Beautiful* curriculum reflects a political orientation and a set of purposes that he does not share. It is conservative in its viewpoint, and it attempts to teach an uncritical patriotism rather than a critical and questioning attitude toward American society. Milton regards the curriculum's intense "America first" tone as offensive. He indicated that he was perfectly willing to allow teachers whose convictions were consistent with the curriculum to teach it. But to compel him to use it was to compel him to deny his deepest political convictions. The content of Milton's views about his subject matter are intimately related to his selection of what to teach. Therefore, one could not compel him to teach something he did not wish to teach without violating his academic freedom.

A second point concerns Milton's discipline. He has had considerable training in history. As a consequence of that training, he is aware of certain facts or accepted professional opinions that *America the Beautiful* either ignores or treats incorrectly. He has an obligation to, as he puts it, "teach the truth"—a truth that in his professional opinion is misrepresented in the texts. For example, he knows that many American historians accept the idea that this country's founding fathers were motivated not so much by their love of liberty as by their love of money—their primary intent was to protect the interests of their own economic class. This notion, and all others like it, is entirely missing from the book. Hence the text does not represent historical truth as best that truth can be discerned. The teacher might further argue that he is the only party in the dispute who is competent to make the final choice of what to teach. This is probably the intent of his remarks that selecting a text is an academic matter.

The third point is that Milton's choice of how to teach has the same connection to his views on his subject matter as his views on what to teach. He believes that the primary reason for teaching social studies is not to transmit facts about government or to inculcate patriotism; it is to communicate the skills of political participation. While these skills certainly involve learning how the political system works, they also involve a facility with political argument and with the political process. This view of social studies requires an active and participatory approach to teaching the subject matter. Such an approach is demanded not only because it is an effective way to teach but because it is also the only way to teach the subject that is consistent with the teacher's view of the subject.

Finally, John Milton might claim that his view of teaching is more consistent with the freedom of students than is the content and implied methodology of the *America the Beautiful* series. The curriculum tends to reflect a single point of view. Moreover, the method of teaching envisaged in the program focuses on transmitting that viewpoint rather than making it an object of discussion and reflection. Since students who take high school social studies are young and politically unsophisticated, this one-sided approach is particularly unfortunate and unfair. In this case, to protect the teacher's academic freedom is also to protect the freedom of his students.

These arguments show that the scope of application of academic freedom extends from research to teaching and from the content of a teacher's beliefs to what will be taught and how it will be taught. John Milton has the right to claim the protection of academic freedom to protect his choice of what and how to teach.

Constraints on Academic Freedom

We do not, however, conclude that this is the end of the issue. Even though academic freedom does extend to a teacher's choice of what and how to teach, it may be necessary to balance John Milton's right to academic freedom against other legitimate rights and interests. We must consider what these rights and interests might be.

Let us put the question in the following way: What interests does Cook represent that are important enough that he should be entitled to have authority over Milton with respect to such central functions of education as curricular choice? Why should we not view Cook (and all administrators) as simply "facilitators" of the teaching process (a view, incidentally, espoused by some administrators as well as teachers)?

Consider that in our discussion of zones of acceptance, we noted that teachers were generally most willing to accept the authority of administrators over "administrivia" and least willing to accept their authority over the things that really matter, such as curriculum and teaching. We may regard John Milton's argument for academic freedom as a justification for this view. That is, Milton could be seen as having claimed that the arguments for academic freedom provide reasons why core educational activities belong outside the zone of acceptance. It is precisely these activities that require the protection of academic freedom.

Such a view of the administrative role is tantamount to seeing the administrator as a servant of teachers rather than supervisor of teachers. The administrator is the person who is responsible to see to it that the supplies are ordered, that the heating system works, that student records are kept, and, generally, that the teacher has available the resources that are necessary to teach. It is not, however, the responsibility of the administrator to interfere with the professional judgment of the teacher with respect to central educational decisions.

It is worth noting that this view of the administrative role is precisely the view of administration that is held by many university professors. Such a view, however, is (arguably) more appropriate to a university context than to a public school. University professors are characteristically more highly trained and specialized in their subjects than public school teachers. Moreover, the educational decisions made by university professors require a higher level of expertise in the subject matter. It is less likely that a university administrator will know what counts as a suitable curriculum in nuclear physics than it is that Sam Cook will know what counts as a suitable curriculum in civics. Also, the purposes of a university may be more strictly academic in their character than the purposes of a public school. Public schools may be as interested in transmitting parental and community values as in promoting the dispassionate pursuit of truth. Finally, the university student may be presumed to be more mature than the public school student and as a consequence less in need of protection from the teacher who wishes to give a one-sided argument or to indoctrinate the student in a personal point of view.

We may now return to our central question. What interests does Sam Cook represent that entitle him to some authority over John Milton's educational decisions and must be balanced against Milton's claims for academic freedom?

Perhaps the most important thing to suggest is that Cook represents the authority of parents and the community over the education of children (see Chapter

6). To argue that John Milton has complete freedom to determine what and how he will teach is, in effect, to say that parents and the community have no say over what and how their children will be taught. Thus, insofar as we believe that parents and the community have some legitimate say over the education of their children, we cannot consistently believe that teachers have complete authority over educational decisions. Cook is not just an administrator. He is the representative of the authority of the community. His decisions concerning educational matters represent the authority of the community.

A related point is that one may reasonably see the public school as a device to transmit parental and community values as well as a marketplace of ideas. We will discuss this issue more fully in the next chapter. Here let us note that John Milton's view of academic freedom is also tantamount to holding that decisions about the values to be realized in education are entirely the prerogative of professionals. Only they may determine what is worth learning and what values should be passed on to children. If one believes that parents and communities have some right to influence the values that are transmitted to their children, one must also recognize some limits on academic freedom.

It is worth noting in this respect that John Milton seems to have a confused notion of educational authority, one that we believe to be rather common. He has been an advocate of parental participation in educational decision making. But he also believes that his right to academic freedom entitles him to the final say on all substantive educational matters, and he especially seems to believe that parents may not properly see the school as a means to transmit their *political* values to their children. These views are fundamentally inconsistent.

We should also ask whether John Milton's view of academic freedom is consistent with the rights of students. Public school students are both immature and a captive audience. These facts strongly suggest that the public that compels students to attend school also has some duty to protect them from abuse while they are there. Surely among the various forms of abuse from which students require protection are indoctrination, instruction that is inappropriate to their age or maturity, and inept or inappropriate teaching methods. We have suggested that to a considerable extent the question of how to teach cannot be answered apart from the nature of the subject matter being taught. However, no one believes that every public school teacher is so imbued with the intellectual standards of his or her subject that indoctrination or inept and inappropriate instruction are nonexistent. John Milton's view of academic freedom seems to give total discretion over educational matters to teachers. Such a view of academic freedom protects not only the marketplace of ideas but also the teacher who wishes to indoctrinate students in a favorite ideology. To recognize that the maturity of students and their status as a captive audience should entitle them to some protection against potential teacher abuse is to recognize that there must be some limits to teachers' claims to academic freedom.

The final value that must be balanced against the right to academic freedom is the efficient management of the school and the coordination of its educational program. It is reasonable to suppose that students will learn more if there is some coordination between what they are taught from class to class and from grade to grade. Moreover, any organization that expects to provide an effective service requires the capacity to make and implement plans in an efficient manner. Efficiency has preconditions. Individuals need to be willing to subordinate their desires to collective direction. Leadership must be possible, and leadership sometimes requires that others be willing or compelled to obey appropriately made decisions regardless of whether they agree with them. Insofar as academic freedom entitles a teacher to make educational decisions without considering the rest of the program or the overall efficiency of the school, it may be educationally dysfunctional. Indeed, the scope of academic freedom demanded by John Milton seems to entitle teachers to operate schools as intellectual anarchies, where any coordination between various components of the program will occur only because of voluntary cooperation or luck.

Summary

John Milton's argument for extensive academic freedom seems to depend on an image of the public school as a place where people come together to pursue truth under the guidance of someone who is thoroughly trained in some intellectual tradition and who alone is able to make competent decisions about what and how to teach in terms of the intellectual demands of that subject matter. It is in some ways an appealing view of what schools should be. It is not, however, a complete view of what public schools should be, and it is certainly not a complete picture of what they are. Schools are also places created by parents and communities to transmit their values and what they deem to be appropriate and necessary skills to their children. They are places that immature children are compelled to attend and to be taught by teachers, few of whom have attained high degrees of expertise in their fields and some of whom are hardly more learned than their students. Finally, they are complex organizations that require coordination and efficient management if education is to happen in efficient ways. A view of academic freedom must accommodate itself to these realities. Good administration is not equivalent to facilitating the actions of teachers.

Consider now how Sam Cook might respond to John Milton's views on academic freedom. He might begin by granting prima facie validity to Milton's argument. Other things being equal, academic freedom should protect a teacher's right to free choice of teaching materials and methods.

However, other things are not equal. Milton's arguments are predicated on two assumptions that Cook cannot grant. The first is that the parents and the community who hired Cook, who gave him the responsibility to oversee the operations of Jefferson High, and who have participated in the selection of the *America the Beautiful* curriculum, have no right to an effective say in what their children are taught. Giving parents a say in curricular matters must mean something more than merely permitting them to voice an opinion. Cook, in this case, can properly see himself as representing the authority of the community over the educational process. Parents, after all, were on the committee that selected the curriculum, and the Board of Education has approved their choice. Second, Milton's arguments assume that Cook has no right to insist that the teachers at Jefferson collectively provide a coordinated and efficiently run program of instruction. The point of the Curriculum Committee is to coordinate the program. The *America the Beautiful* curriculum was the product of a collective choice involving not only parents but John Milton's colleagues. Cook's authority does not in this case represent some abstract "tyranny of the majority" imposed on Milton's intellectual freedom. It represents the need to have a coordinated and effective educational program. In short, the right of parents and community to have an effective voice in the education of their children and the need for an efficient and coordinated program outweigh the teacher's claim to academic freedom. Therefore, Cook might argue Milton must be made to cooperate.

In our opinion, Cook does have a right to expect Milton to adopt the *America the Beautiful* curriculum. This does not, however, mean that the teacher has no right to academic freedom. It is surely unreasonable, for example, to expect Milton to behave as though he believes everything in the book. And it is even more unreasonable to expect him to attempt to get his students to accept uncritically everything in the book.

What follows is that while Cook may be entitled to compel Milton to use the text and actually to teach from it in good faith, Cook does not have the right to confine Milton to the text or its viewpoint. Academic freedom here should mean that the teacher may comment on the text, challenge its ideas, discuss its inadequacies with his students, and supplement the text with other material critical of its views. To deny the teacher these privileges is to grant the principal and the Jefferson Curriculum Committee more than the right to set the curriculum. It is to grant them the right to determine what may be thought about or believed. The arguments against John Milton's expansive view of academic freedom seek to promote efficiency in instruction. But to constrain the teacher in his use of the required material is to seek to police thought; it is the central purpose of the concept of academic freedom to prevent this.

Democracy and Reason in Administrative Leadership

You may have noticed that we failed to use the terms *democratic* and *autocratic* in our discussion of leadership. The failure is deliberate. We do not believe that describing an administrator in those terms is particularly enlightening, nor that "democratic leadership" (whatever that might be) is necessarily superior to "autocratic leadership" (whatever that might be). We are well aware that these terms are bandied about in educational circles and that practitioners are frequently praised or condemned by the use of one or the other. We think, however, that these terms merely confuse an already complicated matter. After all, just what would it mean to say, for example, that Sam Cook is a democratic principal? Does it mean that he consults with his faculty on important matters? With parents? With students? Does "consulting" mean calling for a binding vote on an issue or simply informally soliciting opinions from a few friends on the faculty? On what matters should opinions be solicited? Over curricular choice? It was just such "democratic" behavior that created the problem at Jefferson High School. Perhaps "democratic" means simply promoting the interests of the ruled rather than those of the rulers. If so, who are the ruled? Teachers? Articulate students would scoff at that idea: It is they, not teachers, after all, who require permission even to relieve themselves. Perhaps being "democratic" simply means practicing a kind of equality. But are Cook and Milton equals? Surely not in the power they wield over events at Jefferson.

The point is simply this: A school is not a political democracy, a government by the ruled, exercised directly or through their elected representatives. Schools are sharply hierarchical organizations, with a steep gradient of authority and with ultimate power resting in elected school boards and state legislatures, not teachers, pupils, or administrators. Moreover, if one believes that parents have a right to influence educational decisions, it is surely inappropriate for schools to be self-contained democracies. Cook's power and authority as principal of Jefferson comes ultimately from the electorate of his community and his state, not from the people he "rules."

It is a mistake, then, we think, to confuse schools with miniature polities. There are real and legitimate power differences between teachers and principals, just as there are real and equally legitimate power differences between teachers and students (see Chapter 3 concerning students' rights). To be confused on this matter is to run the risk of encouraging a kind of hypocrisy in which administrators encourage teacher "participation" in decision making when such participation is really a thinly disguised attempt to "sell" employees on a decision already made at higher levels in the organization—to clothe power in the garments of political equality. To consider desirable school leadership as "democratic" may be to foster cynicism or confusion among subordinates and guile or self-deception among administrators.

All of this is not to say that a school is no different from the local bank or factory, where administrative power may be exercised with relatively few restraints. Indeed, our discussion of academic freedom was intended to illustrate an important, unique, and legitimate constraint on administrative action that is not present in those other organizations. Further, and also unlike them, schools, of all institutions in our society, are committed to the growth and maintenance of rationality, to reason. Perhaps their primary purpose is developing in the young the capacity to reason effectively. With such a purpose, it is incumbent on educators—teachers and administrators alike—to exemplify the role of reason in human affairs. Thus an administrative action is more properly judged by the quality of the reasoning that undergirds it than whether or not it is "democratic" or "autocratic." An action carried out for sound and explicitly stated reasons is preferable to its opposite, even if the former is "autocratic" in the style of its execution.

Early in this chapter we briefly noted the distinction between organizational authority and persuasion. The latter, we said, is not a form of authority. Instead, compliance is based on the reasons given for an intended action; there is no requirement that one's critical faculties be suspended in advance of a request. The academic freedom and tenure enjoyed by educators, the institutionalized commitment of schools to the free expression of ideas, and the belief that out of the clash of conflicting views a semblance of truth will emerge, all commend persuasion as a peculiarly appropriate style of "leadership" for school administrators, albeit not a style captured by LBDQs, *Managerial Grids,* or LPC scales.

Although the Cook-Milton case is fictional, the participants' inability to articulate the rationale for their actions is, we fear, all too common among both teachers and administrators. Among the latter this is doubly unfortunate. In an institution devoted to the development of rationality, administrators must be capable of expressing a principled basis for their actions. However, we also believe that they have a responsibility for understanding and expressing the principles that undergird the actions of their subordinates when, as in John Milton's case, those subordinates are unable to do so for themselves. In this sense, in a dispute with a teacher, an administrator is obligated to be his or her own worst enemy. It is too bad that John Milton only dimly grasped the nature of his right to academic freedom. It is far worse that Sam Cook "couldn't see that academic freedom had much to do with choosing high school textbooks."

Ultimately, if graduate training in educational administration is to improve the management of schools (and there is cause to doubt that it does; see Gross & Herriott, 1965), it will be because novice administrators gain the technical and ethical concepts necessary to reason more adequately about their own and their subordinates' responsibilities and to express those reasons in a competent manner.

Questions

1. If you were John Milton, what might you do in order to teach as you liked while maximizing you chances of gaining legal protection for your behavior?

2. If you were Sam Cook, how far would you permit John Milton to go in modifying the curriculum, assuming that he could be convinced to adopt the disputed book? Suppose that he used the book as a foil, treating it as an example of chauvinistic writing and, as a result, induced some of his students to have substantial doubts about the value of patriotism, loyalty, and America's role in history—all of this in direct opposition to the implicit wishes of the board. Would you support him in such a usage?

3. To what extent do the arguments given for academic freedom apply to elementary and high school teachers? Is tenure the best mechanism to protect their job security?

4. Was it a mistake for Sam Cook to allow parents to participate in curriculum decisions? Should professionals always maintain ultimate control?

5. Can the academic freedom of teachers ever be inconsistent with the academic freedom of students?

6. We have said that principals generally lack significant rewards and punishments to have much influence on teacher behavior. Can you make a contrary argument?

7. Why should academics and public school teachers enjoy the particular protection afforded by tenure when that protection is not extended to other salaried professionals? What, really, is the difference between teachers and social workers?

CHAPTER 2

School District Conflict and the Matter of Censorship

A Case of Censorship?

Puddly-in-the-Slough School District is a small, rural district in the mountainous section of one of our eastern states. Its citizens have traditionally been coal miners or farmers—although lately a number of suburban tracts have been built in the community. Many of these newer homes, owned by middle- and upper-income people who commute to a nearby city, stand in sharp contrast to the somewhat down-at-the-heels residences in the older parts of town.

These changes in population have generated some stress in the district. Because of the influx of new students, the school system was compelled to undertake a building program. The longtime residents (the "locals") were less than pleased to find their taxes increasing in order to pay for the education of the more affluent "newcomers."

Nor was concern limited to fiscal matters. The locals had a different set of educational values than the newcomers. Their children generally did not aspire to college. Indeed, many did not finish high school. After school they returned to the farm, found a job in the mines, or took a blue-collar job in the nearby city. Their parents' idea of education was the three R's, discipline, and vocational education. The newcomers, however, assumed that their children would attend college and expected the Puddly schools to prepare them to do so. They wanted their schools to provide college preparatory classes and to emphasize creativity and critical thinking.

There were other differences between the two groups. The newcomers were oriented to the cultural and economic life of the city and ignored local community activities. They were less inclined than the locals to be religious, and the majority of those who had some religious convictions attended either one of the liberal Protestant congregations in the city or the Reform synagogue. The locals, however, were community-oriented. They turned out for the Maple Festival and the woodcutters' contest. They shopped in the village. Their religious life was dominated by two independent churches, the Steadfast Baptist Church and the Holiness Pentacostal Church.

The teachers in Puddly generally identified with the newcomers. Although some of the teachers, particularly the older ones, had been born and raised in town, a significant percentage of them had been hired during Puddly's period of rapid growth. They saw themselves as professionals and identified with the interests of the newcomers. They were also newly unionized.

Over the past few years the locals had come to feel vaguely alienated from the school's program and staff. The town paper, the Puddly *Splash,* had recently contained several letters commenting on unionization, which had suggested that the teachers' union would make sure that the school was run for the benefit of teachers and not students.

These community tensions were not, however, reflected in the deliberations of the Puddly school board. For years the board's meetings had been relatively brief and amicable, principally concerned with financial and building issues or other items put before it for decision by the superintendent (whose recommendations were almost always followed). Its public sessions were sparsely attended, and typically the only representations made to it were those of the PTA delegate, the teachers' union delegate, and someone speaking for the taxpayers' association when the annual budget was under consideration. Board members, who were primarily drawn from the business and professional classes of Puddly, viewed themselves as representing the entire community. As the board saw it, its duty was to make decisions in the interest of all the children of the district. Of its nine members, seven had been chosen in yearly at-large elections, while two had been appointed by the board itself to fill vacancies that had occurred in midterm. Board members knew and generally liked one another and tried to conduct their meetings in a "businesslike and professional manner." If they were aware of the growing disaffection of some segments of the public, they did not let that awareness intrude on making rational, "nonpolitical" decisions.

Now this quiet had been shattered. It had all started innocently enough. Jane Pious, a student in Andrew Mill's eleventh-grade English class, complained to her mother that she did not wish to read a book assigned to her because it was "dirty." Mrs. Pious looked over the book, J. D. Salinger's *Catcher in the Rye,* and found that it was indeed, by her standards, a dirty book.

Mrs. Pious went to school, book in hand, and presented the matter to the Puddly High principal, Edward Smart. Mr. Smart read a few choice passages selected by Mrs. Pious and concluded that he saw what Mrs. Pious was getting at. Later that day he discussed the matter with Mr. Mill. Mr. Mill indicated that the book had been assigned for a book report and that if the student did not wish to review that one, he would assign her another. Mr. Smart called Mrs. Pious to inform her of the decision. When she expressed thanks for his concern, Mr. Smart assumed that the issue was ended.

He could not have been more wrong. As fate would have it, Mr. Pious was a deacon of the Steadfast Baptist Church. At one deacon's meeting he happened to mention the incident to Rev. Stone, the pastor of the church. Rev. Stone thought little of the matter until the next day when he was talking with his son, who was also a student in Mr. Mill's class. He asked to see what his son was reading for his book report. That, as it happened, was Kurt Vonnegut's *Cat's Cradle.*

Rev. Stone was outraged. He regarded the book as obscene, anti-American, and antireligious. He did not, however, go directly to Principal Smart. Rather, he took it upon himself to review the other books on Mr. Mill's list in order to find out what else had been assigned to the children of his congregation.

His inquiry produced a list of three other works that he found to be "inappropriate": Kurt Vonnegut's *Slaughterhouse Five,* Aldous Huxley's *Brave New World,* and

Eldridge Cleaver's *Soul on Ice*. Rev. Stone then made an appointment with Mr. Vacey, the superintendent of schools. In addition to Rev. Stone and Mr. Vacey, the meeting was attended by several parents, Mr. Smart, and Mr. Mill. Rev. Stone asked that different books be assigned to each of the children whose parents objected to their children's assignments. He also expressed the view that the superintendent might wish to take a closer look at what was going on in Mr. Mill's class.

This time Mr. Mill dug in his heels. He announced that he was not going to allow his book selection to be reviewed by a group of self-appointed censors. The session became increasingly heated and ended when the teacher abruptly got up and walked out. Mr. Vacey told Rev. Stone that he would talk further with Mr. Mill and get back to him.

Various events, including a holiday recess, prevented an early meeting of the superintendent, the principal, and the teacher. When Mr. Vacey got around to talking with Mr. Smart and Mr. Mill, he found that the teacher had not been idle. He had talked with the head of the teachers' union, and the union had established a committee to consider the role of parents in curricular decisions. Although its deliberations were not quite completed, the union head said that the committee viewed Rev. Stone and his supporters as attempting to usurp the proper function of teachers and that their actions amounted to an attempt to censor the reading materials selected by the professional staff. As the union official put it, "We are not going to stand idly by while the curriculum is gutted on the whims of a small group of right-wing, religious fundamentalists. If we yield to them on the matter of selecting English books, we may as well turn over control of the schools to these flakes."

Superintendent Vacey then called Rev. Stone and told him that while he personally sympathized with Rev. Stone's concerns, Mr. Mill had refused to change his mind. Mr. Vacey went on to explain that his hands were tied by the union and the courts and that there was nothing he could do. He declined Rev. Stone's request to put the issue on the agenda of the next board meeting, saying that he was sure the issue could be worked out "when everyone had a chance to cool down."

Rev. Stone was not impressed. His reaction was a sermon the following Sunday on immorality in the schools, followed by the organization of the Committee on Morality in Puddly Schools. The committee, which soon became somewhat illogically known as COPS, went to work to find out "just what's really going on in our schools."

In a mere six weeks COPS was ready with a report, which it provided simultaneously to the school board and the Puddly *Splash*. COPS's report was a wholesale castigation of the Puddly curriculum, which was described in one concluding sentence as "promoting anti-American, anti-Christian, Godless, immoral, secular humanism." These are some of its highlights:

1. COPS produced a list of ten titles that were required reading in various classes and that it considered immoral. Another dozen or so optional books were objected to on similar grounds.
2. COPS identified a further set of twenty-five titles in the Puddly High School library that were either immoral or anti-American.
3. COPS objected to the elementary school social studies curriculum, *Man: A Course of Studies*, on the grounds that it taught ethical relativism.
4. COPS objected to a course in values clarification for similar reasons.
5. COPS objected to teaching evolution as a fact rather than a theory and to the failure to give equal time to "scientific creationism."

The report generated several weeks of hostile letters to the editor, as various parties were criticized as "pinkos," "Birchers," or "censors." This period of acrimonious public debate culminated at the next school board meeting. During the normally quiet five minutes set aside for "public presentations," a dozen parents and teachers spoke heatedly about the COPS report, including Rev. Stone and Mr. Mill, who closed the hourlong period with a shouting match. The board seemed taken aback by the virulence of the feelings expressed. Several members questioned Rev. Stone rather closely as to just whom he represented when he used phrases such as "we want" and just how many citizens of Puddly were members of COPS. As one board member put it, "This board cannot serve as a mechanism to satisfy the demands of small pressure groups of doubtful educational standing." The PTA representative said that although his organization had taken no position on the matter, he personally thought that religion and politics had no place in the schools—a view with which Superintendent Vacey fervently (if silently) agreed. At the close of the session, the Puddly board decided to take the matter under advisement and appointed a committee. The public debate continued.

During the ensuing weeks, Superintendent Vacey was notable for his silence. His only public statements were to the effect that he was busy attending to the education of Puddly's children and to getting a bond issue passed. Privately he confided to his friends that he could not afford to become involved. He had to be able to work with both groups. If he took sides, or was perceived as taking sides, he would be ineffective as superintendent and perhaps even lose his job.

Meanwhile, each side was busy developing its views and building its political support. COPS had made contact with similar groups in other communities. Speakers from the Moral Majority had begun to appear in the local churches. The teachers' committee, which had inevitably been dubbed ROBBERS, had expanded to include parents and was holding meetings with an American Civil Liberties Union lawyer.

Finally in mid-April, the board committee released its report. The report took no stand on the merits of COPS's charges. Instead it proposed a policy for dealing with the issues. The policy contained these provisions:

1. No books currently in the library would be removed.
2. No changes would be required in the current curriculum.
3. Any parent could have his or her child excused from any school assignment or any elective course by writing a letter indicating that he or she believed the assignment or course to be offensive.
4. A parent could prevent his or her child from checking out any library book by writing a similar letter.
5. A parents' committee consisting of two members of COPS, two members of ROBBERS, and an additional member appointed by the board would review new books and new curriculum proposals and set future selection policy.

Both COPS and ROBBERS rejected the plan. COPS argued that it was unworkable. It would require parents to have a detailed knowledge of what their children were being taught and of the content of the library. Moreover, having their children excused from some classes would subject them to ridicule and social ostracism. Finally, COPS argued, the education of one child is affected by the education of that child's peers. No solution that allowed for the corruption of any of Puddly's children was satisfactory.

ROBBERS, in turn, rejected the plan because it might result in the censorship of proposed books and courses. No plan that allowed COPS a say in what could be taught or read could be adequate. Moreover, ROBBERS argued, it is doubtful that parents should be allowed to censor what their own children read or study. The children of some citizens especially (by which they meant COPS supporters) *need* a liberalizing and diverse curriculum—a curriculum that presented alternative views to dogmatic, stereotypical, and mistaken beliefs. After all, that is what being educated meant. Finally, ROBBERS held that no teacher could teach when he or she had continually to find new material for students whose parents objected to some assignments or when students were constantly being excused from something to which their parents objected. The proposed policy was a form of teacher harassment, which would soon produce a bland and sterilized curriculum. During the discussion of the committee's report, Superintendent Vacey refused to either support or reject the recommendations, saying that the matter was one of policy, not administration, and hence properly left to the board.

This hardening of positions was followed by another acrimonious school board meeting in which the beleaguered Puddly school board rejected the proposed policy but failed to agree on any other. The matter was tabled ''indefinitely,'' with both sides recognizing that this meant until after the coming school board election.

The next month was one of the most unpleasant periods in Puddly's history. Both COPS and ROBBERS put up a full slate of candidates for the three positions opening on the school board. Numerous vitriolic letters filled the Puddly *Splash*. The election, which produced an unprecedented turnout of nearly 70 percent of the eligible voters, was very close but resulted in a five-to-four COPS majority on the nine-member school board. The new board members promised to clean house and began at their first meeting by removing ten books from the library.

As it now stands, Puddly-in-the-Slough School District has ground to a halt. Two science teachers resigned during the summer to take jobs elsewhere. Some disgruntled parents are organizing a private school. The board has been unable to agree on issues unrelated to the COPS and ROBBERS conflict. The voters in a later election defeated both a bond issue and a school budget. ROBBERS has promised litigation on the banned books, which seemed likely to last for years. Each group in the dispute refuses to talk with the other, and both are preparing for the next election. In the meantime, Mr. Vacey keeps in close touch with the placement office of the state university where he earned his degree, and he is known to have supplied his résumé to several districts that are seeking superintendents.

Introduction

The conflict wracking Puddly is by no means typical, either in its nature or its virulence. Indeed, school district politics is notable not for the passions it arouses but for the stultifying ennui it typically engenders. Although we have no conclusive evidence that shows the extent to which U.S. school districts are beset with strife over educational issues, it seems clear that in most communities and for much of the time, these issues never become political matters in the sense that they galvanize pressure groups into formation and action, produce heated public debate, or result in the wholesale ousting of incumbent school boards. One need only note the very low voter turnout for board of education elections—lower than virtually any other national, state, or local poll, often below 15 percent of persons eligible to vote—to realize that apathy, not ardor, characterizes the public's attitudes toward its schools.

But we do not wish to overstate the case. If the conflict in Puddly is atypical, it is also not rare. Perhaps the sequence of events has gone somewhat further there than is usual, and certainly it has become more rancorous, but the pattern is one that is becoming familiar to an increasing number of school administrators. What began as a minor, even innocuous incident, one easily resolved by the immediate parties involved, suddenly burgeoned into a major issue pitting educators against a vocal, organized, and angry segment of the community. Other, previously unnoticed concerns about the curriculum rose to the surface to become entangled with the original complaint. These issues split the school from a segment of its patrons and opened a deep rift in the community along socioeconomic lines. What began as a concern of one parent ended as a political confrontation in which warring factions, aided and abetted by "outsiders," contest control of the schools and the right to set policy in accord with deeply held ideological views.

This pattern—the transformation of seemingly minor incidents into heated political issues—is discernible in many of the educational conflicts that have convulsed communities in recent decades. "Community control" and "district consolidation" are examples. Sometimes these local incidents rise to the attention of the highest levels of federal political authority and result in the transformation of the nation's entire educational system: The Browns' inability to enroll their daughter in her neighborhood Topeka school was such an incident. Sometimes they sink to the lowest level of hostility and horrify decent men and women whatever their personal beliefs: In Kanawha County, West Virginia, someone fired on a school bus during a conflict not unlike the one we have described in Puddly. That educational issues occasionally engender the noble sentiments expressed in the pages of *Brown v. Board of Education of Topeka* (1954) and the reprehensible ones expressed on a road in Kanawha County is perhaps sufficient grounds for their claim on our attention. If they are to govern their organizations effectively, school administrators must try to understand fully the processes that transform minor incidents into heated political issues—or, perhaps more accurately, the processes that *prevent* such transformations. Why is the apathy that normally characterizes much of school district politics occasionally ruptured by virulent conflict?

Structure, Process, and Educational Conflict

Conflict and Hostility

Conflict has preoccupied philosophers and social analysts for millennia. It has been an important idea in the writings of Hobbes, Locke, Jefferson, Machiavelli, Marx, and Durkheim, to name but a few. Despite this centrality, it has no agreed definition. Each discipline treats the idea in a manner appropriate to its own particular perspective. Here we shall follow Thomas's lead and take conflict to mean the process that begins when one group perceives that another has frustrated or is about to frustrate one of its concerns and acts on that perception (Thomas, 1976, p. 891).

It is important to distinguish between conflict and hostility. Hostility refers to a mental state, an attitude of animosity, dislike, or even hatred, that may or may not be evidenced in overt action. Although hostility may accompany conflict, it need not necessarily do so. There are many everyday instances of intense conflicts that generate little or no hostility. For example, the members of a high school's English and mathematics departments may be in sharp conflict over some matter of school policy without either group feeling hostile toward the other. Similarly, collective bargaining sessions between unions and management may be highly conflictual without evidencing much hostility.

This distinction between conflict and hostility is important because the failure to make it, we suspect, is partly the cause of educators' strong antipathy toward conflict. Administrators and teachers often attach a negative value to community-school conflict; it is something to be avoided. Many textbooks in educational administration, for example, suggest that "good school-community relations" are an important administrative responsibility, and these books offer procedures intended to promote such relations. Implicit (and usually explicit) in such assertions, however, is the notion that "good school-community relations" are *harmonious* relations, characterized by peace and cooperation. In fact, the stated purpose of the procedures recommended in these books is often to secure parental support for the *school's* chosen policies and practices. However, we suggest that good relations between a school district and its public are not necessarily harmonious ones. Indeed, they might be highly conflictual. *Conflict, in itself, is neither good nor bad; it is simply an inevitable consequence of social life in a democratic society.* Whether a particular conflict episode is positively or negatively valued is largely dependent on its consequences. *One* of those consequences might be a high level of hostility, aggressiveness, or hatred. In that case one *might* be willing to say that the conflict had undesirable consequences. However, hostility is seldom the only consequence of conflict, nor is it necessarily undesirable.

The Social Value of Conflict

A major theoretical analysis of the beneficial consequences of social dissension is Lewis Coser's *The Functions of Social Conflict* (1956). (See also his *Continuities in the Study of Social Conflict,* 1967.) In a series of propositions derived from the classic work of the German sociologist Simmel, Coser suggests some of the effects of intra- and intergroup conflict. Some of these help us to put the events in Puddly in a somewhat different perspective than the one often taken by educators.

One of the obvious consequences of community dissension, a consequence visible in Puddly, is an increased cohesiveness *within* conflicting groups. When attacked, group members tend to draw together in mutual defense, new relationships arise, and positive sentiments among group members increase. It is likely that the level of cohesion among the educational staff of Puddly's schools is considerably higher as a result of the activities of COPS. To the extent that this cohesion is conducive to the creation of new working relationships, cooperation, and favorable attitudes among the faculty, the conflict in Puddly may leave a residue of improved organizational functioning. Nor is an increased cohesiveness necessarily limited to Puddly's educators. The attempt to defend their children from "alien values" has also created among a segment of the parents and citizens a cohesiveness that did not exist previously. At a time when there is increasing concern about social disorganization, the effects of the conflict on group cohesiveness in Puddly may be important.

It might be objected that whatever value results from the new social bonds created within the competing factions in Puddly must be balanced against the negative effects of the factional split. Surely there is more ill will between locals and educators now than previously. However, even such sharp social rifts have benefits. As Coser (1956) notes, people must *unite* in order to fight. Two points are relevant here. First, conflict usually takes place under mutually recognized rules and procedures—in Puddly these are the conventions governing ordinary political dissension. In such cases conflict may have the effect of socializing the contending parties to these values and procedures; it binds together groups that previously had little or no relation, reaffirming and bringing to consciousness these overriding norms. Paradoxically, divisiveness creates a kind of union. Second, conflict is a primary means by which new rules and procedures arise or existing ones are modified. It is a mechanism that promotes social change and adjustment to new conditions (p. 128). We do not know what will be the eventual outcome of the events in Puddly. Whatever it is, however, it may reflect a degree of accommodation between the community's educational and religious institutions that did not previously exist.

Further, conflict is an important mechanism for maintaining peace. Conflict involves the exercise of power—the capacity to have one's way despite resistance. But there is no easy way to measure the relative power of contending groups. Unlike wealth, where money provides a common metric, power is often more easily assessed through use. When COPS and educators contest the right to choose what students in Puddly will read, one outcome of that struggle will be a more accurate assessment by both parties of the relative power of each. Such an assessment is difficult to achieve without an actual conflict. But a realistic assessment of an opponent's strength is an important determinant of the likelihood of conflict in the first place; we are not quick to enter a struggle when the outcome is a foregone conclusion or when, because of the near equality between the factions, that struggle is likely to be long and costly. As a consequence, should any future issue arise between educators and the supporters of COPS, it is likely that an accommodation will be reached more quickly than in the current debate. The upheaval in Puddly is likely to lessen the possibility of future discord; it provides a mechanism for balancing and maintaining social relationships.

Conflict may also serve as a mechanism for producing ideas of a higher quality than might otherwise be produced. As Thomas (1976) notes, conflicting demands may be based on different evidence, values, or frames of reference. When these are articulated by dissenting parties, each is confronted with considerations that it may not have otherwise taken into account. This confrontation may help each to arrive at a more comprehensive view of the issue, and hence solutions are more likely to be based on a consideration of a greater number of alternatives and their consequences. One possible result of the aggressive pursuit of initially contradictory ends is that a win-lose situation is turned into one in which both parties win, in which alternatives are discovered that allow each to attain the desired goals. Adopting such an alternative is, in effect, an improvement over the existing situation for both.

This point, that conflict is a mechanism for improving social conditions, is important. School administrators would do well to remember that the political process is very often a process of group conflict and that democracy, as a form of government, is intended to allow such conflicts to be settled in a just manner. We intend that justice be a product of our Congress, our city councils, *and our school boards,* as well as of our courts. Seen in this way, the common administrative approach to school-community conflict—asking, "How can I smooth things over?" or, as in Vacey's case, "How can I get out of the line of fire?"— may be inappropriate. Instead, another proper administrative role is to ensure that the legitimacy of contending groups is recognized, to see to it that their views are presented adequately, and to assist the school board in fulfilling its legislative funtions. In short, another approach is to ask, *"How can I promote a fair fight?"* We shall return to this point later in this chapter.

All of this is not to argue that conflict is everywhere and always a good thing, regardless of the issue involved and regardless of its violence. It is to suggest that we, as educators, cannot have it both ways; if we value and wish to encourage a community's interest and involvement in its schools, we should not expect or even desire that that interest and involvement always be passive in nature. Indeed, the greater the interest and involvement, the greater the likelihood that conflicts will occur. Conflict may have important beneficial consequences for both the school and its community, and administrators may have an appropriate and active role in these conflicts. The heated events in Puddly are not necessarily to be deplored—though Superintendent Vacey surely thinks they are.

A Process Model of Conflict

Two general approaches to the study of conflict are evident in the literature, one primarily concerned with understanding the processes that characterize the development of conflict episodes—process models—and the second primarily concerned with the factors that influence whether or not conflict will occur— structural models (Thomas, 1976). The first seeks to describe the internal dynamics of disputes, identifying the events that triggered them and shaped their course, while the second seeks to describe underlying social conditions that determine their nature, length, or severity. So, for example, researchers attempting to explain the occurrence of teacher strikes might focus on the effects of various bargaining strategies on the propensity to strike—a process approach—or they might instead focus on the degree of community unionization as an explanatory variable—a structural approach. These approaches are obviously not mutually exclusive; they are simply alternative ways of viewing the same phenomenon. Let us first consider a process approach.

In Figure 2.1, we have reproduced Thomas's conceptualization of the basic components of process models of dyadic (two-person or two-group) conflict episodes. In essence, the model directs our attention to five roughly sequential classes of events that characterize a single episode: frustration, conceptualization, behavior, other's reactions, and outcomes.

The first element, *frustration*, is the term used to suggest a common factor that characterizes the initial stage of an episode. Typically, someone's act (or failure to act) frustrates another's concerns, when "concerns" may refer to needs, objectives, or standards of behavior (Thomas, 1976, p. 895). Such acts may be of various kinds: disagreements, denials, interferences, violations of standards. *Conceptualization* occurs as the parties define the issues and their importance

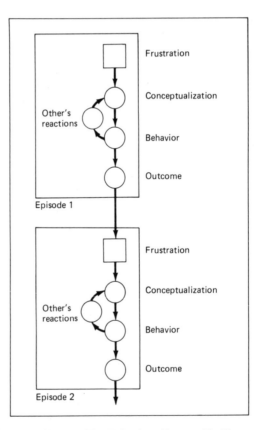

FIGURE 2.1.   Process Model Conflict Episodes. (*Source:* K. Thomas, 1976, "Conflict and Conflict Management," in M. D. Dunnette (Ed.), *Handbook of Industrial and Organizational Psychology,* Chicago: Rand McNally, p. 895. Used with permission.)

and conceive of alternative courses of action and their likely outcomes. The nature of these conceptualizations is critical to the progress of the conflict episode. *Behavior* refers to one party's actions that, as the model indicates, in turn affect the actions of the other party, whose behavior results in a reconceptualization of the conflict and a new set of behaviors. Finally, the end product or *outcome* of the episode may generate a new set of frustrations initiating a second conflict episode.

Thomas's model can help us to understand the events in Puddly. For example, note that no conflict arose when Mrs. Pious requested that her daughter be assigned something other than *Catcher in the Rye*. Her request was granted, and neither she nor Mr. Mill expressed any frustration over the matter. However, when Rev. Stone demanded that substitutions be made for several books and that parental objections be *sufficient* grounds for such substitutions, the teacher experienced frustration. He viewed these demands as illegitimate interference in his right to design curricula. His refusal to accede to these demands in turn frustrated the desire of Rev. Stone and the parents to control the moral influence of the public school on their minor children. Note also how the course of the conflict was shaped by these differing conceptualizations of the issue involved: For Mill and his colleagues the issue was one of censorship and their professional right to select reading material; for Rev. Stone and his allies it was one of children's moral development. Similarly, differing conceptions of the role of literature were involved. For the educators, books were to be judged on the basis of their literary merit; if they also provoked thought and challenged conventional beliefs, so much the better. In contrast, for the parents, literary merit was insufficient; books that contained profanity, that seemed to deride deeply held religious convictions, or that ridiculed patriotism were proscribed. In short, books should promote the traditional virtues, not challenge them.

The model also draws our attention to a common occurrence in conflict episodes: The outcome of one episode frequently serves as the frustration that activates another. In the case at hand, for example, the committee's report, instead of resolving the issue, served to frustrate further the desires of both COPS and ROBBERS. Finally, notice how the COPS report reconceptualized and broadened the issues involved—a frequent process when people get together to share a common grievance. No longer was it simply a matter of Mr. Mill's curriculum; the library's holdings, an elementary school curriculum, a values clarification program, and high school biology were all found to be objectionable. In effect, the issue was no longer one of educators' and parents' respective rights to control what pupils read but one concerning which values the school should inculcate and who has the right to make that choice.

The value of the model for educational administrators, however, lies not so much in providing a broad conceptualization of the process involved in community-school conflicts but in drawing our attention to more specific mechanisms involved in each of its summary terms.

Thomas (1976, p. 896) notes that conceptualization involves at least two important subprocesses: defining the issue and identifying salient alternatives along with their probable outcomes. Perhaps the most important point in regard to the first of these is that "objective reality" does not necessarily govern our behavior, especially in situations where fundamental values are at stake. Each of us acts in terms of how we perceive a situation; those subjective perceptions are its "reality." In Puddly, what was the objective reality of John Stone's reading *Cat's Cradle*? For Mr. Mill, it was a relatively sheltered young man confronting values different from his own and thereby being educated. For Rev. Stone, it was his impressionable boy confronting antireligious propaganda and thereby being corrupted. Actions seen as appropriate in the light of one view may seem quite inappropriate in the light of another. A common mistake made by educators confronted by irate citizens is to assume that their own conception, usually a "professional" one, is not only the correct conception but one that "reasonable" citizens share and that the action they propose will be seen as appropriate by those citizens. Thomas terms this tendency to define a situation solely in our own terms as "egocentricity" (p. 896). An egocentric definition fails to recognize the concerns of others, making their cooperation less likely. In Puddly, both COPS and ROBBERS evidence more than their share of egocentricity.

A related aspect of defining an issue is its "size" (Thomas, 1976, p. 897). Five aspects of size may be discerned: the parties involved, the physical issue, principle, substantive precedent, and procedural precedent. In Puddly, the parties involved can be seen as the affected parents and Mr. Mill, as COPS and ROBBERS, as the entire Puddly staff and the community, or, in the largest sense, as professional educators and laypersons. The size of the physical issue can be conceived as the disputed books in Mr. Mill's class, as all reading materials assigned to students and in the library, or as the entire school curriculum. The size of the principle involved may be viewed as varying from the proper role of parents in selecting books their own children are to read to the respective balance of control between laypersons and educators in public education. Substantive precedent refers to seeing the conflict as determinative for only the immediate parties and issue versus seeing it as determinative for all other parties and similar issues in the foreseeable future—to settling the matter "once and for all." Finally, conceptions of size in terms of procedural precedent may vary from seeing the outcome as setting no precedent for one party's yielding to the other on any future issue to viewing it as establishing dominance on all future issues. The union head in Puddly obviously takes the larger view of the procedural precedent involved: "If we yield to them on the matter of selecting English books, we may as well turn over control of the schools to these flakes."

These conceptions of issue size are important for managing the subsequent conflict. In general, the larger the issue, in any of these five senses, the more rancorous the conflict is likely to become. The lesson, then, is to prevent issues from becoming conceived as large ones or to break down large issues into smaller ones. "The danger inherent in big disputes and the difficulty in settling them suggest that, rather than spend our time resolving big issues, we might better explore the possibility of turning big issues into little ones" (Fisher, 1964, p. 92). In this view, Superintendent Vacey's strategy of staying out of the COPS and

ROBBERS conflict may have been mistaken. Among all of the participants in Puddly's turmoil, he was perhaps the one in the best position to prevent the size of the issue from ballooning in any of these five senses.

A second aspect of the way a conflict is conceptualized that has a direct impact on its course, the rancor it generates, and its aftermath is the extent to which the parties see the matter as involving a necessary conflict of interest (Thomas, 1976, p. 898). Four conceptions are commonly encountered: integrative, zero-sum, either-or (win-lose), and standoff. In Puddly, for example, do parents' desires to protect their children from immoral reading *necessarily* conflict with educators' desires to protect their professional prerogative concerning curricula? If the two groups answer this question in the negative, they are likely to engage in a cooperative search for mutually satisfactory or *integrative* solutions. The level of conflict between them may be minimal. Perhaps the initial meeting between Mr. Mill and Mrs. Pious was the only time in our case when both a parent and an educator sensed no necessary conflict of interest.

As events progressed and Rev. Stone became involved, the dispute took on a *zero-sum* quality. The situation was conceived as one in which there was an inherent clash of interest, and any gain by COPS was seen as involving a corresponding loss for educators. When conflicts are conceived as zero-sum, the level of conflict increases, as a compromise solution is required. Both parties stand to lose something. The board's committee seems to have had such a conception of the conflict in Puddly; their recommendations unsuccessfully sought to strike a compromise.

If the dispute is seen as involving not only an inherent conflict of interest but one in which no compromise is possible, the parties' conception is one of *win-lose*. With this conception of the issue, the level of conflict is likely to escalate still further; both parties stand to lose everything. It is probable that the situation has reached this point in Puddly; both COPS and ROBBERS seem to countenance only total victory for their side and total defeat for the other.

Finally, if the dispute is conceived as a *standoff*, it is viewed as one in which no resolution is possible. This may occur because the issue is defined as one involving such fundamental values that a victory for one side also amounts to a defeat. Neither party can gain. In standoffs the level of rancor may actually subside, but the conflict of interest remains; each group continues to see the other as an obstacle to its success. Thus the aftermath of a standoff may be long-term suspicion, animosity, and distrust.

These considerations lead us to suggest that if school administrators are interested in keeping conflict in their districts to tolerable levels, levels at which mutually accommodative solutions are sought, they would do well to expend an effort to shape the parties' perceptions of a dispute as one that involves no necessary conflict of interest or, at worst, one that represents a zero-sum situation. Viewed in this way, the search for compromises can continue, and while neither side may win absolutely, neither is likely to lose absolutely. Again we see that Superintendent Vacey's almost immediate withdrawal may not have been in his own or the district's best interest.

We turn now to a consideration of the behavior–other's reaction nexus depicted in Figure 2.1. Escalation of a conflict may take several forms. It may include an increase in the number of issues or parties involved, greater hostility or competitiveness, an increase in the number or stringency of demands made, or the use of more coercive tactics. What behavior in Puddly contributed to the escalation of that conflict?

Reevaluation   As Follett (1941) noted years ago, disputes are not often resolved by one party giving in to the other. Rather, they reevaluate their preferred alternative in the light of new information—information provided by their opponent or by third-party mediators. In essence, what occurs is that opponents (or "neutrals") point out undesirable consequences of the alternative that its proposer had not foreseen. Such information causes proponents to reconsider and shift to a new option. The reevaluation is most likely to occur when adversaries are operating in a climate of open communication, trust, and persuasion (rather than coercion). The strategy to prevent escalation, then, is not so much to argue for your case as for your opponents'—to identify and bring to light consequences of their position that they would find undesirable. Doing so tends to deescalate the conflict and promote finding accommodative solutions. Not doing so leaves each side arguing for its own case, often more and more vociferously. From the evidence we have, we see no instance in which either COPS or ROBBERS took the trouble to point out some of the dysfunctional consequences of the other's positions.

Self-fulfilling Prophecies   The response we receive from others is in part a function of our own expectations of what their response will be. If we assume that our opponent is characterized by goodwill and motivated to seek a fair solution to the issue that divides us, and we act accordingly, the opponent is more likely to behave as if those perceptions were correct. Conversely, if we assume the opposite, our expectations are also likely to be fulfilled (Walton & McKersie, 1965). This process is further exacerbated by selective perception. If we are suspicious of others' motives, we are more likely to look for *and see* deviousness and duplicity, even where none exists. Acting on those mistaken perceptions, we make deviousness and duplicity more likely and hence escalate the conflict. It is unlikely that COPS wanted to "take over the schools" in Puddly. However, acting as if that was their motive served to increase the probability of actions consonant with such a desire.

Cognitive Simplification   Under stress or threat, not only do issues tend to become viewed in simplified terms, but the parties themselves begin to see each other as "good guys" and "bad guys." Such distortions promote a crusading atmosphere in which vanquishing the opponent may take on more importance than the original matter in dispute. It is doubtful that there were many "atheists" or "Birchers" on either side in Puddly; perceiving each other in such terms, however, helped to justify extreme demands and actions—to escalate still further the level of school-community conflict.

Distortions of Communication   Stereotypes such as "atheist" and "Birchers" are effectively nullified through open communication. But communication becomes distorted and trust diminishes under conditions of extreme competition or when conflicts of interest are sharp. With trust in short supply, the opinions and reasons of opponents are listened to less and less, and each group concentrates on getting its own view presented. Listening disappears, and communication occurs only through actions. In such situations, actions indeed speak louder than words. The shouting match between Rev. Stone and Mr. Mill at the board meeting is illustrative. Such breakdowns in normal communication channels allow stereotypes to go unchecked, and actions become coercive since reasoning is no longer effective.

Issue Multiplication   As the foregoing mechanisms increasingly characterize a conflict, it becomes more likely that other, apparently extraneous issues will be dredged up and added to the initial ones (Walton, 1969). Matters that, taken singly, might have been easily resolved become untractable when bound together. As opponents become viewed as villains, it is easy to blame all of the perceived flaws in a system, past and present, on them. The appearance of evolution, values clarification, and *Man: A Course of Study* as matters of dispute in Puddly illustrates this process.

These mechanisms suggest various strategies that administrators might find useful in the management of conflict. For example, they might motivate the parties to resolve a dispute by providing incentives for doing so or pointing out the costs of continuing it. A second procedure involves acting as a communication link, ensuring that each group understands fully the reasons for the other's positions, bringing the parties together, acting to reduce stereotypes, and encouraging a collaborative approach to the dispute. Finally, and in line with our suggestion that conflict may have functional consequences, when it is apparent that two groups are avoiding an issue for the sake of apparent harmony, it may be appropriate to induce a confrontation while simultaneously promoting a problem-solving approach to it (Thomas, 1976, p. 912).

Structural Aspects of Conflict

As we have said, process models represent only one approach to understanding the causes of social dissension. Structural approaches seek to identify underlying social conditions that make conflict more or less likely. In recent years, a rich literature has begun to develop concerning school district dissension from this second viewpoint.

Let us first consider the normative view of school governance held by the majority of Americans. Legally, of course, education is a state function. However, each state (except Hawaii) has delegated responsibility and authority for the actual operation of its schools to local school districts, of which there are roughly

14,000 in the United States. The vast majority of these districts are governed by a lay board of education, elected by the residents of the district. (A few boards are appointed, particularly in some of our larger cities.) These boards have broad powers to control the education of youngsters in the community: They have the authority to set educational programs, to assign pupils to those programs, to construct and maintain facilities, to hire and fire teachers, to make appropriate policy, and to levy taxes to pay for all of these functions. While boards may, if they wish, carry out these activities themselves, for many years almost all have seen fit to hire a full-time professional administrator, the superintendent, to carry out the actual task of operating their schools. Nevertheless, in a legal and normative sense, the superintendent is very much the servant of the board. He or she serves at its pleasure and may be dismissed virtually whenever it sees fit to do so.

In this system, the board of education makes policy, and the superintendent executes that policy. As an elected body, the board formulates educational goals and procedures in response to the will of the district's voters. When its actions no longer conform with that will, the mechanism of the ballot provides citizens with the opportunity to replace board members with other citizens who will presumably better reflect the public's wishes. *School districts, then, are a form of local government.* As such, they are subject to the same norms that govern other forms of government in a democracy. Most notably, they are governed by the norm that the people who rule are supposed to be responsive to the people who are ruled. As Eulau and Prewitt (1973, p. 24) put it, "In a democracy the degree to which the governors are responsive to the preferences of the governed is the *sine qua non* of whether democracy, in fact, exists." This normative view, then, engenders an image of government processes that involve citizens stating their preferences or expectations and of groups making (often conflicting) demands while school boards attend closely to these communications, mediate instances of conflict, formulate alternatives, deliberate, and finally arrive at decisions binding on the entire community. While these decisions usually do not completely satisfy the interests of any one segment of the public, they are supposed to balance the interests of all segments. If enough of the public becomes dissatisfied, every few years it has the opportunity to "vote the rascals out." Until that time, the superintendent is supposed to execute faithfully the public will, as that will is formulated by its elected officials.

We should not expect that these processes of government will always be decorous and polite. Anyone who has ever attended a city council meeting, a state legislative session, or a congressional hearing, for example, knows that they are often lively, even tempestuous affairs. Heated debate, shouting, and name-calling are not uncommon. We are not surprised at this because these are *political* arenas and there are strong interests at stake. We *expect* that people in a democracy will vigorously pursue their own interests. Indeed, if people did not do so, it is unlikely that democracy could survive. The alternative would be to allow our governors to decide among themselves what is in our interest—which, as some have argued (e.g., Tucker & Zeigler, 1980; Gittel, 1967; McCarty & Ramsey, 1971; Martin, 1962), is what has happened in many school districts.

More precisely, some have argued that we have allowed educators, particularly school superintendents, to decide what is in the public interest. Contrary to the image of the beleaguered superintendent beset on all sides by competing citizen demands and contentious boards, the evidence suggests that "the overall picture is one of public and school board deference to education experts" (Tucker & Zeigler, 1980, p. 232). To be sure, many school districts experience episodic crises of one sort or another, but the general state of affairs is one of quiet demurral to expert opinion. At base, what is informative about the events in Puddly is how unusual they are.

Seen in the light of the normative view of democratic governance, what is happening in Puddly is no more than quite ordinary political processes: Citizens are making demands of their governors, organizing to pursue their interests more effectively, and using the ballot to sanction their representatives. Politics has been defined as the procedures for deciding "who gets what, when and how" (Lasswell, 1958). The irate citizens of Puddly, both COPS and ROBBERS, are engaged in the commonplace politics of pressing their demands on their governors. If we hold the normative view, their activities should neither surprise nor alarm us. They are merely vigorously pursuing what they perceive to be in the best interest of their children. Indeed, what could be said to be more surprising and alarming in Puddly is the apparent inability of a *designedly political body*, the school board, to handle effectively these ordinary political processes. Our first approach to the conflict, therefore, will be to examine the structure of school governance, noting especially the points at which empirical reality departs from the normative view we have outlined and how an avowedly political institution, the school board, has become relatively apolitical in its functioning.

U.S. school districts were not always headed by a professional educator. For most of the nineteenth century, districts were actually operated by their elected boards. The board itself decided on curricula and facilities, purchased books, hired teachers—performed all the activities that are now duties of the superintendent. With the increasing urbanization of the country, the rapid growth in size of districts following consolidation, compulsory attendance laws, and the rise in the legal age of leaving, among other factors, the job of day-to-day management became too burdensome for otherwise employed persons to do part-time. The profession of school administrator was born.

Further, at the turn of the century, school districts, like other forms of local government, were caught up in the urban reform movement. In attempts to curb rampant political corruption in the nation's cities, numerous reforms were instituted; city manager forms of government were adopted (which are analogous to the lay school board–professional educator form), nonpartisan and at-large elections were initiated, and key governmental sources of patronage—the hiring of personnel and the purchase of goods—were strictly regulated and separated from the direct control of politicians. All these urban reforms now characterize school district governance. These changes had the laudable goal of curtailing political corruption; in practice and in the case of schools, however, they also had the effect of insulating education from normal political processes and contributing to the rise in power of the superintendent (Zeigler, Jennings, & Peak, 1974).

Several studies, most notably those by Zeigler and his associates (Zeigler et al., 1974; Tucker & Zeigler, 1980; Zeigler, Kehoe, & Reisman, 1985), have documented the manner in which the reality of school governance departs from the normative view and the consequences of those departures. Consider first people who occupy seats on boards of education and how they come to do so. In comparable legislative bodies (e.g., city councils), political parties put forward candidates who publicly and actively campaign against incumbents. These candidates raise issues, criticize the records of their opponents, and offer alternative goals and procedures in an attempt to educate voters and appeal for their support at the polls. (Of course, not all political campaigns are of this sort: Mudslinging or vacuous ones are hardly unknown. However, the fact that we recognize these as departures from the norm supports the assertion that our expectations are otherwise.) In contrast, one-third of the members of elected school boards gain their position through appointment (as when an incumbent resigns and the board itself appoints the successor) or without facing any competition. Indeed, since candidates are often hard to find (board service is unpaid, time-consuming, and not particularly useful to the politically ambitious), many run at the urging of the board itself or, more significant, of the superintendent, thus giving a self-perpetuating quality to these elected bodies. When opposition for a seat is involved, in one-fourth of the cases neither candidate is an incumbent, making evaluation of a candidate's voting record on educational issues impossible. Further, there is often little difference among candidates on issues—all are in favor of "good education"—and when differences are involved, these are unlikely to concern the critical elements of educational programs and personnel. Instead, physical plant, fiscal affairs, and the role of the board itself more often provide the substance of campaigns (Tucker & Zeigler, 1980, pp. 44–45). Thus the processes by which many board candidates come to office—through appointment by the incumbent board with the advice of the superintendent, or election without facing an incumbent or even an opponent, without having to formulate a position on difficult educational questions—serves to insulate board members from the sorts of political experiences we find in other arenas of government. This insulation weakens their socialization to the political aspects of their role. It provides no training in political conflict.

Nor is this weakened socialization the only or most important difference between school boards and other elected bodies. In the structure of the electoral process itself, several features of school board elections, legacies of the reform movement, tend to decrease voter interest in educational politics and the intensity of competition for seats. The scheduling of elections—in most cases separate from other local, state, and national balloting—serves to decrease voter turnout. The further separation of school concerns into distinct components (e.g., the separation of budget votes, referenda, and school board elections) probably has a similar effect and may serve to create an artificial distinction between office-holders, the programs they propose, and the financial implications of their choices. At-large elections ensure that, even when incumbents are involved, no candidate is running *against* an incumbent. Hence there is seldom head-to-head competition for office. Whereas at-large procedures were instituted to curb the power of "ward bosses," they also deprive both aspirants and incumbents of an identifiable constituency to whom to appeal and whose interests must be represented. Instead, every candidate is supposed to represent the interests of all the voters in the district. In socially heterogeneous communities (such as Puddly) that may become a difficult, if not impossible, task for ordinary mortals. Rather, the at-large election often provides a means whereby a small majority of citizens can achieve complete dominance of a board to the exclusion of other groups and their interests. Since board members have always had a decidedly middle-class WASP complexion (Campbell, Cunningham, Nystrand, & Usan, 1975), the interests of the poor and minorities are particularly likely to be slighted by at-large elections. As in our case, if lower-status members of the district share particular educational views, they are required first to organize themselves politically and put up candidates if these views are to be represented; the machinery of ward-based elections is not available to facilitate the process. (Zeigler, Jennings, & Peak, 1974, found that board turnover is decreased where at-large procedures exist.) Similarly, nonpartisan elections contribute to lowering the intensity of the competition. Political parties tend to ensure that candidates are put forward; few elections for other political offices go uncontested (as they had in Puddly). Parties also provide a mechanism for monitoring the performance of incumbents. The outs have both the organization and the motivation to keep a watchful eye on the voting records and public statements of the ins.

The party system has another effect on this competition. While helping to ensure the presence of competition, parties also tend to moderate its nature and intensity, keeping it within acceptable bounds. That is, they are capable of disciplining both officeholders and candidates. Platforms, for example, are not vacuous documents designed to appeal to all voters; they have served as effective guides to elected officials regarding the proper position to take on various issues (Lindblom, 1968). In addition, parties have a vested interest in ensuring that their candidates refrain from reckless charges and untoward actions that may return to haunt them in subsequent elections. Thus the nonpartisan nature of educational politics may have served to mute the public's interest and participation in its schools while simultaneously providing fertile grounds for general domination by professionals punctuated by occasional eruptions of very heated and relatively undisciplined conflict.

Next consider the role of interest groups in the ordinary political system and in education. While the term *interest group* has often taken on a negative connotation, many political scientists see these as essential aspects of a democratic system (Lindblom, 1968). They provide legislators with information regarding the preferences and expectations of their members and with facts to buttress their arguments regarding relevant issues. No one is alarmed, after all, if the opinion of the American Association of Manufacturers is sought regarding a proposed change in import duties, if the AFL-CIO is consulted regarding minimum wage legislation, or if the American Medical Association is invited to testify about the effects of a change in Medicaid. These organizations are viewed as legitimate representatives of groups whose interests should be considered by lawmakers. The situation is quite different with regard to schools. First, by far the most active "interest group" in most districts is the PTA. But controlled by teachers and administrators, the PTA is decidedly "establishment"-oriented, and its activity during elections injects little controversy into the proceedings. Instead, it seems to serve administrators and boards as a resource during times of crisis (Zeigler, Jennings, & Peak, 1974, p. 174). A second active group at the local level, the teachers' association, may confine its attention to a narrow range of issues, such as salaries and class size. Zeigler and his associates (p. 99) concluded that fundamental issues, particularly those concerning educational programs, are more likely to be raised by either "left- or right-wing" groups.

Thus Puddly presents a common pattern. The public appears to take little interest in its schools, and the structure of school district electoral processes serves to mute what interest there is. Public officials—board members and educators—incorrectly interpret this quiescence as evidence of general satisfaction with the status quo. However, in the lower-status segments of the community (which participate less in the political process in any case), dissatisfaction with school policies is widespread but unfocused and unarticulated. When an incident occurs that exemplifies some aspect of the submerged discontent, an interest group forms. This group, initially consisting of only the few people directly involved in the incident, *publicly* articulates a grievance shared by others but perhaps only half recognized by them as such. In seeking redress, media coverage and word of mouth bring the group and its grievance to the attention of other like-minded citizens, and the personnel and resources available to the group to prosecute the issue swell. As its activity and criticism of board policy increase, public support for the board declines; the group's political resources are further incremented at the expense of those of the board. This process may be exacerbated as additional grievances are joined with the initial one. At some point the group's potential success in achieving its goals alarms other citizens whose interests are threatened, and another pressure group is activated in opposition to the first. The board is now presented with conflicting demands that it must mediate. If unsuccessful in doing so, its support declines further, the struggle becomes more heated as the activities of both groups intensify, and the board's support continues to decline. "And so it goes," to quote one of the (absent) principals in the Puddly affair, Kurt Vonnegut, until a resolution is reached, often through the medium of the ballot. As Tucker and Zeigler note (1980, p. 15), interest groups thrive in an atmosphere of conflict between the rulers and the ruled.

Another important aspect of the role of interest groups in local educational politics concerns board members' and superintendents' attitudes toward these actors. A large proportion of the former do not view themselves as representing any particular segment of the community or as speaking for any particular interest. It is a rare board member who views himself or herself as "speaking for labor," for example (Tucker & Zeigler, 1980). Board members tend to see themselves not as representatives but as trustees. Further, they are not inclined to treat such groups—other than the PTA and the teachers' association—as legitimate. While communications from *individuals* are treated as important and are attended to, demands made by *organized groups* are often viewed with distrust (Zeigler, Jennings, & Peak, 1974, p. 78).

Superintendents are even less likely than boards to extend legitimacy to group demands—and not without reason. In districts where group activity is high, financial defeats are more common, firing of teachers more frequent, and superintendent turnover more likely. When superintendents insist that education and politics do not mix, at least when "politics" means active demands from community interest groups, they are not just mouthing platitudes (Tucker & Zeigler, 1980, p. 76).

The upshot of all these structural features—apolitical recruitment patterns; fragmented and nonpartisan electoral processes; the absence of strong, institutionalized, and legitimated interest groups; and the trustee orientation of board members—is to render a nominally political body peculiarly apolitical and thus to depoliticize education. Such features help to sustain the widespread belief that education is somehow "above politics," that providing good schooling to children is too important a community function to be subject to the rough-and-tumble system that democratic societies have evolved to decide "who gets what, when and how." But it is not manifestly obvious that the importance of schooling is a reason for depoliticizing it. As one of the more acerbic political scientists has put it, "Thus does the public school, heralded by its champions as the cornerstone of democracy, reject the political world in which democratic institutions operate" (Martin, 1962, p. 89). Schools may be among the most important institutions in our society in determining "who gets what, when and how." If so, it is inappropriate to "liberate" them from the political arena.

In the balance of power between school boards and their superintendents, a major resource of the board (in addition to its legal authority) is its claim to represent the interests of the electorate. We have seen how the features discussed so far tend to weaken that claim. That is, in a conflict of views on some educational issue between board and superintendent, the board's claim to represent the will of the people is a powerful resource rendered weak. On the other side, the superintendent's resources are not inconsiderable. First and foremost is the superintendent's professional expertise—the claim that as an extensively trained and experienced professional, he or she understands a problem better and hence can offer the better solution. Americans generally accept this claim of expertise (Martin, 1962), though, as we shall see in Chapter 6, it is an arguable one. Further, the view that politics and political solutions are inappropriate in education serves to strengthen "technical" solutions relative to political ones. Second, the tenure of superintendents is generally longer than that of board members in the same community (Zeigler, Jennings, & Peak, 1974, p. 68), allowing the former to assert greater familiarity with the matter under discussion. Third, the superintendent has more ready access to the tools of decision making: information, staff, lines of communication throughout the organization, funds, and time (pp. 152–154). Fourth, and very important, it is typically the superintendent who sets the agenda for board meetings. As in Puddly, this agenda-setting function can be and is used to focus the board's attention on the items of business the superintendent deems "appropriate" and to prevent other items from coming to the fore. Hence boards are presented with a problem *as conceptualized by the superintendent,* coupled with the information the latter believes to be relevant and with a proposed solution to which the board must react. Significantly, board agendas are much more likely to contain items concerning "tangibles" of physical facilities and finances than they are to contain items concerning educational programs and curricula (p. 154). Finally, novice board members, many undoubtedly ignorant of their authority, are commonly tutored in their new roles by the superintendent, making it possible for the latter to socialize them "properly" to their responsibilities (Kerr, 1964). These considerations, when placed alongside the weakened political power of boards, serve to tip the balance of power significantly toward professional educators.

The point of all of this is not to argue that professionals have everywhere assumed powers that rightfully belong to the public and its elected representatives, though there are some notable and well-documented cases when just that seems to have occurred (see, for example, Rogers, 1978; Peterson, 1976). Rather it is to suggest some of the complexities of school governance and, in particular, to note some of the ways in which reality departs from the normative model described earlier. The view that boards make policy in response to citizen preferences and superintendents faithfully execute that policy is not entirely in accord with school governance as practiced in the United States.

These structural considerations help to explain the sudden and relatively virulent outbreak of school-community conflict in Puddly. They suggest that this board (like many others) was unaware of and unprepared to fulfill its political functions. To paraphrase that consummate politician, Harry S Truman, it was not prepared for the heat but neither could it flee the kitchen when the politics of education in Puddly became less than prosaic. The board's difficulty was exacerbated by the common pattern of decision making encouraged by Superintendent Vacey, in which it generally considered only technical matters placed before it by the superintendent and on which it acted only after he had made a recommendation. When Vacey, who immediately recognized the potential for conflict inherent in Rev. Stone's complaint, decided that his best strategy was to remain as uninvolved as possible, the resulting power vacuum created by his withdrawal was filled by fractious and intemperate pressure groups, who were themselves politically inexperienced and undisciplined. Faced with these warring groups making seemingly incompatible demands and without guidance from their chief school officer, the board effectively collapsed as a functioning legislative body.

Preachers, Politics, and the Curriculum

A second prominent structural aspect to the conflict in Puddly bears discussion. The protest against the district's curriculum arose from a particular part of the community, the fundamentalist Protestants, and was spearheaded by one of its religious leaders. This pattern is by no means atypical. Across the country, independent Baptists particularly, and fundamentalist Christians generally, have been at the forefront of attacks on the public schools, especially in regard to curriculum matters (Park, 1980). We do not believe, as some writers imply (Brodinsky, 1982), that members of these groups, in collusion with other "right-wing" organizations such as the Moral Majority, are out to destroy American public schools. Nevertheless, their prominence in affairs like that in Puddly requires explanation, and school administrators should understand why many fundamentalists are so sensitive to educators' choices about what to teach.

Perhaps the first point to understand is that historically Baptists and fundamentalist sects have been strong advocates of the separation of church and state. Along with Quakers and Puritans, Baptists had their origins in the revolt against an established church in England and in the American colonies. Roger Williams fled the Massachusetts settlement for Rhode Island for this reason, among others, and is generally credited with founding the first Baptist church there in 1639 (Skerry, 1980). As a group, then, fundamentalists are particularly alert to governmental actions that impinge on religious beliefs and practices; the First Amendment's guarantee of religious liberty—that the state shall make no law respecting the establishment of religion *or the free exercise thereof*—is taken very seriously.

While respect for this tradition of separation of church and state may have eroded a bit among some fundamentalists, it is inappropriate to see them as engaged in a wholesale attack on the separation of church and state. Neither are they engaged in any attempt to "Christianize" the nation by imposing their religious views through the public schools. Rather, most fundamentalists perceive the schools as attacking their religious convictions (Page & Clelland, 1978). "Dirty" or "un-American" books are objectionable because they corrupt children. The absence of prayer and Bible reading in schools is problematic because this constrains the religious freedom of people who wish to pray. Fundamentalists often respond to schools with the consciousness of a minority group; they seek curtailment of perceived attacks on the values and legitimacy of the group's views.

Second, the fundamentalist churches are strongly congregationalist in nature. That is, they are relatively devoid of an overarching denominational hierarchy that sets policy, pays for and assigns ministers, or formulates interpretations of religious doctrine. Instead, each congregation settles such matters for itself. As a consequence, a church's leaders and its minister are particularly attentive to the wishes and beliefs of the congregation and are relatively free of constraints imposed by higher ecclesiastical authority. Further, independent Baptists, and fundamentalist groups generally, tend to insist on literal interpretations of the Scriptures. For example, when the Bible says that God created the earth in seven days, it means just that; evolutionary theory, then, is seen as clearly contradicting the word of God. In addition, religion and church affairs play a prominent role in family life; religious beliefs and practices are not confined to Sunday mornings. Finally, the members of these sects tend to be drawn disproportionately from the poor and the lower middle class, and most of their adult adherents have not had a college education.

Taken together, these structural characteristics of fundamentalist groups help to explain their prominence in curricular controversies. Because these groups are relatively poor, the compulsory public school has been the primary vehicle for their children's education; private sectarian schooling has not been a realistic option (although their dissatisfaction with public education has recently put them at the forefront of the growing trend to set up private schools, often at considerable financial sacrifice; see Skerry, 1980). Seen from their viewpoint that a public *compulsory* institution is inculcating ideas directly contradictory to deeply held beliefs derived from the received word of God, it is understandable that some of these parents become irate. The congregational structure of their churches may serve to make their ministers particularly responsive to these concerns among their flocks, not moderated by settled policy positions adopted in any church hierarchy. Further, it seems likely that experience with elected church governing boards, which are highly responsive to members, may lead to similar (but less easily met) expectations for local school boards. Thus if one understands the right to the free exercise of religion to include the right to raise one's children in the family faith, the compulsory teaching of contradictory ideas by a state institution can be viewed by fundamentalists as infringing on their First Amendment rights. Put less legalistically, it is easy to imagine the fear these parents may experience when their children begin to question, as a consequence of a compulsory school curriculum, beliefs thought to be essential for the welfare of their souls.

The decentralized structure of American fundamentalism can serve to enhance these fears. As we have noted, fundamentalist groups generally lack the bureaucratic structures that coordinate and make policy for most major Protestant denominations. They are not, however, devoid of centralized leadership or means of communication. Leadership among fundamentalists is often exercised by "religious entrepreneurs," men such as Oral Roberts or Jerry Falwell, who are charismatic leaders and who make contact with individuals through radio, television, newspapers, and the mail rather than through denominational structures or local churches.

The lack of denominational structures and the existence of entrepreneurial leadership has two consequences of interest. First, fundamentalists are more likely to be victims of religious fads and religious hucksters than are other Christian sects. They lack institutions that stabilize and deliberate, and they are more open to media persuasion. Second, the entrepreneurial leadership of fundamentalism has a considerable set of incentives to promote and enhance the fears of its constituents. Unlike the leaders of other denominations, who are supported by the contributions of local churches, fundamentalist entrepreneurs depend on the direct contributions of individuals. To survive they must build an audience of individuals who are loyal enough to their cause not only to heed but also to contribute regularly. It is likely that simply running a video church doing what every church does every Sunday is insufficient. That is, it is helpful to present oneself as playing a unique and crucial role in the struggle against the forces of evil. It is thus understandable if the evils one is fighting, including the evils besetting the public schools, become a bit larger than they really are. This is not to say that fundamentalist leaders are insincere or deliberately exploitative individuals. A vast majority are not. But the need to "rally the troops" does provide an incentive to find an "enemy without" and enlarge its evil. When the enemy without is the public school system, it is not overly surprising that an occasional "dirty book" can be transformed into the demon of secular humanism.

Legal Aspects of Textbook Controversies and Curriculum

The Law and the Curriculum: General Principles

Authority over the curriculum generally and over textbooks specifically is best viewed as a power delegated by the state to local school districts. School boards have the basic power of decision over what shall be taught and over the choice of textbooks.

This choice is, however, subject to a number of constraints. For example, states have a variety of legislatively mandated curriculum requirements with which districts must comply. They may also forbid certain things, such as textbooks that are obscene or subversive. Even in the case of a mandated curriculum, states generally do not require that school districts purchase any particular textbooks. Some, such as Texas, do require school districts to purchase textbooks from an approved list. These states play an especially important role in determining textbook content. Publishers are highly motivated to have their texts included on these approved lists. Hence they are also motivated to expunge from their texts any material that may cause them not to be approved. In this manner the mechanism of state textbook approval gives some leverage to individuals such as the Gablers and their textbook evaluation organization (see Hefley, 1976) who are willing to critique and lobby against texts they perceive as offensive.

There are fewer restrictions on the selection of books for school libraries. Many states, such as New York, require schools to maintain libraries but do not regulate their content. Operational constraints on libraries are the district's budget and the recommendations of teachers and librarians. These groups may also be influenced by organizations such as the Gablers' that review and recommend books. Since few school boards have the time to check the books recommended by teachers and librarians, effective power over choice rests with the professional staff.

Within these constraints, what goes into or comes out of the school curriculum must be decided in accordance with constitutional principles. What are the principles involved? We suggest that much of the relevant legal literature expresses and is to a large extent an attempt to balance four potentially conflicting ideas.

The Marketplace of Ideas   Federal courts have held with considerable regularity that a central purpose of the First Amendment is to protect the free exchange of ideas. This right involves not only the right to speak or write freely but has been regarded as containing a right to listen and a right to know (*Meyer v. Nebraska*). The state may neither suppress nor deny access to unpopular ideas.

The Right to Uphold Community Values   Courts have also held that local control of schools is an important value worthy of judicial notice *(San Antonio In-*

dependent School District v. Rodriguez). Local control is valued because it permits communities and school boards to pursue and inculcate local values. This is seen as a liberty interest. The assumption appears to be that individuals will be freer to preserve their individual values in education when those values are subject to democratic control and when the political entity exercising that control is geographically small rather than large. Local autonomy is seen as promoting a higher level of individual freedom with respect to education than control at the state or national level (see Bull, 1984).

Religious Neutrality   The curriculum must be religiously neutral. It cannot establish anyone's religious views as those of the school, nor can it restrict the free exercise of religion.

Parents' Rights   Courts have given some protection to the right of parents to control the education of their children in cases where parental values conflict with those of the school. Generally, this consists of the right to withdraw one's child from instruction regarded as offensive and the right to make alternative arrangements for the education of one's child *(Pierce v. Society of Sisters).*

Educational administrators should be familiar with some of the cases that established these principles. In *Meyer v. Nebraska,* the Supreme Court struck down a Nebraska statute prohibiting the teaching of modern foreign languages in the elementary grades. The intent of the statute was to promote civic development by protecting students from foreign tongues and foreign ideas. The Supreme Court's rejoinder was that a state may not act so as to "foster a homogeneous people." In general, courts have not been willing to tolerate regulations that seem arbitrarily to restrict reasonable forms of pluralism in the curriculum. Nor have they been willing to tolerate attempts to socialize students in a narrow mold.

On the other hand, courts have not been overly solicitous of the sensibilities of people who feel that they or their group has been maligned by something in the curriculum. In a case *(Rosenberg v. Board of Education of the City of New York)* where parents had charged the Board of Education of New York City with using books alleged to be anti-Semitic, the court commented:

> *Public interest in a free and democratic society does not warrant or encourage suppression of any book at the whim of any unduly sensitive person or group of persons, merely because a character described in such book as belonging to a particular race or religion is portrayed in a derogatory or offensive manner. (p. 543)*

The books in question were *Oliver Twist* and *The Merchant of Venice.* It is worth noting, given current sensitivity to allegedly racist books such as *Huckleberry Finn* and the sensitivity of many fundamentalists to various curricular matters, that the statute at issue in *Meyer v. Nebraska* was primarily intended to prevent the teaching of German and came just a few years after World War I and that *Rosenberg* followed the slaughter of European Jews during World War II.

Courts have insisted that the curriculum must be religiously neutral. In *Everson v. Board of Education,* the Supreme Court held that an Arkansas statute prohibiting the teaching of evolution was unconstitutional in that it violated the "establishment of religion" clause of the First Amendment. Other attempts by religious groups to influence the curriculum in a way favorable to their viewpoint have fared similarly. Federal courts have refused to permit prayer and Bible reading in the schools *(Abington School District v. Schempp),* they have refused to permit the Ten Commandments to be posted in classrooms, and they have been unwilling to let stand laws mandating equal time for evolution and scientific creationism *(McLean v. Arkansas Board of Education).*

Courts have not, however, been willing to order the removal of otherwise secular material from the curriculum simply on the grounds that it is offensive to someone's religious viewpoint. In a case where the court found that the use of certain materials (including materials concerned with values clarification) did in fact offend the religious views of some parents, it nevertheless saw the use of such materials as neither constituting the establishment of any secular religion nor as violating the right to free exercise of religion. In *Williams v. Board of Education of the County of Kanawha,* the court maintained that "these rights are guaranteed by the First Amendment, but the Amendment does not guarantee that nothing about religion will be taught in the schools nor that nothing offensive to any religion will be taught in the schools" (p. 96).

Textbook Censorship

In a recent case *(Island Trees Union Free School District Board of Education v. Pico),* the Supreme Court laid down a set of principles central to the issue of censorship. The case came from the Island Trees School District of New York. The school board had ordered nine books removed from the school library on the grounds that they were "anti-American, anti-Christian, anti-Semitic, and just plain filthy" (p. 2803). The board was challenged in court on the grounds that its action violated the First Amendment rights of students.

Writing for the majority, Justice William Brennan treated the case as a matter of balancing the right of a local board to inculcate local values against the First Amendment right to know. Concerning the rights of local boards, Brennan wrote:

> *We are therefore in complete agreement with petitioners that local school boards must be permitted "to establish and apply their curriculum in such a way as to transmit community values," and that "there is a legitimate and substantial community interest in promoting respect for authority and traditional values be they social, moral, or political." (p. 2806)*

Brennan goes on to argue, however, that the First Amendment includes the right to receive or have access to information. This right does not deny to boards of education the right to "significant discretion to determine the content of their school libraries." It does, however, preclude the use of that discretion in a narrowly partisan way. He concludes:

> *We hold that local school boards may not remove books from school library shelves simply because they dislike the ideas contained in those books and seek*

by their removal to "prescribe what shall be orthodox in politics, nationalism, religion, or other matters of opinion." (p. 2810)

The application of this standard appears to turn on motivation. If the motivation is to deny access to ideas, the removal of the books would be illegal. However, their removal would be permissible if they were judged to be *educationally* unsuitable. The Court sheds little light on the question as to how we are to distinguish the intent to suppress ideas from the intent to eliminate educationally unsuitable material. Brennan does, however, regard as suspicious the fact that the Island Trees board violated its own procedures for considering books. The case was remanded to a lower court for a judgment concerning the facts regarding board intent.

It should be noted that the law often permits parents whose values are offended by some portion of the school curriculum to withdraw their children. *Pierce v. Society of Sisters* gave constitutional protection to the right to establish private schools and to send one's children to them. Parents may also have the right to educate their children at home provided an "equivalent" education is provided. Parents may exclude their children from any portion of the curriculum or deny them access to any library books that they find offensive. In general, this right is restricted only when it threatens the state's fundamental interests in education. Thus parents are able to exclude their children from classes in values clarification or from reading offensive books, but they are not permitted to keep their children from instruction in reading, since the state has a compelling interest in the literacy of its citizens. (For a detailed account, see Peterson, Rossmiller, & Volz, 1978, Chapter 13.)

These four ideas—the free exchange of ideas, the preservation of community values, religious neutrality, and the rights of parents—are important values to be realized in the design and implementation of curricula. The problem is, of course, that they are in potential conflict. The full realization of one is almost certain to impair the realization of the others. The events in Puddly illustrate just such an instance. Most people in that community would probably endorse each value individually. The issue for school administrators such as Vacey is to develop procedures that allow their joint realization.

Textbook Controversies: Censorship and Parents' Rights

The Case against Censorship

What are some of the issues that characterize textbook disputes? The most obvious ones pertain to the concepts of censorship and parents' rights. The teachers and their allies view COPS as censoring the curriculum. They conceive of the issue as a standard case of intellectual freedom. COPS members are likely to see the issue as one of parents' rights and of defense of community moral standards. Let us formulate the issue from each point of view.

Often educators view attempts by parents to remove books from the library shelves or from the curriculum as censorship pure and simple. Consider the following comments by Allan Glatthorn (1979):

> *But finally, I believe, we must take a stand. After all the dialog has been held and after the needed changes have been made, we must at some place draw the line. For the battle has been joined. We are locked in a struggle over the fundamental principles of freedom and liberty. Is is not simply the struggle to defend our professional freedom to choose books. It is the larger struggle to ensure that the public school classroom remains a forum for free inquiry. If angry parents can turn the public school into a closed system for inculcating their narrow vision, then surely we are all in trouble. (p. 52)*

In his discussion of the issue, Glatthorn indicates that teachers need to employ reasonable judgment in what they select for students. Not everything is appropriate. And they need to be solicitous of the concerns of parents. But at the bottom line, parents who challenge the books selected by teachers are censors to be resisted in the name of liberty. Consider some of the assumptions embedded in Glatthorn's view.

The first assumption is that the values of free inquiry are the appropriate and prevailing ones for the classroom. The curriculum is to be a place where students can follow the argument where it leads and discover truth from a multitude of tongues. Presumably, Glatthorn would say that underlining this commitment is a more fundamental one, a commitment to the free choice of the student.

Second, Glatthorn must believe that the intellectual freedom of students should take precedence over the views of parents concerning the education of their children when these conflict. The schools are not to be places for "inculcating the narrow vision of parents."

Third, Glatthorn must believe that maintaining the prerogatives of teachers and educational professionals to determine the curriculum is the best protection for the intellectual freedom of students.

Given these assumptions, the position of Puddly's ROBBERS is persuasive. These assumptions allow the full weight of our society's commitment to free choice and free inquiry to be brought to bear against COPS. ROBBERS, then, have a strong case for their view.

What Counts as Censorship?

Before we move on to discuss what can be said on behalf of COPS, a few observations on the idea of censorship are in order. What is to count as censorship? The question is important because "censorship" is a loaded term. It has strongly negative connotations. Thus any group that succeeds in stigmatizing its opponents with the term will have won an important victory. What, then, is censorship, and who are the censors in this case?

The obvious response is that COPS are the censors. They wish to restrict the availability of reading material to their children. Consider, however, a divergent perspective.

Note first that anything that is in the school library or in the curriculum reflects a choice or, more accurately, a series of choices. Textbooks, for example, involve choices by authors about what material is appropriate. They involve choices by publishers about what will sell. And they involve choices by school boards, administrators, or teachers about which competing text to use. Any choice involves not only a commitment to include something but also a commitment to *exclude* something. Even texts that present different points of view ignore some viewpoints. The reason for this is simple. The public school curriculum, like radio or television, is a limited-access forum. There is not time to present every view. Not everyone who might wish to present an idea can do so. Choices are necessary. Are such choices censorship?

We may refocus the question. Why is it that making a choice about what is to be included in or excluded from the curriculum does not constitute censorship while objecting to that choice does? The answer is not obvious.

People who make curriculum choices and those who object to them differ in at least two important ways. First, they disagree about what is educationally worthwhile. Each group has a set of educational values and goals that it would like served. These values and goals lead to different choices.

Robert Small (1979) provides a quotable commentary on the difference in educational values that is often reflected in discussions of English literature:

> *What we have here is a clear and probably unresolvable clash of ideas. Sometimes we act as if our opinions about the values of literature study are true and these others false; but we must remember that by rejecting cultural heritage for critical thinking, greatness for relevance, the truth for each reader's truth, answers for questions, we reject the main reasons why society has put us there to do what we do. In addition, when censors condemn some literary works as morally corrupting, we often treat those claims with ridicule. No one was ever corrupted by a curse word, we say. Just because that story contains a character's argument against the existence of God doesn't mean students will stop believing. A story about sex doesn't provoke students to sexual activity. Is that right? Can we be the same people who maintain that literature can give readers insights into life? That literature can change people's lives? That the pen is mightier than the sword? We have been caught in our own inconsistencies and should admit it. It makes no sense to believe that literature can make people better but that it cannot make them worse. Either it has power, or it does not. And if it does have power, then it is to be feared as well as admired. (p. 59)*

Small presents the heart of textbook controversies as a conflict of educational values. Indeed, it is seen as a conflict about moral education and the role literature is to play in it. One group wishes students to read works designed to convey what it sees as the best values of the cultural heritage. The second group wishes to use the curriculum to present current issues and to allow students to discover some personal truths about them. One might represent the substance of conflicting values in other ways, but this will serve for our discussion.

The second way in which people who make curriculum choices and those who object to them differ is in their power to determine the choice. Rather obviously, people who make the choice have the power to do so. People who disagree with the choice lack the power to make it. When choices contrary to their educational values are made, their recourse is to acquiesce or to protest.

Now, what is it about these two differences—the difference in educational values and the difference in power—that makes one group censors and the other not? Our response is simple: Nothing. People do not become censors simply because their educational values differ from those held by professionals. Nor do they become censors because they are powerless. *Protesting the choices of educators does not make people censors.*

What, then, constitutes censorship? We suggest two criteria. First, censorship is a choice or rejection of a choice motivated not by the desire to serve a set of educational values but by the desire that a certain set of educational values be neither served nor considered. This criterion is meant to convey the idea that part of what constitutes censorship is the desire to suppress someone else's viewpoint rather than to promote one's own. Putting this point somewhat differently, censorship is the attempt to promote the victory of one's views and ideas through the use of power or coercion against one's opponents rather than through the use of reason and persuasion. But this definition is not adequate. It would, for example, make it difficult to explain why the failure to teach astrology in public schools or universities is not an act of censorship. There are sometimes good reasons for excluding things from the curriculum. That an idea is known to be nonsense is surely one of them.

Thus we add a second criterion. Censorship occurs when a choice or the rejection of a choice is motivated by reasons that are not legitimate educational concerns but rather are intended to prevent acquaintance with a serious idea because it might be adopted. This criterion embodies two points. The first is that when something is excluded or removed from the classroom for good educational reasons, that is not censorship. The fact that comic books and *Playboy* are not commonly used in literature classes can be given good educational justification. Neither Bugs Bunny nor *Playboy*'s bunnies have cause to complain of censorship if they are unrepresented in school curricula.

The second point is that censorship is, in essence, motivated by fear of thinking. It is the desire to isolate our views from serious challenge or prevent the consideration of threatening ideas that is the key ingredient of censorship. Censorship is at heart the attempt to pursue truth with power, not thought.

This concept of censorship is not particularly easy to apply. This is not a problem with the concept. It is a product of the complexity and ambiguity of the phenomena. The definition does, however, have two noteworthy advantages. First, it focuses attention on the key issues. Is this act motivated by legitimate educational concerns or by fear of thinking? Second, it is neutral to the question of power. It leaves open the question of who the censors are, the people who make the choice or those who object to it.

The Case for COPS

We now turn to the case for COPS. We believe that there are basically two kinds of arguments COPS might make. First, COPS might argue that it is not a censor. Rather, its members are simply attempting to get the schools to reflect their educational values and are employing the democratic process in order to do so. They might wish to argue that their exclusion of certain books, courses, or programs was motivated either by the desire to reorient the educational values being served or by the belief that the materials excluded failed to meet reasonable standards of educational value. We leave it to you to appraise the merits of such arguments. We suggest only that arguments of this sort are not inherently defective and must, therefore, be judged on a case-by-case basis with full attention to particular details.

Second, COPS might wish to argue a case based on parents' rights. The essence of such an argument is that in a free society, the right to determine how a child is to be raised belongs to the child's parents, not to the government. Public schools are, however, governmental agencies. Thus when a school assigns or makes available to students material disapproved by the students' parents, the school has usurped the rightful place of parents. The school is behaving as though the government rather than parents were entitled to control the education of children.

It is important to note the limits of this argument. Such an argument, if successful, may justify a parent's restricting what the school may teach or make available to his or her *own* child. It does not show that any particular parent or group of parents should have anything to say about what schools teach other people's children. As it stands, therefore, the argument cannot justify COPS's wholesale exclusion of some books from the Puddly library. It can only justify the rights of parents to have a say about what their children are taught.

Further Considerations on Censorship

Three additional topics are relevant to these issues. One is the question of how one goes about deciding whether or not some curricular material has educational merit. Here there are, no doubt, a large number of criteria. One criterion is whether or not the curricular content has standing in the professional community concerned with the topic. We have suggested that excluding astrology from the curriculum is not censorship for the simple reason that astrology is considered to be wrong. How do we decide this? One response is that this is the opinion of a professional community, astronomers, that is in a position to know about astrology's hard scientific aspect. This is to say that questions about what is and is not known to be true in various subject areas must be appropriately refereed. It is not to say that we should teach only the views of experts to the exclusion of debate and questioning. But even here experts can help us to decide what issues are genuinely open in a field and what issues have been decided. When we want to know what ideas are worth teaching and what issues are worth debating in areas such as biology, chemistry, or mathematics, the opinions of professional biologists, chemists, or mathematicians are important to consider (see Strike, 1982b).

Second, we need to consider the relationship between parents' rights and the public interest. If we assume that parents have a prima facie right to govern the education of their children, what limits are there on this right? One limit is suggested by the concept of the public interest. Some kinds of educational services provide benefits that are important not only to their immediate consumers but also to the welfare of the community. A student who learns to play a musical instrument derives primarily personal benefits. A student who learns to read, however, benefits the entire community, for that student becomes a better and more productive citizen. Moreover, a student who fails to become a competent violinist does not thereby threaten the welfare of the community in the same way as a student who cannot read.

When a particular kind of educational service has significant effects for the welfare of the public, the public gains a right to a say about the matter. Thus a parent may decide without opposition that his or her child shall not study music. A parent may not, however, decide without opposition that his or her child shall not learn to read. In the latter case a significant public interest is involved; consequently, the public gains a right to exercise some authority over such decisions.

The final point is that the notion of the public interest might be used to support the argument advanced by COPS. COPS parents had argued that some of what students were asked to read was immoral and morally corrupting. One response to them is that if they believe this, they have the right to prevent their children from reading such material, but they have no right to deny the material to other people's children. COPS may, however, respond that what other people's children read is of considerable import to them. The moral education of their own children is surely affected by the values of their children's peers. Moreover, the moral education of the community's children must have an effect on the welfare of the community. Does not the community have a significant interest in having citizens who accept such values as honesty, tolerance, and truthfulness? May it not have an interest in other values as well? The concept of the public interest, then, provides a mechanism for expanding the scope of arguments concerning moral education, for it gives each an interest in the moral education of all.

Conflict and the Administrator's Role in Textbook Controversies

School Policy

Superintendent Vacey has tried to avoid the controversy in Puddly. His reluctance to become involved is understandable. Feelings about textbook conflicts tend to run high. Such conflicts touch people's fundamental values; concern is likely to be great and room for compromise small. An administrator who becomes involved in such a conflict can expect to exhaust his or her political capital rapidly. Mr. Vacey's fears of losing his ability to work with the citizens of his district, and possibly his job, are not unrealistic.

What might he have done? As we suggested earlier, perhaps the first rule of thumb is not to ignore the issue in the hope that it will go away. Textbook controversies have a way of not going away. Moreover, they can quickly become very visible and emotionally charged. We suspect that it is better to deal with them at the outset. Keep in mind that most such cases do not begin with letters to the editor or organized pressure groups. As in Puddly, they begin with particular inquiries by particular parents into something that has been assigned to their child. Parents usually do not "go public" or seek organizational support until they begin to feel the schools are not being responsive.

The second rule of thumb is to have a policy. It helps immeasurably in dealing with such cases to have an agreed set of procedures that all parties consider fair and workable. Such a policy prevents decisions that are (or appear to be) arbitrary or ad hoc and goes a long way in securing the agreement of all parties to the resulting decision. Moreover, the existence of a set of procedures to be followed allows the matter to be discussed privately and provides an automatic cooling-off period in which the parties involved can reflect dispassionately on the issues, without any need to maintain postures, defend public statements, or keep political allies happy. Finally, such a policy should be hammered out prior to the eruption of a conflict, not in the midst of one.

We do not intend here to describe such a policy; instead, we shall discuss some of the criteria applicable to judging or constructing one (for a specific example, see Bartlett, 1979).

A Policy Should Legitimate the Participation of Everyone Legitimately Concerned   Parents have a right to an opinion about the education of their children, and they have a right to express their concerns about what their children are reading. A policy that excludes people who feel aggrieved can be neither fair nor successful.

The question of whom else to include is more difficult. Aggrieved parents may wish to be represented. Administrators may, however, wish to exclude some groups (such as the Moral Majority) whose aspirations and agenda may go well beyond the selection of schoolbooks. Generally, a policy must recognize that parents will not always be sophisticated concerning their own views and may rightfully desire a spokesperson. Perhaps this is particularly the case in curriculum protests because they may originate among a segment of the community that may be less well equipped to articulate and defend its position in the face of professional educators' opposition. A policy might, however, encourage parents to seek help among friends and local agencies and should discourage initial representation by organizations with broader objectives from outside the immediate community.

The Threat to Involved Parties Should Be Minimized   As we shall argue shortly, parents should not have to deal with inappropriate labels such as "censors" or "Birchers." They also need to be assured that their standing in the community or their child's standing in the school will not be jeopardized by their raising an issue. Teachers, administrators, and board members should likewise be free from pejorative labels and threats to livelihood and status. Thus a policy ought to incorporate expectations for the behavior of individuals on any committee to determine the fate of books and programs. Civility, so notable for its absence from both sides of the dispute in Puddly, is a minimal expectation.

Deliberations Should Be Confidential   No policy will work if the deliberations of the people implementing it are debated in the local newspaper or if participants must constantly account to their supporters. Any committee executing a policy should feel the obligation to report recommendations and a rationale for them for public discussion. Actual committee deliberations, however, should be confidential so long as they are in process.

Attention Must Be Focused on the Content and Educational Suitability of the Material in Question   It is surprising how many censorship cases begin with an argument between a parent and an administrator over something neither of them has read. Works should be read and discussed. They must be judged as a whole rather than on isolated passages. Moreover, deliberations should be preceded by some discussion of relevant educational standards. Agreement on such standards is useful but not required. People deal more reasonably with one another if they have some understanding of their educational aspirations. Parents and teachers may come to see one another as people who are genuinely concerned about education rather than as "religious zealots" or "secular humanists" conspiring to undermine basic values.

Informal Discussion Should Precede Formal Procedures   It should be expected that a parent who objects to something his or her child has been assigned should discuss that concern with the teacher who made the assignment. It is always to be preferred that a conflict be settled informally between the parties most directly involved, when that is possible.

Policies conforming to these standards will not make textbook cases go away. These disputes arise because Americans persist in the somewhat inconsistent beliefs that values are private matters over which the state should have no control, that public schools should be state-operated majoritarian institutions expressing democratic consensus, and that schools should be operated by professionals with expertise in educational matters. When the members of a diverse society must function in a common institution, there will be irreconcilable conflicts that no amount of procedural reasonableness will cause to go away. What we hope for from our suggestions is that reconcilable conflicts will be resolved and that disputes that remain will be settled fairly. The following remarks by Stephen Arons (1983) put the matter in context.

> *The growth of professional control of school administration and the eclipse of meaningful relationships between parents and teachers have left families with the feeling that they have lost custody of the child who goes to school.*

Parents who want their values and concerns for their children expressed in schooling are increasingly met with a wall of professional hostility and bureaucratic lethargy. It is not surprising that these people . . . should turn to organized battle to regain control of the schools. Political action is a reasonable answer to the lack of responsiveness of schools to the endlessly varied needs and aspirations of families. (p. 28)

The Administrator's Role

When the hostilities in the Puddly School District arose, Mr. Vacey beat a hasty retreat. We believe that strategy was mistaken on both practical and ethical grounds, for several reasons.

The most important reason is that a real issue between individuals with real and legitimate concerns is involved. We have argued that most cases of censorship—and indeed most other disputes concerning education—involve differences between individuals who have a legitimate stake in education and who have different viewpoints on what education should be. One group is not in favor of competent open-minded education while another benighted group seeks to impose dogmatism on the schools. Nor is one group seeking to corrupt the nation's youth and the other upholding America and God. Both groups, by virtue of being teachers and parents, respectively, have a right to a say about educational policy in their community and have views on education that deserve consideration.

Second, a democratic decision-making mechanism is a suitable and appropriate means for resolving conflict. Matters of educational policy—particularly those that express differences concerning educational values and preferences (see Chapter 6)—are not appropriately decided by experts. In a democratic society, conflicts of values are appropriately worked out by political mechanisms that recognize everyone's right to pursue personal values and provide fair ways for individuals to participate in conflict resolution.

Finally, conflict can have desirable consequences. Conflict need not bring only or primarily hostility and unpleasantness. It can promote group and community cohesiveness, participation in education, valuable political socialization, and fair and mutually acceptable decisions.

What, then, is the administrator's role in conflict? We suggest that in many instances it is to help the involved parties to have a fair fight. That is, it is to attempt to make the political process work well. The following are the kinds of things that contribute to promoting a fair fight.

Help to Identify and Gain Recognition for the Legitimate Parties to the Dispute   Who has a right to participate in a given dispute? Certainly teachers, administrators, school board members, and parents have a legitimate concern for education. It is normally inappropriate to exclude them. The administrator can promote a fair fight by helping each party to recognize the right of the others to participate.

Create a Climate of Civility and Respect   A most important component of having a fair fight is to get people to respect the worth, dignity, and sincerity of those with whom they disagree.

Promote Forums for Direct Communication   Letters to the editor and exchanges at school board meetings tend to harden positions and increase hostility. Direct contact and discussions are more likely to promote mutual comprehension and respect.

Create a Fair Mechanism for Decision Making   Create a process in which the interested parties can participate and to which they agree.

Educate Board Members to Their Political Role   School board members are the elected representatives of the community. They should be encouraged to play this role. Conflicts are less likely to erupt into hostility if various groups in the community feel that their views are represented on the board. The administrator should help the board to have informal debates on policy issues rather than attempt to steer them toward the "correct" decision.

Focus the Issues   Generally, disputes are more easily settled when the issues are clearly understood by the participants and when the scope of the issues is contained. It is easier to decide if a given book is suitable for junior high school English than to decide if one individual or another is willing to tolerate censorship or secular humanism.

   In short, school administrators must deal with conflict by showing respect for the combatants and for democratic institutions. And they must encourage others to do likewise.

Questions

   1. Not every issue is appropriately refereed. An issue is appropriately refereed only when there is an established body of knowledge concerning it and a recognized group of experts who process this knowledge. Which of the following issues is inappropriately refereed?
   a. The question of whether to teach both evolution and creation
   b. Questions about moral education
   c. Questions about the best teaching methods
   d. Questions about sex education
   2. Members of organizations such as COPS are often accused of representing the views of outside groups such as the John Birch Society. Is this relevant?
   3. What rights should parents have in the education of their children? Why?
   4. Are educators legitimate referees of pedagogical questions?
   5. COPS and ROBBERS represent not only different ideas but different social classes. Does this make any difference?
   6. Mr. Vacey has attempted to keep out of the dispute. Is this an effective strategy for him? Should an administrator attempt to influence public debates about educational policy?

7. Is there anything in our recommendations concerning policy that might raise legal problems?

8. Which of our suggestions did Mr. Vacey violate? Is there any reason to believe that things might have turned out differently had he responded differently?

9. Our recommendations are based in part on our analysis of censorship. If you disagree with any part of our analysis, how would you change our recommendations?

10. Might someone who followed our suggestions sometimes create a problem where one might not otherwise have occurred?

11. Should professional educators have any right to overrule a parent's wishes concerning the education of his or her child? If so, when?

CHAPTER 3

Discipline and Students' Rights

Disorder at Rankled Memorial

"He's got to go." Ms. Parker could not tell if Andrew Burns was demanding or begging. "He's driving me crazy and has reduced my class to chaos. If you'll only suspend him for a few days, I can regain control of my class. If you don't support me in this, my class will go right down the drain."

Ms. Parker considered that more than Mr. Burns's class seemed to be going down the drain. A good case could be made that the whole school was. Rankled Memorial High School, of which she was principal, had more than its share of troubles. Though these troubles manifested themselves in numerous ways, they could be summed up in one word—*discipline*. Actually, *indiscipline* would be more precise. Andrew Burns's problem with one of his students, Karl Trotter, was merely the tip of an iceberg whose dimensions were fearsome to contemplate.

The first of these was attendance. Rankled Memorial had the poorest attendance rate of any high school in the city. On any given day, fully 20 percent of its students were absent. Many students seemed to come or not as they saw fit, and attempts to counter this by building a home-school cooperation program had been notable for their lack of success. Many students' homes were headed by a single working parent (almost always the mother), who often seemed to be so preoccupied with the task of making ends meet that she had little energy left for the school's problems. Tardiness and class-cutting were endemic.

A second dimension was drugs. Like most urban schools, Rankled Memorial had a drug problem, but of late this had become significantly worse. "Substance abuse" (the current term for alcohol and/or drug abuse) was widespread among the students. Teachers complained that a number of their charges regularly appeared to be under the influence of one drug or another. Indeed, only last week the daily paper had headlined a major police "bust" of drug traffickers in the city. One of these, Ms. Parker learned from the article, was a student at Rankled.

A third dimension was vandalism, which was reaching alarming proportions. The head custodian complained that one of his staff was occupied nearly full-time simply replacing broken windows. The installation of wire mesh grills had helped but had not completely eliminated breakage. Graffiti appeared nearly as fast as they could be removed. (Ms. Parker secretly cursed the inventor of the aerosol paint can.) Furniture, chalkboards, projectors, and assorted other pieces of school equipment were in a chronic state of disrepair from deliberate abuse. Rankled Memorial, once a beautiful example of postwar school architecture, had become a littered, decrepit, and ugly shell of its former self.

Last but not least was the matter of violence. Although Ms. Parker had not been forced to ask for regular police patrols of her building (as have many urban schools), she feared it would come to that. Fights were common—so much so that the vice-principal seemed to spend much of his time trying to settle student disputes. In one a knife had been brandished, but fortunately no one was injured. The recent appearance of youth gangs in the neighborhood was ominous. Several cases of students extorting money from other students were known to have occurred, and Ms. Parker had every reason to believe that many more were occurring but going unreported. Finally, six weeks ago a teacher had been badly beaten as he left the building after dark and headed for his car. The culprits had not been apprehended, hence it was unclear whether students were involved, but the staff was up in arms. They demanded action—a tough crackdown on all forms of misbehavior and immediate expulsion of any student who physically threatened a teacher. Further, they viewed the widespread use of drugs as a major cause of the other problems and demanded that Ms. Parker clear the school of drugs and drug users.

But if all these were simply some dimensions of the iceberg, its tip, Karl Trotter, was her immediate problem. Karl was a bright, troubled boy from a working-class family. He had a history of conflict with the school. He had been suspended several times for incidents as diverse as fighting, theft, and smoking marijuana. Students such as Karl were not rare in Rankled Memorial.

This year, however, Karl was a different sort of problem. He had become radicalized. Somewhere he had gotten involved with a leftist organization that had explained to him that his feelings of alienation and his conflict with the school were a consequence of the evils of capitalist domination. Karl had become not only a true believer but a vociferous one.

Most of Karl's teachers had found Karl's conversion to be an improvement. Despite an occasional harangue on the Marxist interpretation of the issues of the day, Karl's behavior had improved, and he no longer seemed to be in constant trouble. His penchant for Marxist rhetoric was perceived by teachers and students alike as nothing more than a minor irritation. At least that was how it was until the drug raid.

In an attempt to crack down on drug usage, a surprise drug bust had been organized. Initially, Ms. Parker had been against it, but the teachers were insistent. Ms. Parker had given in, hoping that even if it accomplished little, it might at least calm the faculty and perhaps even assure some parents that the school was trying to do something. One afternoon during sixth-period classes, a locker search was conducted. All of the students' lockers were opened and inspected. The search was quite productive: It turned up several stashes of marijuana and liquor, a few knives, and, alarmingly, one gun. Students with contraband in their lockers had been immediately suspended.

Many of the students had been furious at having their lockers searched. They were particularly upset about the suspension of John Sweet, a very straight young man who had made the error of allowing another student to use his locker to store ''some stuff.'' The stuff, it turned out, included a bag of marijuana. Most students believed that it did not belong to John. Ms. Parker had, however, ordered a mass suspension and had not investigated individual circumstances. Students believed that John's suspension was unfair and wondered about others.

Had it not been for Karl, student anger would likely have dissipated. Karl, however, responded to the locker search like a Moses at a convention of pharaohs. He found himself a mimeograph machine and a typewriter and went to work.

Karl first attempted to organize a strike. That did not work out well. He managed to get a few dozen students to boycott a few classes, but most students could not be effectively mobilized in that way. So he turned to sponsoring classroom debates. In each of his classes, he insisted on having the class discuss the locker search. Some teachers permitted this; others did not. The result was the same either way. Karl was succeeding in raising the level of student indignation. When a teacher permitted the discussion, Karl was successful in making his peers feel victimized and exploited by the school. When the discussion was not permitted, Karl was able to use that to make students feel repressed.

Andrew Burns had permitted the discussion in his math class. Indeed, since he had had considerable reservations about the locker search, he found the matter of some interest and had hoped that an open discussion would help students to work through their anger. Karl, however, was not willing to let it go. He had managed to keep a better part of the school discussing locker searches for almost a week. Students were increasingly angry and unruly. Things were tense.

This morning when Mr. Burns had arrived in class, he found Karl giving out a mimeographed paper that he expected the class to discuss during the period. When Mr. Burns politely suggested that he thought the class should get back to geometry, Karl argued that the class be allowed to vote on what they wanted to do. Mr. Burns had more than a suspicion as to how that would come out. Geometry was not universally beloved among his students. He "pulled rank" and told the class that they had spent enough time on the locker search and that they were going to study geometry. He collected Karl's handouts and deposited them in the trash. Words followed. Mr. Burns recalled that among them the word "fascist" figured prominently. He then collected Karl and his handouts and proceeded to Ms. Parker's office, where he now sat demanding Karl's suspension.

Ms. Parker had no idea how to proceed. If she failed to suspend Karl, Mr. Burns and the rest of the teachers would be outraged. They would expect Ms. Parker to back up a teacher's judgment in this sort of situation. So would many parents. On the other hand, she was not at all sure that suspending Karl would do the least bit of good in calming the students. She rather suspected the opposite. They would see it as simply another violation of their rights. Things could get worse.

Further, she was not sure that she could suspend Karl. The school district's attorney had come by the other day to inform her that she was legally on thin ice with the locker search and the suspensions and to give her a quick sketch of students' rights, with ominous references to due process and free speech. For all she knew, Karl had a legal right to say whatever he wanted in geometry class and Mr. Burns had violated some constitutional right by confiscating Karl's papers. Karl and Mr. Burns were waiting. She had to think of something quickly.

Introduction

Rankled High is not alone. Across the United States, in small towns as well as large cities, a general atmosphere of indiscipline characterizes many schools. In some districts, uniformed police are to be seen in classrooms, corridors, and offices. Indeed, the problem of discipline was deemed of sufficient magnitude to provoke the attention of a subcommittee of the U.S. Senate, which issued a "report card" awarding our schools an "A in violence and vandalism" (Subcommittee to Investigate Juvenile Delinquency, 1975). The problem is not simply one of a greater incidence in the breaking of school rules; qualitative changes have occurred as well. Educators have always had to deal with student crime in its milder forms: Schoolyard fights, broken windows, and profanity directed at teachers are hardly new phenomena. What seemed to be new was the increasing occurrence of major felonies: Murder, rape, armed robbery, and arson are no longer unheard of. Nor are such crimes confined to high school pupils; middle school and even elementary children are committing them as well.

Simultaneously, this apparent wave of indiscipline has been accompanied by judicial decisions that have extended important constitutional safeguards to pupils, protecting them from school administrators who in attempting to deal with student misbehavior have acted in what the courts judge to be illegal ways. Thirty years ago it is doubtful that a school principal would have hesitated to search student lockers if he or she felt so inclined or summarily to suspend students for relatively minor rule infractions. Today, Ms. Parker is well advised to be careful in doing so, lest she violate students' fundamental rights. This has provoked some school administrators to complain that the courts have made it unreasonably difficult, if not impossible, to enforce ordinary standards of decorum.

The public is also alarmed. The annual Gallup polls of citizens' attitudes toward their schools consistently show that "lack of discipline" is perceived as the most serious problem facing public education (Gallup, 1984). The erosion of parental trust implied in these polls is worrisome: An absolute desideratum of parents' support of public education is the belief that their children are physically safe while at school. In fact, for years the schools' ability virtually to guarantee the daily security of millions of children stands as one of their more remarkable accomplishments (though usually taken for granted). But as the statistics suggest, in many schools that virtual guarantee can no longer be assumed.

Finally, it is plausible to suppose that schools characterized by disorder (not to say violence) are also characterized by climates that are inimical to the academic achievement of even well-behaved students, that the morale and average competence of their staffs decline as good teachers flee, and that a significant proportion of their budgets is diverted to such "unproductive" uses as insurance, the repair of vandalized property, and school security requirements. For all these reasons, school administrators need to be cognizant of the explanations and issues pertaining to student discipline. While Rankled High is surely not the worst of the nation's "blackboard jungles," neither is it a hushed and reverent "grove of academe." In short, educational administrators will do well to contemplate the causes and consequences of school indiscipline, as well as the legal and ethical concepts that should guide their actions concerning it.

The Roots of School Crime

There is no dearth of explanations for the difficulty in maintaining an orderly school environment. In examining some of these, we will first attend to some of the structural features of schools themselves. These features characterize virtually all public schools; they help us to understand why discipline of youngsters is more problematic in educational institutions than in other organizations that also serve children and youth. Next we will turn our attention to several sociological theories that can be useful for explaining variations in the degree to which individual schools present problems to teachers and administrators.

Client and Institutional Choice

More than twenty years ago, Richard O. Carlson (1964) proposed a useful typology of client-serving organizations (e.g., schools, hospitals, welfare agencies) that calls attention to two distinguishing characteristics among these organizations. Carlson noted that some organizations are able to select their clients, while others are not. Further, some have clients who come voluntarily, and others do not. In Table 3.1 we have created a four-celled table by cross-classifying these two characteristics, and we give a few examples of organizations found in three of the four cells. (In modern American society, no organization appears to be of type 3.)

Each type of organization created by this typology can be characterized as having a predominant problem. For example, those of type 1 have the problem of *attractiveness.* Since their clients may or may not choose to come, organizations such as private schools must find ways to attract them in sufficient numbers to allow the organization to continue to exist. Carlson terms these organizations ''wild,'' meaning that they must adapt to their environments and compete with one another for clients. Type 2 organizations confront the problems of *standards.* When clients are free to come and may not be refused, expectations for their performance may have to be tempered by the quality of those who choose to participate. Thus public two-year colleges may offer courses that would be considered ''inappropriate'' in a private college (e.g., macramé, auto mechanics) in

TABLE 3.1
A TYPOLOGY OF CLIENT-SERVING ORGANIZATIONS

May Organizations Select Clients?	Is Client Participation Voluntary?	
	Yes	*No*
Yes	Type 1 Private schools and colleges, law firms	Type 3 —
No	Type 2 Public two-year colleges, adult education programs	Type 4 Public elementary and secondary schools, prisons and reformatories, state mental institutions

SOURCE: Adapted from Richard O. Carlson, 1964, ''Environmental Constraints and Organizational Consequences: The Public School and Its Clients,'' in Daniel E. Griffiths (Ed.), *Behavioral Science and Educational Administration,* 63rd Yearbook of the National Society for the Study of Education, Chicago: University of Chicago Press, p. 265.

order to attract students and may award passing grades for work that would be considered unacceptable in a private institution able to select its students.

Type 4 institutions are of primary concern to us here. This cell of the table includes public schools, public mental hospitals, prisons, and reformatories. It may be disconcerting to see schools grouped with prisons and asylums. However, they share the common attributes of being unable to refuse admission to their clients, who in turn have no choice over their participation. Carlson terms these organizations "domesticated." They need not compete for clients; a steady supply is assured. Funds are more closely tied to the numbers of persons served than to the quality of the service provided. They cannot "go out of business" and need not adapt as quickly as type 1 organizations to changes in the social and political environment. In this sense they are "domesticated"—protected by the larger society.

The salient problem of type 4 organizations is *control.* They are required to provide a service to unselected clients, some or most of whom do not desire that service. In prisons, of course, virtually all inmates are there involuntarily, and mechanisms to control their behavior play a much larger role in organizational life than do mechanisms serving other organizational ends, such as rehabilitation. In high schools many students are there voluntarily much of the time, so mechanisms of social control are less obvious than in prisons. However, it is virtually certain that in all high schools some students would prefer to be elsewhere most of the time and that all students would prefer to be elsewhere some of the time. This fundamental characteristic of public schools—the lack of choice of both the organization and students—makes problems of discipline so significant to teachers and administrators.

Both organizations and clients need to adapt to this involuntary relationship. For the school two major adaptations are *segregation* and *preferential treatment* (Carlson, 1964). Segregation refers to mechanisms designed to separate unselected and unwilling students from the rest of the student body. Special classes for students with "behavior problems" is an example. Similarly, difficult pupils are more often assigned to vocational than to academic "tracks," at least partly on the grounds that more practical, job-oriented training may improve their willingness to participate. Sending pupils to the principal's office or to see a counselor and suspending students are examples of this form of adaptation.

Preferential treatment, on the other hand, refers to the dispensing of organizational sanctions differentially according to student cooperation. It is well documented, for example, that grades are not based entirely on academic performance; a substantial component reflects students' willingness to conform to rules and various personality traits that are desirable from the school's perspective. Bowles and Gintis (1976) concluded that conforming to rules, dependability, and punctuality, for example, are nearly as important as academic ability for earning good grades. In schools, good behavior pays off in a very tangible way (Jackson, 1968). These mechanisms, then, make the processing of reluctant clients more tolerable from the school's point of view.

Students, too, evidence forms of adaptation to their involuntary participation. Carlson (1964) describes several. Students who participate willingly most of the time evidence what he terms a *receptive adaptation,* meaning they accept the school's objectives and procedures as their own. At the other extreme, the *dropout adaptation* is evidenced by truancy, tardiness, and leaving school at the earliest permissible age. Between these two extremes lie *situational retirement, sidebetting,* and *rebellion.* The first of these is characterized by the student who is physically present but mentally absent. One study, in which high school students were monitored with paging devices, concluded that, on the average, pupils were inattentive to instruction more than half of their classroom time (Csikszentmihalyi, Larson, & Prescott, 1977). The second form of adaptation, side-betting, involves mitigating the involuntary nature of the student role by redefining the purposes of the school. The institution becomes a site for athletic achievement, contacts with the opposite sex, or opportunities to engage in valued (but nonacademic) activities such as music or drama. Situational retirement and side-betting are likely to present only minor problems of control to educators. Indeed, such students may be models of deportment, though their academic performance may leave much to be desired. A more problematic form of adaptation is rebellion. The rebellious adjustment is by far the most conspicuous. Such students reject the purposes or the procedures of the school, or both. They frequently test the limits of permissible behavior. "The perspective taken by the students is one of seeing the whole situation as a game of wits; and the object of the game is to see how much one can get away with" (Carlson, 1964, p. 275). The obvious implication of Carlson's analysis is that some student rebellion and indiscipline is inevitable, just as some inmate defiance of authority is inevitable in prisons— and for the same reason. Both the institution and the individual have no choice concerning their relationship.

Crowds, Praise, and Power

Although the involuntary nature of the relationship for both organizations and students provides a start toward helping us to understand the prevalence of indiscipline in schools, it is not the only relevant attribute of the relationship. Another is the persistent themes of *crowds, praise,* and *power* that characterize schools (Jackson, 1968).

An important and often overlooked aspect of schools is their sheer population density: As Jackson notes, schools are crowded places, perhaps more so than any place of adult work. Thirty or so minors are placed in a single room under the supervision of one adult. This high density sharply increases the need for conformity to rules and, in addition, creates the requirement for rules peculiar to the institution. Schools often require that one obtain permission to speak, to get up out of a seat, or to chew gum. A concomitant of this crowding is a lack of privacy. As we shall discuss later, in a sense an act violates a rule only when it is perceived and defined as a violation. Because of the overwhelmingly public nature of life in schools, actions that might go unnoticed or unpunished elsewhere become sanctionable in classrooms (fidgeting in one's seat is a prime example). Further, crowding and the high minor-adult ratio mean that much of students' time is necessarily spent waiting—waiting to be called on, waiting for help with a problem, waiting to sharpen a pencil, waiting in line for lunch (Jackson, 1968). It is plausible to suppose that unoccupied time spent in a crowded and public situation contributes to the frequency of disciplinary incidents.

Coupled with the matter of crowding is that of evaluative judgments. Judgments—praise or disapprobation—are the everyday stuff of student life (Jackson, 1968). The daily cycle of academic assignments and evaluations, the frequent opportunity for rule breaking, and the observability of behavior help to ensure that praise or blame are meted out regularly and publicly in classrooms. The sheer frequency with which judgments are rendered in schools probably exceeds that of any other institution in the lives of either minors or adults. As a consequence, there is plenty of opportunity to become recognized by teachers (and peers) as a "good student" or a "troublemaker." As we shall see, this evaluative atmosphere of schooling contributes to the problematic nature of school discipline.

Finally, we should note the sharp disparity in power between students and teachers (Jackson, 1968). The bases of teachers' power are several: the formal power invested in them by the state, the power that derives from being *in loco parentis*, the power resulting from professional training, the general power of adults over minors, and the power that accrues from possessing a virtual monopoly over classroom resources, most notably, perhaps, grades and time. The teacher role is primarily one of activity and dominance; that of pupils, passivity and submission. Thus Jackson concluded that some of the most useful qualities students can develop for success in such a milieu are patience, docility, and relative quiescence. It seems plausible to suppose that such qualities are difficult to achieve for adolescents, many of whom are rapidly on the way to physical, social, psychological, and sexual maturity. In addition to the involuntary nature of schooling itself, classroom life undoubtedly contributes to the difficulty of maintaining order.

Youth Culture

A third perspective on schooling and adolescence can help to further our understanding of the prevalence of discipline problems in schools. First stated most comprehensively in James Coleman's *The Adolescent Society* (1961), it has received extensive attention in recent years.

Coleman's thesis might be summarized as follows: There exists a strong peer culture among adolescents that is in some respects antithetical to the adult culture and to the professed goals of the school. This culture arose as a consequence of large-scale historical trends that have displaced the family as the basic productive unit in society. Simultaneously, the increase in productivity that resulted from this change enabled modern societies to free themselves from depending on young people to contribute to the labor force and freed families from depending on the income thus generated. Having lost their economic function, adolescents increasingly spent their time in schools preparing to take on adult roles. In a sense, society "invented" the adolescent in the later stages of the industrial revolution and then required a "holding ground" to accommodate him. Schools provide such a place, as well as a role, that of student, not tightly connected to adult institutions. Thus high schools are not simply crowded places; they are crowded with young people who have few of the commitments and responsibilities that mark adulthood. As a consequence of this "disconnectedness" and the crowding together in a single institution,

> the student is forced inward toward his own age group, made to carry out his whole social life with others his own age. With his fellows, he comes to constitute a small society, one that has most of its important interactions within itself, and maintains only a few threads of connection with the outside adult society. (Coleman, 1961, p. 3)

This intensified interaction has led to the development of a somewhat distinctive culture that at least in part separates young people from adults. The culture is impossible to describe adequately, not only because of its variation from place to place but also because it changes so rapidly. During the last decades it has at various times and places included relatively distinctive forms of music (e.g., "heavy metal"), sports (surfing), religion (Hare Krishna, The Way), dress ("punk"), and recreation (smoking "pot"). Coleman (1974) described this culture as inward-looking, prizing attachments to others of the same age, admiring autonomy from adults, sympathizing with the underdog, and valuing change.

To the extent that such values characterize adolescents in a school, the discipline problems of teachers and administrators are further exacerbated. First, activities and attributes that give a student status among his or her peers—athletics, a car, the right clothes—do not directly contribute to achieving status in the school's view (academic success). Indeed, they may militate against it. Further, the subdivision of a student body into cliques, which themselves have a status ranking (e.g., "jocks" may have more status than "grinds"), may serve to depress students' motivation to excel academically, and this may be particularly true for girls, for whom very high academic achievement may actually stand in the way of "popularity," which is a predominant value (Coleman, 1961). Finally, some of these cliques consist of students who openly or covertly reject the value system of the school. For example, students who make the rebellious adaptation noted by Carlson often form cliques that develop a subculture of their own, a subculture that awards prestige for toughness, indiscipline, and independence from all adult authority. Similarly, cliques with their associated subcultures grow up around the procurement and use of drugs. Such subcultures among adolescents provide rewards for rule violations that may more than offset any punishment the school attaches to them.

The publication of *The Adolescent Society* in 1961 touched off considerable academic debate and research, both of which continue to the present (see Boocock, 1980, for an informative discussion and review of the evidence). In particular, the assertion that a nearly monolithic youth culture antithetical to adult and educational values exists seems questionable. It appears that most young people have internalized adult and school values at least to the point of aspiring to educational success defined in conventional terms. However, it seems equally clear that in most schools a significant (and prominent) minority of students have not, and the size, importance, and nature of such groups varies from school to school and over time. (You might compare the interesting case studies, spanning decades, in Waller, 1932; Cusick, 1973; Stinchcomb, 1964; and Gordon, 1957.) Such groups, when they reject school values, provide support for their members (and others) to do likewise.

We have tried to suggest that the roots of school discipline problems are not entirely individual in nature. The behavior of Karl and other rebellious students at Rankled Memorial High School cannot be understood by attributing their actions entirely to idiosyncratic personality or character "defects." Neither should their behavior be attributed solely to incompetent parents, urban poverty, racism, or any other favorite cause. The social structure and culture of the school and its inhabitants must also be considered. The involuntary nature of the school-student relationship, the character of the institution's demographics and its authority relations, and the development of student subcultures are prominent among these considerations.

It nevertheless remains true that these factors cannot be sufficient explanations of school indiscipline. If that were so, all schools would be equally disorderly, since these factors are characteristic of most public high schools in this country as well as in most other countries. Yet it is clear that disorder is much more prevalent in some schools than in others and in some countries more than others (Friday, 1980). It is necessary, therefore, to consider other explanations of school disorder to account for variations in indiscipline rates among schools. Explanations for the variation in rates of any educational phenomenon are especially relevant to the study of school administration, for such explanations must necessarily focus on characteristics of social systems and not on the individuals who make them up.

Theories of Deviant Behavior

To consider discipline problems in schools as examples of deviant behavior, it is perhaps best to begin by defining the term *norm*. Norms are the rules people use to express what they expect of one another; they define what behavior is appropriate and inappropriate in a given group (De Fleur, D'Antonio, & Nelson, 1977, p. 37). In schools these rules are of several types: Some establish identity and requirements for participation (e.g., students may not enter the teachers' lounge); some govern face-to-face interaction ("politeness rules," e.g., students should be respectful of teachers), and some are civil-legal, formally enacted by governments as laws or by its agencies as legitimate rules with specific sanctions attached (e.g., "Students found smoking in the building will be suspended for one day"; Birenbaum & Lesier, 1982). Deviance, then, involves the violation of a norm.

Human behavior is deviant to the extent that it comes to be viewed as involving a personally discreditable departure from a group's normative expectations, and it elicits interpersonal or collective reactions that serve to "isolate," "treat," "correct," or "punish" individuals engaged in such behavior. (Schur, 1971, p. 24)

Finally, it is important to note that norms (and hence pupil deviance) in schools are not simply expressions of educators' expectations for student behavior. They also express pupils' expectations for themselves and for their teachers.

There are numerous theories of deviance, each with several variations. Like the equally numerous theories of personality, it is probably pointless to ask which is "correct." From the practitioner's perspective, it makes more sense to ask which is more useful in a particular situation. All provide differing perspectives and approaches to the question "Why do people violate rules?" In this chapter we will briefly examine four theoretical answers: anomie, differential association, labeling, and deterrence.

Before turning to these particular explanations of deviance and how they might be applied to schools such as Rankled Memorial, it is useful to remind ourselves of a point made by Durkheim (1950) before the turn of the century. Simply stated, Durkheim suggested that crime is both normal and inevitable. He noted that deviance from socially prescribed behavior has been present in all societies and in all ages. Further, he argued that such deviance served socially useful purposes: the punishment of a rule-breaker provides a dramatic opportunity for collective reproach and to reacknowledge the rules that bind the society together, thereby increasing social cohesion. Indeed, Durkheim believed that some level of crime was socially necessary and desirable; a society of saints would be required to invent sins, no matter that they be entirely venial in the eyes of ordinary mortals.

At a less abstract level, it is also wise for school administrators to remember that young males in this society (and probably all others) commit a vastly disproportionate number of offenses (Wilson, 1983) and that high schools amount to "holding grounds" for millions of these persons. Taking these points together—that crime seems to be inevitable in all societies, that high schools house a high percentage of people in the age group most likely to offend, and that schools themselves are structured so as to make some level of indiscipline almost certain—suggests that it is pointless for educators to expect to eliminate crime and misbehavior in schools. It is more realistic to consider ways of reducing the rate of juvenile offenses and to effect qualitative changes in their nature than to hope to eliminate them entirely.

Anomie Theory

Perhaps the most influential sociological theory of deviance was one formulated by Robert Merton (1957). Merton suggested that every society may be characterized by a set of culturally prescribed goals and a set of culturally prescribed means for attaining them. Thus, for example, U.S. society has always stressed economic success as an important goal and education, hard work, and thrift as legitimate routes toward achieving it. Similarly, institutions within a society may stress particular goals above others and prescribe socially accepted means for their realization. In the case of education, schools stress academic achievement as an end to be sought by all pupils and studiousness, good attendance, careful work habits, and attentiveness, for example, as legitimate mechanisms for attaining it. Merton's insight was to call attention to the situation that arises when individuals or groups are systematically blocked from attaining goals through legitimate means, a situation he termed *anomie*. While most Americans have internalized the goal of economic success, some groups have historically been denied the means to achieve it—for example, blacks. Nearly all high school students value academic proficiency as measured by grades, but a few of these students will fail despite their best efforts, and most will succeed but at relatively modest levels. Any system of marking that relies substantially on a relative standard for meting out grades (comparing students' work with that of others or treating A's as a scarce resource) necessarily requires that some will not attain the success to which they aspire. The school, then, like the wider society, pressures individuals to come to terms with having internalized a valued goal and their inability to achieve it.

Merton argued that nonconforming behavior—deviance—is a *normal* reaction to such situations. He identified five sorts of responses—conformity, innovation, ritualism, retreatism, and rebellion—depending on whether or not the individual accepts the culturally prescribed goal and the socially legitimate means of its achievement and whether or not new values are substituted. Table 3.2 illustrates this typology.

Conformity, accepting the value of academic success and the normally legitimate methods for attaining it, is probably the most common student adaptation to the disjunction between means and ends. Despite continued relative "failure," most students continue to strive for success, though undoubtedly over time their definition of success is revised downward. *Ritualism* essentially consists of abandoning the goal altogether while continuing to "go through the motions"—it is the logical end point of a process of continual downward revision of aspirations. Although ritualism represents a severe educational problem, students who adopt conformity or ritualism as modes of accommodation present no especially severe discipline problems for teachers or principals.

Not so the *innovators*. Probably the most common sort of innovative adaptation in schools is cheating. Students caught between the pressure of their educational aspirations and their own limitations in fulfilling those aspirations may turn to various illegal procedures—crib notes, plagiarism, and copying from others' test papers are examples. Cheating is not an uncommon activity in U.S. schools. From this perspective, however, it is not simply a matter of individual morality, a failure of character. It is, in part, a consequence of students' holding a value for themselves—high educational achievement, which schools and parents have urged them to hold—and being unable to attain it. Further, it is likely that the general devaluation of manual labor in this society and the belief that school success is the route to a "good" job also contribute to the incidence of this sort of innovation in schools.

Cheating, however, is not the kind of innovation that currently troubles Ms. Parker. Drug dealing and extortion are better examples of her immediate problem. These are also examples of innovations in Merton's analysis. Recall that deviance is a product of established values and socially blocked routes to their realization. The value involved in this case is not that of educational success but

TABLE 3.2

TYPOLOGY OF REACTIONS TO GOALS-MEANS DISJUNCTURES

Is Approved Goal Accepted?	Are Legitimate Means Accepted?		
	Yes	No	No; New Values Substituted
Yes	Conformity	Innovation	—
No	Ritualism	Retreatism	—
No; New Values Substituted	—	—	Rebellion

SOURCE: Adapted from Robert K. Merton, 1957, *Social Theory and Social Structure*, New York: Free Press, p. 140.

the even more widespread one of economic achievement. It is doubtful if many American youths can escape internalizing this as a value. The consumer orientation promoted by media advertising constantly reinforces it; cars, clothes, and the good life in general are products of economic success. But as Coleman (1974) and others have argued, the young have lost their economic function. With the steady rise of compulsory school age and the labor market's demand for increased levels of education for entry-level jobs, the legitimate means of attaining economic success have been systematically denied the young. One response to this disjunction of means and ends, according to Merton's view, is the spread of innovation—crime—among high school-age youth. According to self-report studies, as much as 90 percent of adolescents have engaged in behavior that, if discovered, would warrant an appearance in juvenile court (President's Commission on Law Enforcement and Administration of Justice, 1967). For various reasons such statistics are highly suspect; undoubtedly much of this so-called crime is relatively trivial "status offenses" such as truancy and running away. Nevertheless, as Rankled Memorial illustrates and as the reports on violence in the schools document, economically motivated crime is no longer rare in U.S. high schools (Goldstein, Apter, & Harootonian, 1984; Subcommittee to Investigate Juvenile Delinquency, 1975, 1977). According to Merton,

> It is when a system of cultural values extols, virtually above all else, certain common *success-goals* for the population at large, *while the social structure rigorously restricts or completely closes access to approved modes of reaching these goals* for a considerable part of the same population, *that deviant behavior ensues on a large scale. In this setting, a cardinal American virtue, "ambition," promotes a cardinal American vice, "deviant behavior." (Merton, 1957, p. 146; italics in original)*

Rather dramatic evidence for this point can be inferred from a study conducted by Elliot (1966), who found that delinquency rates declined by up to two-thirds *after* boys dropped out of school. Similarly, in New Zealand, McKissack (1973) found that property thefts were correlated with the legal school-leaving age. As that age is raised, the rate of theft in the final compulsory year also rises. Thus delinquency is at least in part a response to economic "needs" that cannot be met legitimately while in school.

A fourth response to the goal-means disjuncture, according to this view, is to reject both goal and means. Merton terms this *retreatism*. In its milder forms, retreatism is illustrated by the youth culture discussed earlier—the substitution of success at music, sports, or popularity for educational or economic achievement. In its more virulent forms, retreatism is exemplified by chronic alcohol and drug abuse among students. Individuals adapting in this manner are *in* the society of the school but not *of* it (Merton, 1957, p. 153). If they earn few of the rewards it has to offer, they also experience few of the frustrations and anxieties that attend seeking those rewards.

Finally, the last mode of adaptation is termed *rebellion*. Here individuals not only reject both the prevailing goals and their accepted means of attainment but also substitute new goals and means in their place. Such an adaptation is very uncommon and arguably becoming more so. Perhaps the decades of the 1960s witnessed more concerted attempts to replace both the goals and the means of the public school with different visions than any other time in our history. It is likely that Karl has such a vision. However, the difficulties in doing so are formidable, and the "alternative schools" movement was not notable for its success. Nevertheless, Karl and others like him remind us that achieving high grades and extended education through diligence and study are not universally accepted by students as appropriate values for themselves or others.

Perhaps the major implication for educators such as Ms. Parker of Merton's conception of anomie is to call into question the desirability of a single-minded focus on academic achievement as the proper goal for students to strive for. This is particularly important now, when educational "excellence" is being touted as a national priority. This is not to say that students should not attempt to excel academically. It is to say that educators must remember that many students are simply unable to do so. No amount of hard work and application is likely to get some pupils successfully through an increasingly demanding academic curriculum. Many will fail to excel; some will simply fail. There is now abundant evidence from this country as well as others that delinquents are drawn much more frequently from among students who have done most poorly in school (see Friday, 1980, for a review). Further, even if delinquency was not a likely consequence of repeated failure at school, such failure would be objectionable on moral grounds because of the psychological abuse it involves for some pupils. Thus anomie theory is important in reminding administrators that it is important to provide alternative ends. Excellence in competitive and noncompetitive sports, the arts, and productive labor, to name but a few, are desirable goals for adolescents to work toward in schools.

Anomie theory has been criticized on various conceptual grounds. For example, the degree to which students innovate (e.g., commit a crime) or retreat (e.g., become drug abusers) is dependent on the availability of *illegitimate* means. That is, just as the availability of legitimate means to attain values varies, so does access to illegitimate means. Indeed, Ms. Parker's strategy of locker searchers operates on precisely this view. More fundamentally perhaps, Merton's analysis has the same deficiency we noted for Carlson's—its monolithic view of culture assumes that all individuals subscribe to the dominant values equally. In addition, the picture that emerges from anomie theory is one of abrupt change from conformity to deviance. It does not account for the progression from commitment to generally accepted norms to deviant behavior. It lacks, in short, a sociopsychological component. Theories of differential association provide such a component.

Differential Association Theory

While anomie theory is principally concerned with the impact of social structures on deviant behavior, differential association theories are instead concerned with the learning process involved in becoming deviant. Undoubtedly the most influential version of these views is the one proposed by Sutherland and Cressey (1978). An important aspect of Sutherland and Cressey's conception is that individuals acquire deviant behavior in exactly the same ways as they acquire conventional behavior. People learn values, norms, and techniques that are favorable to criminal behavior *and* unfavorable to it. Whether or not criminal behavior is enacted, then, is a function of an individual's definition of a particular situation as being one appropriate to enactment (Traub & Little, 1980, p. 174).

Sutherland and Cressey (1978) formulate this theory as a series of propositions. Among these are the following:

1. Criminal behavior is learned behavior.
2. It is learned in interaction with other persons in a process of communication.
3. The primary part of such learning occurs in face-to-face groups. (Hence mass media portrayals of crime and violence have only minor effects on individual deviance.)
4. What is learned in such groups is two sorts of things: specific techniques of deviance; and motives, rationalizations, and attitudes regarding criminal behavior.
5. The motives, rationalizations, and attitudes that are learned concern definitions of the legal code that are either favorable or unfavorable to deviance. (That is, in some groups the code is always defined as rules to be observed, in others as rules that should be violated. In most groups in this society, definitions are of both sorts. For example, drinking by minors is illegal, but it is permitted by many parents in special circumstances, e.g., tasting champagne at a family wedding.)
6. An individual becomes delinquent because of an excess of definitions favorable to violations over those unfavorable to it. (This is the principle of differential association.) Delinquency becomes more likely as the adolescent experiences a preponderance of definitions favoring violation.
7. All definitions, whether favorable or unfavorable to delinquency, vary in fre-

quency, duration, priority, and intensity. (Priority refers to the idea that definitions learned early in life are likely to be more powerful than those learned later. Intensity refers to such things as the prestige of the source of definitions and emotional reactions to the learning situation.)

Several points about this theory and its recent modifications are important. First, it is not simply a formalized version of the folk wisdom that falling into "bad company" explains delinquency. A mother who punishes her son for taking money from her purse but who knowingly pockets the change from a cashier's mistake, who "samples" the fruit in a produce market, and who makes no effort to return a lost article is providing an excess of definitions of the legal code favorable to its violation. The ratio of favorable to unfavorable definitions is critical. Further, what is learned is not some generalized predisposition to behave in a deviant fashion but rather specific situations in which such behaviors are acceptable. In the example, the son has learned that he may steal from a stranger with an untroubled conscience but not from a family member.

A second important idea in considering differential association theory was contributed by Sykes and Matza (1957). They point out that it is a mistake to view the theory as essentially one of delinquent subcultures—that is, that youth groups with values that are the inverse of those held by law-abiding citizens influence and induct nondelinquents. If that were the case, they note, we would expect that delinquents would evidence no guilt or shame when detected in a law violation. But in fact they often do. Further, delinquents commonly evidence admiration and respect for nondelinquents, which is inconsistent with an inverse value system. Still further, Sykes and Matza argue that in the typical pattern of increasingly frequent delinquent acts, the offender occasionally will be caught. In such instances the adolescent must face the demands for conformity that originate from parents, teachers, or police. It seems implausible to believe that these demands can be completely countered by an entirely new value system, particularly when the demands originate from adults on whom the offender is largely dependent. In short, it is a mistake to view most delinquents as miniature hardened criminals. The problem is to explain why they violate rules in which they believe.

In addressing this question Sykes and Matza (1957) suggest that what is learned via differential association is a set of justifications for deviant acts—*justifications seen as valid by the delinquent but not by society at large or the legal system.* Further, these justifications are not trotted out after the fact; *their learning precedes the deviant act and makes it possible.* These justifications allow the youth to render his own internalized norms inoperative, freeing him to engage in a delinquent act without damage to his own self-image. Sykes and Matza suggest five classes of these justifications:

1. *Denial of responsibility.* The individual sees himself as acting out of reasons beyond his control—inadequate parents, bad companions, a slum neighborhood, or the like.
2. *Denial of injury.* Acts may be defined as permissible if no one will be injured, hence they are not "really" wrong. Vandalism and thefts from corporations

("they are insured") and from the wealthy ("they can afford it") are examples.

3. *Denial of a victim*. Acts planned against another may be justified because the person "deserved it" (e.g., "The teacher was unfair to me").

4. *Condemnation of the condemners*. Here the delinquent shifts the focus of attention to the people who might condemn his acts. They are hypocrites or are motivated by spite; "police are crooked" and "schools are boring" are examples.

5. *An appeal to higher loyalties*. In this case the deviant act to be committed is justified on grounds of a higher morality, often loyalty to an immediate group of friends. Violating a rule was necessary in order not to violate the trust or confidence of a friend.

Differential association theory, then, provides a conception of the *process* by which initially conforming students come to violate the rules of school and society. It has several practical implications for educators. First and most obviously, it suggests a view of conforming students and staff as providing a kind of "curriculum" for delinquents and potential delinquents. That is, its emphasis on the learning that takes place in face-to-face groups makes the composition of student peer groups an important *educational* resource to administrators. It suggests that potential delinquents will be less likely to act out that potential if the preponderance of the definitions they receive from friends and acquaintances favor conformity to normative standards. Clearly, administrators cannot legislate whom students have for friends. However, no one's friendships develop at random. Friends are chosen from among those with whom one interacts, and interaction patterns in schools are constrained in important ways by administrative actions: class assignments, track choices, team sports, and extracurricular activities. These are fully or partially under educators' control. School personnel can influence with whom students interact and hence, indirectly, the nature of the messages they receive concerning conformity and deviance. Thus it suggests that a propensity to deviance is an important *educational* criterion—in addition to test scores, grades, and other conventional standards—in making student assignments. At the very least it calls into question the common practice of "dumping"—placing discipline cases together in special classes or in lower tracks—and using exclusion from team sports and group extracurricular activities as a form of punishment.

Second, the theory's notion of the priority of definitions, meaning that those learned early are likely to be more potent than those learned late, stresses the importance of active delinquency prevention as well as delinquency control. There are numerous practical programs intended for use in schools to teach prosocial values and behavior. For example, the Character Education Curriculum (Mulkey, 1977), Values Clarification (Raths, Harmin, & Simon, 1978), and Moral Education (Kohlberg, 1973) are all attempts to shape the values of young people and, thereby, their behavior. Still other programs (e.g., Structured Learning; Goldstein, Sprafkin, Gershaw, & Klein, 1979) are aimed directly at behavior. These programs are complex, all have their critics, and it is impossible to treat them adequately here. (For an overview and evaluation of those programs, refer to Goldstein, Apter, & Harootonian, 1984.)

Finally, the notion of source prestige has implications for teacher behavior and parent-school cooperation in preventing delinquency and discipline problems. There is evidence (Boocock, 1980, pp. 229–236) that parents and teachers are respected sources of information on certain topics—most notably for our discussion, moral issues and school problems. It follows that if these sources are equivocal concerning such matters, and in particular if they lend credence to the sorts of justifications discussed by Sykes and Matza, students will be more likely to commit delinquent acts. In effect, they increase the ratio of definitions favoring delinquency to those opposing it. For example, in class discussions of the events at Rankled Memorial High School, students are likely to justify delinquent behavior by denying a victim or appealing to higher loyalties, as in not reporting a drug dealer. Indeed, such justifications are precisely the sorts used by relatively unsophisticated minors (and adults) for deviant acts. If teachers treat such justifications "neutrally"—as of equal worth to justifications for legal behavior— they lend legitimacy to them and thereby make delinquent behavior more likely. This is precisely the problem created by some values clarification approaches to moral education in the classroom. Differential association theory thus suggests that when teachers (or parents) take a nonjudgmental position on the rationalizations students offer for deviant acts, they are behaving in a miseducative manner and are likely to increase the amount of indiscipline a school experiences.

As with anomie theory, differential association explanations for delinquency are not without their critics. The theory has been criticized for, among other things, its apparent dismissal of the media's effects on lawbreaking and especially violence because it does not explain impulsive acts, does not take adequate account of biological or personality factors, and oversimplifies learning theory.

Labeling Theory

Where anomie theory takes its cues from social structural considerations and differential association theory from social psychological ones, labeling theory concentrates on the behavior of nondeviant individuals. Where the first two are concerned with the conditions and processes that lead to deviant acts, labeling theory is principally occupied with what happens *after* an act has been committed. It concentrates on the consequences of identifying a person as a "delinquent," a "discipline problem," a "slow learner," or, for that matter, a "good student."

Labeling theory has been expressed in the works of a number of writers but was first detailed most completely in *Outsiders* by Howard Becker (1963). Essentially, Becker argued that a deviant act is not intrinsically different from a "normal" one: There is nothing inherent in criminal behavior that can be used to distinguish it from permissible actions. For example, physically striking another person may be defined as a felony and punished or as a sport (as in boxing) and rewarded. The difference between the two is not in the act itself but in how others define the act. Further, such definitions vary from culture to culture and over time. Homosexuality is a criminal offense in some societies but not others; moderate social drinking was an offense in this country just a few decades ago but draws little or no attention today. Thus the core of this approach is not the behavior of an individual but our reactions to that behavior. It focuses on the people who make the rules, the application of those rules to some people but not others, and the reactions of the former to having the rules applied to them. The theory shifts attention to the institutionalized processes of social control and the ways in which "definers"—educators, the police, the courts—decide what and who is deviant.

From the labeling perspective it becomes possible to consider deviance as a career pattern—a succession of statuses through which an individual passes on the route to becoming a "shoplifter," a "drunk," or a "juvenile delinquent," for example. The theory distinguishes between primary and secondary deviance, which may be illustrated using the case of delinquency. During the stage of primary deviance, the individual considers himself and is considered by others to be a conforming member of society. Though he may have occasional brushes with authorities, these are dismissed by himself and others as pranks, youthful exuberance, or instances of immature judgment. Each act that comes to the attention of authorities may be informally punished, but no one considers their perpetrator a delinquent. As such acts continue, however, it is likely that increasingly severe punishments will be applied and that resentment and hostility will begin to be focused on the penalizers. At some point the tolerance of authorities will be exceeded, and *official* action will be taken, say, an arrest and conviction.

What is important about this official action, though it may be in response to an act no more serious than others previously handled informally, is that it amounts to a *successful* labeling of the adolescent as an offender. Henceforth, it is argued, others will react to the individual as a delinquent, a boy gone "bad," a person of proven moral inferiority, no longer one who is simply somewhat more mischievous than others. This labeling, or "stigmatizing," simultaneously causes the juvenile to reformulate his conception of himself to that of a delinquent. Thus officially attaching the label results in an abrupt and significant qualitative change in the youth's self-concept and in his relations with others. He now enters the stage of secondary deviance; he continues delinquent acts as a consequence of *being* a delinquent. Finally, this self-identity as a delinquent is stabilized by movement into a group of other boys similarly labeled, a group that provides moral justification and technical expertise for criminal acts. The critical step in this whole process, then, is the action taken by institutional actors in attaching the label "delinquent."

Why should some labels have such a powerful effect? In addressing this question Becker draws attention to Hughes's (1945) classic distinction between "master" and "subordinate" statuses. Although everyone occupies numerous statuses simultaneously (e.g., male, student, brother, and athlete), master statuses tend to override others' perceptions of us and to govern social interactions. For instance, in the United States, race and sex are master statuses. A black female physician, mother of four and member of the local country club, is first and foremost a black and a woman; the subordinate statuses of physician, mother, and club member may not protect her from being treated as a black woman in daily interactions with others. "Delinquent" is such a master status. Further, master statuses have associated with them a number of other attributes: A delinquent, unlike the rest of us, is someone who flouts the laws; who is irresponsible, untrustworthy, and deceitful; and who may be violent if his desires are thwarted. This constellation of attributes controls others' reactions to him. In effect, arrest and conviction signify the successful attaching of a master status and its related attributes to a youth, and that status governs others' interactions with him. Treated as such a person, he becomes one.

Variations on labeling theory have been applied extensively to educational phenomena, but almost entirely as an explanation for social class and racial differences in academic achievement (e.g., Rist, 1970) or for the consequence of mistaken perceptions (e.g., Rosenthal & Jacobson, 1968). This is curious, for the theory has several obvious implications for school administrators and school discipline. Most important, perhaps, its focus on teachers' and administrators' responses to misbehavior provides a necessary balance to the natural tendency to focus attention on the behavior of the offending students. What the student has done (or not done) is important, of course, but so are our reactions to it—perhaps more so, since the latter are under our control, while we may only hope to influence the former. In any case, labeling theory draws our attention to a school's rules, the handling of students who misbehave, and the ways we think about students.

Numerous observers (e.g., Silberman, 1970) have commented on the multitude of rules that some schools promulgate and their sometimes petty nature. Regardless of the accuracy of such claims, what is certain is that every rule defining some act as "illegal" in schools creates a class of "offenders" where none previously existed and requires the "treatment" of those offenders. Labeling theory suggests that administrators and teachers faced with disorderly schools might profitably review their disciplinary codes and practices with an eye toward "decriminalizing" certain student behavior when that is appropriate. Naively interpreted, of course, the theory suggests that dissolving all rules would automatically eliminate discipline problems, but few people would consider that a serious option. More sensibly, the labeling perspective suggests that many types of student behavior, though it may offend adult sensibilities, may be profitably ignored, some may be best handled on an ad hoc discretionary basis as it occurs, and some deserves formalized rules and specified penalties.

In the case of the last category, the theory also suggests that most disciplinary cases be handled privately, with knowledge of the case and its outcome restricted to people who meet a clear "need to know" criterion. To do otherwise risks attaching such labels as "truant" or "cheat" to students, labels that may unnecessarily color their subsequent interactions with staff and peers and ultimately create a confirmed "discipline case."

Similarly, this view of the genesis of disciplinary problems calls attention to the professional behavior of teachers and administrators in informal discussions among themselves. Just as a patient or a client has the right to expect discretion from a physician or lawyer, students with disciplinary problems might reasonably expect that their cases not serve as the topic of faculty lounge gossip.

Along with the theory of differential association, a labeling perspective also suggests caution in setting up and assigning disorderly students to special classes. Such procedures publicly proclaim to others and to the students that they are judged unfit to be schooled with "normal" students. Finally, the distinction between master and subordinate statuses alerts us to the dangers of stereotyping that may accompany affixing labels to students. Not all students at Rankled Memorial who were caught with drugs are addicts, dangerous people, or poor students.

As with the explanations for deviance previously addressed, labeling theory is not without its critics (see, for example, Mankoff, 1971; Downs & Rock, 1982; Gouldner, 1968). It is unclear, for example, to what range of behavior the labeling process applies. In addition to delinquency (perhaps its most common application), it has been used to explain the behavior of skid row residents (Spradly, 1970), blind persons (Scott, 1969), and homosexuals (Humphreys, 1970). Further, the approach may well attribute much more power to a label than most labels have. The theory does not admit of the possibility that individuals may commit to a deviant career well before a label is affixed to them (Mankoff, 1971). Perhaps the most commonly voiced criticism notes that the theory ignores the power relations in society and the prevalence of white-collar crime. Despite these deficiencies, the theory provides a useful counterperspective to educators' tendency to view student behavior as *the* problem to be dealt with and to focus attention on educators' reactions to that behavior. It suggests that in dealing with the events at Rankled Memorial, Ms. Parker would do well to consider the ways in which her own and her staff's reactions create disorder in the school.

Deterrence Theory

Deterrence theory (theories, really) has a long, honorable, and popular history tracing back to Aristotle, who noted that the greatest crimes are the result of excess, not necessity. That is, the problem of deviance is rooted in human nature, because it is in people's nature not to be satisfied. Thus the curbing of appetites, not the equalization of material goods or opportunities, is required to prevent it. But how are appetites to be curbed? At their heart, deterrence theories posit two basic mechanisms, fear of punishment and its converse, desire for gratification. Hence they are closely tied to utilitarian views of human conduct: We seek to minimize pain and maximize pleasure. We can reduce delinquency or indiscipline in schools, therefore, by making it more "costly" to engage in or by making conforming behavior more rewarding. Some such view is undoubtedly held by most people, educators included. It finds expression in the popular demand to "get tough" with students who misbehave (or adults who commit crimes). It is reflected by Rankled Memorial's teachers, who press Ms. Parker to punish student misconduct severely.

As James Q. Wilson, perhaps the most articulate exponent of this view, notes, it will probably surprise many people to know that scholars are deeply divided over the correctness of deterrence theories, especially over whether or not punishment deters crime. Many sociologists believe that crime rates will not go down if society gets tough on would-be lawbreakers, nor will they go up if we take a "soft" or more "therapeutic" view of violators (Wilson, 1983). Indeed, implicit in the theories we have already discussed is the notions that the causes of deviance are something other than fear of punishment, and hence its control is to be found in other mechanisms. The reasons for this skepticism are not hard to find.

At base, control theories rely on an individual's rationality. They assume that each potential lawbreaker calculates (however roughly) the costs of breaking a rule and the benefits of doing so and behaves according to the resulting balance. But the benefits of lawbreaking are often immediate and obvious: The mugger gains the content of his victim's wallet; the student extortionist at Rankled Memorial gains his peer's lunch money. However, the costs of such behavior are by no means always so obvious. Apprehension is not certain. Indeed, in the case of the mugger, the probability of being caught in many communities is less than one in ten (Wilson, 1983). We do not know the analogous probability for the student extortionist, but it is certainly less than one in ten. Further, even if the perpetrator is caught, punishment is not certain and may take place far in a necessarily cloudy future. In the United States, no more than three felonies out of a hundred result in a prison term, and incarceration is usually months or years away. We know of no data regarding the analogous possibility for punishment of student malefactors. Still further, the severity of any punishment that might be received is usually unknown. Thus the potential rule-breaker, adult or student, cannot easily estimate the costs of violating some rule. Many are undoubtedly ignorant of these potential costs. And some of those who break rules may do so on impulse; this may be particularly true of young people.

During the past decade there have been a great many studies of whether or not punishment deters crime. Despite its simplicity and obvious practical importance, this question is extraordinarily difficult to answer. In part this difficulty is a product of the imprecision in its asking: We are likely to get better answers if we ask whether particular punishments will deter a specified class of people from particular crimes. Even when focused more specifically, however, most research has dealt with the effects of changes in the law on *aggregate* populations—for example, did New York's tough 1973 drug law, which mandated prison terms of up to fifteen years for selling heroin, cut down on the incidence of that crime? Such studies are dependent on highly imprecise estimates of the offense in question (e.g., the number of drug sales occurring before and after the law's passage), can only partially control for a few of the numerous other factors that might affect the crime's rate of occurrence (e.g., unemployment, inflation, recession), and are plagued by statistical difficulties (e.g., multicollinearity in the data). Further, it seems plausible to suppose that most people, adults and students alike, refrain from breaking many rules not so much because they fear punishment but because they have internalized prohibitions against lawbreaking, perhaps very early in their lives. For this group, getting tough on miscreants by increasing the severity of punishments may be largely irrelevant. What is required, of course, are studies of individuals who *might* commit crimes or break school rules—who are "at risk," so to speak, because they have few internalized prohibitions—as these individuals respond to changes in the penalties for deviance. There are few such studies and, to the best of our knowledge, none concerning students and school rules.

Despite these caveats, there is something for school administrators to learn from the studies that have been done. In thinking about deterrence it is important to keep in mind three distinct aspects of punishment: certainty, celerity, and severity. Variations in any or all of these may deter student disorder. Punishment may be made more certain; as the probability of apprehension increases, individuals seem less willing to violate rules. It may be made swifter; as the time between the commission of an act and its punishment is perceived to shorten, violations appear to decrease. Finally, it may be made more severe; as the stringency of discipline increases, violations may decrease (Wilson, 1983).

It is wise to bear these points in mind, because getting tough with disorderly students is often equated with dispensing increasingly severe punishments. Such a strategy may be self-defeating, for harsh punishments may work against certainty and celerity. This is so because teachers and administrators may be more likely to overlook an infraction on the part of some students if they believe the penalty for it to be so severe as to be counterproductive or lacking in mercy. When teachers refuse to report student misconduct, certainty of punishment is decreased. Similarly, when the stringency of an offense's punishment is made greater, there is often a concomitant move to delay its imposition in order to ensure that procedural due process criteria are met. For example, when punishment involves dismissal from school, a formal hearing may be required; hence celerity is sacrificed. (Indeed, it was apparently for these reasons that New York's drug law failed to work; judges seemed unwilling to impose fifteen-year prison sentences on young people caught selling an ounce of heroin, and defense attorneys strove to exhaust all avenues of appeal and plea bargaining to avoid such sentences for their clients.) Thus getting tough may be more effective in deterring student misbehavior if efforts are directed primarily at ensuring that offenders are caught and swiftly disciplined, even if the discipline itself is rather mild.

In regard to serious crime, the weight of the evidence seems to be that deterrence works, but only marginally (Gibbs, 1975; Wilson, 1983). Getting tough will reduce crime in our streets, but not by much. But it is important to remember that such a pessimistic conclusion applies to the small proportion of criminals, perhaps less than 10 percent, who account for the large proportion of our felonies, perhaps 80 percent. This is not because criminals are irrational but because they apply standards to their behavior different from those applied by the rest of us, and such standards have their roots in constitutional and family influences that are beyond the reach of civil authorities (Wilson, 1983). Further, it is important to distinguish the acts to which this conclusion applies, serious felonies, from the vast majority of the acts which collectively characterize disorderly schools—truancy, tardiness, minor vandalism, profanity, smoking, and fistfights. Research suggests that standards regarding these acts can be set and enforced by school authorities (e.g., Coleman, Hoffer, & Kilgore, 1981; Rutter, Maughan, Mortemore, & Ouston, 1979; Subcommittee, 1977) and that doing so is important in creating an orderly environment that is, in turn, conducive to learning. For such behaviors, deterrence probably works. In the end, of course, that may not be the critical consideration. Penalizing misbehavior and rewarding its converse are right acts in themselves, regardless of their deterrent value. We now turn to these considerations.

Legal Aspects of Student Discipline

Were the actions taken or contemplated by Ms. Parker legal? We will look at three specific questions: First, could Ms. Parker rightfully suspend Karl for his actions in Mr. Burns's class? Second, were her actions in suspending the students whose lockers contained some contraband legally correct? Third, was she legally entitled to search the students' lockers?

Free Expression

The lead case concerning the civil rights of students is *Tinker v. Des Moines.* This case concerned several students who were suspended for wearing a black armband to school in order to protest the Vietnam War. The Supreme Court overturned the suspensions, employing the following reasoning: First, the Court held that the wearing of the black armbands was an act of symbolic speech, which, as a form of speech, enjoys the protection of the First Amendment. Second, the Court held that students are persons so far as the Constitution is concerned and that neither students nor teachers abandon their constitutional rights at the schoolhouse door. They added to this idea, however, the claim that First Amendment rights must be "applied in the light of the special characteristics of the school environment."

The justification for this view of student rights rests largely on the Court's view of education for citizenship. Justice Abe Fortas, writing for the majority, quotes with favor the following phrase from *Keyishian v. Board of Regents of the State of New York:*

> *The classroom is peculiarly the "marketplace of ideas." The Nation's future depends upon leaders trained through wide exposure to that robust exchange of ideas which discovers truth "out of a multitude of tongues, [rather] than through any kind of authoritative selection" (p. 512)*

What are the limits on students' freedom of expression? Here the Court prescribes what is often referred to as the "material and substantial disruption" standard. In Fortas's words:

> *Conduct by the student, in class or out of it, which for any reason—whether it stems from time, place, or type of behavior—materially disrupts classwork*

or involves substantial disorder or invasion of the rights of others is, of course, not immunized by the constitutional guarantee of freedom of speech (p. 517)

The emphasis placed on the words *materially* and *substantial* in this doctrine is best understood in relation to its opposite. The Court maintains that undifferentiated fear or apprehension of disruption is not a sufficient reason to interfere with the student's right of free speech.

These ideas seem to indicate that the school would be within its rights to take disciplinary action against Karl. Karl's actions would have resulted in the disruption of Mr. Burns's geometry lesson. Moreover, there was a shouting match in which Mr. Burns was referred to as a "fascist." Thus the disruption of Mr. Burns's class seems real. We should also note that other federal court decisions have made it quite clear that schools may regulate the distribution of literature by students as to time, manner, and place of distribution so long as the purpose is not to stifle freedom of expression (*Vail v. Board of Education of Portsmouth School District*). It seems clear that in this case Mr. Burns is motivated by the desire to teach his subject matter rather than to prevent Karl's views from being expressed. It is unlikely that Karl would have a case unless the school acted in such a way as to prevent him from distributing his leaflet altogether.

Due Process

How about the suspensions? In *Goss v. Lopes* the Supreme Court dealt with the question of suspensions for ten days or less. The argument before the Court was largely whether a short suspension should be considered *de minimus,* that is, whether its consequences were too insignificant to be concerned about. The point of this argument is that the Fourteenth Amendment says that persons cannot be deprived of life, liberty, or property without due process of law. The question, then, is whether a ten-day suspension constitutes a sufficient deprivation to require the protection of the Constitution. The Court held that students facing suspension had a nontrivial property interest in their education and a nontrivial liberty interest in their reputation.

These interests are not, however, substantial; thus the scope of due process requirements is not large. The essential requirements are expressed as follows:

Due process requires, in connection with a suspension of 10 days or less, that the student be given oral or written notice of the charges against him and, if he denies them, an explanation of the evidence the authorities have and an opportunity to present his story. (Goss v. Lopes, p. 565)

The due process requirements imposed are therefore not extensive. It appears that they can be discharged in a brief conversation. Be aware, however, that the due process requirements for longer suspensions or expulsions can be more extensive.

Hence it appears clear that Ms. Parker erred when she suspended the students with contraband in their lockers without giving them an opportunity to defend themselves.

Search and Seizure

Was she entitled to the locker search in the first place? The law on this topic is not settled. Nevertheless, we can provide some insight into the topic.

In a recent case concerning a search of a student's purse (*New Jersey v. T.L.O.*), the Supreme Court dealt with the issue of the standard to be used in searches in public schools. Here the Court held that students did have a legitimate expectation of privacy. Schools may not, therefore, search their property or persons capriciously. On the other hand, the Court also held that the school has a legitimate need to maintain an environment in which learning can take place. This need must be balanced against the students' right to privacy.

In the Court's view, this balance is not effectively struck by the normal requirements for a search. Public school officials need not obtain warrants, nor must they meet the test of probable cause. The Court provided the following text for the reasonableness of a search.

> *The legality of a search of a student should depend simply on the reasonableness, under all the circumstances, of the search. Determining the reasonableness of any search involves a determination of whether the search was justified at the inception and whether, as conducted, it was reasonably related in scope to the circumstances that justified the interference in the first place. Under ordinary circumstances the search of a student by a school official will be justified at its inception where there are reasonable grounds for suspecting that the search will turn up evidence that the student has violated or is violating either the law or the rules of the school. And such a search will be permissible in its scope when the measures adopted are reasonably related to the objectives of the search and not excessively intrusive in light of the student's age and sex and the nature of the infraction. (*New Jersey v. T.L.O., p. B472)*

On the surface it might appear that Ms. Parker's search of the lockers would meet this standard of reasonableness. Given the evidence of drug use in Rankled, it seems plausible to hold that Ms. Parker had a reasonably grounded suspicion that a search of students' lockers would turn up evidence of illegal drugs and that the search was not intrusive beyond the need to discover the drugs. (Note, however, that *all* lockers were searched and that Ms. Parker lacked a reasonable suspicion concerning any particular student.)

Unfortunately, such a conclusion cannot be drawn, for the Court saw fit to include a note that explicitly disavows application of this case to locker searches (*New Jersey v. T.L.O.,* p. B754). Lower courts have not exhibited a consistent approach to the issue. Some courts have given fairly free rein to administrators to search students' lockers (*People v. Overton*). They have argued that the school and the student share joint control of the locker and thus the school has free access to it. Others have held that the student does have an expectation of privacy in the content of his or her locker (*State of New Jersey v. Engerud*). Lower courts thus have taken different approaches to the problem.

Despite its disavowal, however, the Supreme Court's decision does affect the question. Note that there are two issues here. The first involves whether there is an expectation of privacy. The second concerns the standard to be used in justifying a search. The second issue arises only if one assumes that students have some right to privacy in their lockers. The lower courts cited disagree about the first question. The Supreme Court does not address the question. However, given the assumption of such a right to privacy, it is difficult to see why the Court's standard of reasonableness would not apply.

We may then fairly (if speculatively) conclude that the standard for searching a student's locker is no more demanding than that of reasonableness (although it may be weaker). If that is correct, it is very likely that Ms. Parker's search would prove legally permissible.

Ethical Aspects of Student Discipline

The Moral Basis of Rights

Human beings owe one another equal respect. The phrase "equal respect" incorporates two further ideas. The first is that human beings are objects of intrinsic worth. I may not, therefore, treat another human being as though that person were merely a means to my own ends. I must recognize the other person as valuable in his or her own right. I must therefore treat the other person with dignity. I must regard others' wants and needs as worthy of fulfillment. I must not exploit them or treat them unfairly.

Second, I must regard others as equals so far as their status as human beings is concerned. While I may (or may not) be smarter, stronger, or better-looking than some, I am not on that account more or less valuable a person than they. No one is inherently entitled to better treatment than anyone else. We must therefore treat others not only with respect but with equal respect. No one is more valuable a person than anyone else; everyone is entitled to equal rights.

These ideas are abstract. We can, however, move one step closer to concreteness by suggesting some particular classes of rights to which these abstract moral principles appear to lead.

If we believe that other persons are ends and not means, we must be concerned for their autonomy and their growth. We must see them as responsible moral agents who have the right and duty to decide how they will act, what they will value, and what kinds of persons they will be. These are not decisions we are free to make for them. If people are to decide such matters for themselves, they will require the capacity for independent thought and judgment, that is, autonomy; and they will need the resources required to think things through and to make competent choices.

Intellectual Freedom

These sentiments are the basis of arguments that show that it is morally offensive to manipulate or indoctrinate people and that people have rights such as those of free speech and a free press (Strike, 1982b). Manipulation and indoctrination are wrong because they are forms of psychological coercion. When a teacher indoctrinates a student, the teacher, in effect, says, "I have the right to decide whether you shall believe this. Since I have this right, I am going to rig the game so as to make it psychologically difficult for you to think other than in the way I wish." Indoctrination (see Snook, 1972) is a way of denying people freedom over their own thoughts.

People who are responsible for their own choices also have a right to the information relevant to those choices. They must have access to ideas and have the opportunity to discuss and debate these ideas. Rights such as freedom of speech and freedom of the press serve to provide the kind of access to ideas that free people require if they are to be responsible for their own choices.

Competent choices, of course, depend not only on the availability of ideas and information but also on the competence to assess them. If we are to respect other persons, we therefore have to show concern for their competence.

These arguments indicate that intellectual freedom is vital in education. They suggest that students have a right to be free from indoctrination and manipulation and that they have a right to free access to ideas and to discuss those ideas freely. The arguments do not, however, have much to say as yet about the forms this intellectual freedom should take in an educational program. We will come to that momentarily.

Due Process

Consider another class of rights. People have the right to protection from arbitrary decisions. Decisions are arbitrary when they are made without evidence, when they are based on improper or irrelevant considerations, or when they lack any consistent or known standard. These ideas of rationality, consistency, and publicness are the basis of the idea of due process and are designed to ensure that decisions are based on reasonable and relevant evidence and that they are made on the basis of the application of a consistent and known standard. To punish someone when you have not followed proper procedures to determine guilt or to judge someone according to a shifting or unknown standard is to violate that person's right to due process.

Privacy

A third right is the right to privacy. Part of the idea of showing respect for persons is allowing people control over their own lives. This involves more than not interfering with their choices. It requires that we give people control over information about themselves. We are not entitled to know information about others, especially if that information is potentially damaging or deeply personal, unless that individual chooses to share it with us. We are not entitled, capriciously, to pry into others' affairs or to know things about them that they do not choose to reveal.

This control over information entails control over personal space. If I am entitled to control information about myself, this means that you are not free to search through my possessions or my personal space without my permission.

The Ethics of Teaching

These rights suggest a great deal about the ethics of teaching and of operating an educational institution (see NEA, 1984). They suggest first of all a duty to respect students' opinions and to give students reasons for what they are asked to believe.

The idea of respecting students' opinions does not require that teachers agree with everything a student says or pretend that no opinion is better than any other. Students are in school to learn how to make competent judgments. This is a skill that depends on criticism. It is difficult to improve in any skill if we do not receive feedback on our mistakes.

What is required is that teachers not respond to students' ideas with derision or sarcasm and that teachers provide students with relevant and comprehensible reasons for the ideas presented to them. Students too are moral agents. They must ultimately become responsible for themselves. They do not belong to teachers. Thus teachers have no right to determine what students will believe or what they shall be in any coercive way. The teacher who wishes to promote the growth of students into responsible moral agents will need to help students learn to make competent choices for themselves. Teachers will thus need to give students the evidence on which they may base a choice while also helping them to acquire the skills required to assess that evidence.

Part of the process of learning to make competent choices is that of reflecting on one's current beliefs. If the classroom is to be a marketplace of ideas, the purpose is not so much that students will fashion truth out of a multitude of tongues as it is that students will learn the skills of making reasonable choices by engaging in the process of critical dialogue. Failure to show respect for student opinions marks the end of critical dialogue. The idea that students should have the rights of free speech and a free press makes the most sense in an educational context if it is understood as imposing on teachers a duty to respect students' opinions in a way that makes possible the sort of critical dialogue on which growth depends.

In an educational context, the idea that students have the right of due process imposes on teachers and administrators an obligation to be fair in assigning grades and in discipline. If a student is to be punished, the teacher or administrator has an obligation to take reasonable precautions to ensure that the student committed the act for which he or she is being punished. At the minimum, the student ought to be allowed to know the reason for the punishment and to explain his or her side of the matter. Students are also entitled to know what the rules of the school or the classroom are, and punishments must fit the offense.

Grading is an area in which standards of due process are frequently violated. Teachers have a duty to employ valid measures of students' abilities and to base grades on them. Students have a right to know what is expected of them. Grades ought to be unrelated to any personal characteristics beyond relevant performance.

The right to privacy deserves considerable emphasis in schools. Students are at an age when they are most vulnerable to being hurt by what others think about them. Moreover, school environments are most unprivate places. Students rarely are away from the scrutiny and evaluation of their peers or their teachers. For students who are in some way personally unattractive or academically less talented, schooling can become a relentless barrage on their sense of dignity and self-worth, offering little place to hide. Many students are in desperate need of more control over how they are seen by others and of a piece of private personal space in the school. Teachers and administrators have a responsibility to provide such privacy for students. This is not primarily a matter of not rummaging capriciously through students' lockers. Nor is it primarily a matter of not revealing confidential information about students. Often it is a question of how teachers deal with students in a public context. When a student cannot do something required in a given subject, teachers should act in such a way so as to minimize the possibility of calling public attention to that fact. We believe that the practice of calling on students in class (as opposed to allowing them to volunteer) can often amount to an invasion of privacy. Certainly, teachers or administrators have no right to question a student about any personal or family matter in a public context. Teachers who use values clarification or other techniques designed to help students reflect on their values need to be especially cautious not to allow students to feel pressured to reveal information about themselves. The expectation that people be honest with one another can easily evolve into a kind of coercion to "tell all" and from there into an invasion of privacy. Students are fragile people who deserve a higher level of privacy in schools than they often receive.

Application to Rankled Memorial

How have these rights fared in our case? Consider some arguments showing that each of these three sorts of rights has been violated.

First, it might be claimed that Karl's rights of free speech and a free press were violated when Mr. Burns prevented him from distributing his leaflet and discussing it in class. Karl was, after all, attempting to facilitate a discussion of an issue that had become of considerable interest and concern to the students of Rankled Memorial. Arguably, the discussion would have been of more educational value to students than a lesson in geometry. Moreover, Mr. Burns was motivated by more than just the desire to get on with teaching geometry; he wished to shut Karl up. He had come to the opinion that Karl's advocacy of leftist ideas was beginning to be troublesome and was the source of student unrest at Rankled. His motivation, therefore, appeared to be to repress Karl's views.

Second, the due process rights of the students who were suspended following the locker search may have been violated. The students who were suspended after the locker search were suspended entirely on the basis that contraband was found in their locker. They were neither given an opportunity to explain how the contraband had gotten there nor to defend their innocence. They were simply sent home. Thus Ms. Parker failed to take adequate steps to establish guilt.

Finally, the locker search constituted a violation of the students' right to privacy. A locker is one of the few private spots granted to a student. It is given to the student for his or her own use. Moreover, it is provided with a lock. Clearly the expectation established is that it is the private space of the student to whom it is assigned and that neither other students nor teachers and administrators have a right to enter the locker uninvited.

One can therefore construct a plausible argument that each of the rights under discussion was violated. Obviously, however, there is something to be said on behalf of the school as well. What we need to do is ask ourselves what the limits on the various rights in question are and how these limits apply to the facts in the case.

Concerning Karl's rights of free speech and press, it is clear that there must be some limits on freedom of expression. People cannot say whatever they wish whenever they wish. To allow them to do so would be to allow people to impose themselves on others or to be generally disruptive. The point of freedom of expression is to prevent the state from enforcing some orthodoxy and (especially in schools) to promote the kind of environment in which people can discuss and grow. It is not to allow people to make nuisances of themselves whenever they wish. It is thus consistent with the right of free expression to allow institutions to regulate expression in order to protect the rights of others so long as the effect is not that only ideas of which the institution approves can be heard.

In the case at hand, Mr. Burns might argue that he was not attempting to repress Karl's right of free expression. He was trying to protect his right to teach geometry and the right of his students to learn geometry against Karl's disruptive behavior. Karl is free to distribute his paper and to advocate whatever views he wants, so long as he does so in a proper place at a proper time. The school may have to provide a time and a place, but it need not turn over its geometry classes to anyone who wishes to discuss something else.

Another kind of argument should be discussed here. Arguably, some kinds of rights have a competence requirement. We do not permit people to vote until they have reached a certain age, because we believe that voting requires certain abilities that are unlikely to be possessed by younger people. Do the various rights of free expression have any competence requirements?

Recall for a moment John Stuart Mill's arguments for intellectual liberty, sketched in Chapter 1. It is noteworthy that Mill (1956) follows his first formulation of the idea of liberty with the following remarks:

> *This doctrine is meant to apply only to human beings in the maturity of their faculties. We are not speaking of children or of young persons below the age which the law may fix as that of manhood or womanhood. Those who are still in a state to require being taken care of by others must be protected against their own actions as well as against external injury. . . . Liberty, as a principle has no application to the time when mankind have become capable of being improved by free and equal discussion. (pp. 13, 14)*

Mill clearly believes that there ought to be a competence requirement for various liberties, among which he appears to include the right of free expression.

Why? Partly because he appears to believe that free expression can do harm. No doubt he is right here. But this does not explain why children should have different rights than adults. Mill also, however, appears to believe that the purposes of free expression are not well served unless the exchange of views is between equals. Recall that Mill's basic defense of free expression was linked to the notion that it was one of the social conditions required for the pursuit of truth. The marketplace of ideas produces truth out of a process of debate. Mill apparently believes that this process is not likely to work unless both parties to the discussion "have become capable of improvement by free and equal discussion."

It might then be argued that most students, given that they are likely to be considerably less advanced in school subjects than their teachers, are also likely to have much less to contribute to the process of criticism and debate from which truth is supposed to emerge. Perhaps truth is likely to be discovered in the classroom when students attend to the views of their teachers. However, we have not argued for free expression for students on the grounds that society's store of knowledge will be increased as a result. We have argued that the process of free and open discussion promotes the growth of students. It is not required that students contribute to the growth of knowledge. What is required is that they grow into responsible and competent people. It might be responded that this is not so much an argument for extending the civil rights of free speech and a free press to students as it is an argument for the value of classroom discussion. We may have a duty to respect the opinions of students, but the point of doing so is to show respect for their worth as persons and to help them learn. We are hardly likely to achieve that result if we regard their views as on a par with the views of the teacher. The relationship between teacher and student is not like the relation between two scholars trying to hammer out a position of some topic. It is more like the relationship between master and apprentice, where the point of the apprentice's participation in the activities of the craft is to learn how it is done.

All of this suggests that the respect teachers are supposed to show for students' opinions must be tempered with the recollection that in order to teach, teachers must be in control of the process of dialogue in the class.

There are, therefore, lines of argument that can be used to show that the rights of free expression of children in schools have a different set of purposes than the rights of adults and that owing to the immaturity of students and to the fact that they are novices in the subjects they are studying, the scope of these rights for students might differ from those of adults (see Strike, 1982b). Mr. Burns might appeal to such arguments to show that his treatment of Karl was perfectly justifiable.

Can similar arguments be made for the right of due process and the right to privacy? We think not. It is hard to see why there should be any sort of competence requirement for these rights. It is hard to see how it might be argued that because a person is immature, that person is more reasonably subjected to arbitrary or capricious judgments or to invasions of privacy than anyone else. Indeed, it seems more likely that we ought to be more judicious in protecting these rights for the immature, because immature persons are more vulnerable and less capable of defending themselves than are adults.

We might, however, explore another line. It might be argued that schools cannot be expected to provide rigorous protection of these rights while simultaneously serving their educational purposes efficiently. Innumerable articles have been written ascribing the schools' loss of disciplinary control over students to judicially mandated due process requirements. Such requirements, it is argued, are beyond the power of school administrators to comply with. Administrators respond to excessive judicial encumbrances by not taking action where action is required. An administrator who cannot search students' lockers is not likely to be able to control drug traffic. Likewise, an administrator who cannot suspend a student without first having some form of hearing is severely limited in controlling student behavior.

Ms. Parker might use these arguments in defending her behavior in the locker searches and suspensions. She could not have dealt with the drug problem without the locker searches. Moreover, since there were quite a number of students who had some form of contraband in their lockers, it was simply impossible to give each of them a hearing before suspending them. Had she had to comply with the niceties of due process, she would have had to take no action or to proceed arbitrarily against only some of the students involved.

Two Ways of Thinking about Rights

It is worth commenting on the structure of these arguments, for they raise an issue that pervades ethical decision making. That issue concerns the extent to which it is morally permissible to deny the rights of a single individual if the overall consequences of doing so are desirable. Let us make two factual assumptions about our case. Let us suppose first that John Sweet was unjustly suspended. John, in fact, had been guilty of nothing more than being overly trusting of one of his friends. Let us assume also, however, that Ms. Parker is correct in holding that it was not possible to check the innocence or guilt of each student who had been suspended and that her behavior has, in fact, had a desirable effect on student drug use and student discipline.

What follows from these facts? Consider two ways to think about the matter. One might reason that the main consideration is whether or not people are on the average better off as a consequence of the violation of some individual's rights. The fundamental question is what serves the greatest good for the greatest number. It is unfair to have the majority lose out because the rights of one individual or of some minority stand in the way.

This sort of appeal to the greatest good for the greatest number has some intuitive difficulties. Perhaps most problematic is that it seems capable of justifying some morally abhorrent behavior (see Rawls, 1971). Suppose it turned out that on the average, people would be better off if a small portion of the population were enslaved, would that suffice to justice slavery? We hope not.

We should thus take care in agreeing that individual rights can be waived whenever it serves the general welfare to do so.

Another way to think of the issue is to hold that rights can be waived only when the individual receiving the lesser right would, when capable of a rational decision, agree to it. This suggestion seems to work well in some cases. A drunken person who wishes to go for a drive is quite likely to agree in a sober moment that he or she ought to be interfered with when drunk. Generally, it seems morally appropriate to interfere with the liberty of people who are incapable of rationally judging their own welfare, when we do so for their best interest rather than for our own. This way of thinking about the issue will, of course, often result in denying us the right to trade one person's rights for the welfare of the group. Few people will be willing to waive their right to due process in order that discipline might be more efficiently exercised. Most of us, we suspect, would agree to a proposal that allowed our right to due process to be abridged for the sake of more efficient discipline only if we believed that we were better off running the risk of being unjustly punished than we were in putting up with the lack of discipline. We leave it to you to decide if this kind of restriction on trades between the rights of the one and the welfare of the many is reasonable.

The Issue of Citizenship

One more consideration ought to be mentioned. We should ask about the educational consequences of how rights are dealt with in schools. One aspect of this concern is citizenship. Among the more important roles of schools is to train students to be competent members of a democratic society. It is often suggested that school functions as the first and most important model to children of what social organizations outside the family are like. Moreover, students learn adult roles and behavior patterns by modeling the behavior of adults. If we wish to have schools produce good citizens, we must expect schools to provide adequate models of the workings of a democratic society. Students are hardly likely to gain an understanding of the value and point of democratic social institutions from the lessons preached in civics and problems of democracy classes if what they are told is routinely contradicted by how they are treated.

A second aspect of the educational consequences of how rights are dealt with in schools is student alienation. The discussion of student rights and the ethics of teaching began with the assumption that we decide what rights people have by determining what counts as showing equal respect for persons. The other side of that idea is that in denying people their rights, we fail to show respect for them as persons. The psychology as well as the philosophy of this idea seems correct. When teachers or administrators fail to respect the rights of their students, they convey a message that students are somehow not worthy of fair treatment. People who believe that their worth as persons is being denigrated have a way of becoming alienated. It is unlikely that students will respect their teachers or administrators if they are not first respected by them.

Mutual trust and respect are the moral basis of education. Learning is unlikely to thrive in a contentious or litigious atmosphere or in one where students believe they are being used as means to promote the ends of others. The central issues of student rights and student discipline are how an environment that creates and sustains such trust and mutual respect can be developed.

Student Control and the Ethics of Punishment: Ethics, Administration, and the Social Sciences

The Issue

We shall conclude this chapter with what we believe to be a most perplexing and difficult issue. This chapter seems to involve two quite distinct ways of dealing with questions about student rights, discipline, and punishment. Indeed, it might be argued that it contains two different ways of thinking about administration. The first section provided a discussion of the causes and cures of deviant behavior. It seemed to regard the student as a creature of his or her environment. Deviant behavior was seen as a product of the structure of the student's environment—of various social forces. Insofar as advice was given about how to deal with student behavior problems, the advice had the general form of recommendations to change student behavior by changing the student's environment. Either remove the cause of deviant behavior or respond to deviant behavior in a way that will deter further instances.

What seems missing in this sort of analysis is what might be termed a "moral point of view." Concepts such as fairness and rights, moral and immoral action, or guilt and innocence are largely missing from the account. The student is not seen as doing something that is morally wrong for which he or she is responsible and thus appropriately punished. Rather, the student is seen as doing something "deviant," engaging in behavior that departs from the desired norm for the institution. The task is to alter the environment so as to produce the desired outcome. The student is not seen as a moral agent expected to behave in a morally proper fashion. Instead, the student is seen as a management problem to be controlled and brought into line with the norm.

The legal and ethical portions of the chapter, however, dealt with a much different set of concepts, and they viewed the student in a much different light. The student was seen as a moral agent, as someone who is responsible for his or her actions. The issues concerned rights and duties. What may a student rightfully do without adult interference? When may a student rightfully be punished? The concern for guilt and innocence was at the heart of the matter. If students are to be punished, they must be punished for doing things that they have no right to do, and their guilt must be reasonably established. The issue about punishment is more whether it is appropriate, whether it fits the crime, than whether it is deterring. The primary issue is not management, it is justice.

Let us label these two viewpoints the "management" perspective and the "moral" perspective, respectively. Having sketched them briefly, several questions arise. Are they incompatible or just different? If they are incompatible, which should be adopted? How different are they really, and in what does the difference really consist? If they are notably different, what are the implications for the practicing administrator?

We can begin to think about these topics by discussing how these two perspectives differ on three questions:

1. What is the view of the person in each perspective? Are persons moral agents, or are they products of their environments?
2. Is the primary purpose of school discipline to serve justice or to promote efficient management of the school?
3. Is the purpose of punishment to provide retribution for morally wrong behavior or to change deviant behavior?

Perspectives on Persons

Consider first what we assume when we view a person as a moral agent who is morally responsible for his or her actions. We can begin to get a grasp of this idea by asking what is required in order to hold people responsible for something they have done. We suggest that there are at least two conditions.

The first is that *the person must have the ability to choose.* A phrase popular among philosophers captures this idea well: *Ought* implies *could.* The point is that we cannot reasonably hold people responsible for what they have done unless we believe that they could have done something else. If, for example, we believe that Karl was so strongly influenced by his background of poverty or that he was so thoroughly indoctrinated into his radical beliefs that he was simply unable to do anything other than what he did, we ought to conclude that he could not help himself and that therefore he is not responsible for his behavior. If people cannot choose—and are not, therefore, responsible for what they do—we should regard any harm they do us not as a wrong but as a misfortune. Extortion by a person who cannot do otherwise should be experienced as similar to losing our money through a hole in a pocket. It is unfortunate, but since the extortionist could not choose to do otherwise, we have not been done any wrong. We may wish to prevent further occurrences, just as we would wish to sew up the hole in our pocket, but there is no moral culpability involved.

The second condition that must obtain is that *the person must be able to choose for moral reasons.* The person must understand the difference between right and wrong conduct and, indeed, must have some idea how to decide what counts as right or wrong in the case at hand. A person who can choose but who does not understand or cannot apply the concepts of right and wrong (if there are such persons) cannot choose for moral reasons. They may choose for reasons of personal interest or gain, but they cannot choose to do something because it is the right thing to do. Perhaps more important, a person who does not understand what is morally at stake in some action cannot be held fully morally responsible for the choices made. This seems often to characterize children. Small children, for example, often seem to enjoy hurting one another's feelings. It is common to excuse them by observing that they do not understand what they are doing.

In such cases, it is probably not sensible to mean that they do not know that their actions are painful to the other child. Normally they do understand that hurt is a consequence of their action. Indeed, that is usually why they do it. What we mean is that they do not appreciate the moral significance of deliberately causing hurt to another person. They have not learned to see what they are doing as wrong. To the degree that a person does not understand the moral significance of an action, he or she is not fully responsible for it.

To be a responsible moral agent, then, it is necessary that a person be able to choose and be able to choose for moral reasons. That does not, of course, mean that the person will make the morally correct choice. People can be evil. What it means when these conditions are fulfilled is that people may be held responsible. When they choose morally, their actions are properly praised. When they do not, their actions are properly condemned. Such, at least, are the assumptions built into the idea of moral agency.

Now, why might the views discussed in the earlier sections of this chapter suggest that people are not moral agents? There are two reasons. The first is that the way in which the causes or cures of deviant behavior are understood is such as to preclude the idea that people could freely choose to do other than what they did. People are products of their environment in a way that precludes choice. The second reason is that the relationship between people and their environment is understood in such a way as to preclude choice on moral grounds.

What might the first case be like? First, it is important to be clear that we are not claiming that the mere fact that a person's environment does influence his or her behavior is a *sufficient* reason to believe that the person's choices are not free. It is not so much *whether* the person's choices are affected by the environment that is important but *how*. Consider the following explanations of a person's decision to buy a car.

Person A needs a car. He proceeds by determining what sort of car fits his family's needs and what he can afford to pay. He then reads consumer magazines on the range of cars that satisfy his needs and that he can afford. Having reduced the choice to three cars, he buys the one for which he was able to negotiate the best deal.

Person B has an unconscious need to think of himself as a macho lady-killer. He has recently seen ads for a car that associate owning it with a macho image and that portray people who drive it as having great success with women. Person B buys one of these cars although he cannot really afford it. If asked why, he could not give a clear answer.

How can we distinguish these cases? There are two important considerations. The first is that it seems intuitively more plausible to treat person A as having made a free choice than it does person B. The second is that person A seems to have made his decision on the basis of relevant evidence. Person B, however, is more accurately described as the victim of influences over which he has no control.

We suggest the following interpretation of these observations. We believe that people are moral agents responsible for their choices when they are able to respond to their situations as providing evidence for what they should do. When, however, people respond to their environments in such a way as to suggest that they are not able to treat their circumstances as evidence for their choices, they are not behaving as moral agents. They are instead victims of processes that they do not understand and cannot control.

If this is correct, the very suggestion that people are influenced by their environment does not carry the implication that they are not moral agents. This is implied only when they do not understand or have the capacity to respond rationally to their circumstances. Coleman's (1974) account of youth alienation from the adult world and adult values tends to suggest that young people are not moral agents, whereas the view that crime can be deterred by raising its cost to the criminal carries no such implication. Coleman's account views the values and culture of youth as formed by social structures and institutions that organize their values in ways that young people are unlikely to be able to observe or understand. It suggests that values are not freely chosen. The view that crime can be deterred by raising its cost, however, assumes that people reflect on the consequences of their behavior and act in a way to maximize their well-being. This may not be a model of the best in moral reflection, but it is a case of people responding to their environment as evidence. What such people do or what they value is a consequence of forces they can understand.

The view that crime may be deterred by raising its cost to the individual may, however, suggest that people are not moral agents for another reason. People who decide whether or not to commit some offense may be rational agents, but it is less than clear that they are moral ones—that they are responding to moral reasons. They seem to be responding to a calculation of their own well-being rather than to any viewpoint as to what is right. If the view suggests not only that people are often motivated by such considerations but that this is how people necessarily make decisions, the question is raised as to whether people can be moral agents. There is no doubt that they are rational agents. They can make choices on the basis of reason. But can they respond to moral reasons? Views of human beings as motivated solely by calculations of their own well-being are not comforting in this regard (see Parfit, 1984). At least they are not comforting if one views moral behavior as requiring something beyond calculations of self-interest.

Thus one can understand many of the theories of deviance and crime discussed in the first part of this chapter as carrying the implication that people are not moral agents. Some carry this implication because they suggest that deviant behavior does not involve reason or deliberation on the part of the individual. Others do so because they suggest that the reasons that individuals have for what they do are not reasons of a moral sort. There are, however, grounds for thinking that this is not the entire story.

First consider that it is very likely inappropriate to treat these various theories of crime and deviance as sufficient accounts of deviant or criminal behavior. They are best seen as ways to account for why some people are more predisposed to engage in unacceptable conduct than others. Indeed, a person whose behavior was not only influenced by the factors pointed to in these various theories but was entirely dominated by them would very likely be thought of as not just deviant or criminal but as pathological. Many youths may tend to reject adult values because their social niche isolates them from the adult world and from adult institutions. Alienation from adult values may thus be a factor in their behavior. But this does not require us to believe that young people are therefore incapable of considering a moral case for adult values or of acting for moral reasons. Coleman, for example, has argued that among the consequences of the exclusion of young people from the adult world is that "it creates a warmhearted, sympathetic, and open political stance, one which focuses on certain principles like equal opportunity and civil rights but ignores others, such as honesty, reward for merit, and the rule of law" (Coleman, 1974, p. 124). The experience of youth may, therefore, predispose young people to be less inclined than adults to appreciate the moral point of honesty. This is not to say, however, that the average adolescent is incapable of understanding or being motivated by a moral argument that appeals to the concept of honesty.

The conclusion to be drawn from these considerations is that the fact that these accounts are not seen as sufficient explanations of deviant or criminal behavior is also a reason to believe that the truth of such a theory leaves room for moral agency. It is, perhaps, only the pathological fringe of individuals who are so dominated by the factors pointed to by these theories that they must be seen as incapable of responding to moral reasons and therefore as failing to be moral agents.

A second factor to consider in this matter is that in schools it may be especially important to see students as people who have not become fully capable of acting as moral agents but as individuals in whom the *potential* for moral agency resides. The discussion to this point strongly suggests that whether or not a person is a moral agent should be seen as a matter of degree. It is affected by mental health, degree of independence from "determining" environmental influences, and ability to understand and apply moral reasons. All of these things come in degrees. Certainly, the last is something that is a learned capacity. Perhaps, then, as educators, it is better for us to see our students as people who are learning to be moral agents rather than as individuals whose acts are determined by environmental factors. We believe that educators who take this view of their students will have a sounder view of education as a result.

A second issue that is important to this discussion is the extent to which we should see behavior problems as matters of justice as opposed to issues of management. Here we may distinguish these stances by looking at the concepts employed to understand student behavior by looking at the kinds of questions asked.

Justice or Management

A management perspective is best characterized as one in which the basic questions asked concern the most efficient means to accomplish a given end. Objectives are identified, the way in which the current state of affairs differs from the desired state of affairs is noted, and the most efficient means to bring reality into conformity with the desired state of affairs are pursued. Administrative behavior is judged entirely in terms of the efficiency with which identified objectives are perceived.

We may illustrate the point of this view and something of its weakness by inspecting a somewhat stereotyped debate about "philosophies" of discipline. It is common to hear discussions about discipline that are based on a contrast between the "law and order" view and the "humanistic" view. The former emphasizes the strict enforcement of rules, "running a tight ship," and swift and efficient discipline. The latter emphasizes dialogue with students and student participation in setting and enforcing rules and tends to prefer counseling or "therapy" to punishment as a way of securing compliance. The debate between these views usually concerns which of them is more effective in producing an orderly learning environment. They are judged in terms of their efficiency.

From our perspective, what is most striking about these two views is how alike they are, not how different. Neither is much concerned with issues of fairness. Nor is either much concerned with the educative role of the school in teaching the concept of justice. Instead, both focus on how to deal with students in order to produce a desired outcome: How can the school environment be managed so as to maximize such worthy outcomes as safety, orderliness, and learning? Certain questions seem excluded: What rights do students have to govern their own conduct in an educational setting? What constitutes sufficient evidence to establish whether or not a student is guilty of violating a school rule? What rights of due process does a student have in matters of school discipline? How do we fit the punishment to the crime? These are the sorts of questions that characterize a "justice" perspective. Its primary concern is not efficiency but fairness—to judge guilt and innocence fairly and to assign punishment fairly.

We do not, of course, claim that the managerial and the justice views are always mutually exclusive. Nor do we claim that they cannot be integrated into a more inclusive perspective (although, frankly, it is beyond our ability to do this). It is worth noting, however, that the perspectives can conflict in ways that produce frustrating dilemmas for educational administrators. Consider Ms. Parker's mass suspension, which included John Sweet. Ms. Parker might very well argue that this mass suspension was required by the situation. There was simply no way to restore an orderly school environment and to combat Rankled Memorial's drug problem while simultaneously attending to the niceties of due process and privacy. If Ms. Parker had been required to assure herself that everyone whom she suspended was in fact guilty of possession of drugs, the suspensions would have been impossible. Discipline could not have been restored. It is too bad that innocent people such as John Sweet had to suffer, but that was a requirement of restoring order that, in her judgment, had to be made. When they conflict, the greater good is to be preserved over fairness to the individual.

Punishment

We can perhaps shed a bit more light on this issue by looking directly at theories of punishment. Two general classes of views can be distinguished. The first holds that the point of punishment is to secure some socially desirable outcome. The usual candidates for such socially desirable outcomes are the reform of the male-factor, the deterrence of further crime, and the protection of society by removing potentially dangerous people.

The second view holds that the point of punishment is to respond to a morally reprehensible act by inflicting a suitably corresponding quantity of pain. The point of punishment is retribution.

Let us refer to these views as the consequentialist and nonconsequentialist theories of punishment, respectively (see Strike & Soltis, 1985). These labels point to the fact that one major difference between the managerial view and the justice view is that the former justifies punishment in terms of its consequences, while the second does not.

On initial reflection, it may appear that consequentialist views have a good deal to be said for them. They seem oriented to using punishment to make the world better, while the nonconsequentialist view seems merely to respond to evil by adding to it an additional quantity of suffering.

There are, however, a number of difficulties with consequentialist views. Let us consider three.

First, consequentialist views do not require us to punish the guilty. In many instances the desirable outcomes of punishment can be achieved by punishing the innocent. A quite common case of this is the practice of teachers' punishing an entire class of students because they cannot identify the source of a given disruption. Such punishment may be effective—perhaps because it organizes the peer pressure of the innocent against the guilty. But many of the punished are innocent. Even when punishment is viewed as a "lesson" to deter similar behavior by others (a kind of public demonstration of the cost of crime), it is not required that the guilty be punished. All that is really required for deterrence is that others *believe* that the guilty are punished. While it is reasonable to think that it will often be more efficient in deterring crime to punish the guilty, there is nothing inevitable about this. Moreover, in cases where the facts suggest that crime can be deterred by punishing innocent people, consequentialist theories will justify doing so.

Second, nothing in consequentialist theories of punishment requires that the punishment fit the crime. Indeed, in the consequentialist view, the relevant factor in determining the quantity of punishment required in a given case is not the character of the offense but the amount of pain required to deter further instances. In cases where the threat required to deter crime is substantial, the punishment required by consequentialist theories may be substantial, even when the crime to be deterred is trivial. For example, littering is a crime in most states. But notices of small fines for doing so posted on roadside signs seemingly have little effect in deterring the practice. However, if convicted litterers were summarily hung from those signs, we suspect our highways would rapidly return to a more pristine state.

Third, the view that punishment is supposed to deter crime or to separate people who might engage in socially harmful behavior from society renders it perfectly reasonable to punish people because they *might* commit a crime. There is no special reason why they must already have done something. All that is required is that they be known to have the tendency to criminal behavior. We can then deter crime and protect society in advance by punishing those with criminal tendencies.

These difficulties all result from a common source. They all stem from taking a purely consequentialist approach to punishment. Once we make the commitment to think about punishment in this way, all that matters is that we produce the desired consequences. Matters of guilt and innocence enter in only accidentally. They are not essential to thinking about the character of punishment.

Nonconsequentialist views of punishment, by contrast, are not sensitive to the consequences of punishment. Rather, they are sensitive to the moral quality of the act. Punishment is not intended to produce any set of consequences. It is intended to provide retribution for evil deeds. That being the case, what is essential is that the punishment be fair. Fairness consists primarily in punishing the guilty and in having the punishment fit the crime.

The Primacy of the Moral

Let us summarize: We seem to have two very general ways of thinking here. It is important to note that these are not just views of discipline or punishment. They are closer to being general ways of thinking about dealing with human beings with important implications for teaching and administrative practice. One view starts with the assumption that people are moral agents. They are free to choose and have an obligation to choose for moral reasons. In dealing with them, there is a prima facie obligation to respect their moral automony and thus to give them reasons why they are expected to behave in a given way. This view emphasizes various moral concepts as central to thinking about human behavior. In matters such as student discipline, the primary issues to be solved concern rights, fairness, guilt, and innocence. Consequences need not be discounted in reflecting on behavior, but justice is the prime consideration. Justice is not to be decided in terms of consequences. Nor is it to be traded off against them.

The second general view does not emphasize the status of persons as moral agents. It is more likely to regard people as products of their environment and to emphasize management of the environment as the basic concept in dealing with people. Neither the idea that people are free to choose nor the idea that people should be dealt with by giving them reasons is likely to be emphasized. Moral concepts are not very likely to play an important role in conceptualizing problems. The concerns are for the efficient production of desired consequences. Questions of justice, when they arise, are quickly assimilated to issues concerning what sorts of outcomes are desirable and how to produce them.

It is important to recognize here that we have presented two rather sharply opposing stereotypes. Few serious thinkers on matters of ethics or administration are likely to fall cleanly into one of these groups. Moreover, surely the truth of the matter lies in some integration of these views. We accept the nonconsequentialist arguments that justice cannot be defined entirely in terms of the production of desirable consequences. But neither does it seem reasonable to think of justice as entirely divorced from consequences. Likewise, it is important to treat people as moral agents and thus give them reasons for what they are asked to do or believe. But it is naive to think that the nonmoral features of the social environment have no effect on behavior. Neither can one responsibly ignore the character of these effects. Being a responsible moral agent surely includes taking responsibility for the consequences of one's actions.

It is beyond our ability in the few remaining pages of this chapter to develop such an integrated view. Let us suffice with a more modest effort. We wish to argue that no view of administration that does not emphasize what we have termed a moral point of view can be adequate. Why? We can suggest three reasons.

First, most of our experience with ourselves and with others suggests that people really are moral agents. We all appear to respond to the world as evidence and to employ and respond to moral considerations. Granted that there are many philosophical perplexities as to how this is possible and some psychological and sociological theories that suggest that it is illusionary. Nevertheless, our common experience with other human beings makes a strong case for their status as moral agents.

Second, our political and legal system assumes such a view. As we progress through this book, we argue that a variety of political concepts, such as liberty, equality, and democracy, are inextricably linked to the notion that people are moral agents. It would be a strange educational system that sought to educate children to be citizens in a liberal democracy and at the same time administered its schools in a way based on other views. As will become apparent in chapters 6 and 7, we are not arguing anything quite so simple as the claim that schools in a democratic society must be run democratically. We are not quite ready to allow students the right to elect their teachers or teachers to elect their administrators. Rather, the point is that our theory of administration must be based on the same concepts that underlie our political system. We cannot expect to teach our students to be responsible citizens of a democratic society if we are not willing to govern our relations with them with the same concepts concerning rights and justice that define human relations in a democratic society.

Finally, we must not lose sight of the rather ancient idea that "the laws educate." Our rules and regulations do not only regulate conduct; they also teach lessons about what we believe concerning how human beings ought to relate to one another. Perhaps foremost, it is the responsibility of education to create human beings—people who understand what it means to be a moral agent and who are capable of treating other people as such. Perhaps we should learn to think of our schools as moral communities that above all else are responsible for exemplifying the values that we wish our children to acquire.

These arguments do not lead to any very detailed recommendations for administrative behavior. They are instead intended to promote a way of thinking about administration that we believe is insufficiently represented in current administrative literature. Perhaps we can put the point cryptically as the eleventh commandment for administrators: "Thou shalt not allow thy sense of justice to be overcome by thy desire for efficient management."

Questions

1. Could Karl have been suspended if he had been giving out his papers in the hall and his leaflets led other students to become disruptive in Mr. Burns's class?

2. Suppose John Sweet had been given a hearing but was suspended anyway. Would he have had any recourse? Should he?

3. How might search and seizure issues differ when they concern searching an individual's person rather than a locker? Is it ever appropriate to conduct a strip search? When? What safeguards should be insisted upon and why?

4. Might another approach to the drug problem have been taken before engaging in the search of students' lockers? Is there another approach that might have been taken with Karl?

5. Ms. Parker seems to be motivated in part by a desire to display support for the faculty and to bolster faculty morale. Is that a legitimate concern in this case? How else might she have proceeded? When ought faculty not be supported?

6. Why might there be competence requirements for some rights and not others?

7. Is free discussion more important in a math class or in a civics class? Why?

8. Are there times when it might be important to be able to suspend a student before meeting normal standards of due process?

9. Suppose Karl had been distributing his leaflet between classes but students came into class generally interested in Karl's leaflet rather than in the subject matter. Would that be grounds for taking disciplinary action against Karl?

10. Are there any circumstances under which school administrators should be able to control the behavior of students away from school or to suspend them for something that happened outside of school?

11. When would you be willing to have students' lockers searched? Would you be willing to search a student's person if you believed he or she was concealing something? What is the appropriate role for police in such matters?

CHAPTER 4

School Desegregation

Integrating Mason-Dixon High

Mason-Dixon High School was the product of court-ordered desegregation. It was located in Banneville, a city of approximately 100,000 in a Middle Atlantic state. Like many such cities, Banneville had seen a rapid growth in its black population over the past two decades. In 1954 it was 15 percent black; in 1984, 55 percent. Moreover, since its black citizens were younger on the average than the white residents, the black school population was approaching 75 percent.

Although Banneville had not had legally mandated segregation in its public schools for nearly a quarter of a century, the city seemed to find it natural to maintain racially distinct schools. It encouraged real estate practices that maintained residential segregation, and it built its school buildings and drew its attendance boundaries in such a way that attendance zones corresponded to divisions between racially distinct neighborhoods. One consequence of this was that few black and white children attended school with one another. A second consequence was that a federal court ordered the district to desegregate its schools. A third was Mason-Dixon.

Mason-Dixon High was new. It had been built deliberately on the border between two racially distinct neighborhoods as part of the district's attempt to comply with the court's order. It had been open for four years, with Mr. Frederick Kipplinger as its head. Kipplinger was strongly committed to providing a high-quality integrated education to his students. Indeed, this commitment was one of the reasons for his selection by the board. That same commitment had now created a serious problem for him.

During his second year as principal, Kipplinger had become increasingly aware that despite the almost equal racial proportions of Mason-Dixon's students, those proportions were not evident in many of its classrooms and corridors. Fully 75 percent of the school's white students could be found in the academic track; an analogous proportion of its black students were to be found in the vocational one. In its honors and remedial courses, the hoped-for balance was nonexistent. Mrs. Clark's calculus class, for example, was lily-white; Mr. Robinson's review of arithmetic course was virtually all black. Further, this pattern of internal segregation reached deep into the social fabric of the school. The north end of the cafeteria was clearly the black end, the south clearly the white. Many of the extracurricular activities were substantially segregated. Mason-Dixon's basketball team was nearly all black, its tennis team all white.

This pattern of internal segregation seemed largely a matter of voluntary choice. This was obvious in the case of team sports, but Kipplinger's careful investigation of the school's tracking system failed to reveal any overt discrimination in pupil assignments. Students claimed to be in the courses they wanted to be in. If teachers or guidance counselors were discriminating against minority pupils, they were doing so in such a subtle way as to go undetected. Besides, Kipplinger doubted that this would happen. Mason-Dixon's staff had volunteered to teach in the school and had been personally selected by him. He doubted that he had recruited a corps of clever bigots.

Further, a careful study of student grades and test scores led inevitably to the conclusion that his school had done nothing to improve black students' achievement levels. There was a substantial gap between the academic performance of black and white students when they arrived at Mason-Dixon. That gap was just as evident after nearly two years of what the principal had hoped would be a quality integrated education. Kipplinger believed that these two facts were related; that is, he believed that his minority pupils' initially low achievement was due to the segregated education they had received in their elementary schools. The integration they were to experience at his school was to remedy that. However, it was now obvious that there was little if any integration at Mason-Dixon. Hence, his black students were attending a high school that was, in this critical respect, no different from the elementary schools they had come from. It was little wonder that there had been no effect on their achievement levels.

By the end of the second year, Kipplinger and a committee made up of staff and parents had devised a plan to desegregate their ostensibly already desegregated school. Essentially, the plan contained the following provisions:

> *No extracurricular activity would be permitted to exceed 65 percent of either race.*
>
> *The English, mathematics, and science programs would remain tracked, but teachers and counselors would "strongly encourage" minority students to enroll in the college-bound courses. All other programs were untracked and would follow the "65 percent rule."*
>
> *Students would be required to enter the cafeteria from the north and fill in from that end to the other. While this might not eliminate racial groupings at individual tables, it would eliminate the distinct black and white ends of the lunchroom.*
>
> *The Social Studies Department would offer a seminar titled "Human Relations at Mason-Dixon High" to all current students and each year thereafter to incoming students. This seminar was intended to improve intergroup attitudes.*

Mr. Kipplinger worked hard to sell his program to a dubious school board and an anxious community. The most common reservations expressed were that race was being employed as a criterion for many decisions regarding placement and that students might feel pressured to change their programs if racial quotas proved difficult to meet. The board acquiesced, at least in part motivated by a fear of yet further intervention in their affairs by a federal judge. It established the provision, however, that the program would be evaluated before the end of its second year by an outside evaluator. It contracted with Educational Systems and Testing, Inc. (EST), to carry out this assessment.

The program was implemented with less stress than anyone (including Kipplinger) had anticipated. The extracurricular activities were integrated without difficulty. There was some grumbling among students about having to take courses they might not have elected, and there were a few fights in the cafeteria, but the strains were few.

Things appeared to be going well until the evaluation appeared. Mr. Kipplinger had agreed with a representative of EST that the evaluation would focus on four questions:

What was the effect of the program on academic achievement? What was its effect on students' aspirations? What changes resulted in student self-concepts? What effect was there on racial attitudes?

The results of EST's assessment had appeared a month ago. They were a great shock and disappointment to Mr. Kipplinger. His program had had negligible effects on academic achievement. There may have been some slight improvement among black students in the academic track of English, but EST's statistical experts thought these to be random variations. The rest of the report was unrelenting bad news. The academic self-concept of Mason-Dixon's black students had declined markedly, and this was especially true of those in the newly untracked social studies and foreign language programs. Moreover, the percentage of black students expressing a desire to go to college had declined. Most disturbing of all, EST's survey indicated a sharp increase in hostile attitudes among both student groups.

When the results of the evaluation had appeared in the city's newspaper, many parents felt that their children had been exploited by what one letter to the editor termed "Mr. Kipplinger's penchant for social engineering."

Kipplinger often asked himself whether EST's results were to be believed. Perhaps they only represented the short-term effects of doing something new. But his faith in integration was seriously weakened. Suppose the results were correct? Did it follow that it would be better to go back to the old system and allow Mason-Dixon to resegregate? In any case, Kipplinger knew that these questions were academic, as far as he was concerned. His contract as principal would be up at the end of the year, and there was one statistic that he did not need an EST statistician to compute for him: His chances of reappointment were zero.

Introduction

Desegregation is in trouble. Since 1954 and the *Brown* decision, America's struggle to rid itself of its legacy of bigotry has been a shattering experience for many communities. For nearly a decade following *Brown*, very little school integration took place. Through an often ingenious series of maneuvers, many southern states managed to evade the law's grasp. Strategems such as "freedom of choice," the conversion of public schools to "private" ones, and the outright closure of entire school districts were used to maintain historical patterns of racial separation. Each of these schemes and their numerous variants had to be tested in a federal court, where, sometimes after years of litigation, they were struck down. The Supreme Court's admonition to move with "all deliberate speed" provoked much deliberation, the transfer of large sums of the public's money to the pockets of lawyers, and very little speed. Years passed before any substantial numbers of black and white children attended class together in most southern communities.

Northern citizens had no cause to feel righteous, however. Although few districts in that region had practiced de jure segregation (or at least the variety imposed by southern law), integrated schools were also rare. Sometimes northern segregation was the result of covert reasons clothed in the rhetoric of "neighborhood schools"—schools whose attendance boundaries "just happened" to coincide with racially identifiable areas of the city. Sometimes racial isolation was a consequence of private, biased decisions made in the offices of bankers and real estate agents. And sometimes it was the product of impersonal ecological forces that encouraged the migration of whites to the suburbs, leaving the cities largely black. Banneville's segregation appears to be a product of all three. In any case, by the mid-1960s it was obvious that many northern districts were more segregated than those in the South. Thus the civil rights movement and the federal courts turned their attention north, and the passions that had attended the desegregation of Dixie's schools spread to such cities as Boston, Chicago, and Detroit.

Our large northern cities have stymied legal remedies for segregation. When 80 percent of a district's school population is black, no amount of busing, voluntary transfers, or magnet schools will eliminate virtually all-black schools. Since the Supreme Court has shown little stomach for "interdistrict" remedies (e.g., mandatory busing between city and suburban districts, the abolition of district boundaries), little more can be accomplished in large metropolitan areas. In a few places, such as Rochester, New York, voluntary busing plans that shift pupils between the urban core and its surrounding suburbs have been worked out. But such situations are rare. Even where there are substantial proportions of majority students left, popular resistance to "forced busing," absent a court finding of de jure segregation, has made further progress politically difficult. It is in the more moderate-sized communities like Banneville that desegregation is still possible.

As if all of this were not enough, there is a growing suspicion that desegregation, voluntary or not, has not worked. Early in the history of the effort, there was a widespread belief that desegregation would have strong salutory effects. It would improve the academic achievement, aspirations, and self-concepts of minority pupils, and it would reduce or even eliminate racial stereotypes and ill will. The first significant attack on this prevailing orthodoxy came with the publication in 1972 of David Armor's article in *The Public Interest*, "The Evidence on Busing." Armor concluded that not only were these laudable goals not achieved by busing, but their achievement was actually hindered. The article set off a storm of controversy, and it helped to trigger an avalanche of studies on the effects of school integration. (We shall examine some of the more prominent of these in this chapter.) By the mid-1980s, few people continued to believe that simply ensuring some arbitrary balance in a school's racial demography would automatically achieve these goals.

One response to these disappointing findings is found in the claim that integration has not worked because it has never been tried. Proponents of this view point out that desegregation is not integration, by which they mean (among other things) color-blind friendly social relations among pupils in a desegregated school. They note that the all-too-common result of desegregation plans is the internal *resegregation* of students within a "racially balanced" institution. Black and minority students are disproportionately found in the lower academic tracks of officially desegregated schools. They may dominate some extracurricular activities and be virtually absent from others. "Minority sections" of cafeterias and corridors spring up. Many newly desegregated schools come to acquire, in small, the pattern that existed in the district prior to its "integration." Indeed, the social relations within them resemble those within the community itself. Just as there is a "black section" of town, there is a similar section of the school. By such a process the term *black English* has taken on a bitterly ironic meaning in some high schools; it refers not to a dialect but to the lower-track English classrooms reserved for the academically untalented. Such is the situation at Mason-Dixon.

Few more virulent problems face educational administrators today. A small number of desegregated schools teeter on the edge of racial warfare. Occasionally one goes over the edge. In some the appearance of peace is maintained, but there is little real interaction between minority and majority students. They might as well be attending separate institutions. Indeed, as Mason-Dixon illustrates, it is arguable that they might be better off doing so. In only a few instances has desegregation fully realized the goals intended for it. It is critically important that school administrators be familiar with the evidence surrounding this great social experiment and the legal and ethical theories that bear upon it. The actions that these persons take—or do not take—are likely to have significant consequences for achieving equality of educational opportunity (to say nothing of racial harmony) in the United States.

The Evidence on Desegregation

Desegregation and Minority Achievement

Perhaps the single most influential study ever conducted on race and student achievement was the massive project carried out for Congress by James Coleman and his associates and published in 1966 as *Equality of Educational Opportunity (EEO)*. The study's findings were to reshape for decades our thinking about schools in several important respects. Of principal concern was that it documented, on a national scale, what many had suspected for a long time: The achievement of children of all minority groups (with the notable exception of Asian-Americans) was below that of the white majority. What was shocking, however, was the magnitude of this gap—about one full standard deviation on the tests used. This was no trivial amount. This finding, and the conclusion that minority children who attended integrated schools outperformed those who attended segregated ones, provided the first substantial scientific evidence supporting the desegregation movement. Coleman's further conclusion, that the achievement gap was *not* due to differences in expenditures per pupil, school facilities, or teacher quality, seemed to sound the death knell for explanations of racial differences in educational success that rested on the belief that schools attended by black children were of inferior quality to those attended by whites. Separate was, seemingly, inherently unequal, just as the Supreme Court had said.

This is not the place to dwell on the controversy that *EEO* set off. (The U.S. Office of Education, apparently in an effort to mute its impact, released the report on the eve of July 4, hoping that few reporters would spend a holiday slogging through hundreds of pages of dull prose and regression tables; Hodgson,

1975, p. 27.) Here we wish simply to note that the report put education at the forefront of social scientists' concerns and provided ammunition for the supporters of school desegregation. What followed was more than a decade of strenuous legal and political battles intended to ensure that American children of different races went to school together and equally strenuous academic battles over how to assess the effects of their doing so. Thus in part due to Coleman and his colleagues, not only do we have a large number of instances in which a major social policy was implemented, but we have a large body of scientific literature that purports to tell us whether or not that policy worked. We see through its glass darkly.

The opacity of this research has numerous causes. Perhaps the most important is the almost inevitable confounding of socioeconomic status and race: Although the majority of blacks are not poor, many of the poor are black. Hence, it is often unclear if achievement benefits are a consequence of mixing students of different races or of different social classes. (Coleman was clearer on this point than many who have cited his work as conclusive proof of the benefits of racial desegregation. He attributed achievement gains to socioeconomic heterogeneity.) Thus if achievement gains result from an SES effect, we should not expect that ensuring that black children attend school with relatively poor whites would have any effect at all. It seems certain that some desegregation plans accomplish just that and hence may appear to be ineffective. In addition, a major problem arises because many studies are cross-sectional in design, a particularly debilitating weakness in this area. Further, even when studies measure students' achievement before and after the implementation of a desegregation plan, the follow-up period is often only a year or two. It seems unlikely that substantial effects would occur so quickly. Even if effects are very small in the first year, cumulatively they may be substantial. Finally, qualitative factors, such as the community turmoil that sometimes accompanies desegregation, may affect its results. Thus we must approach this social science literature with a more than usually jaundiced eye. In the following synopsis we shall rely primarily on the recent syntheses of the research that have been carried out.

One of the earliest studies that attempted to integrate this literature was carried out by Jencks and his associates (Jencks et al., 1972). They concluded that any reduction in the gap between black and white pupils' achievement brought about by desegregation must necessarily be small. This was because the variance in achievement *between* schools is much smaller than that *within* schools. This is a critically important point for school administrators to understand. If only 20 to 30 percent of the variation in achievement scores lies between schools (a commonly accepted estimate), this sets an upper bound on the effects that *any* districtwide policy can have on pupil achievement. Jencks et al. estimate that any improvement in the performance of black students on standardized tests brought about by desegregation must be on the order of 2 or 3 points. "Eliminating *all* predominately black schools might therefore reduce the overall black-white gap from 15 to 12 or 13 points. Such a gain would not be completely trivial, but it certainly would not have much effect on the overall pattern of racial inequality in America" (p. 106).

St. John (1975) reviewed over 100 investigations that had been conducted up to the early 1970s. She concluded that while there were a somewhat greater number of studies suggesting positive effects on minority achievement, the results were so mixed and many of the studies so methodologically flawed that nothing approaching a definitive conclusion could be reached. She did find some support for an effect when arithmetic achievement was considered, especially among pupils who had experienced desegregated education for longer periods of time. Another reviewer was less equivocal. Weinberg (1977), surveying virtually the same research as St. John, concluded that desegregation improved minority achievement. Bradley and Bradley (1977), in a careful review, were so struck by the methodological difficulties inherent in attempting to assess desegregation's effect on achievement that, like St. John, they declined to reach any conclusion other than that.

Recently, a quantitative technique ("meta-analysis") for integrating the results of numerous studies has been developed by Glass (1976). This procedure may be helpful for "teasing out" from many investigations the effects of some treatment and for providing an estimate of the magnitude of those effects. This technique was applied to studies of desegregation by Kroll (1980), who concluded that if minority achievement was enhanced, any gains were small and not statistically significant. In our judgment, Crain and Mahard's (1981) application of this procedure provides one of the most useful integrations of the desegregation literature from an administrative perspective, for they explicitly consider the possibility that variations in the implementation plan (as well as methodological considerations) may account for differences in the conclusions others have reached.

Crain and Mahard found ninety-three studies (many of which were doctoral dissertations) concerning the effects of formal desegregation plans implemented in various communities. They grouped these studies according to their methodological rigor (true experiments, control group designs lacking random assignment, etc.), indexed the number of years students had experienced desegregation prior to being tested, and recorded the grade level at which implementation took place. Several of their conclusions are noteworthy:

1. The design of a study was important in determining effects. The more rigorous the design, the more likely a positive achievement effect would be found.
2. *When* desegregation takes place seems to be critical to its outcome. Nearly all the cases involving kindergarten and the early primary grades showed positive effects. Studies involving upper elementary or high school students were much less likely to report achievement gains.
3. If desegregation takes place in the primary grades, and if students hold on to the achievement gains made there, they will score about one grade level higher, on the average, in the later years of schooling than if desegregation had not occurred. If integration takes place in kindergarten, the later gain will be approximately two grade levels.
4. The length of time students spend under a desegregation plan makes no difference. Apparently desegregation "creates a sudden burst of achievement growth," which is merely maintained in later years. (Crain and Mahard find

this "surprising"; we find it dubious—it makes neither theoretical nor common sense.)

5. The type of desegregation plan—mandatory or voluntary or the nature of any busing involved—made no differences in achievement.

6. The racial composition of the desegregated school makes a difference. The presence of too few or too many minority students seems to lessen effects. Crain and Mahard suggest that approximately 20 to 30 percent is optimal. Two possible explanations for this are offered: (a) The desegregation effect is really an SES effect. High proportions of low-income students negatively influence the achievement orientation climate of the school, while overwhelmingly white schools are hostile environments when very few minority children are involved. (b) A smaller black population cannot be resegregated into lower-ability groups or tracks, which presumably would have negative effects on achievement.

7. Metropolitan desegregation (city-suburban exchange plans) has more positive effects than plans involving a city or its suburbs separately. Presumably this is also an SES effect.

8. Although few studies explicitly considered Hispanic students, the foregoing conclusions seem also to apply to them.

Finally, we should mention that desegregation per se seems to have little or no effect on nonminority students' achievement (Levine & Havighurst, 1984, p. 433). However, two caveats are relevant. First, when desegregation plans involve altering a school's racial balance drastically, the phenomenon of "white flight" may appear (Coleman, 1976): Some white families may either move out of the city or send their children to private schools. We do not wish to make much of this argument, since it is highly debatable that such dispersion occurs at all beyond the first year of desegregation or that any substantial numbers of families are involved (see, for example, Rossell, 1975; Farley, 1976). In schools in which white achievement declines followed desegregation, the cause appears to be that teachers lower their expectations of and demands on all students, which would tend to lower the achievement of *both* majority and minority students (Patchen, 1982).

What is to be made of all this? What may one conclude when, for every study reporting minority achievement gains, there seems to be another reporting no effects or even losses? It is important to put these findings into perspective. First, remember that no reputable scholar believes that desegregation of any sort will, of itself, eliminate the black-white achievement gap. Even some of its strongest advocates consider that reducing that gap by 25 percent would be about as much as one might hope for (Pettigrew, Smith, Useem, & Normand, 1973). Of course, that is not a trivial amount. For many students a gain of that magnitude represents a step over the threshold of functional literacy. Second, it seems likely that socioeconomic status, not race, is at the root of the problem. So far as effects on achievement are concerned, integrating schools without attending to the relative SES of the students involved is misguided. (Some researchers would disagree with this; see, for example, Pascal, 1977.) Third, the differences in black-white achievement have been declining—whether one measures such achievement with standardized tests or in more practical (and important) terms such as high school completion and college attendance rates (Levine & Havighurst, 1984, p. 442). Fourth, any effect from desegregation probably depends primarily on concomitant changes in teaching and administrative practices: strong leadership, a concentration of effort and resources on student learning through relatively structured classroom practices that emphasize the expectation that all students will learn, and the involvement of parents in furthering such expectations (Coulson, 1976). We shall have more to say about such practices shortly.

Desegregation and Prejudice

Regardless of the effects of desegregation on achievement, an important impetus for the movement has been the belief that it would reduce racial prejudice in America. The separation of children according to their race could only continue to exacerbate the suspicion, stereotyping, and ill will that has characterized race relations in the United States. Ideally, the true "common school," in which children of all classes and races shared a common experience, would build a sense of respect and brotherhood possible in no other institution.

As with educational achievement, there have been numerous studies of the effects of desegregation on students' racial attitudes and behavior. And as with the achievement literature, when taken in toto, the results are inconclusive. The number of studies that report positive effects seems to be equaled by the number that report no effects or even negative effects. But this should not surprise us. In itself, simply bringing groups into contact with each other may serve to confirm stereotypes as well as disconfirm them. For example, it seems obvious that if minority students with lower levels of educational achievement are simply placed in majority schools, any white stereotypes concerning minority students' lesser academic abilities may be strengthened, not weakened. Further, there is a large body of literature concerning the effects of education on social (including racial) tolerance (see Hyman & Wright, 1979; Serow, 1983). This literature, which is not concerned with desegregation per se but with the effects of additional increments of schooling, is largely unequivocal: Increasing levels of education lead to increasing levels of social tolerance. Thus we need to look beyond simpleminded comparisons of social attitudes in segregated versus desegregated schools. We need to consider specific aspects of desegregation programs and their effects. In this regard, McConahay's (1981) review is useful. It can be summarized as follows:

1. The length of time that students experience desegregation may be important. Negative outcomes are likely to be most common in the first year. This is not only because the process may generate turmoil in the community that is reflected in the school but also because the process itself is simply disruptive to students (McConahay recommends against short-run evaluations, which, he believes, are likely to show negative effects on tolerance even when a program is working.)

2. With regard to the racial composition of a school, approximately equal proportions of majority and minority students seem to lead to more intergroup contacts and greater tolerance. If these proportions are radically out of balance, minority students (regardless of race or ethnic group) tend to isolate themselves from the majority. However, some self-isolation occurs in nearly all instances. (Note that this conclusion conflicts to some extent with that concerning achievement.)

3. Despite mixed evidence from the desegregation literature itself, McConahay (1981, p. 43) concludes that other research on the growth of tolerance supports the idea that early is better than late. Integrating primary-grade pupils is likely to have more positive effects than integrating students of upper elementary and high school age.

4. There has been virtually no research on the effects of multiethnic textbooks, and the one study that touched on this matter (Slavin & Madden, 1979) found that they had no effect on attitudes and behavior. Since many of the recent textbook changes that have attempted to incorporate minority life and history are essentially "cosmetic" in nature (pictures of blacks, Mexican-Americans, etc.), this conclusion seems plausible. Further, it seems unlikely that textbooks, in themselves, would have much effect on such matters. Similarly, courses in minority history have, at best, very weak effects on racial tolerance among whites and no effect on blacks. Neither of these conclusions should be taken to mean that all-white books and ignoring the history of minority peoples in schools is all right, only that school administrators should not expect their effect on tolerance to be notable. Such practices are to be justified on other grounds.

5. A very common practice in desegregation procedures has been to include teachers' workshops as part of the overall strategy. Presumably one purpose of such workshops is to reduce prejudice among the professional staff. McConahay (1981) finds such expectations chimerical—a workshop of a few days seems unlikely to change deeply held attitudes and values. We would add that the assumption that a substantial proportion of teachers and administrators are prejudiced seems dubious. Perhaps the primary import of these workshops is to send a clear signal of the board's and administration's commitment to integration. Similarly, Slavin and Madden's (1979) study of the effects of interracial committees of students and teachers intended to promote tolerance and settle grievances found that these had no effect. The level of prejudice in schools with such committees was no lower than in those without them. As with textbooks, their justification is to be found elsewhere.

6. Interracial athletic teams promote tolerance among both minority and majority students (McConahay, 1978; Slavin & Madden, 1979). Indeed, the magnitude of their effects seem to be among the largest of the various desegregation practices studied. Further, there are good theoretical grounds to expect such effects from other integrated extracurricular activities as well, such as drama clubs and orchestras, though these have not been studied. We shall see shortly why this expectation is reasonable.

7. The question of integration at the classroom level presents a dilemma. Ability grouping and tracking practices are often justified on the grounds that faster pupils are not bored by instruction geared to less able students, nor will the latter experience frustration or unnecessary anxiety as a consequence of competing with their more talented peers. The research on these presumed effects is far from unequivocal. There is, however, some reason to believe that while faster students will learn more under homogeneous grouping practices, slower students will learn less (Esposito, 1973). In any event, ability grouping and tracking are correlated with race and SES—minority and lower-status students are more frequently found in lower tracks, creating an internal resegregation of desegregated schools. It is important to remember, however, that the relation between SES or race and track is not high (typical correlations are on the order of .3 to .4; see Haller & Davis, 1980; Davis & Haller, 1981), nor should such a relation necessarily be taken as prima facie evidence of teacher bias (see Heynes, 1974; Haller, 1985). Nevertheless, tracking tends to produce somewhat more segregated classrooms, and there is some evidence that such classrooms have a negative effect on behavioral tolerance (Schofield & Sagar, 1977). Thus McConahay suggests that administrators may face a trade-off: Slightly higher overall achievement may have to be balanced against a decreased opportunity for improving interracial attitudes and behavior. We suggest that in any given instance, administrators implementing a desegregation plan should look closely at the degree of racial imbalance likely to be created by existing tracking schemes. Where such imbalance seems high, the tracking plan should probably be modified or scrapped in favor of integrated classrooms. This is not only because in the sometimes volatile atmosphere of school desegregation, improving interracial tolerance seems more important than any marginal improvement in achievement, but because integrated classrooms provide perhaps the most important condition necessary for improving race relations, as we shall see.

8. The most notable procedures for improving race relations in schools may consist of some variant of cooperative work groups. (If you are interested in these techniques and their effects, see Slavin & Madden, 1979; Weigel, Weiser, & Cook, 1975; De Vries, Edwards, & Slavin, 1978; Aronson & Bridgeman, 1979.) Essentially these procedures consist of organizing students within classrooms in deliberately interracial teams. Team members sit together, and each person is responsible for tutoring teammates in a particular topic. Competition, when it exists, is among teams rather than individuals, and each person is forced to become "expert" in some particular area.

Such team arrangements have been shown to improve student attitudes and behavior toward one another substantially. These improvements seem to come about because cross-race interaction and cooperation for achieving common goals is required and status differences that arise from differing levels of academic achievement within a team are minimized. Further, overall academic achievement is not adversely affected. We shall have more to say shortly regarding the theoretical justification for these approaches. For the moment let us simply note that cooperative work groups are impossible to devise when classrooms are not themselves integrated, hence our suggestion that administrators and staff carefully examine the effects of tracking and grouping practices when desegregation plans are being considered. But these approaches are not without their problems (see especially Schofield & Sagar, 1977).

Desegregation and Self-evaluation

A third area in which desegregation has been presumed to have positive benefits, particularly for minority children, is that of self-evaluation. By this term we mean to include the ideas of self-concept, achievement orientation, racial identity, and self-esteem—the aspects of our psychic life that concern our idea of self, what sort of person we are. One of the major concerns running through the research on desegregation deals with such matters. Indeed, no less a social science authority than the U. S. Supreme Court (*Brown v. Board,* 1954) seemed to believe that racial separation in schools would have devastating consequences for the self-evaluation of black children:

> *The policy of separating the races is usually interpreted as denoting the inferiority of the Negro group. A sense of inferiority affects the motivation of a child to learn. Segregation with the sanction of law, therefore, has a tendency to retard the educational and mental development of Negro children. (p. 494)*

In the next few pages we will examine some of the evidence bearing on this and similar beliefs.

Keep in mind that there is no agreed-upon definition of *self-evaluation,* and various researchers have used this term in differing ways. For example, one of the leading researchers on self-concept distinguishes between that term, which refers to one's image of oneself, and self-esteem, which refers to one's evaluation of that image (Coopersmith, 1975). Further, it is widely recognized that a pupil's self-concept is differentiated into many components that may be variously valued, specific concepts of self as "student," "athlete," and "son" or "daughter," each of which is probably even further differentiated and judged. Such complexities mediate against generalizable conclusions concerning desegregation's effects on students' self-evaluation.

These complexities are illustrated in the research on racial self-identity. For some time it was believed that black children (and adults) came to devalue their race as a consequence of de jure segregation and from simply living in a racist society. Perhaps the most famous series of studies reaching this conclusion were those carried out by the Clarks in the 1940s and cited by the Supreme Court in *Brown.* In these studies, very young black children were asked which doll, black or white, they preferred to play with. Their preference for white dolls was interpreted as evidence of a developing race hatred. Similar studies have used pictures of potential playmates or asked children to choose the most attractive child. More recent research (Spencer, 1976, cited in Epps, 1981) seems to indicate that black children who evidence a preference for white dolls, children, or playmates do not necessarily denigrate their race. Spencer concluded that children may learn that being white is preferred by others without preferring that for themselves. Other recent studies (Banks, 1976) suggest that earlier researchers reached the wrong conclusions because of faulty methodologies. Perhaps the times have simply changed. In any case, studies of the effects of school integration on racial self-awareness seem to indicate that children attending desegregated schools are more likely to choose same-race pictures as "most like" themselves after several years in an integrated setting and that preference for own-race peers increases (Epps, 1981). It is possible, then, that what Mr. Kipplinger observed in his school—voluntary social groupings of students of the same race—is in part a product of his attempts at integration. The evidence in these matters, however, is so limited that such a conclusion remains highly speculative.

Reviewing the research on desegregation's effects on self-esteem, Epps (1981) determined that some studies found blacks' self-esteem higher in desegregated schools, others found the reverse, and some found no differences. Further, race differences in this matter may be a result of variations in specific aspects of self-esteem, as noted earlier, or they may be a function of concomitant differences in socioeconomic status. In the latter case, differences may not be in the direction commonly expected. Cicirelli (1977), studying primary-age children, found higher self-esteem scores for lower-SES pupils. Still further, sex differences may account for the findings of some researchers, as may variations in instrumentation. Noting that Weinberg's (1977) review of the research in the area led him to conclude that desegregation on balance may be slightly helpful to blacks' self-esteem, Epps more cautiously concludes that it is probably not harmful (p. 92). Our reading of the literature on the relationship between self-concept and school achievement leads us to a similarly cautious conclusion. That is, while it is not obvious that desegregation affects self-esteem either positively or negatively, neither is it obvious that self-esteem affects academic performance. Although many believe that a high self-concept leads to higher achievement, there is no conclusive evidence of this (Scheirer & Kraut, 1979). Thus the empirical claims advanced by Chief Justice Warren in *Brown* are now suspect. A priori it seems to us that any simple causal relation between the racial proportions of a school and its students' general self-concepts is unlikely. Students' evaluations of themselves are surely dependent on a myriad of more powerful and interacting factors than whether a high school is 20, 50, or 100 percent black.

If general self-concept seems relatively unaffected by school integration, this may not be true of black students' *academic* self-concept—their evaluation of themselves as students. One important finding is that in segregated schools (or tracks within schools), minority pupils' academic self-concept is as high as and sometimes higher than that of white students. This is significant because the actual achievement of black students is often below that of white students. Brookover et al. (1979) suggest that this phenomenon may be a consequence of inappropriate feedback in largely black schools and classrooms. That is, if teachers lower their expectations because they assume their charges' achievement will be low, they will praise substandard work, perhaps under the notion that to do so is kinder than to be critical and demanding. As a consequence, many black pupils may justly (but incorrectly) conclude that they are good students and develop a very positive academic self-concept. (It is almost certain that students' academic self-concept develops as a consequence of feedback from teachers and from observing the performance of their peers in the classroom.) However, when these same students are integrated into white-majority schools and face demanding teachers and better-prepared classmates, the result may be a sharp (and painful) downward reevaluation of personal academic competence. This seems likely to be the cause of the decline in black students' self-concept observed at Mason-Dixon High by the EST evaluation. Teachers and administrators do minority students no favor by such "kindnesses."

Successful Integration: What Works?

Although the literature on desegregation's effects is replete with contradictory and negative findings, students should not conclude that its pursuit is therefore pointless. We shall examine some of the legal and ethical justifications for integrating our schools. However, we stress that there are now enough cases of successful school integration to warrant cautious optimism, especially if professional and community expectations are kept within reasonable bounds. (We suspect that Mr. Kipplinger's hopes were unrealistically high.) In particular, it should be clear that mere juggling of minority-majority proportions in schools will not, of itself, attain quality integrated education. Unfortunately, from an administrative perspective, proportion juggling is relatively easy and has dominated far too many desegregation plans. As Mr. Kipplinger has learned to his sorrow, there is nothing magic about "65 percent." In part, the problems of Mason-Dixon stem from a failure to distinguish desegregation from integration.

The conceptual foundation of school integration was laid by Gordon Allport in his influential book *The Nature of Prejudice* (1954). His formulation, commonly termed "contact theory," has explicitly or implicitly guided America's attempts to integrate its schools. Allport put it this way:

> Prejudice (unless deeply rooted in the character structure of the individual) may be reduced by equal-status contact between majority and minority groups in the pursuit of common goals. The effect is greatly enhanced if this contact is sanctioned by institutional supports (i.e., by law, custom or local atmosphere), and if it is of the sort that leads to the perception of common interests and common humanity between members of the two groups.

School administrators should note several important things about this formulation. First, and most important, it is a theory about the reduction of *prejudice*, not about improving academic achievement. Some desegregation plans guided by this formulation may also result in improved academic performance, but such gains are likely to be the result of *educational* practices implemented in conjunction with them. At the present time there remains a substantial gap between the school achievement of most minority groups and that of the white majority, though that gap seems to be closing (Levine & Havighurst, 1984, p. 442). Thoughtfully wrought implementations of school integration plans may marginally close that gap further; they are unlikely to erase it.

Second, note that two necessary conditions are specified in Allport's formulation if interracial contacts are to result in the reduction of prejudice: equal status and common goals. Simply bringing students together in the school is insufficient. Indeed, it may be counterproductive. Consider equal status. What is meant here is that situations must be so structured that interactions between majority and minority students are interactions among equals. In much of the research we have reviewed, "equality" has meant equal socioeconomic status. It seems doubtful to us that many students assess equality in such esoteric terms. It seems much more likely that perceptions of equality are founded on the immediately relevant task at hand: in the classroom, academic prowess; in the drama production, the ability to act; on the gym floor, the capacity to sink a shot from twenty feet out. There is probably little that needs to be done in regard to the latter sorts of activities. Extracurricular activities tend to bring together students with similar interests and roughly equal talents. Further, as we shall see, these activities are very often characterized by the other necessary condition, common goals. It is in the classroom that difficulties arise.

The classroom presents a dilemma. On the one hand, contact theory requires that there be contact. Hence it is imperative that classrooms, not simply schools, be integrated. On the other hand, it also requires equal status, one important aspect of which is equal academic performance. However, newly integrated minority children may not be performing at a level equal to that of their majority peers. In educational practice, the usual solution to wide variations in pupil achievement is some form of tracking or ability grouping. But while these practices may decrease within classroom achievement differentials, they also effectively resegregate courses within the school. "Advanced" English becomes white English, and "remedial English" becomes black English; contact between the races is reduced, and existing prejudices remain intact or are exacerbated. Eliminating tracking creates more heterogeneous classes and exposes the relatively poor academic background of minority students, and existing prejudices remain intact or are exacerbated.

The solution to this dilemma seems to lie in the other condition required for contact theory to work, common goals. Prejudice is reduced when people are required to work together in order to achieve a common end. It is no accident, we believe, that one of the strongest effects emerging from desegregation research is the influence of integrated athletics. Team sports may be the *sine qua non* of cooperative endeavors in a high school. Individual competition must be submerged in favor of team performance. Though research on the effects of integrating other extracurricular activities such as school newspapers, clubs, and intramural sports is lacking, we would be surprised if similar results would not be obtained. The trouble with the traditional classroom, then, is that it is precisely the forum in which individual competitiveness is exalted. Students' individual success and failure in the struggle for grades is highlighted. Successful school integration may well require that this characteristic of classrooms be reduced or eliminated in desegregating a school.

It is here that the studies on cooperative learning take on considerable importance. As we have noted, these schemes are founded on the idea of pupils working together in carefully constructed interracial teams, with individual pupils taking responsibility for particular aspects of the subject matter to be mastered and rewards going to teams rather than to single students. There is no question that these schemes are difficult to implement. They require a fundamental reorientation of most teachers' approaches to classroom instruction. Considerable time, money, and effort in teacher in-service training is required, as well as considerable supervisory effort, to ensure that implementations "take." The alternatives, given the present state of our knowledge, seem to be inadequate or even counterproductive.

In reviewing the research on desegregation, McConahay (1981) finds strong support for Allport's contact theory. In cases where desegregation was accompanied by careful attempts to structure integrated classrooms along the lines suggested by cooperative learning strategies, racial prejudice was reduced. Such attempts are relatively infrequent, however. Hence, taken in toto, the research is equivocal. At this point it is unclear whether these strategies will also help to eliminate mean achievement differences between minority and majority students. To us, the prospect seems doubtful. It seems more likely that these differences are a consequence of a multitude of factors, none of which are thoroughly understood. As we shall argue, there are good reasons to pursue school integration, whether or not it also alleviates achievement differences.

What, then, in the way of practical advice can be offered to administrators like Mr. Kipplinger, who are striving to integrate their schools? Willis Hawley is perhaps this country's foremost authority on the problem. After reviewing numerous studies (Hawley, 1981, 1983), several of his conclusions are worth noting:

1. Integration should take place in the earliest grade possible. Kindergarten and the first grade are better than the upper elementary levels and certainly better than the high school. This is because achievement differences between minority and majority pupils are smaller then than they may be later, and prejudices are least. The possibilities for positive interactions, therefore, are at their highest.
2. Tracking and ability grouping should be avoided. Where they seem educationally essential, monitor them to ensure that racial diversity is maintained to the maximum extent possible. "Pullout" programs for remedial instruction should be monitored for the same reasons.
3. In heterogeneous classrooms, employ cooperative learning and peer teaching strategies. Ensure that the teaching staff is well trained in using these approaches.
4. Within classrooms, strive to achieve a critical mass of minority students—approximately 20 percent. Less than this and students tend to segregate themselves. However, there is some evidence that intergroup conflict increases as parity is attained.
5. Increase the opportunities for interracial contacts in situations requiring cooperation rather than competition. Expand extracurricular activities and do not make participation in them contingent on academic performance or behavior.

6. Create a relatively stringent disciplinary policy and enforce it evenhandedly. Parents are particularly concerned about the potential for race conflict in desegregating schools and should be involved in setting school disciplinary codes.
7. Reduce the anonymity fostered by large schools and classrooms by creating smaller learning environments, and within these attempt to inculcate shared norms of academic achievement and good decorum. There is evidence that smaller class sizes lead to improvements in achievement, and these may be particularly important for integrating schools.
8. Once a plan is implemented, stick with it for a reasonable period of time. Desegregation plans are typically disruptive to students, teachers, and parents. Modifications coming rapidly one on another create additional disruption. Do not expect even good plans to bear fruit in only a year or two. (Hawley, 1983, p. 335)

One issue remains to be discussed: integration versus separation. In recent years, many black leaders have called for an end to school integration. For example, Barbara Sizemore, at one time superintendent of Washington, D. C.'s public schools, has argued that school integration has deflected attention from attaining quality schools for minority children (Sizemore, 1972). She concludes that integration cannot work until the black community has attained status and power equal to that of whites. In the meantime, diverting resources to integrated schools effectively precludes their use in black-majority schools, where additional resources are desperately needed. Given the lower achievement levels of minority pupils, the first priority should be improving those schools, not improving further schools where the majority of the students are middle-class whites.

In many cities this issue is now moot. Without voluntary city-suburban transfers in those communities, the possibility for school integration is now past. Improving the quality of all-black schools is the only alternative remaining. Where it is not, the case for quality integrated education remains strong. Pettigrew (1971, cited in Levine & Havighurst, 1984) argues that the case for black separatism is unsound. Racial separation is the cause, not the remedy, of the current problem. Further, white racism is currently declining; to halt our attempts at integrating our schools will simply breathe new life into it. Finally, effective integration, whether of schools or jobs, hastens that decline. In any case, we think that there are better reasons for integrating our schools than the empirical evidence cited by Pettigrew or that we have reviewed. These reasons are legal and moral in nature.

Legal Aspects of Desegregation

The Meaning of Brown

The Fourteenth Amendment to the United States Constitution says in part that the states may not deprive any of their citizens of the equal protection of the laws. The amendment was passed shortly after the Civil War and was intended primarily to protect the civil rights of newly freed slaves. Its force is to prevent the states from employing irrelevant characteristics or illegitimate classifications in legislation or in dealings with citizens.

The legal standard used historically to apply the equal protection clause of the Fourteenth Amendment to education was the "separate but equal" doctrine announced by the Supreme Court in *Plessy v. Ferguson*. Though the case dealt with railroad cars, not schools, its ruling was the basis of legally mandated dual school systems.

In the 1954 case *Brown v. Board of Education of Topeka*, the Supreme Court rejected the "separate but equal" standard so far as education was concerned, holding that "in the sphere of public education the doctrine of separate but equal has no place. Separate facilities are inherently unequal" (p. 495).

Consider some of the remarks of Chief Justice Earl Warren in his expression of the Court's opinion. "In these days, it is doubtful that any child may reasonably be expected to succeed in life if he is denied the opportunity of an education. Such an opportunity, where the state has undertaken to provide it, is a right which must be made available to all on equal terms" (p. 493). Warren then quotes with favor these remarks from a lower court:

Segregation of white and colored children in public schools has a detrimental effect on the colored children. The impact is greater when it has the sanction of law; for the policy of separating the races is usually interpreted as denoting the inferiority of the Negro group. A sense of inferiority affects the motivation of a child to learn. Segregation with the sanction of law, therefore, has a tendency to retard the educational and mental development of Negro children and to deprive them of some of the benefits they would receive in a racially integrated school system. (p. 494)

Warren's remarks appear to exhibit considerable concern for the effects of segregation on the self-esteem of black children and for the effects of low esteem on education. The view represented in these comments might be illustrated by the following diagram:

SEGREGATED → FEELINGS OF → LOW   → LOW LIFE
SCHOOLS   INFERIORITY   ACHIEVEMENT   SUCCESS

Although the Court did entertain some evidence from various social scientists that seemed intended to justify such a theory about the connection of segregation, schooling, and achievement, there is some doubt that this is the primary basis on which *Brown* was decided. Judge William Doyle (1977, p. 13) comments thusly on the issue:

No person would argue that any race or group is inferior to another, that it is to be considered unworthy to associate with the excluding group. I submit thus that this is the actual key to the Brown *decision. . . . * Brown *[and others] were not predicated on the studies of sociologists and psychologists. They are all based on the fundamental invalidity of isolating people from other people.*

Note that this passage suggests not only that *Brown* was not decided primarily on considerations of social science but also that the decision was not first and foremost intended to promote equality of educational opportunity. Instead, it is seen as directed toward a violation of freedom of association, which in turn was seen as rooted in an official state presumption of the inferiority of blacks. On this reading of *Brown*, its primary message is that government agencies may not restrict the freedom of association of any citizen on the grounds that some people are less worthy than others.

This philosophical difference in what *Brown* is fundamentally about has some bearing on Kipplinger's program. If we are primarily interested in equal opportunity, it seems reasonable to attempt to generate an equitable distribution of the human and material resources for learning even if we must override the voluntary choices of some students in order to do so. Mr. Kipplinger's attempt to achieve a racial balance in Mason-Dixon classrooms might be argued as necessary in order to promote equal opportunity. However, if we are primarily interested in freedom of association, we have little reason to override the free choices of students even if some racial imbalance results. For in this case the injustice of segregation is not that black and white students do not go to school together but that they are compelled to go to school separately. Freedom of association is not offended, however, if the racial imbalance results from voluntary choice. The reading of *Brown* that sees it as having to do primarily with freedom of association thus gives little support to Mr. Kipplinger's aspirations.

We should also note that judicial sentiment has not been kind to the idea that an important point of desegregation is to distribute human resources equitably. Judge Sobeloff (*Brunson v. Board of Trustees*) comments concerning the testimony of Thomas Pettigrew, a Harvard sociologist, in *Brewer v. School Board of City of Norfolk*:

> *Pettigrew's central proposition is that the value of a school depends on the characteristics of a majority of its students and superiority is related to whiteness, inferiority to blackness. . . . It rests on the generalization that, educationally speaking, white pupils are somehow better or more desirable than black pupils.*
>
> *The . . . proponents of this theory misapprehend the philosophical basis for desegregation. It is not founded on the concept that white children are a precious resource which should be fairly apportioned. . . . Segregation is forbidden simply because its perpetuation is a living insult to the black children and immeasurably taints the education they receive. This is the precise lesson of* Brown. (p. 826)

These comments suggest that Mr. Kipplinger is not alone in his perplexity concerning what desegregation ought to mean for his school. Educational scholars and the legal community exhibit significant disagreement concerning the moral point of desegregation.

Refining the Standard

While *Brown* declared segregation to be illegal, it failed to answer two important questions with which the Court has been grappling ever since. The first concerns what exactly is to count as illegal segregation. The second concerns the remedies for illegal segregation.

Following *Brown*, few segregated school districts rushed to desegregate. Many adopted policies designed to give the appearance of having abolished legally mandated (de jure) segregation while nevertheless maintaining schools substantially attended by members of one race. In Prince Edward County, Virginia, the school board decided to close the schools rather than to desegregate them. A private school was established for the white children of the county, which was subsequently partly funded through tuition grants provided by the Virginia general assembly and the Prince Edward County Board of Supervisors. In this case (*Griffin v. County School Board of Prince Edward County*) the Supreme Court, holding that "whatever nonracial grounds might support a state's allowing a county to abandon public schools, the object must be a constitutional one, and grounds of race and opposition to desegregation do not qualify as constitutional" (p. 231), ordered the reopening of the county's public schools and empowered the district court to require the levying of taxes "adequate to reopen, operate, and maintain without racial discrimination a public school system in Prince Edward County" (p. 233).

Perhaps the most popular device to eliminate de jure segregation while maintaining separate black and white schools was the "freedom of choice" plan. Students were assigned to the school they had attended the year before unless they specifically asked to be reassigned to a different school. Such plans tended to maintain prior patterns of racial segregation while giving the appearance of a racially neutral pupil assignment policy.

In such cases, the response of federal courts has been to require desegregation plans that succeed in disestablishing dual school systems. In striking down one such plan in New Kent County, Virginia, the Supreme Court (*Green v. County School Board*) commented:

> *The New Kent School Board's freedom-of-choice plan cannot be accepted as a sufficient step to "effectuate a transition" to a unitary system. In three years of operation . . . the school system remains a dual system. . . . The board must be required to formulate a new plan and, in light of other courses which appear open to the board, such as zoning, fashion steps which promise realistically to convert promptly to a system without a "white" school and a "Negro" school, but just schools. (p. 441)*

Such cases indicated that once a history of de jure segregation has been established, a school district has more than a duty to create a racially neutral pupil assignment policy. Rather, the district must eliminate its dual schools. It may no longer maintain schools that are identifiably white or black.

The courts have not, however, abandoned the distinction between de facto and de jure segregation. It is not racial imbalance per se that is illegal, but racial imbalance that results from action of the state. Nor have courts required school districts found guilty of segregation to achieve a racial balance in each school that reflects the racial composition of the district as a whole. Neighborhood residential patterns may still be taken into consideration so long as doing so does not serve to maintain a dual school system. The courts' overall philosophy seems to have been to attempt to restore things as they would have been had the illegal segregation not occurred.

The case that has perhaps been most important in defining illegal segregation and specifying permissible remedies for it has been *Swann v. Charlotte-Mecklenburg Board of Education*. This case concerned a situation in which an earlier desegregation plan based largely on a neighborhood school policy and voluntary transfers had failed to achieve meaningful desegregation. The district court had ordered a plan that involved substantial redrawing of attendance zones and a significant degree of pupil transfer (busing). This action was challenged with the argument that the Constitution does not require anything beyond a racially neutral pupil assignment policy such as is involved in a neighborhood school policy. The case thus required the Court to be more clear both as to what precisely constituted illegal segregation and what remedies were permissibly used by courts once illegal segregation had been found.

In dealing with the nature of illegal segregation, the Court made it clear that while there was nothing illegal about de facto segregation, the meaning of de jure segregation is broader than legally mandated segregation. It includes other actions by public officials that are intended to create or maintain a racial imbalance. Commenting on the location of school buildings, the Court noted:

> *In ascertaining the existence of legally imposed school segregation, the existence of a pattern of school construction and abandonment is thus a factor of great weight. In devising remedies where legally imposed segregation has been established, it is the responsibility of local authorities and district courts to see to it that future school construction and abandonment are not used and do not serve to perpetuate or reestablish the dual system.* (Swann v. Charlotte-Mecklenburg, *p. 21*)

As to remedies for illegal segregation, the Court was clear that while it did not require every school to reflect in its composition the racial composition of the district as a whole, remedies such as busing and redrawing of attendance zones were permissible where they were necessary to eliminate a dual school system. *Swann* thus accomplished two things. It effectively defined illegal segregation as racial imbalance caused by state action (later cases, such as *Keyes v. School District No. 1*, were to add the idea that the segregatory effect must have been intentional), and it gave courts a wide range of weapons to be used in remedying illegal segregation. In doing so, it paved the way for federal courts to move north and to deal with segregation in northern cities. Such segregation often lacks a recent history of legally required dual schools. Segregation is instead maintained in large part by drawing attendance zones to correspond with racially homogeneous neighborhoods.

Pupil assignment is not the only issue involved in remedying desegregation. Courts have also required school districts undergoing desegregation to desegregate their teaching staffs (*Brown v. Board,* 1955) and have held that where staff cutbacks are required by desegregation, they cannot be unfairly borne by black teachers (*Singleton v. Jackson Municipal Separate School District*).

Tracking

The issue with which we are most directly concerned in this chapter is the problem of tracking and internal resegregation. Mr. Kipplinger has acted to prevent internal resegregation in Mason-Dixon High by assigning students to classes in a way that is sensitive to race. Is this practice legally permissible? Might it be legally required?

We should note at the outset that tracking is one issue that has not been thoroughly explored by courts. What follows is thus based on a few lower court cases and should not be considered well-established law (see Drowalzky, 1981).

Note that no court has held tracking per se to be illegal, even when it appears to lead to some degree of racial segregation. Tracking may, however, be legally problematic should it be seen as perpetuating segregation in a recently desegregated school or as perpetuating the harm done to black students under segregation. Even here the issue is not likely to be tracking per se, but the flexibility of the tracking system or the accuracy of the system whereby students are assigned to tracks. In the desegregation case *Hobson v. Hanson*, the court held that "ability grouping as presently practiced in the District of Columbia school system is a denial of equal educational opportunity to the poor and a majority of the Negroes attending school in the nation's capital" (p. 443). Here the court expressed concern that the tracking system provided a significantly inferior education to students in the lower tracks who were assigned to them more on the basis of race or socioeconomic class than on the basis of ability. In the court's words:

> These then are the significant features of the tracking system: separation of students into rigid curricula, which entails both physical segregation and a disparity of educational opportunity; and, for those consigned to the lower tracks, opportunities decidedly inferior to those available in the higher tracks. . . .
>
> A precipitating cause of the constitutional inquiry in this case is the fact that those who are being consigned to the lower tracks are the poor and the Negroes, whereas the upper tracks are the provinces of the more affluent and the whites. (p. 513)

In another case (*Moses v. Washington Parish School Board*) concerning a recently desegregated school district, a court objected to the use of tests to assign students to various tracks when that led to internal resegregation:

> It becomes readily apparent to anyone familiar with the nature of white and black schools in the South that the children going to the white schools would be provided with better facilities, faculties and educational materials than their counterparts in the black schools. It is equally apparent, given the obvious reluctance and recalcitrance of school boards to establish unitary schools, that the school board in deciding to use testing probably anticipated that most whites would score well and thus used testing to maintain as many segregated schools as possible. Testing used to resegregate students in a recently desegregated school system is not permitted. (p. 1345)

These cases suggest that in the context of desegregation, tracking will become problematic under some of the following conditions:

1. When tracking perpetuates an inferior education for black students
2. When tracking leads to resegregation
3. When students are assigned to tracks on the basis of tests that are sensitive to race as well as ability
4. When the tracking system is rigid so as to become self-perpetuating for the individual student

On the other hand, these cases also suggest that tracking is unlikely to raise legal difficulties if classification is accurate and flexible and if the education provided to each student regardless of track is a quality education suitable to the student's needs.

How would the courts see Mr. Kipplinger's system for dealing with internal resegregation at Mason-Dixon? Here we can only speculate. Our best guess is that what Mr. Kipplinger is doing would be legally permissible. Despite the fact that it attends to the racial composition of classes and activities and can deny admission to some classes and activities on the basis of race, the system is designed to prevent something that courts have deemed worth preventing, internal resegregation. Moreover, the plan seeks to provide a quality education for each student and seems to possess sufficient flexibility such that no student faces being permanently consigned to a poor or inappropriate education on the basis of race. In short, the Kipplinger plan seeks to implement a constitutionally permissible and perhaps required objective, and it does not possess any of the flaws that have plagued other tracking systems.

On the other hand, it is doubtful that the Kipplinger plan is legally required. It might be the case if Mason-Dixon's tracking system had led to a high degree of internal segregation that provided black students in the lower tracks with a poor or an inappropriate education. Under such conditions the school might have found itself under some legal compulsion to do something about the matter. The fact that assignment to tracks was voluntary renders even this judgment suspect. The main reason, however, to suspect that Mr. Kipplinger's plan would be unlikely to be legally obligatory is that it seems to go beyond the legal expectations for tracking in a desegregated school. There is little reason to suppose that a court would require anything quite as enthusiastic as Mr. Kipplinger has provided.

Our best judgment, thus, is that given current law and the facts of the case, Mr. Kipplinger's plan is legally permissible but not legally obligatory.

Ethical Considerations

Segregation and Freedom of Association

Note that Mr. Kipplinger has done some things in his program of desegregating Mason-Dixon that are not self-evidently called for by the idea of desegregation. Most obviously, he has acted in such a way as to disregard the voluntary choices of some students as to with whom they wished to associate or what courses they wished to take on the grounds that those choices led to what Mr. Kipplinger regarded as an unacceptable racial mix. In order to alter the racial mix, Mr. Kipplinger has interfered with the curriculum choices of some students and has gone so far as to dictate with whom students may eat or what clubs they may join. Is there anything that warrants this extreme sort of intervention into the lives of Mason-Dixon students?

A negative answer might be argued in the following way. It might be claimed that what is wrong about segregation is that blacks are prevented from going to school with whites. It is the element of coercion in segregation that makes it morally obnoxious. No harm and no injustice are involved in a situation in which racial imbalance results from the voluntary, uncoerced choices that people make. If the segregation in Mason-Dixon's lunchroom or in its curriculum really does result from voluntary, uncoerced choices of students, no moral problem arises, and there is no reason to interfere with the results of such choices.

This argument is not, however, entirely convincing. We might ask, for example, if we would not be disturbed by a society in which people of different races routinely declined to associate with one another or where their choices routinely led to racially segregated social patterns. We might at least wonder if something ought not be done about the level of distaste such people were exhibiting for others different from themselves. We might even begin to wonder how voluntary their choices were. It seems odd that skin color should affect people's preferred activities in such a way that their choices routinely lead people of different colors to separate lives. We might wish to know why they choose in this way. Why should black students disproportionately prefer a vocational course of studies? If they do, we might at least wonder how free the choice is. Perhaps, for example, the choices of black students are influenced by their belief that they will be denied access to professional jobs no matter how well they do in school. Or perhaps they choose nonacademic tracks because they cannot afford to go to college. If black students choose under different and more restrictive conditions than white students, are such choices voluntary?

To deal with such matters, we have to have a clearer picture of what is at stake in desegregation. What is it supposed to do? What is its moral point? And what is the moral evil of segregation?

Let's begin with a few observations on the idea of discrimination. The word *discriminate* has a neutral use. Whenever a choice is made to do one thing and not another, some sort of discrimination is involved. If one student is admitted to a university and another not, discrimination between the two students has taken place. Choices are not possible without discrimination.

Discrimination becomes obnoxious when it is done on inappropriate or irrelevant grounds. Grounds for choice are not simply relevant or irrelevant. They are relevant or irrelevant to some purpose. Moreover, purposes may be legitimate or illegitimate. Thus a reasonable and justified decision is one made on the basis of grounds or criteria that are relevant to a legitimate purpose.

Let us assume that education is a legitimate purpose. What kinds of personal characteristics are relevant to the kind of education made available to a person? Three things are commonly suggested: ability to profit, individual aspirations, and willingness to put forth appropriate effort. A university, for example, would be within its rights to deny admission to a student on grounds that the student could not or would not do the work or that the student had no interest in the program of studies. It would be a strange world in which people who could not do the work and who had no interest in being physicians were nevertheless admitted to medical schools.

On the other hand, characteristics such as race, sex, and religion are irrelevant to the majority of legitimate purposes we might have. To base a decision on them is ordinarily wrong and is discriminatory in the negative sense of the word. When such criteria are employed, it is surely appropriate to expect the user to meet a high standard of proof in showing that the criteria in fact have a relevant connection to a legitimate purpose. Moreover, when a person employs an irrelevant criterion, we are usually safe in assuming that something morally dubious is afoot.

Segregation seems a particularly offensive form of the use of an irrelevant criterion in dealing with people. Why? Let us return for a moment to equal respect. We have argued that our fundamental moral duty to other persons is to treat them with equal respect and that the reason for this is that no matter how people may differ from one another, as persons they are objects of value and of equal worth. Consider how this idea might be applied to education and to the issue of segregation.

Segregation is morally obnoxious because it is a violation of freedom of association and is stigmatizing to the persons segregated. What, after all, is segregation? It is the refusal of one group of people to associate with another because they find doing so to be distasteful to themselves.

Each of us, we suppose, knows of someone whom we find unpleasant and with whom we would just as soon not associate. Segregation, however, is not rooted in individual reactions to the personality or particular characteristics of another individual. It is rooted in the rejection of the worth and value of an entire group of people on grounds that pertain not to anything they have done or anything that they are except the color of their skin. The presumption must therefore be that such persons, simply by virtue of their membership in some racial group, are inherently unworthy of being associated with.

Segregation thus brands the segregated with a stigma of inherent inferiority. The message communicated by the denial of freedom of association is that the members of the excluded group are not entitled to the same respect and are not of the same inherent value as persons as the members of the group doing the excluding. Segregation seems based on a direct denial of the idea of equal respect and virtually requires the assumption that the segregated are less fully persons than the segregators.

When segregation is a matter of law or public policy, these messages and assumptions are linked with the power of the state and partake of the authority of the state. Segregation makes the denial of equal respect, the assumption of inherent inferiority, and the stigma resulting from such views a matter of public commitment. It is as though the government were to edit the Declaration of Independence to read, "Some men are created equal."

Equal Opportunity

We can also look at the idea of segregation from the perspective of equal opportunity. Mr. Kipplinger might wish to argue that his policies for Mason-Dixon High were designed to give each student an equal opportunity to learn and to succeed in life. Such an argument would not, of course, self-evidently justify everything that Mr. Kipplinger has done. For example, it is not obvious that integrating the cafeteria or clubs promotes equal educational opportunity. Moreover, it is arguable that interfering with the voluntary choices of students in order to overcome the segregatory effects of the tracking system interferes with equal opportunity in that it denies to some students the right to pursue their own well-being as they conceive it. Should not equal opportunity mean that black and white students have equal access to educational opportunities of their own choosing? It is not obvious that equal opportunity requires a common educational experience for everyone or that it requires a higher level of integration than the level that would result from voluntary choices under conditions of equal access.

To examine these questions, we must get a clearer view of what equality of educational opportunity means. Our approach will be to treat the idea of equal opportunity as part of a set of questions about distributive justice. Such questions concern fairness in the arrangements a society makes for distributing social goods to its members. We will view the school as part of a social system that functions to distribute goods and services, jobs and income, and other things that seem linked to them, such as social position or status. We might capture these things under the general label "life success."

What, then, constitutes fairness with respect to the social institutions that determine life success? We shall begin our discussion by proposing the following candidate for a principle that defines economic justice: *Fairness as pertains to success in life consists in the existence of a set of social institutions for the distribution or allocation of social goods such that social goods are allocated according to relevant rather than irrelevant criteria.*

Race is not a relevant basis for the distribution of any social good. But what is a relevant basis for the distribution of social goods? Consider the following sketch of a theory of relevant reasons.

One assumption is that people should gain from society roughly in proportion to what they contribute. People are entitled to what they earn. In a society whose goods and services are distributed primarily by free markets, economic benefits will be primarily a function of social contribution as measured by the free choices of consumers. That is, what a person will get is determined by his or her ability to provide something valued by others. The scarcity of the service provided in relation to the demand for it is supposed to determine its actual price. People will then be rewarded according to their realized and applied talent for meeting the needs of others.

This account provides some systematic basis for the intuitive assumption that applied talent or ability is a relevant basis for social rewards, but race is not. Talent has a plausible connection with the satisfaction of the wants and needs of others; race does not. The view does, though, have its difficulties. For one, it makes no provision for the care and feeding of those who through no fault of their own have no marketable skill. The view is at best an incomplete account of economic justice.

For our purposes, however, its chief deficiency is that it makes no provision for fairness in the acquisition of marketable talent. Imagine a society that was scrupulous in making sure that rewards were attached only to an individual's productivity, not his or her race, but at the same time allowed only members of a given race to acquire those talents that pertained to the better-rewarded economic niches. Such an arrangement seems clearly unjust. Fairness requires not only that economic rewards be allocated according to relevant criteria but also that the opportunity to acquire talents and skills be allocated according to relevant criteria.

Thus we need a second theory of relevant reasons. This time we need to know what counts as relevant grounds for assigning opportunity. This question can be addressed much along the lines of its predecessor. That is, a society whose goods and services are distributed by free markets may also wish to allocate its opportunities in ways that yield optimal social benefit, again as measured by the free choices of consumers. This leads to the conclusion that a relevant basis (though not the only one) for allocating opportunities for the acquisition of a given talent is the ability to acquire talent. Race can again be assumed to be irrelevant.

This analysis leads to a view of economic fairness that can be summarized in the following four points:

1. Fairness in the distribution of economic goods and services is viewed as fair competition rather than as a function of some property of the actual distribution of goods and services. This kind of equality is quite consistent with significant variation in actual economic benefits so long as the competition for these benefits is fair.
2. Fair competition has two components: (a) Economic benefits need to be assigned on relevant grounds, and (b) the opportunity to acquire talents and skills must be assigned on relevant grounds (see Rawls, 1971).
3. What counts as relevant in each case is determined by what best serves society as measured by free markets, which in turn are thought to represent the expressed desires of consumers.
4. The consequence is to justify attaching economic rewards to scarce talents and skills and attaching opportunity to acquire these talents and skills to ability to profit.

This view describes a meritocratic view of social justice in which the basic value is the satisfaction of consumer preferences and equality is valued primarily because it is an efficient way of achieving this goal.

Before looking at how this view of fairness in the economic realm can be treated as a theory of equal educational opportunity, we should note at least two points at which it fails to provide a sufficient account of social justice and, consequently, a suitable guide to educational policy. First, the view as sketched fails to attend to the distribution of noneconomic goods. Societies distribute not only opportunities and income but also liberties and political rights. A view of justice that attends to fairness in the economic realm but fails to attend to such matters as freedom of speech or religion and to the right to participate in political affairs is an incomplete view. This point becomes important in education when we recall that schools exist not only to produce people who are economically competent but also to create people who are competent citizens of a democratic society. It is entirely possible that when we look at how educational resources ought to be distributed in order to secure a fair distribution of the competencies required for citizenship, we will get a different view of how they ought to be distributed than we would if we attended simply to the matters of economic efficiency (see Strike, 1983).

In the case at hand, Mr. Kipplinger may not be motivated primarily by a desire to provide each student with an equal opportunity to acquire some economically desirable talent. He may be more concerned to provide a fair distribution of the educational resources on which political participation depends. He might argue, for example, that vocational courses fail to provide students with the capacities, such as the ability to speak and write persuasively, that allow people to be effective in pursuing political goals. He may feel that, should a significantly disproportionate number of black students fail to do academic work, the black community will be deprived of adequate political leadership. In short, Mr. Kipplinger may be motivated by what philosopher John Rawls (1971) has termed the fair value of equal liberty rather than by an overriding concern for economic fairness.

The second shortcoming of the view we sketched is that it fails to attend to the possibility that productivity is not a sufficient basis for the distribution of economic rewards, even when equal opportunity obtains. From an ethical point of view, the idea that people are ends and not means and that they are entitled to equal respect and dignity suggests that what they are entitled to in life cannot be solely a product of the value of what they produce nor solely the result of fair competition. To allow people to share in society's store of goods and services only in a way that is proportional to what they have produced would be to treat them only as a means to serving the needs of others, not as ends in themselves. Moreover, such a view makes no provision to meet even the marginal needs of those who, through no fault of their own, are unable to be economically productive. To allow those who cannot be productive to starve is not consistent with treating them as ends in themselves. These considerations do not suggest that the view we sketched is wrong, only that it is incomplete.

To see the impact of this view on public education, we need merely note that public schools are thought to be our society's central institution for distributing opportunities for success in later life. Such a view assumes that whatever is learned in school is a central ingredient in life success. It is also easy to assume, since schools are primarily concerned with cognitive attainment, that cognitive achievement is the relevant variable. Although we are not convinced of this, these various ideas generate a view of how schools should function in our society. Figure 4.1 is meant to suggest that schools distribute the opportunity for achievement on relevant rather than irrelevant grounds, that ability to profit is the primary relevant ground and race the primary irrelevant ground, and that schools distribute cognitive achievement—the basis of life success.

It is also worth noting that the sketch of equal opportunity to this point does not incorporate a view as to what exactly about the school environment makes a difference so far as achievement is concerned. Such a view is necessary, however, if we are to decide whether we are providing equal opportunity. For example, we would be unlikely to feel that equality of opportunity was being denied if we were to discover that the walls in predominantly black schools were painted blue while the walls in predominantly white schools were painted yellow. There is no inequality here because wall color makes no difference to learning. We would not draw a similar conclusion concerning a difference in the quality of teachers because we are likely to believe that teachers make a difference. Inequality of opportunity is not just any difference between black and white schools; it is a difference that makes a difference.

Does any of this discussion of the structure of equal opportunity help us to decide whether or not Mr. Kipplinger is justified in his rather aggressive attempts to overcome the internal segregation of Mason-Dixon High? It does suggest at least two possible lines of argument.

First, Mr. Kipplinger might justify his internal desegregation plan by arguing that the mix of students in the individual student's learning environment is in some way a part of that student's opportunity. If students themselves are considered an educational resource for other students, an unequal distribution of

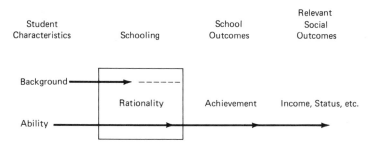

FIGURE 4.1.   Equality of Opportunity. (*Source:* K. A. Strike, 1982, *Educational Policy and the Just Society,* Urbana, IL: University of Illinois Press, p. 190. Used with permission.)

these students constitutes a denial of equal opportunity. Mr. Kipplinger might, then, argue that the racial composition of a classroom was itself a part of the students' learning environment and that by creating a reasonable racial mix, he was creating equal opportunity.

Second, Mr. Kipplinger might argue that he is entitled to ignore to some extent the choices of students concerning their program because those choices were affected by earlier inequalities. Students from the previously black school were denied the same educational resources available to the students attending the white school. As a consequence, they are less well prepared to succeed in the college preparatory curriculum of Mason-Dixon and less inclined to attempt to do so. By insisting that each component of Mason-Dixon's curriculum be integrated, Mr. Kipplinger is attempting to create an environment that will serve to restore to some of Mason-Dixon's students the educational opportunity they would have chosen had they not been denied a quality education at some earlier period. He is refusing to accept the consequences of prior injustices.

One final line of argument is available to Mr. Kipplinger. He may argue that the point of attempting a thorough integration of Mason-Dixon is to teach tolerance and respect for members of other races. If this line of argument is to succeed, Mr. Kipplinger must show at least two things. First, he must be able to show that teaching tolerance is a sufficiently overriding concern that it justifies interfering with student preferences. Second, he must show that tolerance is in fact learned by interaction with members of other races of the sort that he is promoting at Mason-Dixon. (Review our discussion earlier in this chapter for evidence relevant to these suggestions.)

Mr. Kipplinger has one further dilemma to deal with in defending his program. The EST evaluation of his program has discovered very little evidence to suggest that his efforts are working and some that suggests that they are not. Achievement has not changed much since the program was initiated, nor have the aspirations of black children. The self-concept of black children has apparently declined. Finally, the result of enforced contact between black and white students has apparently been an increase in mutual distaste. Much in Mr. Kipplinger's plan appears to have gone wrong. Does he have any defense?

Two arguments are worth making. First, Mr. Kipplinger's plan has been in force only a bit longer than a year. But few highly complex operations can be made to run well in a year. Moreover, Mr. Kipplinger was attempting to implement his plan under very trying circumstances. There was a great deal of confusion in Mason-Dixon resulting merely from the fact that it was a new school. Teachers had not settled into their new jobs. They had not been trained to function in a racially integrated situation and felt that they had to get their own acts together before they could attend to Mr. Kipplinger's pet project. Few students knew each other. All were concerned about racial tensions in a potentially troubled and unfamiliar situation. Conditions were hardly ideal for doing something new. Indeed, Mr. Kipplinger thought not that his plan had not succeeded but that it had hardly been tried. Many of the evaluation's results were quite possibly consequences of a new and unfamiliar situation. It was not at all clear that his plan was based on unreasonable assumptions or that it could not be made to work. Indeed, Mr. Kipplinger believed that the first question to ask of any innovation was not whether it had worked but whether it could be made to work. He was not inclined to abandon his program until he had had a chance to debug it.

The second issue Mr. Kipplinger might wish to argue is whether the results of the evaluation are even relevant to the merits of his program. He had to admit that despite his arguments to the board about equal opportunity and the effects of an integrated environment on achievement and tolerance, his basic motivation for the plan was not its educational results. He simply believed that segregation was wrong. It was wrong for the members of one race to refuse to associate with the members of another race. He did not see that the evaluation really changed much. Discrimination and intolerance are still wrong, even if their remedies have a negative impact. Mr. Kipplinger was not really trying to improve test scores. He was trying to run a school that was as untainted with racial prejudice as he could make it. Segregation was simply immoral, period! What could EST have to say about that?

Questions

1. Are there any purposes of integration or desegregation on which we have not touched?
2. Is it ever appropriate to intervene in education to eliminate a racial imbalance that results from voluntary choice? If so, when?
3. What kinds of problems is Mr. Kipplinger trying to solve? To what extent are these problems rooted in differences in social class in addition to or instead of race?
4. What do you think of Mr. Kipplinger's response to the EST evaluation? Does the evil of segregation depend on its consequences?
5. Practically speaking, does Mr. Kipplinger have any choice but to terminate his program? If he wishes to defend it, how should he proceed?
6. What is meant by tolerance? What would you count as evidence that it had been achieved?
7. How important is self-concept to these issues? If a program had a positive effect on achievement and a negative effect on self-concept, would you consider that to be a gain or a loss?
8. What might Mr. Kipplinger have done in order to have given his plan a better chance of success?

CHAPTER 5

Resource Allocation and School Achievement

Quality and Inequality in El Dorado

Bob Bender imagines the solution to his dilemma: His state's supreme court would drop dead, preferably last year, and the citizens of El Dorado would have more children, preferably last decade. Then his troubles would be over, and his life as superintendent would be simple. But the members of the court seemed disgustingly healthy for elderly jurists, and it was unlikely that the women of El Dorado had successfully concealed their childbearing from him. Thus Bob Bender has a big problem.

The problem stemmed from two sources. First, the court had discovered that there was considerable variation in property wealth among the school districts of the state. As a consequence, there was also a considerable variation in the amount those districts spent on educating their children. The court found this to be in violation of the state's constitution. Accordingly, it had directed the legislature to remedy the situation by designing a more equitable system for funding schools. While the legislature had not yet completed its work, it was already clear that El Dorado would get much less state aid than it had in the past. Because of some large industrial facilities, the district was property-rich, though its residents were no wealthier than the average.

The second source had to do with the decline in the school population. El Dorado's schools had about 30 percent fewer students than they had ten years ago. This had already caused a significant decline in state aid. Further, all of its schools were well below their capacity.

These problems pointed to a simple solution; indeed, they virtually demanded it. The solution was school consolidation. Bender had known this when he had taken the job as superintendent two years ago, and unlike many communities, El Dorado recognized the necessity for doing so. There would be no problems from the community on that score.

Further, the decision about which school to close was easy. El Dorado had one building that could only be called a geriatric case. Dolmen Elementary School would have to go. It was old and poorly insulated, had the fewest pupils, and was in need of major repairs. If it were left open, the district would have to spend an exorbitant sum to refurbish it; shutting it down would produce a windfall in lowered fuel costs and would save the salaries of several clerical and service employees.

Bender's problem was what to do about Dolmen's principal and staff. Since the district had only three elementary schools, there were only two other places they could go: Left Bank and, on the opposite side of town, Steinbeck. The former was newer and had generally better facilities, but between them they could easily absorb the students and staff of Dolmen. Unofficially, both had pupil-teacher ratios of approximately 26 to 1. The difficulty was that Bender could not think of any fair or politically acceptable way to decide who was to go where.

Left Bank Elementary served a generally upper-middle-class clientele. Its students and their parents valued education. Pupils there always did well on standardized tests, and they seemed to enjoy school. Despite this, it was Bender's opinion that their success was more a consequence of their advantaged background than the school's program or its staff. This was not to say that Left Bank's program or its teachers were inadequate. They were not. It was just that they were not better than average, in Bender's judgment.

In contrast, Steinbeck served the poorest of the district's children. But its relatively new principal, Sarah Lighthall, and her staff were dedicated to their pupils' education. The school was a "tight ship," as far as Bender could tell, where kids worked hard, did well, and liked their school. A great deal of stress was placed on the basics, and it was expected that all children would master them. Contrary to what some might expect, discipline was actually less a problem at Steinbeck than at Left Bank. And although the test scores at Steinbeck were not quite as high as at Left Bank, they seemed considerably higher than those of most other schools with a similar clientele. In fact, on balance, Bender thought that the pupils at Steinbeck did a lot better than their designer-clad peers across town.

In any case, perhaps the root of Bender's current problem was Dolmen's principal, Kathryn Loobies. Loobies had been hired and tenured by Bender's predecessor. In the two years that Bender had been in El Dorado, he often wondered why. She seemed to him to be relatively incompetent. Loobies was likable enough, but she was entirely unassertive. For example, she obviously disliked having to evaluate her teachers. She did it as seldom as possible and never found serious deficiencies among them. Further, planning was not her forte; to Bender, the school seemed adrift. He could not exactly put his finger on it, but everyone there seemed to go about their business with little sense of what anyone else was doing. Each year a scattering of parents would complain that there seemed to be no connection between their children's previous work and what they were required to know for their present teacher. One manifestation of this seemed to show up in the school's standardized test scores. Bender had taken the trouble to dig out the records of Dolmen's students for the past ten years—the time that Loobies had been principal. These showed a substantial and steady decline, beginning three years after her arrival on the scene. At bottom, Bender considered Loobies just a little stupid.

If he had doubts about her intellectual competence, he had none whatsoever about the staff she had hired in her years as principal. Loobies seemed to hold a remarkable theory about hiring new staff: Their personnel records suggested that she refused to employ any teacher more able than herself. For example, their SAT scores and college GPAs were well below average. Several had gone to schools that Bender considered less than second-rate. While the district encouraged its teachers to take graduate courses (and rewarded them modestly for doing so), few of Dolmen's staff had chosen to avail themselves of the opportunity. Bender suspected that not a few of them would be unable to pass a modestly demanding graduate course.

It was not just a matter of credentials, however. In the few chances that Bender had had to visit classrooms since his arrival, he had been least impressed with

Dolmen's. In many rooms he thought that an excessive amount of time was being wasted. Dolmen's children were, in general, somewhat disadvantaged (though not so much as Steinbeck's). Their teachers seemed to accept low achievement as an inevitable consequence of this. It was not that they were harsh to disadvantaged children. In fact, the opposite seemed to be the case. They struck Bender as excessively kindly and forgiving of wrong answers and low test grades, and they seemed to want to make school as pleasant as possible. If that meant not demanding that some pupils master the intricacies of fractions, so be it.

Finally, despite Loobies's reluctance to be assertive with her staff, it was abundantly clear that the staff was unhappy with her as principal. Dolmen produced more grievances than any school in the district. Several of the more experienced teachers, who had not been recruited by her, had privately complained to Bender about one or another of her actions—or more precisely, her inactions. Whenever a vacancy occurred in one of the other elementary schools, Bender could count on a majority of Dolmen's senior staff requesting reassignment.

These characteristics of Dolmen's professionals interacted in an unfortunate way with the district's collective bargaining agreement. That agreement, which covered both teachers and principals, provided that seniority be a major consideration in staff reassignments. Bender was not required to adhere to the seniority provision, but he would have to provide very good reasons if he did not. If he lacked such reasons, a grievance was certain—and he would lose.

But the outcome of following a seniority rule was clear to Bender. First, Loobies would choose to go to Steinbeck. This was because she was senior to Sarah Lighthall but not to the principal of Left Bank. Hence she would assume that school's principalship, and Lighthall would have to go back to the classroom, unless Bender could get the board to agree to create an assistant principalship for her. He could do that, he knew, but he was highly reluctant to remove Lighthall from her job. Bender considered her the key to Steinbeck's success.

Second, if Loobies went to Steinbeck, many of Dolmen's teachers, especially the more experienced ones, would grab the opportunity to go to Left Bank. Thus if seniority were followed, the net result would be that an inept principal and the district's least experienced and least talented teachers would descend on Steinbeck. That seemed to Bender to be unfair. Steinbeck's pupils were clearly more in need of a quality program than those in Left Bank. On the other hand, it was likely that if he successfully overrode the seniority provision and sent Loobies and her weakest staff to Left Bank, not only would he provoke a fight with the union, but the parents at Left Bank, who were much more attentive to such things, would be likely to howl in protest. He would take a great deal of heat from his board, perhaps seriously damaging his future credibility.

But what were his alternatives? How does one go about fairly distributing ineptness? He would have to have a convincing answer to that question, a convincing set of reasons for rejecting seniority. He needed a theory of fairness in resource allocation. Or else he needed a place to hide.

Introduction

Bob Bender has a difficult choice to make. He has a weak principal and a generally incompetent teaching staff at one of his schools, and the collective bargaining agreement of his district requires him to allocate these people to the remaining schools. It is not a pleasant or easy choice. How should he think about it?

The first problem Bender needs to address is what kind of question he is faced with. We suggest that it is a question of resource allocation. Like money, books, programs, and facilities, teachers and administrators are educational resources. Given that they can be assigned in various ways, they are resources that can be allocated. Bender can approach his problem as one of how best to allocate resources.

Why think of teachers and administrators as educational resources? Part of the answer is that the attainment of educational goals depends on personnel. Teachers and administrators make a difference for student learning. Making a difference in what students learn is one of the qualities that defines an educational resource. We would not, in contrast, ordinarily think of the color of classroom walls as an educational resource, since wall colors do not usually affect educational outcomes.

If something is to be thought of as an educational resource, it must also be capable of being distributed in some way. Consider, for example, that a child's IQ makes a difference for the child's education. It is not, however, an educational resource, because it is not something we can make available to the child. On the other hand, if being in the same class with able classmates affects learning, it makes sense to think of the *mix* of students in a room or a school as an educational resource. The mix of ability is something that can be distributed.

Since principals and teachers affect educational goals, and since these personnel can be assigned, they are educational resources. Hence their assignments can be thought about in the same way as we think about distributing dollars, books, and facilities.

What Makes a Difference?
The Search for Important Resources

Surely one of the most important streams of research that emerged in the 1960s, and continues to the present time, is the large number of studies referred to collectively as the "school effects literature." We cannot hope to review this vast outpouring in detail, but it is essential that anyone who administers educational organizations be familiar with at least the broad outlines of this work.

We will begin our discussion with what, in our judgment, is the single most influential piece of educational research done in this country, that conducted by James Coleman and his colleagues in 1966 for the U. S. Congress. That massive investigation literally defined the field.

Equality of Educational Opportunity: The Coleman Report

To understand something of the importance of the study *Equality of Educational Opportunity* (Coleman et al., 1966), it is necessary to put the research in the context of the times. The work was commissioned by Congress as part of the Civil Rights Act of 1964. Ten years after the *Brown* case, it had become clear that the pace of desegregation in the South was considerably slower than what many people thought seemly. It is likely that what Congress had in mind was for Coleman and his associates to demonstrate that many of the nation's black children still attended essentially segregated schools, that the schools they attended were deficient in obvious ways when compared with those attended by white children, and that those deficiencies were the cause of lower academic achievement among blacks. Certainly Coleman himself thought that his study would document these "obvious" facts: "The study will show the difference in the quality of schools that the average Negro child and the average white child are exposed to" (Coleman, quoted in Hodgson, 1975). What "quality" meant in reference to schools seemed equally obvious: Buildings would be less adequate, teachers less experienced and less well trained, and supplies and equipment in shorter supply.

However, the facts turned out to be not so obvious at all. Regarding the first (that black and white children continued to attend separate schools), the survey's results showed that while this was still true in many areas of the South, it was also true in the North, especially in our large cities. Racial segregation was not simply a southern phenomenon. More important for our discussion, however, *EEO* failed to uncover substantial differences in facilities, teacher quality, or equipment in the schools attended by pupils of either race. Thus the second prediction turned out to be false. Obviously, then, if the schools attended by children of the two races were basically of equal quality, the third prediction must also be false; differences in school quality could not account for differences in the achievement of black and white pupils. And that is what Coleman and his associates found. The basic conclusions of *Equality of Educational Opportunity* can be summarized as follows:

1. Substantial differences existed in the measured academic achievement of black and white students at all grade levels tested.
2. Family background (that is, parental socioeconomic status) had a very great influence on student achievement.
3. The relationship between family background and achievement did not diminish over the years that students spent in school.
4. There was relatively little variation in achievement between schools when compared to the amount within schools.
5. Little of the variation in student achievement could be attributed to variations in school facilities or curricula.
6. Variations in teacher attributes (as in level of training or verbal ability) accounted for a bit more of the variation in student achievement than did variations in school facilities, but this amount was still small.
7. The social composition of the school (that is, the average socioeconomic status of its student body) had a larger effect on achievement than either the quality of its facilities or the quality of its teachers.
8. The extent to which students believed that they could control their environment had an important effect on their achievement.

On the basis of these findings, Coleman concluded, in perhaps the most quoted statement ever made in a piece of social science research:

Taking all of these results together, one implication stands out above all: That schools bring little influence to bear on a child's achievement that is independent of his background and general social context; and this very lack of an independent effect means that inequalities imposed on children by their home, neighborhood, and peer environment are carried along to become the inequalities with which they confront adult life at the end of school. For equality of educational opportunity through the schools must imply a strong effect of schools that is independent of the child's immediate social environment, and that strong independent effect is not present in American schools. (Coleman et al., 1966, p. 325)

Students of educational administration must thoroughly comprehend what Coleman was saying, for his conclusions and his interpretation of them go to the very heart of the American belief in the importance of education. They challenge the ideal that schooling serves to break the link between where a child starts out in life and where he or she eventually ends up. Coleman was saying that public education does *not* enable the children of the poor to get a start in life equal to that enjoyed by their more advantaged peers. They begin school at a disadvantage, and they emerge twelve years later as disadvantaged as when they began. It is little wonder, then, that *EEO* was perceived by most observers as a dagger pointed at the heart of the Jeffersonian ideal of the common school.

But in addition to the political and philosophical importance of this overriding conclusion, *EEO* directly challenged many of the cherished beliefs of school administrators. It suggested that the resources that administrators commonly believed to be important in improving the quality of education—good buildings, extensive libraries, well-designed curricula, and highly trained teachers, for example—had little to do with improving student learning.

If the research on school effects had stopped in 1966 with the publication of *EEO*, Superintendent Bender would have little to concern himself about. Ms. Loobies and her crew of teachers could transfer wherever they wanted. Whether they went to Left Bank or Steinbeck would make little difference to the achievement of the children at either school.

There is a potentially important caveat to this, however. Note that the sixth conclusion on the list indicates that although highly trained and experienced teachers had only a small effect on student achievement, Coleman also found that this effect was somewhat larger where minority and poor children were concerned. Since Steinbeck is populated with such children, teacher assignments to that school might make a difference.

Numerous criticisms of the report surfaced immediately. These tended to be conceptual and methodological in nature. For example, because there had been widespread suspicion of congressional motives, many school districts failed to cooperate with the researchers or provided patently fraudulent data (Jencks,

1972). Thus, although the study contained usable data from a massive sample of respondents (approximately 570,000 students in grades 1, 3, 6, 9, and 12 and 67,000 teachers), there was much suspicion that the sample was seriously biased.

Similarly, considerable attention was focused on a methodological strategy used by the *EEO* researchers. Without delving into the technical details, they had relied heavily on multiple regression procedures to analyze their data. In doing so, they had chosen to enter family background into their equations first, on the grounds that children's family circumstances are temporally prior to any possible effect of school resources. In doing so, however, they necessarily reduced their estimates of the effects of those resources. (This happens because family background is positively correlated with measures of school quality; high-status parents tend to send their children to well-equipped and well-staffed schools. Entering family background first reduced estimates of the effects of school resources on achievement.)

Regardless of such criticisms, with conclusions as shattering as Coleman's, research did not stop. Indeed, the study of school effects became a growth industry in academe. Initially, most of this research adopted a strategy similar to that of *EEO*, a strategy that has come to be termed "input-output analysis."

Input-Output Research on Factors Related to Student Achievement

Part of the work that followed *EEO* immediately consisted of reanalyses of the data collected for that study. Perhaps the most thorough attempt to test Coleman's conclusions by using his own data appeared under the title *On Equality of Educational Opportunity*, edited by Mosteller and Moynihan (1972). In that volume a group of researchers, responding to the many criticisms leveled at *EEO*, attempted to test his findings by carrying out analyses thought to be more adequate than those used in the original report. With relatively minor exceptions, Coleman's results withstood these tests. Variations in school resources seemed to make little difference in student achievement.

In the meantime, numerous researchers began carrying out original investigations of the issues raised by *EEO*. This initial wave of studies were generally modeled on the procedures used in *EEO* and came to be termed "input-output" or "production function" analyses. Essentially, these procedures treated the school as a "black box"—an entity whose workings were not understood or could not be studied directly. Instead, researchers measured various input factors, such as teacher qualifications, expenditures per pupil, and class size, and then related these measures to measures of student outcomes (usually standardized test scores), while holding constant the effects of various confounding variables such as family background and pupil ability. The black box metaphor was apt; the processes by which schools used these inputs to produce test scores remained unknown.

Input-output research focused most frequently on those resources over which administrators might exercise some control. These included expenditures per pupil, various attributes of school personnel, class size, pupil mix, instructional time, and physical facilities.

Expenditures per Pupil

For many years a common assertion advanced by educators was that if a local community, the state, or the national government would provide additional funds for schools, improved student learning would result. If input-output research taught us anything, it was that there is no necessary truth to this assertion. Administrators' pleas for more funds on these grounds are now treated with a healthy dose of skepticism by the public. The problem is obvious. Money is used to purchase various goods and services for schools. These goods and services are then combined in complex ways to produce student learning. However, money can be spent foolishly, and any particular mix of goods and services may be inappropriate for a specific group of pupils (Monk, 1981). Under such conditions, new funding will not improve student achievement. Indeed, more money for schools could lower achievement.

More fundamentally, perhaps, the research on this topic seems to support the conclusion that nearly all U.S. schools are currently operating well beyond the point of diminishing marginal returns (Averech, Carroll, Donaldson, Kiesling, & Pincus, 1972). The notion is that up to some (rather low) level of funding, more money produces more achievement. Beyond that point, however, each additional dollar produces a smaller and smaller increment in achievement. (In fact, it is at least theoretically possible that at some point more money could produce negative increments in learning.) Certainly, the evidence from international studies would suggest that U.S. schools are well into the zone of diminishing marginal returns. In expenditures per pupil we are at or near the top among nations (including the modern industrialized ones), yet we rank much lower in student achievement in virtually all subject areas tested (Lerner, 1982).

Moynihan (1972), in a provocative article on this subject, suggests that the public should be wary of claims by educators for a greater access to the public treasury. Who will benefit? he asks. His answer: teachers. Since salaries and fringe benefits constitute the great bulk of school expenditures, the most likely beneficiaries of increased school spending will be teachers, not pupils. The research provides no compelling reason that simply coming up with more money will have necessarily salutary effects on how much pupils learn.

Clearly, how money is spent is more important than how much is spent. We will look at some of the resources that money can purchase (and some that it cannot) that are commonly thought to make a difference in student learning.

Teacher Characteristics

One of the prominent lines in the input-output studies has been an attempt to identify teacher characteristics that make a difference in pupil learning. For example, do children learn more when they are taught by experienced teachers? Is having a certified teacher better than having an uncertified one? Let us examine four of the more commonly studied teacher characteristics and their effects on achievement: experience, training, certification and tenure, and verbal ability.

Teacher Experience   One way money might be spent is to purchase the services of more experienced teachers, either by recruiting them directly when a vacancy occurs or by structuring a district's salary schedule so as to retain those who might otherwise depart. Does teacher experience have a positive effect on student performance?

The research tends to suggest that it does, though its effects are quite small (Bridge, Judd, & Moock, 1979; Glasman & Biniaminov, 1981; Guthrie, 1970). This apparently small effect of experience is troublesome for at least two reasons. First, it is counterintuitive. That is, conventional wisdom among school administrators is that teachers get better at their work as they gain experience. Indeed, common sense tells us that this is true of most complex jobs, and teaching is certainly a complex job. Second, if the finding is correct, it calls into question a major factor in determining teacher salaries. It suggests that the commonly used salary schedule, heavily based on experience, is economically irrational. It amounts to paying more for a largely irrelevant characteristic.

The small effect of experience may even be inflated beyond its true value. Spady (1973) has suggested that teachers use their seniority to transfer to positions in "better" schools, ones with more able pupils. Since these pupils do better on tests, more experienced teachers seem to be more effective when in fact they are not. On the other hand, Murnane's (1975) analysis suggests that the relationship between experience and pupil achievement is curvilinear. That is, over the first two or three years, increased experience results in higher achievement. From that point on, however, the relationship levels off. If this were true, the experience-achievement relationship would be quite small overall. It is also possible that more effective teachers leave their jobs to take positions outside of education or to take administrative positions in schools. This would also explain the relatively weak association between the two variables. In any case, the general conclusion of studies that have examined the effect of teacher experience on student learning has been that more experienced teachers are only marginally more effective than their less experienced colleagues.

Teacher Training   The other important variable in determining most teachers' salaries is their level of formal education. Does postgraduate education improve teachers' classroom performance in such a way as to increase student achievement? Should Superintendent Bender be concerned about the general lack of such training among Dolmen's staff?

Again, the voluminous research on this matter would seem to indicate that, at best, the effect of advanced training is very modest. For example, Glasman and Biniaminov (1981), Guthrie (1970), Robbins (1975), and a large study carried out by the New York State Education Department (1972) all concluded that there is a small positive effect from advanced training. However, in some studies, the possession of a master's degree seemed to have a negative effect on achievement. Bridge et al. (1979) and Murnane (1980, cited in Educational Research Service, 1983) both reported negative effects from holding an advanced degree.

In this regard, Hanushek (1970) has suggested that it is not holding a degree but the recency of taking advanced work that is important. His analysis indicated that pupil achievement was higher in classrooms where teachers were currently or had recently enrolled in graduate-level courses. Perhaps "recency" is simply a proxy variable for a teacher's commitment to the profession and indicates an interest in trying to improve (Spady, 1973). It is this interest and commitment, then, that characterizes effective teachers, rather than the mere possession of some arbitrary number of credit hours or an advanced degree. In any case, as with experience, there is some indication that school districts are paying teachers on the basis of a generally irrelevant characteristic.

Teacher Certification and Tenure   Some of the teachers at Dolmen lack permanent certification; others are tenured. Do these qualities make a difference? As one might expect from the findings on experience, tenure itself is unrelated to student achievement. Similarly, being certified to teach seems to make no difference in how much students learn (Bridge et al., 1979). At least one study, in fact, reported a negative correlation between these teacher attributes and learning. One must be careful to understand what is being said here, however. It is not, for example, that a person who has never studied chemistry is competent to teach that subject. Rather, given adequate subject matter knowledge, college-level training as a teacher adds no additional increment to a person's capacity to teach that subject. Such findings, of course, are serious indictments of the nature of teacher training courses in colleges and universities.

Teacher Verbal Ability   One of the significant findings in the *EEO* study was that the higher a teacher scored on a test of verbal skill, the higher that teacher's students achieved. Though this correlation is not a large one, in light of the general lack of relationship between other teacher attributes and student learning it has assumed considerable importance. This relationship has continued to turn up since Coleman's original study (Bridge et al., 1979; Glasman & Biniaminov, 1981).

It seems likely that teachers' scores on a test of verbal ability are simply substitutes for some underlying teacher trait that affects their instructional abilities. For example, it is possible that high-scoring persons are characterized by more complex cognitive structures—structures that enable them to be more resourceful, flexible, and creative in managing the rapid ebb and flow of events in the classroom. Several authors (e.g., Harrison, 1976) have advanced this sort of interpretation. It is also important to note that teacher verbal ability may be more important in the case of low-achieving students.

Regarding teachers' mental abilities, it is also worth noting that college education majors are among the lowest-scoring groups on the SAT. Further, many college students who train to be teachers never actually enter the profession; they go into other lines of work after finishing their schooling. Those who do this tend to be among the higher-scoring education majors. Thus, on average, those who actually enter the classroom are less academically talented. Finally, many persons quit teaching during the first five years on the job. These people who leave the profession also tend, on average, to have earned higher scores on the SAT than those who remain. The net result of this selective attrition, then, is that the corps of experienced teachers in the schools is considerably less talented academically than the original group that entered college (Vance & Schlechty, 1982).

Obviously, simply possessing much of the kind of talent measured by the SAT does not ensure that a person will be an effective teacher. On the other hand, and given the findings of the input-output studies, it should be a matter of concern that teachers seem to be generally lacking in this regard. Mr. Bender must consider the possibility that Dolmen's teachers will have a deleterious effect on pupil learning and that this may especially be the case for the children at Steinbeck.

Class Size

Obviously, one method of expending educational funds is to hire additional teachers and thereby reduce the average size of a district's classes. One of the more controversial series of studies in recent years has concerned the effects of class size on student achievement. For a long time it was generally believed that small classes were better in that pupils learned more. This belief was also among those called into question by the spate of studies that followed *EEO*.

The Educational Research Service has published an extensive review of those studies (1978). That review drew several conclusions important to school administrators. Among these were the following:

There is no support for the notion of an "optimum" class size. Effective class size is a function of a number of factors, such as subject area and availability of learning material.

Within the common range of twenty-five to thirty-four pupils, class size has no decisive impact on achievement.

However, there is some evidence that for instruction in reading and math in the early primary grades, smaller classes do lead to improved achievement.

There is some evidence that for low achievers and lower-SES pupils, smaller classes may help.

No benefits are likely to occur if teachers continue to use the same teaching strategies that they use for larger classes.

Many teachers, when given smaller classes, continue to use the same strategies that they used with larger classes. For example, no greater individualization of instruction seems to occur.

Many of these generalizations were challenged in 1978 with the publication of Glass and Smith's "meta-analysis" of the class size research. These researchers concluded that there was a strong negative relationship between class size and student achievement and that this relationship did not vary much with subject matter, pupil intelligence, or other demographic characteristics. They estimated that a student who would score at the 83rd percentile on an achievement test when taught *individually* would score at the 50th percentile if taught the same subject in a class of forty. But no school district could afford to hire a teacher for each student. In the more practical range, between twenty and forty pupils, they estimated that a student would gain 6 percentile points in the smaller class. Only when class size went substantially below twenty did large benefits begin to show up (Glass & Smith, 1978).

At this point, then, conclusions regarding class size must be tentative. It does appear, however, that the sorts of marginal reductions contemplated by many school administrators (who often cite Glass and Smith in justification) are unlikely to produce substantial gains in measured achievement. This is particularly true if the contemplated reductions are not accompanied by effective in-service training designed to change teachers' instructional strategies to ones that would take advantage of the proposed reduction.

Pupil Mix

One of the most important findings in *EEO* was that the social composition of the school had a relatively strong effect on student achievement. That is, Coleman's analyses suggested that if lower-class children went to schools populated primarily by the middle class, the achievement of the former would be higher than if they went to schools populated primarily with others like themselves. This is commonly referred to as a "contextual effect."

This finding had a considerable influence on public policy; it provided the evidence that undergirded the busing strategy to achieve racial integration, for example. However, it was also important because it drew attention to a kind of resource available to administrators that had been overlooked, one that offered the hope of making an "end run" around the generally negative findings concerning other school resources. That is, it might be possible to assign students in such a way as to improve achievement when simply putting more money into schools attended by lower-class and minority students seemed not to work. Perhaps Superintendent Bender could use students themselves to offset any adverse effects caused by Dolmen's teachers and its principal.

Research on pupil mix has focused primarily on either student achievement or student aspirations for further education as the principal outcomes of interest. In general, studies carried out in the 1960s and early 1970s tended to support the idea that the social context of the school (the social-class composition or the academic talent of its student body) had an effect on both achievement and aspirations (see, for example, Wilson, 1967; Herriot & St. John, 1966). More recently there has been a growing skepticism that such effects are *substantively* significant, even when they are found to be *statistically* significant. For example, Hauser, Sewell, and Alwin (1976) and Anderson, Haller, and Smorodin (1976), in relatively large-scale studies, failed to uncover evidence of substantial contextual effects on achievement or aspirations. These conflicting findings may result at least in part from the virtually intractable methodological problems involved in trying to disentangle home, school, classroom, instructional group, and individual level effects.

Despite these problems, there is some recent evidence that the average academic ability (and perhaps the average social class) of the students in a school has an independent (albeit modest) effect on individual achievement (Henderson, Mieszkowski, & Sauvageau, 1978; Summers & Wolfe, 1977; Winkler, 1975; Murnane, 1983a).

Perhaps the most sensible conclusion for a practicing administrator such as Bender, faced with the need to redraw school attendance areas, is to construct the new boundaries of Left Bank and Steinbeck in such a way so as to take advantage of any possible contextual effects. Bender might, for example, consider sending Dolmen's low-achieving students to Left Bank. He should probably not, however, expect large increments in their achievement as a consequence of doing so. We shall have more to say about this shortly.

School Facilities and Supplies

With only a few exceptions (typically among the earlier studies, e.g., Guthrie, 1970), researchers have been unable to demonstrate significant relationships between the quality or quantity of physical materials and pupil achievement. For instance, the age of school buildings, the size of school libraries, the number of science laboratories, and supplies expenditures per pupil all seem to have no appreciable effect on how much students learn (Murnane, 1983b). These findings do not, of course, justify dilapidated buildings and minuscule libraries. Nor are they compelling arguments for keeping Dolmen open. They do tell us, however, that modern, pleasant, and well-equipped schools must be justified on grounds other than pupil achievement.

Time on Task

During the last decade there has been a growing belief that time itself may be a "potent path for policy" (Wiley, 1976). That is, educators (and the public) have been made aware of the apparently important effects that learning time itself can have on school achievement. Students who spend more time "on task"—that is, involved in academic work—learn more. It is hard to argue against such notions; clearly, few students will learn geometry if they never study the subject. This belief has led many to call for longer school years, more hours per day in school, and more time spent on academic subjects. It is not entirely clear, however, that such simplistic strategies will have the effects their proponents envision.

In part the call for more time spent at academic tasks is the result of studies that document the relatively small amount of time currently spent in those pursuits. For example, Fisher (cited in ERS, 1983) found that instructional activities took up about three hours of a five-hour school day at the second-grade level and about four hours of a six-hour day at the fifth-grade level. Another hour was devoted to nonacademic subjects such as music and art. Perhaps the most surprising finding was that at least forty-five minutes of each day was given over to entirely noninstructional activities such as transitions between lessons, house-keeping, and simply waiting for something to happen.

In part, however, the appeal of the time-on-task research appears to result from its seemingly clear administrative applications. Administrators (and school boards) can manipulate the length of the school year and the length of the school day relatively easily. It seemed that time was a resource that offered an easy and direct way to influence pupil achievement. As research has accumulated, however, the results of such manipulations have become less clear.

Regarding the length of the school year, Bridge et al. (1979) concluded that, despite nonsignificant results in some studies, lengthier school years result in higher achievement. It is unknown, however, how great an increase would be required to effect substantial increments in learning. It is also unknown how extensive an increase would be permitted by the public, especially given that any increase will almost certainly require a corresponding increment in salaries and other operating costs.

Heyns (1978) contrasted rates of pupil learning while the school year is in progress with the same rates when they are closed for the summer. Two of her findings are significant for our purposes. First, time in school had a substantial positive effect on learning. Perhaps even more important, she found that rate of summer learning is much more dependent on family background; poor and minority children fall behind much more rapidly than other children when they are out of school than when they are in it. Heyns concluded that while the school has been unable to attain absolute equality of achievement between social classes and races, it makes a significant contribution to doing so.

Alternatively, the school day can be lengthened beyond its current six-hour average. Stallings and Kaskowitz (1974) and Gilbert and Price (1981), among others, have shown that longer days are positively correlated with student learning. The Gilbert and Price study in particular showed that a quite substantial increase in time (up to three hours) resulted in sharp improvements not only in test scores but also in better attendance and greater participation in school activities. On the other hand, Karweit (1976) found only very modest effects on achievement when the amount of instructional time was varied within more typical limits. Further, these effects seem to vary according to the subject matter being taught (Daniels & Haller, 1981).

But school time is not necessarily an accurate measure of effective learning time. For this reason, most attention has been given to time-on-task studies. Typically, these studies attempt to measure the amount of time students are actively engaged in learning. Measuring time on task usually requires that classroom observers make judgments about when students are actually on task and when they are daydreaming, doodling, or simply feigning interest in lessons. Needless to say, such judgments are difficult to make.

Reviewing a large number of the time-on-task studies, Borg (1980) concluded that there were consistent positive relations between time on task and student achievement. However, Karweit (1983), in another review, concluded that there was considerable doubt about the size of these relations and how generalizable they are. As Karweit notes, effects will clearly depend not simply on the amount of time students are engaged in learning but on what they are doing. Learning occurs when the student is engaged in instruction that is *appropriate* for him or her.

It is this focus on instructional activities, and on the more microscopic study of what is actually going on in classrooms, that helps to distinguish the effective schools research from the input-output research. We turn to this literature next.

The Effective Schools Research

In contrast to the "black box" approach that has characterized much of the input-output research, the effective schools movement has taken a somewhat different approach to the study of school effects. Very often this approach has been characterized by an attempt to identify groups of effective and ineffective schools and then to examine in detail the inner workings of the schools in each group. In essence, instead of trying to see if various resources affect learning, the researchers have tried to identify differences in the ways that resources are actually used in schools that are known to be effective and ineffective with the same kinds of pupils. Further, they have tried to trace the flow of resources from the district level to the individual child. It is clear that important resource allocation decisions are made at each level of the organizational hierarchy and that decisions made at one level affect those made at the next (Monk, 1981).

It is difficult to summarize this diverse research, in part because it is hard to compare the results of one study with those of another. This is a consequence of the methodology such work requires—close inspection, observation, and impressionistic accounts of dynamic processes within a small number of schools, rather than the highly quantified, statistically oriented, static, and large-sample methodologies that characterize input-output work. Nevertheless, certain generalizations seem to be emerging (ERS, 1983; Cohen, 1983). These concern teachers and teaching, school management, and school climate.

Teachers and Teaching

Some of the same teacher characteristics that showed up as having positive effects on student learning in the input-output literature also appeared in the effective schools research. For example, teachers with higher verbal scores appear to be more effective; more important, effective staffs were characterized by particular actions and beliefs.

One of the more frequent findings has been that effective teachers hold high expectations for their students and assume that students will meet those expectations. They create a businesslike, task-oriented environment and hold students accountable for their work (Rosenshine, 1979). They minimize time spent in non-learning activities, and they visually monitor their classes, moving about the room frequently (Cohen, 1983). Brophy (1982) depicts these teachers as well organized, seldom having to stop to find materials or not knowing what is to happen next. They are consistent in disciplining students. They do *not* rely heavily on highly differentiated grouping; the numbers of such groups is small, and less time is spent working with them (ERS, 1983).

School Management

The effective schools research has consistently pointed to the leadership behavior of principals as critical to school success. Principals of effective schools were viewed as much more assertive with regard to many aspects of their roles than principals in less effective schools. For example, with regard to the instructional program, they spent much more time in classrooms, they provided frequent and constructive feedback to teachers, they installed in-service programs aimed at improving instructional techniques, and they worked at ensuring that curricula were implemented as intended and that these curricula were articulated across grade levels (ERS, 1983; Greenfield, 1982; Bossart et al., 1982).

Cohen (1983) suggests that another important characteristic of effective schools that has emerged from the research is that they are tightly coupled. That is, schoolwide goals, instructional objectives for each grade level, instructional activities within each classroom, and methods of pupil assessment are all carefully designed to fit together. Thus "students are exposed to a well-ordered and focused curriculum, and the instructional efforts of teachers . . . are consistent and cumulative" (p. 30). Achieving this tight coupling is an important administrative responsibility; indeed, administrators are the only ones who are able to achieve it.

School Climate

The notion of a school climate or ethos is particularly nebulous, yet much of the effective schools research (e.g., Coleman, Hoffer, & Kilgore, 1981; Brookover et al., 1979; Rutter, Maughan, Mortemore, & Ouston, 1979) points to the existence of such a climate. It is the notion of a shared culture, a set of values and expectations, that characterizes good schools. This climate seems to contain several elements. In part, these are academic in nature—they consist of the shared belief that all students can learn regardless of their social background, that academic matters are important, and that hard work is necessary to achieve success. In part, they are social. Effective schools are characterized by a kind of moral order (Grant, 1982) that involves respect for individual rights, trust of people in authority, and willingness on the part of both staff and students to enforce standards of appropriate conduct.

As with the input-output research, the effective schools literature is not without its problems and its detractors. One of the most common criticisms has been that its definition of *effective* is overly narrow—typically, it has meant schools with higher than expected standardized test results. Critics note that schools are judged on numerous criteria besides test scores, such as their ability to meet administrative, social, and emotional goals. Even assuming the adequacy of that criterion, it is often assessed in different ways, making comparisons across studies difficult. Further, standardized tests have often been restricted to a few subjects and a few grade levels, particularly to the elementary grades. Thus generalizations to other subjects and higher grades are difficult to make (Rowan, Bossart, & Dwyer, 1983).

One of the most serious conceptual problems has been researchers' inability to create convincingly a causal ordering of their variables. That is, virtually all of the characteristics of effective schools discussed here could be the consequences of higher achievement, not the causes of it. For example, teachers may have high expectations for their students because those students do well on tests. Similarly, a community that takes a strong interest in education may demand tighter coupling in its schools' curricula and be made up of parents who expect their children to achieve. In that case, both coupling and achievement could be consequences of an external factor, parental interest.

But despite these problems, what is most striking about the research results found in the effective schools literature is how commonsensical they are. With the possible exception of the findings regarding individualization (that less may be better), the behaviors and beliefs of teachers, administrators, and students found to distinguish good schools from bad ones are the stuff that any thoughtful layperson might recommend.

However, to say that these findings are commonsensical is not to say that the behaviors and beliefs found to be important are commonplace. Indeed, it is necessary to recognize just how variable schools are in these regards. For example, consider active teaching (the idea that students learn best when teachers spend as much time as is possible directly teaching a planned sequence of lessons). One researcher found that instruction in reading comprehension averaged ten minutes a day in some elementary classrooms and nearly fifty minutes in others (ERS, 1983). It should hardly surprise us if pupils in the former classrooms are less able readers than those in the latter.

Similarly, to say that good schools evidence a close articulation of goals, instructional programs, teaching techniques, and pupil evaluation (that is, that they are tightly coupled) is in some sense to state the obvious. How can a school be good if it claims certain goals, institutes programs that do not serve those goals, adopts teaching techniques that are inappropriate to those programs, and then tests student learning on things not taught? But it seems that many schools operate exactly that way, if we are to believe the literature on the subject (see, for example, Weick, 1976; Bidwell, 1965). Indeed, to call for tighter coupling is, in effect, to call for greater school bureaucratization and less teacher autonomy—anathema to many educators.

Implications of the Input-Output and Effective Schools Research

Regardless of the problems inherent in both the input-output and effective schools research, these bodies of literature are what current practitioners have to go on. Does this research provide any guidance to people in Bob Bender's position? We believe that it does.

Consider the broad outline of Bender's problem: He has too many teachers, some of whom he suspects to be incompetent; he has an extra principal, of whose incompetence he is convinced; he has two underutilized schools, one serving a middle-class neighborhood and one serving disadvantaged children; the staff and program of the former school are adequate and those of the latter are exceptional; and children at both schools are achieving well, especially those at the second, considering their circumstance. Finally, the pupils at the school to be closed come from a mix of socioeconomic backgrounds, and they seem not to have been succeeding well.

One of the first things Bender might recognize is that while El Dorado will almost certainly suffer some reduction in its state aid in the near future, that reduction should not adversely affect its children's academic achievement. If Bender can successfully manage this decline, if he can ensure that essential resources continue to be secured and are properly deployed, there is no reason to expect pupil learning to diminish. El Dorado, like virtually all U.S. public schools, is almost certainly operating well beyond its point of diminishing marginal returns.

Suppose now that he decides to maintain and strengthen the program at Steinbeck and is willing to let Left Bank take the brunt of any reduction in resources. (We will provide a rationale for this decision later.) How might he accomplish this?

His first action must be to ensure that Kathryn Loobies is transferred to Left Bank as an assistant principal or teacher. This probably means that he will face a grievance. Nevertheless, the research we have reviewed in this chapter is virtually unanimous that a school's principal is critical to its success. Assuming that his evaluation of her is correct—that she has failed to demonstrate adequate leadership—he would be remiss to let her take over the management of either school, perhaps especially that of Steinbeck.

Next he might consider the possibility that his district's declining enrollment offers him the chance to relieve it immediately of the services of its less competent staff. Here he will probably be restricted to releasing untenured faculty. Since Loobies's evaluations of all of her teachers have been generally positive, it is almost certain that Bender will be unable to move against those with tenure. (This is not to suggest that incompetent tenured teachers be retained, only that dismissing them cannot be done without time and planning; see Chapter 8.)

In the case of the untenured, Bender may properly consider their "paper" qualifications as well as their formal evaluations. In this regard, undergraduate records, test scores, and recency of graduate training are all relevant to his decision. As we have seen, each of these shows a small but consistent relation with student achievement and hence is a justifiable criterion to use in deciding on dismissals. Obviously, these cannot be the only considerations; they do, however, deserve his attention.

Next Bender might consider his district's unofficial policy regarding class size. Currently all grades at all three schools are kept in the neighborhood of twenty-six pupils. This policy is inconsistent with the research we have reviewed in two respects. First, the research suggests that classes can be somewhat larger or smaller without affecting student learning. Second, it also suggests that small classes are more efficacious in the lowest grades and with underachieving students.

Given these necessarily tentative conclusions, it would be appropriate for Bender not to increase the staff at Left Bank in proportion to the number of Dolmen's children that it absorbs, at least in grades 4 to 6. If the upper-grade classrooms at that school climb from twenty-six per class to slightly over thirty, little of consequence for achievement is likely to result—though certainly the teachers concerned will experience some adverse consequences. If he adopts this strategy, he may be able to reduce the size of the primary grades at Steinbeck to below twenty, with particularly beneficial results for the disadvantaged pupils at that school.

It should also be remembered that several studies indicate that merely reducing class size would have no desirable effects unless teachers adapted their instructional strategies to take advantage of their new circumstances. This suggests a use for some of the money the district will save with the closing of Dolmen. That is, it would be important for the school system to provide the affected teachers at Steinbeck with appropriate in-service training in pedagogical techniques designed for small classes.

In deciding where to assign Dolmen's staff, the research also suggests that disadvantaged students especially will benefit from having teachers with high verbal scores, good undergraduate records, recent graduate training, and greater experience. Bender should probably consider these teacher characteristics in making his assignment decisions. Again, this is not to suggest that these are the only significant teacher attributes, nor the most important. It is simply to suggest that they are relevant. All other things being equal, Steinbeck's children are most likely to benefit from having such teachers.

Finally, Dolmen's pupils will need to be divided up between the two remaining buildings. How should this be done? The simplest method, of course, is to draw an attendance boundary somewhere in the middle ground between Left Bank and Steinbeck and let the children go to the closer school. There is much to recommend this strategy, especially since the research regarding pupil mix suggests two conflicting procedures.

On the one hand, some studies suggest that disadvantaged students benefit from going to school with their more advantaged peers. This research recommends that the boundary be drawn in such a way as to send such pupils to Left Bank. Steinbeck is contraindicated by such studies. "Gerrymandering" Dolmen's present attendance area in order to obtain this result may be possible, if it contains identifiable socioeconomic neighborhoods. On the other hand, the research also suggests that disadvantaged pupils especially would benefit from the sort of strong, basics-oriented program offered at Steinbeck. On balance, we believe that the latter choice would be better; the contextual effects research seems to us to be much more problematic than the effective schools research on this matter.

The foregoing discussion is not meant to suggest the correct solution to Bender's problem. Nor is it intended to be an exhaustive consideration of the issues involved. Rather it is meant to illustrate one way of applying research results to a practical problem. You may have noticed that we have avoided discussing one critically important matter: We simply took the position that the disadvantaged students at Steinbeck were deserving of the bulk of the resources released by the closing of Dolmen. But couldn't a strong argument be made that those resources should go to the advantaged students at Left Bank?

Obviously, the answer to this question is yes. In the last part of this chapter we will examine competing rationales that underlie a choice such as this. Before we do so, however, we need to turn to some of the legal issues involved in school resource allocation decisions.

Legal Aspects of Resource Allocation

You may recall that Bob Bender's trouble began with the need to close a school, and the need to close a school resulted from a loss of state revenues as the consequence of court-motivated school finance reform. How did this happen? We will discuss briefly where the money for public education comes from and some of the legal questions that arise in its distribution. The kind of problem Bender faces is not uncommon, and it is likely to become more common in the decade ahead. It had its roots in a legal controversy that will be played out in numerous states, a controversy that pits two important values—equality of opportunity and local control—against each other. It is important for school administrators like Bender to understand this issue.

Funds for public schools come from three main sources. The first and usually the largest source of funds is local property taxes. Generally, school boards have the power to tax property in their districts in order to raise revenue for public schools. This power is often regulated, to some degree, by state governments. Moreover, in many school districts, the district's budget must be approved by the voters by direct referendum. In other cases, school district budgets come from municipal or county resources, and their approval requires the participation of the municipal or county governments. Thus the power to set budgets and to tax property is local, exercised by school boards, sometimes in conjunction with local voters or with local governments.

The second source of funds is the state government. In the typical district in the typical state, state funds make up a smaller portion of district funds than that generated locally. There is, however, considerable variation both within and between states. Each state has a funding formula that governs what a given district will receive. These formulas are sensitive to a large variety of factors. Such factors include the property wealth of the local district, the number of its students, its transportation needs, and the number of students in high-cost programs. Generally, some state funds go to each district, no matter how affluent.

The third source of funds, and the smallest, is the federal government. Federal funds generally make up less than 10 percent of a district's budget. Moreover, they are often targeted to meet specific needs identified at the federal level. Some funds go to districts heavily affected by government facilities. Some funds have been appropriated to assist with desegregation efforts. And funds have been appropriated for the educational needs of disadvantaged students.

Since property wealth varies greatly between districts, the ability of a district to pay for the education of its children through local property taxes also varies considerably. Such differences are offset somewhat by state funds. States usually attempt to distribute their funds disproportionately to low-wealth districts. However, state attempts at equalization are not sufficient to offset differences in fiscal capacity between districts. Wealthy districts are able to raise more money for the education of their children than poor districts, and they usually do so.

The figures in Table 5.1 for New York (excluding New York City) can serve to illustrate the magnitude of the problem. The table compares per-pupil expenditures, state aid, and income per pupil for districts in the 2nd and 9th deciles in per-pupil expenditures in New York. (General fund expenditures do not include such things as capital or transportation costs. Therefore, they do not provide the full story about per-pupil expenditures. On the other hand, they are a good measure of the funds directly expended for a child's education.) It shows that districts in the 2nd decile spend substantially less per pupil than districts in the 9th decile, despite the fact that state aid to these districts is higher. In short, state aid tends to be equalizing so far as per-pupil expenditures is concerned, but by no means does it lead to equal expenditures. It also shows that the per-pupil income in the 9th decile districts is much higher than in the 2nd decile districts and that 9th decile districts have higher tax rates. The citizens of 9th decile districts are more able to pay. Depending on one's political philosophy, one can see in these facts either that poor districts are unfairly limited in their ability to raise funds for education in comparison with more affluent districts or that the citizens of poorer districts have less preference for education than those of wealthier districts.

This discrepancy in the ability of districts to raise funds for education raises some obvious questions of fairness. If we believe in equality of opportunity, is it fair to allow the money spent on a child's education to vary with the property values or personal incomes in the district where the child happens to live? Does not equal opportunity require equal funding to be available for each child's education?

TABLE 5.1

ANALYSIS OF SCHOOL FINANCES, NEW YORK STATE SCHOOL DISTRICTS, 1982–1983

Districts	General Fund Expenditures per Student*($)	State Aid per Student ($)	Income per Student ($)	Tax Rate per $1,000 ($)
2nd decile	2,819	1,791	24,608	15.20
9th decile	4,471	1,384	51,861	26.80

*Excludes federal funds
SOURCE: New York State Education Department, 1984, *Analysis of School Finances: New York State School Districts, 1982–83*, Albany, NY, p. 7.

One can also see in these figures that the problem of resource allocation with which Bob Bender has been struggling in his district is writ large in the finances of the state. The ethical concepts we shall explore in the next section of this chapter apply to this larger problem as well as to Bender's.

Before we begin to discuss the legal aspects of this question, we should note that it interacts with another, the issue of local control. It has generally been held that local control of education is an important value to Americans. For example, local control permits people to adapt the education of their district to the particular need of their children, and it makes educators more responsive to local concerns. These are presumed to be good things.

Local control has usually been thought to include the right of people to decide how much of their own money they wish to spend on education. People may reasonably and legitimately differ in their preferences for the quality or quantity of the education they wish to provide for their children. It is their right to decide such matters for themselves.

It would seem to follow from this that although it may be unfair for the amount of money spent on a child's education to depend on the property wealth of the child's district, it is perfectly reasonable for the amount spent to vary because of the preferences of the people of the district. In a free society, people are permitted to have different values concerning such matters.

This raises some difficult issues about school finance, for it seems that the values associated with equality of opportunity can conflict with those of local autonomy. Equality, it seems, requires that educational revenues come from state sources and not from local taxes. The amount spent on education in a given district should be a function of the wealth of the state as a whole, not the wealth of a particular district. But it is the ability to set budgets and to approve tax rates that constitute local control. To have education funded fully from state sources is to undercut the right of local citizens to decide for themselves how much of their money will go for the education of their children. Thus, having a reasonable opinion about fairness in school finance requires one to balance concerns of equity with concerns of local control. As we shall see, both of these facets of the issue have become legally important.

At the federal level, the lead equity case in school finance is *San Antonio v. Rodriguez*. This case spelled the end of attempts to have school finance reformed by federal courts. The Supreme Court overturned a lower court decision, which held that the Texas system for financing public education was unconstitutional. The lower court had ruled that Texas had discriminated against the residents of property-poor districts and was thus in violation of the equal protection clause of the U.S. Constitution.

The case turns largely on the standard of review to be applied. Cases involving claims of discrimination may be judged using the very demanding standard of "strict scrutiny" or the more relaxed "rational relationship" standard. Strict scrutiny requires that the statute under question be necessary to serve a compelling state interest. The rational relationship test requires that the statute have a rational relationship to a legitimate state interest.

To have the strict scrutiny standard applied, it must be shown either that the group disadvantaged by the practice in question is a suspect class or that the right at issue is a fundamental right. A suspect class is a group that has been the victim of a history of discrimination. A fundamental right is a constitutional right or one closely associated with a constitutional right.

The essence of the Court's decision was that the strict scrutiny standard is not appropriately applied to school finance laws, since people living in property-poor districts are not members of a suspect class and education is not a fundamental right. The Texas system for financing education was found to satisfy the weaker test. It had a rational relationship to a legitimate state purpose.

Of greatest interest here is the discussion of education as a fundamental right. The Court understood a fundamental right as one explicitly or implicitly protected by the Constitution. Education is not explicitly mentioned in the Constitution. Is it implicitly protected?

The argument employed by the plaintiffs to show that education is implicitly protected is that education is a presupposition of the meaningful exercise of such rights as voting or free speech. If citizens are ignorant, the right to vote or of free speech is meaningless. Its strong association with these constitutional rights should afford it a high level of judicial protection.

The Court responded with two claims. First, it claimed that the constitutional protection of such rights as free speech or voting is a protection against interference with the exercise of these rights but does not include a guarantee of any particular level of competence to exercise them. In the Court's words:

> *Yet we have never presumed to possess either the ability or the authority to guarantee to the citizenry the most efficient speech or the most informed electoral choice. That these may be desired goals of a system of freedom of expression and of a representative form of government is not to be doubted. These are indeed goals to be pursued by a people whose thoughts and beliefs are freed from governmental interference. But they are not values to be implemented by judicial intrusion into otherwise legitimate state activities.* (San Antonio v. Rodriguez, *p. 1298)*

Second, however, the Court does hold out the prospect that should the poverty of an educational system be sufficiently great to constitute an absolute denial of educational opportunity or of basic minimal skills on which rights are contingent, that might constitute a situation worthy of judicial notice.

> *Whatever merits appealees' argument might have if a state's financing system occasioned an absolute denial of educational opportunities to any of its children, that argument provides no basis for finding an interference with fundamental rights where only relative differences in spending levels are involved and where—as is true in the present case—no charge could be made that the system fails to provide each child with an opportunity to acquire the basic minimal skills necessary for the enjoyment of the rights of speech and of full participation in the political process. (p. 1299)*

In short, variations in the availability of educational resources between the districts of a state are not illegal so long as an absolute deprivation of education does not result. Thus the U.S. Constitution provides no legal remedies for interdistrict inequalities in the distribution of educational resources. It is reasonable to conjecture that the same conceptual framework would be applied to judging intradistrict inequalities. It is unlikely that any constitutional remedies exist for inequalities in the distribution of resources among schools within districts. There are likely to be no significant legal constraints on Bob Bender's decision. There is, however, one noteworthy exception to this point. Should intradistrict inequalities in resources be linked to illegal segregation, that might attract a higher level of judicial attention. Race is a suspect class (see *Hobson v. Hanson,* 1971).

Among several additional reasons for its decision, the Supreme Court noted the value of local autonomy. It observed with approval that "the Texas system of school finance . . . permits and encourages a large measure of participation in and control of each district's schools at the local level" (*San Antonio v. Rodriguez,* p. 1305) and that "the people of Texas may be justified in believing that other systems of school financing, which place more of the financial responsibility in the hands of the state, will result in a comparable lessening of desired local autonomy" (pp. 1306–07). Local autonomy is a value to be weighted against equity in the eyes of the Supreme Court. Some state courts have echoed this view as well (see *Levittown UFSD v. Nyquist*).

Although education is not mentioned in the U.S. Constitution, it is mentioned in most state constitutions. Since *Rodriguez* has been decided, school finance cases have been working their way through many state court systems. The argument that the state's finance system violates the state's equal protection clause was accepted in California (*Serrano v. Priest*) but rejected in New York (where local autonomy was treated as a significant liberty interest; *Levittown v. Nyquist*). In other states, whose state constitutions contain a requirement that the state fund a "thorough and efficient" educational system, issues of school finance have been litigated under the thorough and efficient clause. In the most visible of these cases, *Robinson v. Cahill,* the court struck down New Jersey's system of school finance and mandated the state legislature to create a more acceptable system. Judge Weintraub describes the court's reasoning:

> But we do not doubt that an equal educational opportunity for children was precisely in [the legislative] mind. The mandate that there be maintained and supported "a thorough and efficient system of free public schools for the instruction of all the children in the state between the ages of five and eighteen years" can have no other import. Whether the state acts directly or imposes the role upon local government, the end product must be what the constitution demands. (p. 513)

The round of litigation concerning school finance has focused the attention of state legislatures on questions of equity even in states where no litigation has yet occurred and in states where reform movements have failed in court. Thus it is possible that the result will be a higher level of fiscal equity, even in states whose courts have not required it. On the other hand, when states respond to these issues by equalizing the ability of property-rich and property-poor districts to secure equal revenues for equal tax rates, equality of actual expenditures is not assured unless poor districts are willing to tax themselves at rates equivalent to those of more affluent ones. Taxpayer equity does not necessarily generate equality of educational resources.

In our case, we have suggested that Bob Bender's district, which is property-rich, has lost some state revenues because of a reform movement in the state. Given the philosophical sentiments we shall express in the next section of this chapter, we can only applaud. Bender's problem, however, is how to distribute the resources remaining fairly, given the need to close a school and reassign teachers. We need now to discuss the issues of fairness that he faces.

Ethics of Resource Allocation

Bob Bender's dilemma is first and foremost a question about what is fair. Questions of fairness about how educational resources are allocated are questions of distributive justice. Social institutions determine the distribution of various goods. They affect who gets what. Questions of distributive justice are questions of fairness concerning how social goods are allocated. They concern who is entitled to get what under what conditions.

To view questions of resource allocation in education as questions of distributive justice requires that we think of schools as institutions that distribute important social goods. It is widely believed, for example, that the quality of education one receives or the degree of educational success one experiences makes a considerable difference in life prospects. People who receive a quality education are thought to get better jobs, earn more money, and have more satisfactory lives as a consequence. It is the connection between the distribution of educational resources and such social goods as jobs, income, and status that turns questions of educational resource allocation into questions of distributive justice. Consider how we might structure Bob Bender's difficulty as a problem of fairness.

First, Bender must distribute a scarce resource for which people are in competition. He has a group of teachers and principals who differ significantly in quality. He has not got enough quality staff to go around. Since the resource is scarce and since the groups of students are, in effect, competing for the best teachers and the best principal, Bender must find a fair way to allocate this scarce resource.

If he is to make such a decision reasonably, he will have to justify his choice on the basis of some characteristics of the two schools or their students. He will have to ask whether there are any ways in which they differ that might justify assigning the better staff to one school or the other.

How do the two schools differ? The case suggests that they differ in the following ways: (1) The students at Left Bank are generally from a higher socioeconomic group than those at Steinbeck, and (2) the students at Left Bank are generally more academically capable than those at Steinbeck. To explore the possible relevance of these differences, consider two brief arguments for how they should be taken into account in allocating educational resources.

The Case for Left Bank: Ability to Profit   If a choice must be made about who will get superior educational resources, these resources ought to go to Left Bank. They ought to go to Left Bank because the children at Left Bank are more academically able than the children at Steinbeck and will therefore make more efficient use of these resources. Put another way, a dollar's worth of educational resources (teachers' time, books, etc.) used for Left Bank's pupils will produce more learning than the same dollar spent on Steinbeck's pupils. Hence, the level of educational achievement of the entire school district is raised more than it would be if Steinbeck's children received the resources. To expend resources on these children is to expend them in the way that is most likely to result in the development of people who will become tomorrow's leaders. We are investing in the people who will make the decisions and create the jobs. When we invest in these children, the entire society benefits as a consequence. We should commit our resources to Left Bank because that is where they will do the most good.

The Case for Steinbeck: Educational Need   If a choice has to be made about who will get the superior educational resources, those resources ought to go to Steinbeck. They ought to go to Steinbeck because the children of Steinbeck need them more. These children come from less affluent homes and a less affluent community than the children of Left Bank. If they are academically less talented or ambitious, that is no doubt a consequence of their having been raised under more difficult circumstances. But it is hardly their fault that their parents are less wealthy or less well educated than the parents of the children of Left Bank. If anything, fairness demands that additional resources be committed to these children to help them catch up. Our society is a better and more democratic society when it commits its resources to the people who need them the most. Thus we should commit our resources to Steinbeck because that is where they are needed most.

Note how these arguments differ. No facts are in dispute. Both positions agree that the Steinbeck children are more needy and that the Left Bank children are more academically talented. What is in dispute is the moral relevance of these facts.

Actually, there seem to be two related things at issue. First is the comparative claims that can be made for need and ability to profit as criteria for allocation of resources. Given a choice, do we focus our resources on those who can make the best use of them or on those who have the most need of them?

The second issue is the comparative importance of equity versus efficiency in distributing educational resources. Shall we distribute our educational resources in a way that tends to promote equality, or shall we distribute them so as to promote efficiency?

Two points are important here. First, these two questions obviously have a good deal to do with one another. If we emphasize concerns of equity in resource allocation, we are also likely to emphasize need as a criterion for distributing our resources. One way to make educational outcomes more equal is to concentrate resources on the people who are behind educationally. Likewise, if we are primarily interested in getting the "biggest bang for the buck," we will concentrate our resources on the people who can do the most with them. Thus we will concentrate our resources on those who have the most ability to profit. They will make the best use of our resources.

Second, we should be careful not to pose the problem in an either-or fashion. The issues concern the relative attention to be paid to need and ability to profit or equity and efficiency. No view that attends solely to one side of the equation can be fully adequate. One-sided views have absurd consequences. If we focus entirely on need, we will end up admitting candidates who are least promising into college because they are most in need of education. If we focus entirely on ability to profit, we will end up expelling the least able students from elementary school on grounds that others can learn more rapidly from our instruction. No reasonable view can have such consequences. Indeed, one way to test theories of resource allocation is to see whether, in some cases, they have bizarre results. Reasonable views, however, will tell us how to balance need with ability to profit and equity with efficiency.

How, then, should we think about how to balance these concerns in resource allocation? To address these issues, we will sketch two general viewpoints about distributive justice and show how they might be applied to problems of allocating educational resources generally and to Bob Bender's dilemma particularly.

Any theory of distributive justice has to answer at least two questions. The first concerns what is being distributed. Societies distribute all sorts of things: cars, dollars, Ping-Pong tables, and driver's licenses. To develop a coherent view of distributive justice, a theory must take a position on what sorts of things fundamentally matter. Some order must be imposed on the plethora of goods and services that societies distribute. We need to discover a class of basic goods to attend to. Second, a theory of distributive justice must have a view about what counts as a just distribution of that class of basic goods.

Utilitarianism

The first view we wish to describe is utilitarianism (see Bentham, 1961; Smart & Williams, 1973). Utilitarianism's answer to these two questions is alarmingly simple. We should fundamentally be concerned with the distribution of happiness, and the most just society is the society that produces the greatest happiness for the greatest number of people.

Why happiness? Utilitarians are interested in happiness because they believe happiness to be the basic good and the goal (together with the avoidance of pain) at which all human action aims. Other social goods (such as money or cars) have value because of the happiness they produce. Happiness is the lowest (or perhaps highest) common denominator of distributive justice. If we can determine the effects of social institutions on human happiness, we can thereby measure their worth.

Just institutions are ones that maximize the good. Utilitarians generally refer to their measure of social welfare as the "average utility." The average utility of a given society is determined by summing the total happiness of the members of that society, subtracting the total pain of its members, and dividing by the number of persons in that society:

$$\text{Average utility} = \frac{H_{(n)} - P_{(n)}}{N}$$

Happiness is not an easy thing to measure. After a few rather futile attempts to develop a "hedonist calculus" (Bentham, 1961), utilitarians have generally preferred to look at indirect measures. For example, if one assumes that the amount people are willing to spend for something is a reflection of the satisfaction it would bring them, it becomes possible to treat wealth as a surrogate for happiness and the gross national product as a surrogate for the average utility. Modern-day utilitarians are likely to look at the production and distribution of wealth rather than happiness.

Given this point of view, utilitarians are also likely to see just institutions as those that tend to maximize production of goods and services. This is not to say that they do not value social institutions that enhance freedom or equality. It is to say that they value them as means to an efficient and productive society. They maximize the prospects that as many of us will get as much of what we want as is possible.

Utilitarianism has a number of implications for the distribution of educational resources. First, as noted, utilitarians value equality of opportunity. They understand it as a means of productive efficiency. A productive society requires the development of the productive capacity of its members. People are a form of capital. Education is an investment in human capital. Just as any rational business person will invest his or her resources in the most productive way available, educators should invest educational resources where they will achieve the maximum return on investment.

To use irrelevant characteristics such as race, sex, or national origin as criteria for deciding who is to get what educational resource is to invest inefficiently. A decision to make available some educational resource on the basis of race, for example, is one to neglect to develop the productive capacity of the able members of the group discriminated against and, instead, to invest in development of the capacities of members of the favored group, some of whom are less able to make productive use of the resource in question. This is analogous to a business person who purchases a machine that costs more but produces less than another because he or she prefers its color.

This view of equality of educational opportunity does not require that we distribute educational resources equally. That is, it does not require that everyone get the same amount of educational dollars, teacher time, or facilities. What it requires is that educational resources be distributed on the basis of ability to profit in such a way as to maximize productivity. Ability to profit is the relevant criterion, because it (along with motivation and interest) determines who is most able to make productive use of educational resources. Thus from the utilitarian view, educational resources should flow to the people who are the most able. This does not mean that the less able should be neglected. Having a tiny, well-educated elite and a poorly educated mass would probably not maximize society's productivity. The actual distribution of available resources between the able and the less able will be decided by asking what distribution will produce the maximum gain in productivity.

These arguments suggest that in evaluating the commitment of educational resources to various programs for various groups, the essential questions to ask are those that concern the rate of return on our investment. Where will we get the greatest overall social return on our investment? Thus in evaluating the merits of some educational program, we will want to ask such questions as "How much must be invested in the education of a given person in order to increase that person's lifetime earnings by a given amount?" and "Is there an alternative program that will generate a more favorable rate of return on our educational investment?" In asking such questions, we assume that a person's earnings are a measure of his or her productivity and that a person's productivity is a measure of his or her contribution to the satisfaction of members of society. In short, to express an interest in the rate of return on our educational investment is to express a concern for maximizing the average utility. It is to seek the greatest good for the greatest number and as a consequence to seek justice.

Bob Bender is unlikely to have precise figures on how the assignment of principals and staff will affect the lifetime earnings of the students at Left Bank and Steinbeck. It will be difficult for him to apply utilitarian concepts to his decision with any precision. (One of the difficulties of utilitarianism is that it has a way of requiring information that we do not have in order for us to decide anything.) Perhaps, however, Bender can make some plausible assumptions about the consequences of his choices that will enable him to decide using utilitarian standards. Consider the following argument.

Bender might argue that the most productive use of the best staff members would be to assign them to Left Bank. He does have some reason to believe that the children at Left Bank can make more productive use of these resources. The Left Bank children, after all, usually score higher on achievement and aptitude tests than the children at Steinbeck. Moreover, the children at Left Bank have higher aspirations than the children at Steinbeck. It is the Left Bank children who want to be physicians and engineers. It is they who will seek to enter the occupations that are most crucial to the nation's growth and economic welfare. They will be the ones to develop new products and create new jobs. The children at Steinbeck, by contrast, normally aspire to blue-collar or clerical positions, and even when they aim higher, they are less likely to succeed. Of course, their education cannot be entirely neglected. On the other hand, if we succeed in getting them to acquire basic skills at an adequate level, they will be able to render satisfactory performance at the jobs to which they aspire. Thus it seems clear that the most productive use of the higher-quality professional staff is to assign them to Left Bank.

Bender will have to admit that in making this argument he is, to some extent, trading the welfare of the children at Steinbeck for the welfare of the children at Left Bank. Perhaps, for example, some of the Steinbeck children who might have gone on to college and entered more productive occupations will now not do so. However, the point is that the trade is a fruitful one for society as a whole. More has been gained by the children at Left Bank, and, consequently, by society, than has been lost by the children at Steinbeck. Thus the trade satisfies the average utility criterion. The greatest good for the greatest number has been served.

Objections to Utilitarianism

This argument might be challenged in several ways. We might, for example, object to the facts assumed. Perhaps we really get more return on our investment by concentrating on the slow learners, who, because they are behind, will gain more from our instruction, than by concentrating on the most able students, who will likely learn rapidly anyhow. It is true that if the facts assumed in Bender's argument are incorrect, his conclusions about what follows from the average utility principle will also be incorrect. On the other hand, the facts he has assumed seem plausible. Moreover, the central question really seems to be whether, if the facts are correct, Bender's solution to his resource distribution problem is fair. Given this set of facts (or any other), does reasoning from the average utility principle produce fair results? We suggest two kinds of reasons why it may not.

First, Bender may be reasoning from an overly narrow view of the purposes of education. Presumably, it is reasonable to think of education as having a role in the development of human capital. However, it is also the case that the purposes of education include the personal growth of the student and the development of the student's capacity to function as a citizen in a democratic society. Does not Bender's argument omit consideration of these goals? Why are only economic goals to be considered relevant to Bender's decision?

A utilitarian might respond to these objections in several ways. He might claim that Bender has not really done justice to utilitarianism. Utilitarianism is not just interested in economic productivity. Rather, it is interested in total happiness. If Bender really wants to address his problem in a utilitarian way, he needs to find ways of understanding how personal growth and growth as a citizen contribute to happiness and include these matters in his calculation of the average utility. Or the utilitarian might argue that the way in which Bender judged the effects of his decision on the average utility really did include such goals as growth or citizenship. When we decide that one group of people can make better use of a resource than another, we indirectly include their contribution to the civic life of their community, even if we focus on their economic productivity. Indeed, the idea of economic productivity can be understood broadly enough to include notions such as citizenship. Being a good citizen does, after all, contribute to the welfare of the community.

There is an additional problem concerned with the political goals of citizenship that this discussion does not yet reach. It might be argued that the demands for an equal distribution of resources (or even for more equal educational results) are far more pressing when we are discussing training for citizenship than when we are talking about the development of human capital. Americans are committed to the idea that everyone has an equal right to participate in civic affairs. It seems intuitively offensive, for example, to suggest that one person's vote should count more than another's because he or she is more intelligent and can thus cast the vote more wisely. Presumably, the reason for this is that we believe that political equality requires equal access to the political system.

It might be argued that a society that believes in political equality ought also to seek an equal distribution of the skills on which successful political participation depends. Literacy is one such skill, as is much of what is taught in elementary school.

If this is true, a focus on the average utility may be a particularly inappropriate way to think about elementary education. Utilitarianism promotes the highest average distribution, not an equal distribution. But this may be a uniquely inappropriate way to think about distributing educational resources when they affect skills important to the exercise of basic political rights. There we should be more concerned for equal results than a high average. Bender's utilitarian argument may increase the inequality in politically relevant skills between the students at Left Bank and at Steinbeck. If that is so, it is especially problematic.

This line of thought suggests another important concern about the fairness of utilitarian ways of thinking about the distribution of educational resources. It may be undesirable to increase the average utility with no concern for the equality of the resulting distribution. Consider how utilitarianism might be applied to the education of the handicapped, particularly handicapped children who are also mentally handicapped or who are physically handicapped to the extent that it is unlikely that they will ever be able to hold a productive job. Utilitarian arguments could result in a total withdrawal of educational resources from such individuals. In such cases, there is almost always a more productive use for resources—a better place to put our money or our time that will produce a better rate of return in achievement and long-term productivity.

Indeed, it is surprising that advocacy groups for the handicapped often argue for educational programs by employing utilitarian arguments. Often the claim is made that it is cheaper to educate the handicapped and render them employable than it is to pay for maintenance and custodial programs. No doubt this is often true. Nevertheless, the argument has two difficulties. The first is that there will be many handicapped students for whom it will not be true. Are we to conclude that they are not entitled to any educational services? Surely not. Second, if we are going to use utilitarian arguments and appeal to cost factors, we need to be clear that utilitarianism will not justify an expenditure of educational resources simply because it is economically preferable to welfare. Utilitarianism will justify an expenditure of resources only if its rate of return is higher than the other available alternatives. It is one thing to argue that expending educational resources on the education of the handicapped is more cost-effective than welfare. It is quite another thing to argue that it is the most cost-effective alternative available.

The point of this discussion is not, of course, to argue against expenditure of resources for the education of the handicapped; quite the contrary. The point is to provide an illustration of a situation where the results of utilitarian reasoning seem morally objectionable and to suggest that utilitarianism is problematic as a general theory of resource allocation.

What is the source of the problem? Utilitarianism allows, and even requires, society to trade the welfare of one person for the welfare of another so long as the resulting average welfare increases as a consequence. Sometimes such trades seem highly unfair, even if they result in a higher average welfare. It is as though we were presented with a case where twelve sadists were happily tormenting a victim they had captured, and we were allowed to object to this on moral grounds only if the pain inflicted on the victim exceeded the pleasure of the sadists. If, however, the pleasure of the sadists exceeded the pain of the victim, we must view this as a good thing because the average happiness increased. This is a clear instance where a trade between the good of one and the good of all is morally offensive, even if the average happiness increases.

In such cases, we are treating people whose welfare declines as means to the good of others. To do so is to fail to respect them as persons. It is to treat them as though they were things, rather than persons who are ends in themselves with rights that must be respected. The basic reason for providing educational resources for the education of the handicapped is that by doing so we affirm them as human beings with the same claim to dignity, respect, and decent treatment as ourselves. We need not justify such expenditures in terms of the average welfare.

We can respond to Bender's first solution to his dilemma in these terms. Bender has, in effect, proposed to trade the welfare of the students at Steinbeck for the welfare of the students at Left Bank because he believes that the average welfare will increase as a consequence. Even if he is right about the consequences, the trade may nevertheless be unfair. It may be unfair because it treats the children at Steinbeck as means to the welfare of others. They are to be deprived so that others may gain. The trade is unfair because it fails to show proper respect for the worth and dignity of these children.

There is one final difficulty with Bender's utilitarian solution. Utilitarianism gives preference to ability to profit on the assumption that the people most able to profit are those who will make the most productive use of resources. The children at Left Bank should be preferred to the children at Steinbeck because, on the whole, they are somewhat ahead of the children at Steinbeck and can thus make better use of further instruction. However, we should ask why the children at Left Bank are ahead. Perhaps it is because their educational environment has been superior to that of the children at Steinbeck. Perhaps their home, their community, their prior schooling, or some interaction among these accounts for their being ahead. That would mean that they are ahead because they have benefited from some inequality in their respective educational environments.

The difficulty with Bender's utilitarian solution is that it responds to such inequalities in educational environments not by compensating people who have had the more impoverished environment but by rewarding those who have benefited from a superior environment. People who have benefited from inequalities of educational opportunities will receive preferential treatment with respect to further educational opportunities as a consequence. Arguably, this is unfair.

Perhaps we have raised enough doubts about Bender's first proffered solution. Since we have provided some reasons for preferring the children at Left Bank to the children at Steinbeck in our first try, let us see if we can find some reasons for preferring the children at Steinbeck in our second attempt. Moreover, since we have spent some time objecting to Bender's utilitarian solution, perhaps we should allow him to learn from the criticism and to construct his next view in answer to these criticisms. Also recall that in our initial sketch of the case for Steinbeck, we noted that the argument for Steinbeck differed from the argument for Left Bank in two ways. It focused on need rather than on ability to profit, and it emphasized equity over efficiency. Can we make a more systematic case for a view with these characteristics?

Justice as Fairness

The view we shall use to develop our intuitive defense of Steinbeck was developed by a philosopher named John Rawls, who has characterized his view as "justice as fairness" (Rawls, 1971).

The first question that we asked of utilitarianism was "What are we distributing?" The utilitarian response is happiness. Rawls finds the response too subjective. How are we to measure happiness? And how are we to know what sorts of institutions promote it? He suggests that instead of focusing on the distribution of happiness, we should focus on a set of goods that everyone will find important to their lives, no matter what sort of lives they live. These goods, which Rawls calls primary goods, are universal instrumentalities; they are useful for getting what we want in life, no matter what we want. Primary goods are things that reasonable people want, whatever else they want.

One example of a primary good would be wealth or income. Different individuals in our society may legitimately have very different views about how they wish to live and what sort of life is good for them. However, it is difficult to imagine a way of life that does not require income of some sort. Any reasonable person wants some income, no matter what else he or she wants. Income is a primary good.

There are other primary goods in addition to income. Various liberties and rights of political participation are primary goods. For example, any reasonable person will want the right to act on fundamental personal convictions, whatever they happen to be. Thus liberties such as freedom of religion and freedom of conscience are primary goods. Likewise, reasonable people will want the right to participate in decisions that affect their welfare. They will also want opportunities to learn and to work, since education and economic opportunity are also universal instrumentalities.

Distributive justice should not be concerned so much with how happiness is distributed as with how primary goods are distributed. These central resources consist of things such as liberties, opportunities, and wealth.

If Bob Bender wanted to apply this view to his decision, he might conclude that it is not really his concern to determine how education affected overall happiness. Instead, he should ask himself how schools distribute primary goods or things that determine the value of primary goods.

Bender might reason as follows: The central purpose of an elementary education is to transmit basic skills such as reading, writing, and computation. What makes these valuable and central? They are connected with various primary goods. For example, although various political liberties are protected by the U.S. Constitution, the value of these liberties to any individual depends on the possession of certain skills. The value of the right to vote, for example, depends on our ability to decide which candidate best supports our interests. The rights of free speech or a free press are valuable to the extent that one has something to say and the ability to say it. In short, a prerequisite to the value of one's fundamental rights is the ability to obtain and use ideas and information. Literacy is central to meaningful citizenship.

Basic skills are also important for access to the economic system. It is apparent enough that reasonable proficiency in reading, writing, and computation is a prerequisite for access to or success in further education, which is in turn essential for access to many jobs.

Bender might then reason that he need not be concerned with the consequences of education for the long-term happiness of his students. Rather, he needs to be concerned more directly with providing the opportunity to acquire a basic education (see Strike, 1982a). An elementary education provides an opportunity to acquire certain skills that are crucial because they are essential for effective participation in the political and economic institutions of our society.

However, this answers only the question as to what we should be concerned about so far as distributive justice is concerned. It does not tell us what counts as a just distribution. Thus we need to return to Rawls and ask what principles define fairness in the distribution of primary goods.

Rawls (1971) addresses this question by providing the following two principles:

First Principle
> Each person is to have an equal right to the most extensive total system of equal basic liberties compatible with a similar system of liberty for all.

Second Principle
> Social and economic inequalities are to be arranged so that they are both: (a) to the greatest benefit of the least advantaged . . . and (b) attached to offices and positions open to all under conditions of fair equality of opportunity. (p. 302)

The first principle is concerned with political rights such as free speech, a free press, and freedom of religion. Here Rawls insists that a just society provides everyone with the greatest extent of such liberties consistent with similar liberties for all. Our right of free speech, for example, is limited only when we employ speech to limit the rights of others. Similarly, people are to have freedom of religion or conscience, but they may not act on religious convictions that compel others to accept their views.

The first principle can be realized in two general ways. A just society must, first of all, have a just constitution. That is, it must provide legal protection for rights such as free speech, freedom of assembly, and the right to vote. Second, a just society must provide for the fair value of these rights to individuals. Among other things, this requires an education for everyone such that everyone has the skills necessary to exercise his or her rights meaningfully.

The second principle has two parts. The second part demands that economic opportunity be available to all on the basis of their ability and that equal opportunity be provided. The general idea is that a society's economic positions must be assigned on relevant criteria and that a fair opportunity must be available to acquire the skills required for economic participation. Rawls assumes that this requirement is fulfilled when people with similar aspirations and abilities have equal life prospects.

The first part of the second principle is referred to as the difference principle. It requires that any inequalities in the distribution of primary goods be justified so that such inequalities are to the benefit of all, particularly to the least advantaged members of society. The difference principle is perhaps both most important and most difficult. Some additional comment is required.

Consider Figure 5.1, three diagrams of the distribution of some social good (income, perhaps) among a four-person society. In these diagrams, the size of the circles indicates the total amount of income being distributed. The size of the wedges indicates both the amount and the proportion available to each individual. Note that an underlying assumption is that the proportion of the distribution affects the amount to be distributed. That is, inequalities in the distribution of goods and services affect the amount of goods and services available. One reason

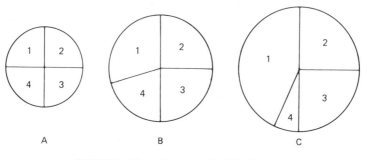

FIGURE 5.1.   Comparative Distribution

for this is that incentives are required to stimulate productivity. People are un-likely to put forth effort in their jobs or undergo extensive training for a difficult position if doing so has no effect on their reward. Thus some inequality in the distribution of social goods is required if people are to be motivated to be pro-ductive.

Rawls insists, however, that such inequalities are just only if they benefit every-one. We can see what this means by looking at the diagrams. Circle A represents an equal division. It is also the smallest of the three. Circle B has some inequality but is also larger. Circle C has more inequality and is larger still.

The key person for Rawls is person 4, since this is the person who, in the unequal distributions of B and C, has the smallest share. The crucial difference for Rawls between B and C is that under the distribution in B, person 4, the least advantaged person, is better off than under the distribution in A, whereas under C, person 4 is worse off. Thus Rawls prefers B to C even though C is larger, because only in B are the inequalities to everyone's advantage. That is, in B, but not C, everyone is better off than in A.

We should note that since its average is higher, C is the distribution that would be preferred by a utilitarian. Moreover, Rawl's objection to C is precisely the one we explored concerning utilitarianism. In C there has been an unfair trade. The welfare of person 4 has been traded for an increase in the average. It is just such trades that Rawls argues are unfair. We should also remember that it was this sort of trade that Bob Bender's utilitarian incarnation wishes to make be-tween the children at Left Bank and the children at Steinbeck.

The rejection of such trades suggests a key feature of Rawls's view and of his argument for his two principles. One may regard Rawls's principles as an attempt to express something of what it means to show respect for the equal dignity and worth of persons. Rawls is, in effect, saying that when we respect persons' worth, we do so by respecting their freedom of choice, by granting them a fair chance to earn their living, and by securing for them a fair share of available social goods. In understanding this system of rights, it is important in each case that respecting people's rights does not permit us to exchange their right for some increase in the average welfare. To have a right is to have it, even if having it is inconsistent with some increment in the average welfare.

Note that this perspective has particular significance when one considers its application to the educational rights of the handicapped. We have claimed that utilitarian arguments about the education of the handicapped can, given a certain set of facts, lead to a complete withdrawal of educational resources. From the perspective of justice as fairness, however, the question is not whether education of the handicapped serves the average utility; rather, the issue becomes one of determining the kind of education that affirms the dignity and worth of handi-capped individuals.

How might the view of justice as fairness be applied to Bob Bender's dilemma? Rawls's second principle requires both that educational opportunity be equal and that any inequalities serve the least advantaged. Consider, first, the notion of equal opportuntiy.

The general idea of equal opportunity is that people who are similar with respect to such relevant characteristics as ability and aspirations ought to have similar life prospects. Conversely, one's life prospects ought not to depend on morally irrelevant characteristics such as race, sex, or family wealth. In Rawls's (1971) words:

> *Those who are at the same level of talent and ability, and have the same willingness to use them, should have the same prospects of success regardless of their initial place in the social system, that is, irrespective of the income class into which they are born. In all sectors of society there should be roughly equal prospects of culture and achievement for everyone similarly motivated and endowed. The expectations of those with the same abilities and aspirations should not be affected by their social class. (p. 73)*

Now recall some facts about the children at Left Bank and at Steinbeck. We know that the children at Steinbeck are less affluent than those at Left Bank. We also know that on standard measures of educational attainment, they are behind the children at Left Bank. Let us add two more assumptions. First, let us assume that the children at Steinbeck do not differ from the children at Left Bank in such educationally relevant things as native ability or aspirations. Second, let us assume that the things that children learn in elementary school are important to their life prospects. They make a difference in how well these children will do in life.

What follows is that the fact that the children at Steinbeck are academically behind the children at Left Bank is prima facie evidence that equal opportunity has not been given them. That they are equal to the children at Left Bank in educationally relevant characteristics yet are behind academically is evidence that their being behind is in some way connected to the fact that they are less affluent. If that is true, the children at Steinbeck have poorer life prospects than the children at Left Bank essentially because their parents are poorer. That is unjust.

This argument does not require that these children have been victims of some form of insidious discrimination by the El Dorado schools. It may well be that the fact that they come from poor homes and a poor community affects their educational attainment quite independent of school. Nevertheless, they have been denied equal opportunity. Their life prospects are less than those of the children at Left Bank because of their social class. The duty of society and, presumably, of public schools is to equalize opportunity, not simply to avoid being the cause of inequality. That being the case, the El Dorado schools have a responsibility to compensate for the educational disadvantages of the children at Steinbeck. This suggests that the children at Steinbeck are entitled to a degree of preferential treatment over the children at Left Bank in the distribution of educational resources.

A similar conclusion can be justified from the perspective of the difference principle. Here the demand is that any inequality in the distribution of such social goods as income or status be justified in that it is to the advantage of those receiving the lesser share.

Notice that in considering the allocation of educational resources, so far as the difference principle is concerned, we must look at their effects on the distribution of social goods. The point is not to satisfy the difference principle directly through the distribution of educational resources but to allocate them so that the resulting distribution of goods such as income and status satisfies the principle.

Think of the matter this way: Suppose that the current distribution of educational resources is such that the children at Left Bank end up with an education that is superior to that of the children at Steinbeck. Also suppose that later in their lives the children at Left Bank will be able to cash in this higher level of educational attainment for a larger share of goods such as income. Is this just, or when might it be just?

The response of justice as fairness is that this resulting inequality is just only if the children at Steinbeck, when they become adults, are better off as a consequence. Otherwise, it is not just.

Now, it is at least logically possible that the children at Steinbeck might be better off under such an unequal arrangement. Perhaps the children at Left Bank will make such extraordinary use of their superior educational attainment that not only will the children at Steinbeck benefit from their accomplishments, but they will benefit more than they would have, had they been the recipients of the superior education.

The more important observation, however, is that although it may be logically possible that distributing educational resources in a way that leads to the enhancement of the affluence and social position of the children at Left Bank benefits the children at Steinbeck, this is, in our judgment, unlikely. We suspect it is far more likely that a distribution of educational resources that produced a higher level of educational attainment for the children at Steinbeck would be in the best economic interest of the children at Steinbeck.

If we assume that this is true, what does the difference principle require? Basically, it requires a preferential distribution of educational resources to the children at Steinbeck until either their economic prospects are equal to those of the children at Left Bank or until the point at which the change in the prospects of the children at Left Bank produces harmful consequences for the children at Steinbeck.

Finally, consider the implications of the principle of equal liberty. Here the obligation of the schools would seem to be to distribute their resources in a way that promotes, so far as is possible, the equal value of various liberties to various groups. It would, for example, be a violation of the principle of equal liberty if the education of the children at Left Bank was sufficiently superior to that of the children at Steinbeck that the former were systematically more able to use the political system to their own advantage.

What kind of distribution of educational resources might satisfy the demands of equal liberty? Our view suggests that an appropriate distribution might have three features.

First, it will seek to achieve a level of education for everyone that guarantees access to a meaningful participation in the fundamental political institutions of a democratic society. In short, it will seek a wide dispersion of basic skills where what counts as basic is defined in terms of a connection with political competence.

Second, insofar as society aspires to provide a level of politically relevant skills beyond the minimum, it will continue to seek as even a distribution of these skills as possible. To put the point negatively, efforts should be made to prevent educational results that generate significant disparities in the ability to use political institutions to pursue one's interests.

Third, insofar as disparities in political competence are likely to result, the educational system should seek to distribute them in such a way that groups of individuals characterized by common interests do not lack for effective advocates. The disadvantageous consequences of political incompetence may be mitigated if people who lack political skills share common interests with those who possess them. To use an obvious example, the rights and interests of the handicapped, even the mentally handicapped, are better protected and pursued when some portion of handicapped persons become effective advocates for themselves. The same point might be made concerning the children at Steinbeck. If the fair value of their liberty is to be protected, it would seem important that some among them become effective advocates for the interests of the less affluent part of the population.

We should note that here, as with the other parts of Rawls's principles, there is a preference for understanding equality in terms of equal results. The reason is not hard to see. If we believe that in a democratic society people should have equal political rights, we ought also to support institutions that make those rights of equal value to different people and to different groups of people. It seems quite plausible to believe that an educational system that produces an equitable distribution of politically relevant skills is a requirement.

Moreover, if we wish to produce equal results, it is likely that we will need to do so by means of an unequal distribution of educational resources. Given inequalities in the backgrounds of children, educational resources will need to be distributed more on a criterion of need than one of ability. We will need to invest in education in such a way as to assure that as many as possible achieve at a minimum level, that there are not significant disparities in politically relevant skills, and that interest groups do not lack for competent advocates.

What solution does this suggest for Bob Bender's dilemma? Just as utilitarianism tended to suggest that the children at Left Bank be preferred in the distribution of educational resources, justice as fairness tends to prefer the children at Steinbeck. In essence, justice as fairness requires a distribution of educational resources that tends to promote equal life prospects. It permits inequalities only when they can be shown to benefit those who receive the lesser share. Since the children at Steinbeck appear to have inferior life prospects than those of the children at Left Bank, educational resources should be distributed in a way that tends to promote more equal life prospects. This seems to require preferred treatment for the children at Steinbeck. The suggestions made at the end of our discussion of the school effectiveness research seem to us to address this objective.

Comparing Utilitarianism and Justice as Fairness

Let us recapitulate the discussion. We have been contrasting two rather general ways of thinking about the ethics of resource allocation: utilitarianism and justice as fairness. The general structure of these views is summarized in Table 5.2, which clarifies but oversimplifies matters considerably. As the foregoing discussion should have made clear, these views can have vastly different implications for how educational resources are distributed. That being the case, it is important for the administrator to have a reasonable opinion concerning the issues these views raise.

It would be presumptuous of us to try to summarize what has become a vast body of argument and discussion in philosophy and economics on these issues. It may, however, be helpful to attempt to distill what we see as the essential issues. Two matters are of great importance.

The first concerns what it means to have a right. Utilitarianism and similar views argue for rights in terms of their consequences. Rights are viewed as social arrangements that must be justified by showing that they promote the general welfare. This view of rights means that rights are seen as tentative things in that their availability depends on their consequences. Rights may be altered or suspended if they do not serve the general welfare. In this sense, rights may be traded for other benefits if the average welfare is enhanced thereby.

Justice as fairness, however, tends to see rights as inalienable in the sense that people are understood to have their rights simply by virtue of their being persons. Their possession of rights is not dependent on the consequences of their possessing these rights. Nor may people be deprived of their rights if their exercise or possession of them does not serve the general welfare.

TABLE 5.2
UTILITARIANISM VERSUS JUSTICE AS FAIRNESS

	Utilitarianism	*Justice as Fairness*
What Is Distributed	Happiness	Primary goods
Central Concept of Justice	Justice requires promoting average welfare	Inequalities are justified only if they benefit those receiving the lesser share
Focus of Distribution of Education Resources	Invest so as to maximize productivity	Invest so as to promote equality of relevant political and economic skills
Favored Criterion for Resource Allocation	Ability to profit	Need
Typical Result	Disproportionate concentration of resources on high-ability students	Disproportionate concentration of resources on disadvantaged students

Second, utilitarianism understands justice in such a way as to permit some people to benefit at the expense of others so long as the average welfare is enhanced. Justice as fairness does not. Inequalities are permissible only when everyone benefits as a consequence.

These issues may be expressed more simply as a single issue. We have frequently suggested that our central moral concepts are captured in the notion that human beings are objects of intrinsic value and, as such, are entitled to equal respect. The issue is, then, the extent to which the value of equal respect of persons permits trades between the welfare of individuals in order to promote the average welfare. To what extent can equality be traded for productivity? Utilitarianism can be regarded as holding that the value of equal respect for persons is consistent with such trades. Justice as fairness denies it.

We cannot help observing, in conclusion, that common practice in educational resource allocation seems to be largely utilitarian in its structure. It seems common to judge educational programs primarily on their effects on economic productivity in a way that is concerned more with maximizing production than with the distribution of the results of production. For example, in our judgment, the argument of *A Nation at Risk* (Gardner, 1983), a document that has received unparalleled attention among educators, is largely utilitarian in its assumptions. The results of this chapter should suggest at least that utilitarian ways of thinking about educational resources are not self-evidently true and that a moral case can be made for patterns of resource allocation that are far more attentive to the needs of the disadvantaged.

Questions

1. Much of the research we have reviewed here looks at the effects of various resources on scores on standardized tests. What kinds of educational goals are not well captured by such tests? If these goals were studied, might a different view of educational resources emerge?

2. Does it follow from the research we have reviewed that too much money is spent on schooling? Does it follow that fiscal equality is unimportant?

3. What are some of the ways an administrator can increase time on task in classrooms?

4. To what extent are inequalities in per-pupil expenditures between districts the result of differences in the willingness of people to tax themselves? Are such inequalities unjust?

5. States vary considerably in the amount spent per pupil on education. Is this a problem? Why is it difficult to address?

6. We have sketched two prominent views of distributive justice. Can you think of others? What implications might they have for Bob Bender's dilemma?

7. We have not discussed the idea of a meritocracy. What is a meritocracy? Is there any sense in which educational resources are earned by students? Are utilitarianism or justice as fairness meritocratic?

8. There has been a lot of talk recently among educators about basic skills or returning to the basics. What makes something basic?

9. Are there cases where our nation's economic goals can conflict with its democratic values? If so, how might that affect our thinking about the distribution of educational resources?

10. How might utilitarianism or justice as fairness be applied to such curricular resources as music or vocational education? Are these opportunities in any way less basic than literacy or computational skills? If so, what difference might that make in what counts as fairness in their distribution?

CHAPTER 6

Democracy, Bureaucracy, and Professionalism

A Problem of Policy

"You did what?" Helen asked, barely controlling her anger. "You and your staff decided that district policy was a bad idea for the kids at Jackson, and you didn't implement it?"

"No, I didn't say that," Alex retorted. "We did implement it. But we modified it to fit the needs of our kids. For God's sake, Helen, you know the kind of children we have at Jackson. They come to us with all kinds of disadvantages. If I retained every pupil who read below grade level, half my school would spend an extra two years in elementary school. And most of them would be our minority kids. Do you call that equality of educational opportunity? These kids need a break, not another kick in the butt from the school system.

"I know I'm responsible to you and to the board to implement board policy. And I've done that. At least I will have done it, as soon as we get the bugs worked out of our procedures. It's not what the policy says that's important; it's what its purpose is. And that's to ensure that our students learn to read. These nine kids will be OK if those damn teachers at the junior high do their jobs. But let's get it straight. Jackson isn't going to have a policy of automatic retention. That idea stinks. You said as much yourself, when we first started talking about it. And I've always said so. It'll destroy the self-concepts of my kids, and building their self-concepts is the overriding goal of our entire program."

The policy that had provoked the heated debate between Helen Aristeme, the superintendent of Centerville School District, and Alex Dumas, the principal of Andrew Jackson Elementary School, was simple and to the point. As passed by the district's board of education, it read:

1. It is the policy of this district that elementary school children who are seriously deficient in their reading skills not be promoted to the next grade.
2. Judgments regarding deficiency shall be made by a principal in consultation with the teacher concerned.
3. No elementary school student who reads more than two grade levels below district norms on the Comprehensive Test of Basic Skills shall enter the junior high schools of the district.
4. Notwithstanding point 3, no student shall be retained more than twice during his or her elementary school years.

Alex was right about Helen's initial reaction. She had opposed the policy. It had originally been suggested by the board's president, and the full board had asked her to look into its merits and make a recommendation. She was still unsure where the idea had really originated but suspected that it had come from some of the teachers and building administrators at the secondary level. (For several years they had been complaining about the poor reading performance of many of the district's elementary school students and the difficulties that created for secondary teachers.) Helen guessed that people on her own staff had informally suggested it to the board. She knew that several members had long-standing personal friendships with teachers and administrators and often saw them socially.

In any case, by the time Helen first heard of it, the board was already solidly behind the idea, as were many of her own staff. As nearly as she could tell, parents were, too. There had been substantial support for it from the community and, to the best of her knowledge, no opposition.

At the board's request, she had brought the idea to her administrative cabinet for study. After protracted discussion, the cabinet had strongly endorsed it. Given that endorsement and the strong support coming from all other sources, she had recommended the policy's adoption to the board. She had, however, conveyed her reservations about it to them and had succeeded in getting the two-failure modification included.

Now, two years later, it turned out that Alex had never really implemented the policy. Instead, he had launched a new reading program at his school, a program that he claimed would reach the same goal of improving reading skills.

Helen remembered Alex's impassioned objections to the policy when it was introduced at one of the weekly meetings of Centerville's cabinet. He had called it "elitist" and claimed that it would not work. He had collected the research on the subject and presented it to his colleagues at one of these sessions. With some exceptions, that research did seem to show that retention seldom had the effect of improving test scores. In fact, one study seemed to show that it lowered them. Other studies claimed that retention had undesirable social effects. Most important, he claimed that retention was damaging to students' self-concepts and that in his professional opinion, promoting a healthy self-concept was a far more significant educational goal than learning to read on some test maker's schedule. However, after all the discussion was over and the final policy hammered out, the board had unanimously adopted it. Helen had assumed that Alex, however reluctantly, had implemented it at Jackson. Obviously she had been wrong.

Instead, Dumas had instituted a special program of his own. That program involved the adoption of a new reading series for the primary grades, a series that had the reputation of being especially good for disadvantaged kids. (This adoption had shown up in Alex's budget as a "supplementary text." Under questioning, however, Alex now admitted that it had replaced the district-adopted basal readers.) He had reduced other costs and used the money to hire a special reading teacher for his school. He had recruited a group of parent volunteers, who came in to work with selected kids on a daily basis. And he had implemented an in-service program on reading instruction for his staff. But he had never retained a single pupil.

Nothing happened for two years. Then the whole issue surfaced again with the arrival of Susan White, Mark Stanford, and Josh Whittier at Centerville Junior High School. When they had entered in September, no one took any special notice of the event, except perhaps the children themselves and their parents. They all seemed to be nice kids who got along well with their classmates and teachers. By the end of the month, however, their instructors began to notice that they were not doing very well academically. For example, in the course of reviewing fifth-grade arithmetic, Susan's math teacher discovered that she was unable to add fractions, a skill she should have mastered long before. Further informal testing revealed that she was ignorant of decimals and that ordinary multiplication and division of whole numbers were difficult operations for her. At about the same time, Mr. Peach, Susan's English teacher, noticed that she could barely read the short stories he assigned and that her spelling was, putting it generously, idiosyncratic. In searching out the cause of Susan's difficulties, Mr. Peach examined her elementary school records. These showed that the girl had progressed normally through the first six grades and that, though her marks were on the low side, she had never failed a grade.

It was her standardized test scores, however, that provoked Peach to turn the whole matter over to Centerville's principal, Margaret Hamilton. Susan's achievement tests all indicated that she was at least two years below grade level in every subject—and three in reading.

At about the same time that Susan's folder landed on Hamilton's desk, Mark Stanford's and Josh Whittier's arrived at the same place, forwarded by two different teachers. Essentially, their records showed the same problem as Susan's. They were well below grade level in all subjects, and more than two below in reading. It was Hamilton who noted that all three were graduates of Andrew Jackson.

Hamilton had phoned her colleague, Alex Dumas, the principal of Jackson, to find out what she could about the three students. What she learned caused her to check the records of all of the new seventh graders from that school and to pass the folders of nine of them up to superintendent Helen Aristeme with a lengthy memo of complaint. All nine were reading more than two years below grade level, and none had ever been retained.

The memo's closing paragraph suggested that the nine were just the tip of an iceberg that could sink the entire curriculum of Centerville Junior High. Hamilton wrote:

> We've spent the last couple of years revising our entire curriculum on the assumption that incoming elementary school students would be reasonably close to grade level in reading. We've adopted new texts on that assumption. The English Department has changed its entire program. What are we supposed to do if Dumas keeps sending kids here who can't read? Since when are principals free to adopt a whole new program without district approval? And since when are we free to ignore board policy? Helen, you'd better get this mess at Jackson straightened out.

When Dumas left Aristeme's office, the issue was still unresolved, and the superintendent was still angry. However, over the next hour she cooled down. She knew she would have to do something—but what? On the one hand, she was concerned about the problem of curriculum articulation; she was reluctant to permit Dumas to continue his own special program at Jackson, although it did seem to her that it might be a good one. And, of course, she could hardly countenance a seemingly obvious violation of board policy. On the other hand, she had never really believed that retention was the way to handle the learning problems of elementary school children. From the perspective of a professional educator, she thought that Dumas's program just might work. Perhaps she could smooth things over for a year or two and give it a chance. She considered setting up a formal program evaluation, perhaps using an outside consultant. If the Jackson program really was successful, such an evaluation might provide the basis for repealing the policy, and Dumas's program might serve as a model for the entire district.

Introduction

From one perspective, the problem in Centerville concerns the effectiveness of reading programs used with disadvantaged children. Is the program instituted by Alex Dumas better than having children repeat a grade? Seen in this way, the problem is empirical—it is a question of fact. It is certainly conceivable that Helen Aristeme, the superintendent, could set up a kind of quasi-experiment to compare the reading performance of Andrew Jackson's students with students at other of the district's elementary schools. After collecting data for a few years, she would know whether or not reading scores were more favorably affected by retaining children or by Dumas's program. She would have a factual basis for making a recommendation to the board.

But more than facts are involved. Indeed, even if Aristeme carried out such an experiment, and even if Dumas turned out to be right (which, incidentally, he probably would), more fundamental issues are at stake. Being right about the facts is not sufficient.

Another issue concerns the requirements of organizational authority and the need to coordinate organizational activities, versus a professional's requirements to make independent judgments about the welfare of his or her clients. Clearly, a school system cannot carry out its educational mission effectively if every principal (or teacher) is entirely free to make judgments about client welfare. Efficiency requires that programs be articulated, that the work of one teacher or one school somehow fit with the work of others. Yet teaching and administration are not mechanical tasks; they cannot be meshed like work on an assembly line. Teachers and administrators need some room to make autonomous judgments, independent of the requirements of the organization in which they work. This issue is usually couched in terms of the supposed conflict between bureaucracy and professionalism. How are we to understand and balance Helen Aristeme's bureaucratic obligation to coordinate the programs of her school district and Alex Dumas's professional obligation to the children at Andrew Jackson?

More fundamentally still, another issue is involved in the conflict in Centerville. It is an issue that only recently has come to the attention of both educators and the public. The retention policy is a policy of the district's board of education. As such, it represents the will of the people, democratically determined. We must assume that the good burghers of Centerville *want* elementary children to repeat a grade if they are deficient in their reading skills. But suppose they are misguided in this want? Suppose Dumas is correct (as the research suggests) that retention is harmful to children? Suppose further that Helen Aristeme follows her inclination and lets Dumas continue his "modification" of this democratically determined policy. The issue raised by these suppositions is not a matter of bureaucratic-professional conflict. Rather, it is a conflict between bureaucracy and professionalism on the one hand and democracy on the other. Is the school system or its professional staff free to modify what the public wants when the public wants the wrong thing?

The central questions of this chapter concern the authority structure of education. Our concern is the extent to which teachers and administrators can be said to be experts or professionals and the extent to which such expertise as they have justifies their authority to make educational decisions. As we consider these issues, it will be evident that we are unimpressed with educators' claims to power over educational decisions based on their expertise. We will argue that education ought to be governed democratically and that the authority of educators must be looked at as an extension of democratic authority, not as something they possess as a function of their expertise.

Schools as Bureaucracies, Educators as Professionals

School systems are often said to be bureaucracies. What is meant by that? Similarly, educators often claim to be professionals. What does that mean? Let us examine these claims.

School Systems as Bureaucracies

The concept of a bureaucracy is an old one, but it was first given detailed attention around the turn of this century by the German economist and sociologist Max Weber. Weber (1947) conceived of bureaucracy as an "ideal type," a set of abstract morphological characteristics that typify this form of social organization. As such, no "pure" bureaucracies exist in real life; all organizations simply approximate bureaucracies to varying degrees. As applied to schools, the ideal type may be taken to consist of four principal attributes (Bidwell, 1965):

A Functional Division of Labor and Specialization   The major organizational task is broken into subsidiary functions, and each of these is assigned to a specialized role. In the case of schools, the overriding task of educating students is divided into such separate functions as algebra instruction, providing career advice, administering the activities in a building, and filing reports. These tasks are assigned to specialized roles: in this instance, mathematics teacher, guidance counselor, principal, and clerk.

A Hierarchy of Authority   The specialized roles are arranged hierarchically so that each is under the control and supervision of a higher one. This aspect of bureaucracy is captured by the familiar organization chart, which depicts the formal lines of authority—who is subordinate to whom. Teachers report to principals, who are in turn responsible to superintendents. The latter, as chief executive officers of the entire system, are responsible to lay boards, who represent the community.

Roles Defined as Offices   Recruitment to a role is based on demonstrated competence and merit. Once recruited, each individual is expected to execute the specific functional requirements of a particular office. For example, the requirements for the office of principal are captured (at least in broad outline) in written job descriptions, and principals are recruited and expected to carry out all of the explicit and implicit tasks of those descriptions. These offices provide a career line, and individuals may spend their working lives as incumbents of various organizational roles. Finally, interaction with clients and with other organizational members is supposed to be universalistic, which implies similar treatment of similarly situated persons. Job performance, not personal relationships, is supposed to govern decisions.

Rules and Regulations   Performance of a role is governed by rules and regulations, often written, that limit individual discretion. Each officer is expected to make decisions on the basis of these rules and to follow official procedures. Rules and procedures are intended to specify the accepted and most efficient manner for accomplishing organizational tasks. For instance, many school districts have "policy handbooks" that detail the district's rules and procedures. These handbooks may specify the criteria to be used for selecting teachers, the recruitment procedures to be followed, how their job performance is to be evaluated, and how incompetent performance is to be dealt with.

Underlying all of these characteristics is bureaucracy's fundamental commitment to two related values, rationality and efficiency. Each characteristic is intended to promote the growth of expertise, and impersonal experts are supposed to make decisions based on technically correct, factual premises—to be rational. In addition, these characteristics of bureaucracy promote efficiency; they provide for the orderly and coordinated execution of organizational tasks. They permit the accomplishment of large-scale endeavors (such as the education of a community's children) in ways that would be difficult or impossible using any other form of organization. Indeed, for Weber, bureaucracy was a mechanism for extending human rationality.

Weber and others recognized that this extension of rationality through bureaucratization was a mixed blessing. Throughout the world, the increasing bureaucratic domination of everyday life has been a cause of despair. One has only to read such disparate writers as Charles Dickens (*Hard Times*) and Franz Kafka (*The Trial*) to be reminded that rationality can be a vice as well as a virtue. But in addition to such overarching criticisms, the Weberian model has been criticized for its internal deficiencies. Two of these should be mentioned.

First, each of the attributes, in addition to promoting organizational efficiency, also seems to promote a corresponding inefficiency. Put another way, the functions of bureaucracy have a corresponding set of dysfunctions.

Consider the division of labor. Certainly, dividing large tasks into smaller ones permits ordinary people to become experts in ways that would be otherwise impossible. Who among us is really expert on the large and incredibly complex task of educating a community's children? Yet many of us could claim to be experts on teaching high school algebra, creating a social studies curriculum, or designing an efficient bus schedule. By conceiving of a complex task as an aggregate of smaller components, people of quite ordinary intelligence can become experts at one of them. Then, by effectively assembling these components (a kind of administrative expertise, incidentally), the complex task can be accomplished.

But at the same time, dividing large tasks into small ones may eventually promote boredom and a decline in motivation. After ten years of teaching ninth-grade algebra, a teacher is almost certainly an expert, but possibly a bored one. The task no longer provides the kind of challenge that serves to maintain motivation and stimulate superior performance.

The hierarchy of authority is essential for organizational coordination. When a multitude of diverse tasks is carried out simultaneously, a mechanism for ensuring that these tasks are done appropriately and on schedule is necessary. Defined authority, clear lines of communication, and a system of subordination accomplish this.

However, the hierarchy of authority also causes a restriction in the upward flow of information. For example, it is rational (from the organization's perspective) for a superior to evaluate a subordinate objectively on the basis of actual performance. But it is also rational (from the subordinate's perspective) to prevent a superior from learning of mistakes or deliberate deviations from established practice. After all, career advancement depends on such evaluations. Hence, upward communication, essential for knowing how well the organization is functioning at the operating level, may be restricted to relatively favorable information.

This may be an especially acute problem in schools, where the work of teachers is carried out in relative isolation, largely unobserved by administrators. A principal's knowledge of events in a classroom is largely a function of what its teacher chooses to tell. Similarly, since school buildings are usually geographically separate, the daily activities of principals are shielded from a superintendent's observation.

Consider also the matter of treating a role as an office. In order to operate efficiently, bureaucrats are supposed to be universalistic, to treat clients and each other fairly and according to established procedures. Personalities, personal relationships, and family ties are not supposed to govern interactions.

But affective neutrality is the other side of the cold impersonality we often complain of in our dealings with bureaucrats. More important from an educational perspective, strict universalism is antithetical to the requirements of good teaching. As Waller (1932) noted years ago, to be effective in a classroom, teachers must "keep their distance" from their charges; they must treat all pupils alike, establishing and adhering to a set of rules governing pupil-teacher interactions. In short, teachers must be bureaucrats. At the same time, however, to be effective, teachers must establish a close relationship with individual children, a relationship governed by warmth and positive affect. In short, they cannot be bureaucrats. Hence teachers are caught in a dilemma, and to watch them at work is to observe them, sometimes from moment to moment, vacillating between being coldly bureaucratic and warmly affectionate.

Finally, bureaucracy requires adherence to organizational rules and procedures; rationality and efficiency are thereby served. Rules specify decisions in cases that otherwise would be problematic. They serve several functions. One of these is to serve as a mechanism for implementing organizational authority without the personal intervention of superiors. Thus supervisors have some assurance that subordinates are discharging their responsibilities properly without constantly observing them at work. Further, rules serve to depersonalize punishment. They may lessen a subordinate's anger at a boss after being "called on the carpet." The boss has simply enforced the rules, which is what bosses are supposed to do. Thus potential anger may be redirected from the supervisor to the rules themselves.

But rules, too, have their dysfunctional effects. In a classic study of industrial organization, Gouldner (1964) noted that rules also serve to specify minimally acceptable performance. For example, a principal may be concerned that a few teachers seem to be out the door before the 3:30 bell has stopped ringing. He or she may feel that staff should be available to students who need extra help. Therefore, the principal may decree that teachers must remain in the building until at least 4:00 in order to provide that assistance. Such a rule, however, helps to ensure that many teachers will be gone by 4:01. It has defined half an hour as the minimally acceptable amount of time to be available to pupils.

Similarly, Gouldner (1964) called attention to the goal displacement consequence of rules. Rules are supposed to be means to organizational ends; they specify efficient actions to be taken in ordinary situations. A good employee (properly) follows the rules and (also properly) is rewarded for doing so. However, such rewards may encourage slavishly following those same rules in unusual situations, when they may be inappropriate. Thus rules may sometimes subvert the achievement of the very ends they were intended to serve.

We can glimpse the operation of some of these dysfunctions of bureaucracy in the events in Centerville. Consider the district's retention policy. That policy was tantamount to an organizational rule; it specified in clear operational terms what was to count as inadequate reading skills and how pupils lacking those skills were to be treated. Its clarity is one of its chief virtues. Vague, ambiguous rules do not promote efficiency. If the meaning of critical terms is unclear or if appropriate actions are left unspecified, a rule may be mischievous in its effects. But note that the rule made no distinctions among students; it was to be applied universalistically—or, as Alex Dumas might have said, it was to be applied rigidly.

In part Dumas's argument rests on his belief that the pupils at Jackson Elementary School should be exceptions. Perhaps retention is a suitable way to handle the majority of the district's children, he might say, but it is unsuitable for disadvantaged ones. Thus a clear rule, rigidly applied, thwarts the district's educational objectives in regard to these children. Note that it does not necessarily help matters much if such an exception were built into the policy itself. Suppose, for example, that the sentence "This policy shall not be applied to disadvantaged pupils" were to be added to the policy. Much of the original clarity is lost. What is to count as a disadvantaged pupil? Since an essential function of rules is to reduce employee discretion, this addition has the defect of simultaneously increasing that discretion. But if wording is added to clarify this term (and hence reduce discretion), it is likely that other ambiguities will be introduced, which in turn would need clarification. By such a process was that model of clarity, our income tax laws, produced.

Consider also the fact that Aristeme continued for two years under the mistaken notion that Dumas had implemented the retention policy. Disregarding for the moment his professed motivation for doing so—that it was an incorrect way to handle the reading problems of disadvantaged children—how was it possible for this to occur? In part the answer to this question must lie in the difficulty any superintendent experiences in supervising geographically dispersed schools. But part of the difficulty may also lie in the fact that it was left to Dumas himself to communicate his actions to Aristeme. In effect, the choice to communicate the intention to violate a policy deliberately was left up to the violator. Since Aristeme has considerable control over Dumas's career, it was understandable that he might fail to tell her of his actions. Gouldner's observations regarding the dysfunctional effects of rules is reflected in Dumas's behavior.

But it can be argued that what has happened in Centerville is a failure to bureaucratize sufficiently. After all, school administrators are not the only executives who are required to supervise geographically dispersed activities. Consider the much worse problem of the U.S. Forest Service, where a bureaucrat must have some idea about what employees are doing in the middle of Minnesota's woods, or the problem of a Washington-based naval commander "supervising" the actions of a submarine captain deep under the North Atlantic. How do these persons know that policies are being followed by their subordinates? The typical solution to such problems is to bureaucratize the system further, designing procedures that permit at least post hoc supervision. Daily reports and logs or meticulous records of objectives and accomplishments are the usual practice in such circumstances.

An adaptation of this kind of bureaucratization would have been possible in Centerville. For example, it would have been easy enough for Aristeme to require an annual accounting of the number of pupils retained in each of the district's schools. With such a report she would have been able to spot what was happening at Jackson Elementary School a year before the principal of Centerville Junior High School reported it to her. However, she would have, in effect, created a rule to ensure compliance with a rule, adding another increment to the district's bureaucratization.

These are some of the problems raised by the Weberian model of bureaucracy; each of its functional attributes gives rise to a corresponding dysfunction. A second line of criticism of the model has noted its relative lack of attention to what has come to be called the "informal organization." Undoubtedly the "classic" description of the operation of the informal organization is Roethlisberger and Dickson's study of General Electric's Hawthorne Plant in Chicago found in *Management and the Worker* (1939). Although that study is now thoroughly discredited (see, for example, Carey, 1967; Franks & Kaul, 1978), it continues to be the standard introduction to the subject.

Years ago, Iannaccone (1964) noted the importance of this other aspect of bureaucracy for understanding how schools actually work. Essentially, Iannaccone called attention to the fact that organization charts, policy manuals, and official lines of authority are poor descriptions of how school bureaucracies and bureaucrats behave. A second social system grows up in all organizations, a social system based on unofficial rules, personal relationships, informal leaders, and the norms of the many small groups that form in the workplace.

This second social system has a direct impact on organizational members and modifies bureaucratically prescribed behavior. Examples of informal organizations include the small friendship groups that arise among teachers who lunch or carpool together and similar groups that cut across a school district's bureaucratic levels, such as cliques composed of teachers and administrators. These informal organizations are probably essential to the effective functioning of bureaucracies. They soften an otherwise impersonal environment and in some cases may provide mechanisms for getting things done more efficiently than the formal organization permits.

We can also glimpse the role of informal organizations in the events in Centerville. If events there had transpired in accordance with the bureaucratic model, the retention policy might never have come into existence. Apparently the idea for the policy emerged from among the district's secondary teachers and administrators. Had they, in the appropriate bureaucratic manner, carried their idea to the superintendent—had they followed the "chain of command"—Aristeme would have been in a position to kill the idea. It is likely that she would have done so. She was (and perhaps still is) opposed to automatic retention. Certainly, it was within her authority as superintendent to decline to expend staff resources in studying the proposal and to refuse to bring it to the board of education for discussion.

However, the chain of command does not describe communication channels as they actually exist in Centerville's school system. The informal friendship groups composed of board members and district secondary staff permitted advocates of the idea to communicate it directly to the board and to persuade its members of the policy's merits. Aristeme was not in a position to refuse even to consider the idea, as she might have done had the proposal come to her from her subordinates. And though she could have still recommended against its adoption, the strong support for it from the board, an influential segment of her staff, and the community itself apparently persuaded her to make a favorable recommendation. Thus a decision based solely on technical expertise—one based on the professional judgment of the senior executive of the organization—was substantially shaped by informal mechanisms of influence and political considerations.

Are Schools Bureaucracies?

Despite these and other criticisms of Weber's formulation, it remains one of the most powerful and influential concepts for understanding this pervasive form of social organization in general and schools in particular. Its power, however, is not that it permits us to ask the question "Are schools bureaucracies?"

We think such a question is naive. First, it demonstrates a lack of understanding of the notion of an ideal type. By definition, ideal types do not exist in the real world. Hence schools are not bureaucracies, at least in the sense that they fully embody each of the attributes noted earlier. Further, to ask such a question is to fail to use the concept analytically. It is more useful for students of educational administration to ask, "In what ways do schools approximate the ideal type, and in what ways do they depart from it, and why?" Used in this way, the concept is capable of informing us about the nature of educational organizations.

Consider the bureaucratic attribute of rules and regulations. Bureaucracies operate according to formally established rules and procedures that specify not only the aims of each office but the acceptable methods for attaining these aims. Are schools bureaucratic in this respect? It is immediately obvious that certain school activities and actors are substantially governed by rules and that other activities and actors are not. Most schools are substantially more bureaucratized for pupils than they are for teachers. There are myriad rules intended to control the actions of students: Rules govern attendance, tardiness, movement between classes (often based on the ringing of a bell), movement within classrooms and in halls, when speech is permitted, attentiveness during lessons, participation in extracurricular activities, homework, smoking (if, where, and what), permissible times and places to eat, and even the chewing of gum, to name but a few of the more common examples. Rules govern virtually all aspects of student life in school, and the large majority of these are directly concerned with students' primary responsibility while they are there—learning. Even those concerning other behaviors are typically justified on academic grounds.

On the other hand, for teachers, schools are much less rule-governed. Of course there are rules regarding teachers, such as those governing absences and vacations, but the sheer quantity of rules is much less. What is more notable, however, is how few of these govern the core aspect of teachers' work, what is done in a classroom (Lortie, 1975). Teachers enjoy considerable freedom in choosing how and what they do in this central aspect of their jobs. Thus what is most striking is not the difference in the sheer number of rules applied to teachers and pupils but that the rules apply to the *work* of one but not the other. Even with regard to the critical matter of mandated curriculum topics, for example, teachers have considerable autonomy. Certainly in the matter of how to teach a particular topic they have a wide latitude within which they may make critical choices. Thus schools vary in both the quantity and the quality of their bureaucratization, depending on whose perspective is adopted, students' or teachers'.

If one goes on to ask why these variations occur, an immediate answer lies in the contrast between the entry aspects of the two roles. In the public schools, at least, student is an ascribed role, teacher an achieved one. Becoming a student has little to do with preferences; it is a matter of attaining some minimum age. Teacher, on the other hand, is a role entered voluntarily based on a prior demonstration of achievement and accomplishment. As we noted in Chapter 3, these differences in entry require the school to confront a large number of often unwilling "clients," making the problem of order paramount. And order—or a semblance of it—can be achieved through rules. But teachers are not unwilling clients. Hence it is not surprising that in schools, rules most often concern the role of student, not that of teacher.

More fundamentally, perhaps, the qualitative difference in the nature of the rules applied to teachers and pupils is linked to the requirement that schools produce a reasonably uniform product (Bidwell, 1965). They are expected to produce persons who are capable of fulfilling adult obligations of citizenship and economic independence. With the spread of "minimum competency" legislation, the requirement for a uniform product is becoming increasingly specific. Yet, because of the ascribed nature of the student role, schools are expected to create this uniform product with widely diverse "raw materials." Public schools, unlike elite universities, are not free to select from among the best available potential clients. It is as if an automobile manufacturer were to be required to produce a car capable of meeting prescribed minimum standards but had no control over the quality of the steel to be used. Given such conditions, workers (teachers) must be allowed considerable autonomy to decide not only what procedures are most appropriate at any given time but also to decide what is to count as meeting the minimum standard itself. Rigid, highly detailed rules governing work performance are inappropriate for teachers.

Finally, it becomes obvious that rules are most appropriate when an occupation's technology is clear—when the procedures for producing some product are known and their effects predictable. Such a technology is absent in teaching. We simply do not know the best way to teach. Without that knowledge, it makes sense to allow teachers considerable autonomy in handling their central task.

We shall have more to say about this matter of autonomy. Here we wish merely to illustrate our contention that a concept such as "bureaucracy" can provide an analytic tool to further our understanding of schools in ways that asking "Are school bureaucracies?" does not.

Educators as Professionals

Just as the concept of bureaucracy is an old one, so too is the notion of a profession. No generally agreed set of criteria allows the unambiguous definition of an occupation as a profession. Numerous writers have specified various characteristics of occupations that make them professions (see, for example, Hall, 1968; Lortie, 1975). Most have mentioned two sets of attributes. Hall (1968) has termed the first set "structural attributes"—characteristics of the occupation itself. The second set is "attitudinal" in nature—characteristics of the persons who practice the occupation. Using Hall's scheme, then, we have the following:

Structural Attributes of Professions
The occupation provides full-time and lifelong work to its practitioners.

It requires a substantial amount of training in preparation for entry. Such training is based on a recognized body of knowledge believed essential to effective practice, and this knowledge is generally imparted in professional schools connected to universities.

There exists a recognized association that speaks authoritatively for its members in the occupation's dealings with the wider society.

A written and enforced code of ethics governs relations between practitioners and their clients and among practitioners themselves.

The occupation and its members enjoy considerable prestige relative to other occupations.

Attitudinal Attributes of Professionals
Professional organizations and other practitioners provide a reference group to individual professionals. They are the source of norms and standards of acceptable practice.

Members are characterized by a belief in service to the public. Client welfare is the paramount value.

Practitioners evidence a sense of calling or commitment to the practice of the occupation. Defections to other occupations are relatively uncommon.

Individuals believe that a very considerable amount of autonomy is required in order to practice their work properly. This involves the freedom to make decisions thought to be in the best interests of clients, relatively free from the wishes of organizational superiors and of the clients themselves.

These characteristics have the same conceptual status as those describing a bureaucracy. They comprise an ideal type. No specific occupation fully embodies each of them, and any given occupation will vary over time and place in the extent to which it fits the description. Further, as with the concept of bureaucracy, it is not very useful to ask if teaching is a profession. It is more informative to ask in what ways teaching approximates each of the attributes, in what ways it does not, and why. We illustrate this process by considering just a few of the attributes listed.

For example, there is a code of ethics for teachers. What is unclear is whether or not the code is enforced. The established professions, especially law and medicine, have regularized procedures for disciplining members. What is notable about this enforcement is that it is initiated and carried out by the profession itself. For instance, in New York, county bar associations have set up regional committees to hear complaints of unethical practice made against practicing attorneys. These committees have rather sweeping powers to investigate and apply sanctions.

Although sanctions for unethical behavior can vary, they include the possibility of initiating disbarment proceedings, a very severe penalty. The imposition of this penalty is uncommon, but it *is* imposed. Suspensions from practice for a specified period (for example, six months) are more common. These are also severe punishments, and not simply because the suspended attorney's means of livelihood is temporarily ended. More important, to ensure compliance, all clients receive written notice of the suspension. Obviously, this is likely to have highly injurious effects on the attorney's ability to maintain that clientele.

It is also worth noting that these committees have nonlawyers among their members, and that the committees focus on charges of unethical conduct; that is, conduct that violates professional canons but that is not illegal. Failure to inform a client of a conflict of interest and neglecting a client's case are examples of unethical but not illegal conduct.

In the case of teachers and administrators, punishments are meted out by employers, not colleagues, and those employers do not have the power to remove a license. Of course, boards of education can and do regularly fire teachers and administrators for misconduct. Indeed, Centerville's board of education would be within its rights to fire Dumas for refusing to implement its policy. However, the distinction is between telling a teacher or administrator, "You may no longer practice here," and saying, "You may no longer practice." The latter is a considerably more severe penalty. Further, we are unaware of a case where an educator's license has been rescinded for *unethical* (rather than illegal) actions.

Consider the matter of commitment. Dropping out of a profession or shifting to another line of work is relatively uncommon. This is not the case with teaching, however. A substantial proportion of people who have trained to teach never actually enter the classroom, and many of those who do enter the occupation leave within the first five years of their practice. This is a much greater turnover than is characteristic of such recognized professions as law, medicine, and architecture. Geer (1966), in an influential paper, analyzes this apparent lack of commitment to teaching.

Geer proposes a kind of "sunk costs" view of commitment; people become committed to a line of work as they accumulate valuable benefits from its practice. At some point this collection of valuables becomes great enough that dropping out or changing occupations becomes too costly; too much must be given up. What sorts of valuables do professionals accumulate?

Perhaps the most obvious is the knowledge and skills required to practice. These begin to accumulate during the training period and continue accumulating throughout the period of practice. This is the case for teachers and administrators as well as other professionals. But as Geer points out, it is important to note the degree to which these valuables are transferable to other lines of work. The less specific the knowledge and skills are to a particular occupation, the less commitment their accumulation produces. The skills and knowledge imparted during teacher training, Geer argues, are less occupation-specific than are those acquired during college training for many other lines of work. In this sense, teacher training more closely approximates a liberal arts degree than a professional one. Hence many people who train to teach find it easy to enter other occupations upon graduation.

If we consider not professional training but subject matter training, an interesting commitment dilemma appears. Take, for example, the preparation of a chemistry teacher. New York, which is reasonably stringent in these matters, requires that a person preparing to teach high school chemistry have at least 15 semester hours in that subject. This is well below the number of hours most colleges and universities require of someone majoring in chemistry. It is also far below the level of training that most firms require when hiring a beginning chemist. If the state believed that to teach this subject a person should have mastered it to the level attained by a chemistry major, it would require many more hours of college instruction in that subject before granting a license to teach. If it did so, however, prospective chemistry teachers would have the option of starting a career in private industry. Since salary differentials between teaching and industry are very substantial in chemistry (as in all of the sciences), any move to upgrade the subject matter knowledge of these teachers would have the effect of lowering undergraduates' commitment to teaching. It would, in short, exacerbate the shortage of science teachers.

We should note that it is not obvious that professional training is essential to teaching or administrative practice. Though all states require such training and license teachers and administrators on its basis, during teacher shortages licensing requirements are routinely ignored. Similarly, training as a teacher is not required to instruct in many of the more prestigious private schools, nor is it required of college and university instructors. We know of no evidence to suggest that teachers in those institutions are less effective than their licensed colleagues. In the case of administrators, it is notable that the United States is one of the very few countries in the world to require extensive graduate-level training in order to practice. But it is not manifestly obvious that our schools are better administered as a consequence than are those of France, Sweden, or the Soviet Union, for example. We shall have more to say about the nature of professional training in education shortly.

Another aspect of the skills and knowledge possessed by teachers that is pertinent to occupational commitment has to do with their speed of obsolescence. The technology and knowledge base of the occupation changes relatively slowly. As a consequence, a practitioner may drop out of the labor market for a period of years (e.g., to begin a family) and reenter with relatively little loss of proficiency. Hence commitment to teaching may be lower than that to other professions where the knowledge base or technology is in rapid flux, such as many branches of engineering.

Again, all of this is not to argue that teaching is or is not a profession but to illustrate how using the attributes of an ideal type may throw light upon the nature of a particular occupation.

The Conflict of Bureaucracy and Professionalism

With this understanding of the nature of bureaucracy and professionalism, we can turn our attention to the interaction between the two. Many writers have suggested that a conflict arises when professional persons work in bureaucratic organizations (e.g., Corwin, 1965; Hoy & Miskel, 1982). It is important for prospective administrators to grasp the nature of this tension.

Perhaps it is useful to notice first the ways in which bureaucracy and professionalism are complementary. Both rest on the application of technical expertise. In the case of the former, expertise is developed through experience and the division of labor, while in the case of the latter, it is primarily a product of formal training. This difference in source, however, seems relatively unimportant. In addition, both bureaucracy and professionalism emphasize objectivity in decision making and an impersonal orientation to clients. However, other aspects of these systems seem to provide the potential for conflict.

One possible source of tension derives from the bureaucrat's orientation to the employing organization as opposed to the professional's orientation to the client. The bureaucrat is expected to make decisions in the best interests of his or her employer, while the professional is expected to place a client's interests foremost. It is obvious that in a given case, these interests may not coincide. For example, faced with some design problem, an automotive engineer must consider both the safety and the cost of any proposed solution. Sometimes the trade-offs involved in these decisions are made in favor of the company and not the client, as the history of automobile recalls illustrates.

This difference in orientation is said to be ameliorated in organizations that deliver a professional service to clients, such as schools. In these cases, since the interests of both the organization (to provide the best service) and the client (to receive it) are the same, professional-bureaucratic tension is reduced (Hoy & Miskel, 1982, p. 112). We think, however, that this view misses an important point: Who is the school's client? It is not always apparent that students are the clients. It is also plausible to argue that the district itself is the client. It is the community that pays for and receives the school's services. In fact, since education is a state not a local responsibility, it is also plausible to argue that the state itself is an educator's client.

In any case, when the identity of the client is unclear, the potential for bureaucratic-professional conflict reappears in another guise: The welfare of one client may have to be balanced against that of another. In a sense, this is what has happened in Centerville. Dumas has conceived of his clients as the pupils of Jackson Elementary School. Their welfare has prompted him to reject organizational policy. But if we consider the community as the educator's client, Dumas's responsibility is to its welfare and that of *all* its children, not simply to the particular students who happen to attend the school he administers.

The major source of tension between bureaucracy and professionalism, however, lies in the control of decisions. In the case of bureaucracies, decisions made at any level are governed by the next higher level. This is the gist of hierarchical authority. In the case of professionals, however, decisions are presumably governed by standards set by a body of colleagues. Dumas and his staff, acting as professional educators, determined what was the appropriate "treatment" for disadvantaged children with reading problems. That treatment was not retention. Put another way, "the ultimate basis of a professional act is professional knowledge; however, the ultimate justification of a bureaucratic act is its consistency with organizational rules and regulations and approval by a superior" (Hoy & Miskel, 1982, p. 113).

The educational research Dumas cited as the justification for not retaining students is an example of professional knowledge. To be aware of this knowledge and not to act in accordance with it is both unprofessional and irrational. Aristeme could be said to have so acted.

If professionalism and bureaucracy are in fundamental conflict in this regard, why is it that tensions such as those in Centerville are not endemic in the schools? There are undoubtedly many reasons for this, but we will mention only a few.

First, there is the matter of the cognitive status of educational knowledge, its "truth value." For example, are research conclusions about grade retention true? If they are known to be true, no professional educator should agree to pupil retention. But very little of educational research (and social science research in general) is on so secure a footing. As we pointed out in the introduction to this book, and as should be obvious from our review of the research on many of the topics we have discussed, dispute about educational "facts" is much more common than agreement. In such a situation, it is always possible to dismiss one set of facts by citing another or to choose one's facts in accord with organizational policy.

Second, it seems likely that if educators were professionals and schools bureaucracies, conflict would be much more common. As should be obvious from considering the attributes of bureaucracies and professionals, neither schools nor educators approximate their ideal types very closely. Since both are such mixed models, the potential for conflict is lowered.

Finally, several writers suggest that the professional aspect of schooling has been "decoupled" from its organizational aspect (e.g., Weick, 1976; Deal & Celotti, 1980; Meyer & Rowan, 1978). Essentially these writers argue that events in schools bear only a tenuous relationship to one another and that this is particularly true of organizational events (e.g., policymaking) and instructional events. What happens in any classroom does not greatly affect and is largely unaffected by organizational activities. This has given rise to an image of schools as "organized anarchies" and the "garbage can model of decision making" (Cohen, March, & Olsen, 1972), which suggest that *existing* solutions are matched to problems as they arise in the organization. This anarchy is abetted by unclear goals, an unverified knowledge base, and a weak technology. Loose coupling characterizes activities within schools as well as between schools. This lack of articulation between organizational structure and classroom activities is said to provide the basis for professional autonomy. We would note, however, that it provides the opportunity for autonomy, whether professional or not.

In any case, bureaucratic-professional conflict is not rampant in American public schools. There is, however, the possibility that the kind of conflict we have described in Centerville is not really a conflict of bureaucracy and professionalism at all but a conflict of both of these with democracy. After briefly examining the legal structure of schooling, we will turn our attention to that subject.

The Legal Context of Schooling

In the United States, education is governed democratically. Indeed, the system of governance of public elementary and secondary education involves a complex, dynamic, often confusing and contentious division of labor among federal, state, and local government. We will describe this authority structure. (Later we will examine what is meant by the assertion that education is governed democratically.)

One caveat is necessary at the outset. To understand how education is governed in our society, it is important to be clear that the legal authority structure is only a part of the real system of governance. Numerous actors affect and influence educational decisions without having legal authority to make them. These include such educators' groups as the National Education Association, legal action groups such as the NAACP and the ACLU, parents' groups such as the PTA, and those who prepare tests such as the Educational Testing Service. Such organizations have had substantial impact on the direction of American education, but they are not part of its formal authority structure. Their influence should not be overlooked.

The supreme law of the land in the United States is the U.S. Constitution. We must begin here to understand the formal authority structure of public education. The Tenth Amendment to the Constitution assigns to the states or to the people powers not assigned to the federal government. Education is among those unassigned responsibilities. Since it is not mentioned in our Constitution, it is primarily the responsibility of state and local governments.

This is not to say that there is no federal involvement in education. State and local practices must be consistent with the requirements of the Constitution and are subject to review by federal courts. Moreover, the "general welfare" clause of the Constitution has been interpreted as permitting Congress to raise taxes for educational purposes. Withholding federal funds for education has become a primary vehicle for enforcing national policy.

The federal government is involved in education in several ways. First, federal courts interpret and apply the Constitution and various federal statutes to the schools. As will be apparent from the other legal sections of this book, this involvement is heavily focused on interpreting the First and Fourteenth amendments as they apply to such matters as freedom of speech, freedom of religion, desegregation, equal opportunity, and due process.

To a considerable extent, the federal statutes that generate court involvement in education deal with a similar range of issues. For example, federal courts have done a good business applying various civil rights acts, most notably the Civil Rights Act of 1964 and legislation concerning the rights of the handicapped (PL 94-142), to schools.

Given that education is seen primarily as a matter for state and local governments, the executive and legislative branches of the federal government have not sought to direct educational policy over wide areas of concern. They have rather focused on matters that have seemed to be national issues. Perhaps the major area of national concern about education in recent decades has been equity. Congress has passed extensive legislation dealing with such matters as racial and sexual discrimination, desegregation, and the rights of the handicapped. Compliance with these statutes is usually secured through threat of loss of federal funds. Other areas in which Congress has passed legislation that has affected education include retirement age, fair labor practices, and career and vocational education.

Congressional legislation has tended to promote various kinds of involvement in education. First, some legislation provides means of enforcement of other federal statutes or court opinions. The 1964 Civil Rights Act, for example, provides for involvement of the Justice Department in investigating and prosecuting claims of discrimination.

A second kind of involvement has been funding. For example, Congress has provided funds for vocational education, voluntary desegregation, and a variety of special programs for disadvantaged students.

A third form of federal involvement in education has been research. The National Institute of Education sponsors research on problems of equity and on basic skills. Research on science and mathematics education is funded through the National Science Foundation.

A final area of federal involvement has been in goal setting. Here the primary technique has been exhortation. Federal agencies are often able to use their ready access to news media to promote various views and reforms. Perhaps the best example of this process is the recent report of a presidential commission, *A Nation at Risk* (Gardner, 1983). Though lacking any formal authority, this report nevertheless seems to have generated a host of reforms (or at least changes) at the state and local levels.

The governance of education in the United States is largely accomplished by a complex shared responsibility between state and local governments. State constitutions characteristically mandate that the state government provide for public education. The state legislature must provide for education within the limits imposed by the state constitution. Education is first and foremost the formal responsibility of the state legislature. Other agencies that are legally authorized to participate in the governance of education must be delegated that right by the state legislature and, for legal purposes, should be thought of as creatures of the state. This is true not only of the various state agencies that exercise authority over aspects of education but of local agencies as well. School districts and boards of education are creatures of the state. States may create or dissolve local districts or redraw their boundaries. Any educational policy made by boards of education must be made within a policy framework produced by the state legislature and must be consistent with it. The authority of the state legislature supersedes that of local government.

Almost every state has a state board of education and a chief state school officer. These may be elected or appointed. Their powers vary considerably from state to state and may range from dealing with the details of administering state aid and setting certification requirements to broad authority over curriculum, textbooks, graduation requirements, testing, and programs. The state board or the chief state school officer may also exercise a quasi-judicial function, ruling on various controversies that arise from local school districts. The chief state school officer is the executive officer presiding over a state department of education, which is charged with administering the state's involvement with local education.

Education at the local level is typically governed by a local school board and a superintendent of schools appointed by the board. Members of local boards may be elected or appointed by some other level of local government. School boards may also exist in a variety of relationships with other local governments.

In some states, school boards exist at the county level; in other states, county school boards are intermediate between the state board and the local board. When school districts are coextensive with municipalities, a variety of relationships are also possible. The school district and its board may be legally distinct from the municipal government. This is the typical pattern. Some school board members may be appointed by city government, although they are generally elected. And the school district may be financially dependent on municipal revenues, although, again, the general pattern is that they are separate taxing agents.

The local board of education is responsible for educational policy at the local level and for the day-to-day operation of the district's schools. The decision-making authority of local boards of education is constrained by federal and state court decisions and by the actions of the state legislature and the state school board. Thus the actual scope of local board authority over educational policy has much to do with how active state government is in making policy. There is considerable variation between states.

Boards' responsibilities include raising funds, construction of buildings, arranging for pupil transportation, and hiring administrators and teachers. In these areas, too, local board decision making is constrained by state regulation.

It is important to be clear that a description of the legal authority structure of education is not necessarily an adequate guide to the actual decision-making process nor to the entities that influence educational decisions. Despite the fact that the system of governance just described has not changed greatly in recent decades, some people would argue that the process of decision making and the locus of effective power have changed considerably. The role of the federal government has generally expanded. It remains to be seen whether that trend will be reversed. The authority of state government has also expanded at the expense of local authority. It is generally believed that educational governance in this century has become increasingly centralized and bureaucratic (Wise, 1979). One issue this raises, which we shall discuss briefly later, is the proper locus of authority for educational decision making.

A second question concerns the professionalization of educational decision making. It has been argued that educational decision making in this century has moved substantially from "the people" into the hands of professional administrators (Zeigler, Tucker, & Wilson, 1976). It may be that while local boards continue to exercise formal authority over educational policy, they are increasingly captives of the administrators whom they hire (see Chapter 2).

Finally, it is important to note that many groups that are neither public officials nor administrators can exert considerable influence on educational decisions. Certainly teachers' organizations can have considerable influence.

One way in which teachers influence educational decisions is through unions; we will discuss this in Chapter 7. A second means is through various professional organizations. A variety of teachers' groups are organized around the subjects taught in schools. These organizations may publish a trade magazine, help develop and circulate new curricula, and provide new ideas or sources of teaching materials. Such organizations may, in conjunction with universities and textbook publishers, have a great deal of influence over what is taught and what there is to teach.

As we noted earlier, a number of other organizations exert influence in a variety of ways. The PTA not only helps out with local endeavors but also lobbies for its educational concerns. The NAACP and the ACLU have had considerable influence on educational policy by assisting in key lawsuits. The Educational Testing Service, the producer of the SAT, has become, by virtue of the widespread use of its examinations, the gatekeeper to some colleges and universities and a monitor of the health of the nation's educational system.

Thus the rather complex and multilayered legal apparatus of formal authority is augmented by an army of groups that seek to influence educational decisions. Actual decisions are the result of a complex interaction among these actors. Perhaps the essential tension concerning educational decisions, however, is that between the people represented by those whom they elect and the professional educators who staff our schools. It is to this tension between democracy and expertise that we now turn.

Democracy: Justification and Limits

The chief protagonists in the impending conflict in Centerville are not Helen Aristeme, the district's superintendent, and Alex Dumas, the principal of Andrew Jackson. They are Dumas and the people of the community (though the latter are not yet even aware that they have a problem). At its core, this conflict reflects the clash of two of our fundamental educational values—democratic authority and professional expertise. Aristeme is caught in the middle. Her difficulty stems from the fact that she subscribes to both, as do most administrators. Ordinarily this presents no problem, because in ordinary circumstances these values do not come into conflict. When they do, however, thoughtful administrators will be sorely tried.

Neither is the issue in Centerville over some substantive matter of educational policy. It is not about the merits of retaining elementary school children at Jackson. It is about who is entitled to decide whether children should be retained.

On the one hand, Aristeme conceives of her role as superintendent as one vested with the authority of her office. That authority comes to her by virtue of her appointment by the district's board of education. It is an authority delegated to her by the board, which has in turn derived its authority from the people. It is her duty to carry out the will of the board and thereby the will of the people. That is what it means to be a civil servant, and a superintendent *is* a civil servant.

A very important part of this duty is to see to it that the community's wishes are not subverted by the employees of the district. If educational choices should be made democratically, the ability of school employees to alter or deflect democratically achieved decisions must be minimized. A teacher or a principal who attempts to substitute his or her judgment for the judgment of the community about what constitutes good education must be viewed as subverting the democratic process. Conceived in this way, Aristeme will consider her staff as employees. That they also may be in some sense professionals is largely irrelevant.

But is it? Aristeme also conceives of her role as that of a professional educator. A side of her is sympathetic to Alex Dumas's actions. His claim to authority over educational issues has nothing to do with democratic authority. He claims authority to make educational decisions because he is competent to make them. Like Dumas, Aristeme possesses the training, knowledge, and skills that are required to make decisions on the basis of reason and evidence. It was they, after all, who were able to assess and interpret the research on retention, not the group of laypersons on the board of education. This side of Aristeme reflects the view of Plato more than 2,000 years ago: "Those who know should rule."

If Dumas's view is right, it follows that teachers and administrators should possess a high degree of independence in educational decision making and that significant limitations on that independence are offensive. For Aristeme to support the community's opinions regarding retention is to substitute the opinions of the untrained for the opinions of the knowledgeable. Under this conception, boards of education, if they should exist at all, should limit their activities to such endeavors as providing buildings and raising funds for education. They should certainly not be entitled to decide important educational matters.

Who is right, or what mix of views is right? How shall we decide? Before we set out to examine some of the arguments that can be made for various views about legitimate educational authority, we need to make a few observations about the nature of the question. First, we shall not treat the issues here as legal or descriptive matters. The issue is not who actually possesses authority but who *ought* to possess it. We wish to provide a perspective concerning what kinds of considerations justify authority and whether the way in which decisions are actually made is justified.

Second, we must separate the question of *who* is entitled to make a decision from the question of *how* that decision might best be made. It is possible that Alex Dumas is perfectly correct in his view that he is more competent to make educational decisions than is the board, and that, as a result, decisions will be better decisions if he makes them. But absent an argument linking competence to entitlement, Dumas has yet to make his case. It is entirely possible that educational professionals make better decisions but that the community nevertheless has the right to make them. We must leave open the question of the relationship between competence and the right to decide.

Finally, we must distinguish between the question of the *right* to decide and the question of *where* a decision is to be located. In complex institutions, decisions are often made by people who are not legally authorized to make them. For example, the board might consistently hold that it has the right to make educational decisions but that it will delegate actual decisions to Aristeme or Dumas. There is no contradiction here. The board remains the legitimate authority. It is entitled to decide. The issue is not where to locate decision making; it concerns who is ultimately responsible for decisions and who, in a disagreement, is entitled to prevail. Many decisions may be located with teachers or administrators while the authority to make those decisions continues to reside with the board.

Given these comments, we must be clear on how the dispute is interpreted. Dumas is not simply asking that the board delegate more of its authority to teachers or administrators because the latter are more competent to make those decisions. He is making the far more radical claim that as a professional he has the right to overrule the board's decisions in cases where they are in error. The maxim "Those who know should rule" is intended to grant final authority to the competent, not merely to delegate decisions to them.

Who, then, should have the authority to make educational decisions? What decisions are rightfully made democratically, by elected representatives of the people? What decisions ought to be made by professional administrators such as Alex Dumas?

Views of Democracy

What is a democracy? Why should we want to have one? What kinds of things should be decided democratically? Who has a right to participate in what sorts of decisions? These questions are so intertwined that it is difficult to discuss them independently.

Let us start by trying to be a little clearer on just what we are discussing. *Democratic* has become something of an all-purpose honorific term. We often use it to praise political institutions or decisions of which we approve, independent of their actual nature. In this chapter, however, when we talk about democracy, we are talking about a way of deciding things. Democracy is a set of procedures or institutions for achieving collective decisions. It is concerned with how to decide, not the content of decisions. It does not concern such matters as the distribution of wealth. A society may have a considerable degree of income inequality. It may for that reason be unjust, but it is not for that reason undemocratic. However, a society that enforces the views of a minority on the majority or that invests decision-making power in some elite may be for that reason undemocratic. Societies that have significant degrees of economic inequality are also undemocratic only when differences in wealth are translated into differences in the power to affect decisions.

What is it about a decision that makes it democratic? We suggest that the following two rules give expression to our intuitive concept of a democratic decision-making procedure.

1. A choice is democratic if the wants of each individual are fairly considered.
2. A choice is democratic if each individual has a fair influence on the choice.

Each rule is required. The first rule by itself is consistent with a benevolent despotism. A dictator might fairly consider everyone's interests and then decide unilaterally what is best for everyone. No one would consider that to be democratic. The second is consistent with a tyrannical majority. If the procedure for decision making is, for example, that in every case the majority decides, it would be possible for the majority to refuse to consider seriously the interests of the minority. That, too, seems undemocratic. The intuitive idea of democracy that these rules express is that a democracy is a way of deciding that takes equality seriously; everyone's interests are fairly considered, and everyone has a fair chance to affect decisions.

Should all decisions be made democratically? Consider the following anecdote. A certain teacher was privileged to hear an eminent educator give a lecture on democracy in the classroom. The teacher was so impressed that she decided to incorporate more democracy in her classroom procedures. It so happened that the very next morning she was expected to teach a unit to her fifth-grade class on European geography. Being democratic, she decided to hold a vote on the location of Rome. Her class voted that Rome was in France.

What is so odd about taking a vote on the location of Rome? One response is that the truth of the statement "Rome is in Italy" is not dependent on a vote. "Rome is in Italy" will continue to be true regardless of the vote of a fifth-grade class or anyone else. It might make sense to take a vote on where Rome *ought* to be. It might even make sense to vote on whether or not to move Rome to France. But it cannot make sense to vote on where Rome currently is.

Why does it make sense to vote on where Rome should be but not on where it is? In voting, one is expressing one's preferences—an opinion about what one wants. Such an expression of preference has a rational connection to what ought to be. That people want Rome to be in France is a reason why it should be there. It is not necessarily a good reason, although we suppose that if enough Italians and enough Frenchmen had this desire, it might be. The point is that good reason or not, it is a reason. The expression of a preference is a relevant consideration as to what should happen.

This is not, however, the case concerning the actual location of Rome. Expressions of preference for the location of Rome have no rational connection to where Rome is. Where people wish it to be is irrelevant to where it is. Voting here makes no sense, not because it is inefficacious (although it is) but because it is logically irrelevant. People's preferences are not a reason for accepting or rejecting the proposition "Rome is in France." We can formulate the force of this discussion in two claims:

1. Voting on a proposition makes sense when the preferences of individuals count as a reason for accepting that proposition. Indeed, usually the point of voting is to aggregate people's preferences so that we discover what, in general, people want.
2. Voting on a proposition does not make sense when the reasons for accepting that proposition are independent of the preferences of individuals.

This leads to the second observation. The problem in applying these criteria for the appropriateness of democratic choice is that there will be numerous unclear cases. Why should that be?

The most important reason is that choices of public policy are rarely simply matters of preference. They are choices embedded in a complex web of assumptions and beliefs, many of which will have truth conditions to which preferences are quite irrelevant. Matters of fact are involved.

Consider, for example, an issue such as nuclear power. Nuclear power is a proper object of democratic decision making because there are preferences involved. We do not want a nuclear power plant built in our neighborhood. Our preferences are relevant considerations against building one there. But people have these preferences in part because they have opinions on matters that are certainly true or false regardless of what they want. We may not wish to live near a nuclear facility because we have certain beliefs about radiation or nuclear hazards. Such beliefs are true or false independent of our preferences.

A similar case could surely be made about education. In many instances, people's preferences are an appropriate consideration in determining what sort of education they or their children should receive. Perhaps the most relevant consideration in deciding whether a district should offer an elective in photography to high school students is whether the citizens of the district want such a course enough to pay for it. Other educational decisions, however, may turn on matters that are true or false independent of our wishes. If there are laws of learning or development, they are what they are regardless of our preferences about them. Such facts are, Alex Dumas might remind us, involved in making decisions about the retention of students.

Democratic decision processes may sometimes focus on aggregating preferences and be inappropriate because what is to be decided is not simply a matter of preference. In the large majority of cases, however, background assumptions that are true or false generate preferences. Because preferences are embedded in a context of such assumptions, democratically achieved decisions can be legitimate but wrong. To say that a decision is legitimate is to say that the decision was made in a fair way. Everyone's interest was considered, and everyone who was entitled to participate had the opportunity to do so. To say that the decision is wrong is to say that the beliefs that generate the preferences expressed are incorrect. Perhaps there is no hazard from nuclear power. In expressing a preference against having a nuclear facility in our neighborhood, we are not really protecting our health. Rather, we are denying ourselves a source of cheap, clean electricity. In the case at hand, perhaps retention does not help children learn to read. Democratic decisions not to build a nuclear facility or not to retain students might be legitimate but wrong.

Most questions of public policy and of educational policy mix matters of preference with assumptions that are true or false. We might, however, draw two conclusions here.

First, insofar as there is an opportunity to structure how a question is put for democratic decision making, it makes sense to focus the question on the issue of preference rather than on the aspects that can be true or false. It makes more sense, for example, for school boards to vote on broad directions for education in a district than it does for them to make decisions as to the adequacy of a certain theory of learning. A school board can more sensibly decide that it prefers basic skills to vocational preparation than decide that behaviorism provides a better description of human learning than cognitive theory.

Second, it seems reasonable to conclude that if a decision turns primarily on what people want, the decision should be made democratically, but if a decision turns on the truth or falsity of some belief, it is not a proper object of democratic choice.

A third observation follows from this. It seems that what is at stake in the debate in Centerville can be understood as a dispute about the status of the decisions involved. Dumas's argument for professional autonomy concerning retention is an argument that the decision turns on beliefs that are true or false. Presumably he would argue that because of his training and knowledge, he is qualified to decide such matters, while others are not. When Aristeme advocates the school board's authority, she is claiming that what is at issue is largely a question of what people want. Centerville's school board is a device to aggregate community preferences concerning the teaching of reading. Such matters are properly made democratically, and professionals who attempt to make these decisions are usurping the right of the democratic majority.

We have sketched a view of what democratic decision making is and when it is appropriate. We now need to consider in more detail some arguments that justify authority over schools.

The Justification of Democracy

Most Americans treat democratic institutions as self-evidently justified. It may come as something of a surprise to them to learn that a large portion of humankind do not find the case for democratic institutions self-evident. Democracy has often been seen, as with Plato, as the rule of the mob or, as with Alexis de Tocqueville, as leading to a society of enforced sameness and mediocrity. What, then, is there to be said for democracy?

Friedrich A. Hayek, in *The Constitution of Liberty* (1960), suggests three common arguments for democracy. The first is that democracy "is the only method of peaceful change that man has yet discovered" (p. 107). It is a civil way of securing agreement between people who have different views but who must achieve a common decision. The second argument is that democracy is an important safeguard of liberty. In a democratic society, people are unlikely to give to others coercive power that might be turned against them. The third views democracy as an educational device. Its chief virtue is that by involving people in decision making, it enhances their grasp of public affairs. By promoting free and open discussion of issues and by thus educating those who may make decisions, it enhances the quality of these decisions, at least in the long run (p. 107).

It should be noted (as Hayek does) that each of these arguments treats democracy as a means to some other end—peace, liberty, competence. None of the arguments treats democracy as an intrinsic good or as an inalienable right. Alex Dumas might find much to approve in the last justification, not because he would agree that democratic decision making enhances competence but because it seems to grant the heart of his argument—that decisions should be made by the procedure that is most likely to produce the best result. We need not reject these arguments because they treat democracy as an instrumental good. At the same time, we might ask whether there is not something more fundamental about democracy. Does it give expression to any right of self-determination that people may have quite independent of whether democratic decisions are always the best or most peacefully achieved decisions?

Consider, then, a line of argument that treats democracy as a kind of inherent right. One theory of government authority that has had immense influence on American institutions is the social contract theory. In the form propounded by English philosopher John Locke (1632–1704), the assumptions of social contact theories pervade the Constitution and the Declaration of Independence. Indeed, the Declaration of Independence as structured by Jefferson was an indictment against King George III for breach of the social contract.

Locke (1963) began the development of his political theory by imagining what he calls the state of nature. The state of nature is a condition in which people live without government authority. Locke describes it as follows:

> *A* State of perfect Freedom *to order their Actions, and dispose of their Possessions, and Persons as they see fit, within the bounds of the Law of Nature, without asking leave, or depending upon the Will of any other man. A* State *also* of Equality, *wherein all the Power and Jurisdiction is reciprocal, no one having more than another: there being nothing more evident, than that Creatures of the same species and rank promiscuously born to all the same advantages of Nature and the use of the same facilities, should be equal amongst another without Subordination or Subjection. . . . The State of Nature has a Law of Nature to govern it which obliges every one: And Reason which is that Law, teaches all Mankind, who will but consult it, that being all equal and independent, no one ought to harm another in his Life, Health, Liberty or Possessions. (pp. 309, 311)*

This description involves three important assumptions. The first is the claim that people have a right to freedom. Their natural state is one of perfect freedom. No one has any inherent right to tell anyone else what to do. It is authority, not freedom, that requires justification.

The second assumption is that people are equal. Here Locke does not mean that they are similar in some empirical way. His point is that they are entitled to equal rights. In the state of nature, people are equal in that no one, by virtue of talent, capacity, or social position, is inherently entitled to rule over anyone else or to give superior treatment to anyone else. In Locke's words, they are equal in sovereignty.

Third, Locke indicates that people in the state of nature possess certain natural rights. Locke lists these as life, health, liberty, and possessions. Jefferson changed the list to life, liberty, and the pursuit of happiness.

One of Locke's central purposes in this discussion is to make the very existence of government appear problematic. If no one has an inherent right to rule over anyone else, how is legitimate governmental authority possible? Can a government ever rightfully compel its citizens to behave as it dictates? How is civil authority possible?

Locke's basic response to this question is embedded in the imagery of the social contract. We should think of governmental authority as resting on a contract among individuals to surrender their sovereignty in return for such benefits as peace, security, and the protection of their rights. They agree to submit to the authority of the government. In turn, they receive the benefits of government.

This doctrine is often expressed by the idea that the authority of a government rests on the consent of the governed. It is the agreement of the governed to submit to the authority of the government that justifies civil authority. This idea of consent and the accompanying imagery of a social contract, however, is problematic. How do the governed give their consent? In most cases, the social contract is a fiction. Few people have the opportunity to participate in the formation of a government and to agree to abide by its decisions. We have not recently been asked by the U.S. government or the state to consent to its authority. Nor, we suspect, would either government be overly impressed by a disavowal of our consent. We would, we suspect, be required to obey all the same. How, then, is consent judged?

One idea that has been expressed in answer to this question is the doctrine of implied consent. We imply our consent to our government by accepting its benefits. Thus when we attend a government school, drive on government roads, or accept any government-sponsored service, we imply our consent to the government.

This strategy does not seem very plausible. The point of the idea of consent is to show that the obligation to obey a government is an obligation voluntarily undertaken. After all, in our society it is rather difficult to avoid government services. School is obligatory. Roads are omnipresent. When one considers that breathing clean (or cleaner) air can be construed as taking advantage of a government service, it becomes difficult to understand how such services are to be avoided. The choice, it seems, is between implying one's consent or leaving. Thus the doctrine of implied consent does not give expression to any reasonable notion of voluntary acceptance of an obligation to obey.

Another response is to argue that the consent of the governed is assured by the provision of democratic institutions. It is in soliciting the vote of its citizens and in acting in accord with that vote that a government establishes that it rules by the consent of the governed. The justification of democracy, then, resides in the fact that democratic institutions are required in order to establish the consent of the governed.

This view seems appealing both as a justification of democracy and as a justification of the authority of democratic governments. However, we do not believe that it succeeds. Indeed, on analysis, it turns out to be a variant of the implied consent doctrine. How is it that democratic institutions are supposed to ensure the consent of the governed? The answer is presumably that in voting, one expresses one's consent for the authority of the government.

It is certainly not clear, however, that this is the case. It is plausible that a vote in favor of a particular candidate or issue might be construed as expressing one's consent for that person or policy. It is less clear, however, why those who have voted with the losing side should be taken as implying their consent. It is less clear still why anyone's vote should be treated as a mandate for the general authority of the government. If this were true, it would seem that failing to vote should be treated as withholding consent. Clearly, however, governments believe themselves to have authority over those who do not vote. Indeed, if they did not, school boards would have to be considered as among the most tyrannical of human institutions since so few citizens vote in most school board elections. Thus we believe that the view that sees democratic institutions as expressing consent is especially implausible in education and would, if true, tend to delegitimize the authority of school boards and their agents.

Let us try another approach. In discussing the Lockean tradition, Benn and Peters (1959) comment:

> *The theory of natural rights had this to recommend it: it recognized the moral principle that every person must be respected as a source of claims, and must not be treated as a mere instrument; and further, that all interests must be weighed impartially. The natural right democrats believed that only a democratic government could be expected to govern in that spirit, not because it ensured that the majority would have its way, but because it conferred on every individual the opportunity to voice a claim which no government could afford to ignore. . . . This suggests two criteria for political organization: that there should be adequate channels through which all interests can make their claims known; and that no interests should be so powerful that a government can safely attend to them alone. (pp. 414–415)*

The central assumption of this argument is that, as persons, all human beings have a right to have their wants and needs fairly and impartially considered. No one is entitled to claim that, by virtue of some natural superiority, their interests count more than those of other people or that they are entitled to get more of what they want than other people. Locke's view of the state of nature was developed, in part, against the doctrine of the divine right of kings. Locke countered this doctrine by a denial of any claim to natural superiority. All persons are created equal. No one has an inherent right to rule. No one has an inherent right to preferential treatment.

This moral right to have one's interests fairly considered becomes an argument for democracy by adding the assumption that political institutions are most likely to attend to the interests of each individual when each individual can exercise some influence on those institutions. The justification of democracy, then, resides in the argument that democratic institutions cause government to attend fairly to the interests of all and that all have a right to have their interests fairly attended to.

We accept this argument thus far. Nevertheless, it seems to us to be lacking in some respects. Although it insists on the right of each person to have his or her interests fairly considered, it makes the justification of democracy contingent on the empirical claim that democratic institutions are the best way to secure the fair consideration of everyone's interests. That argument is logically consistent with a benevolent despotism. If one could discover a potential ruler with the character and competence to consider each person's interests fairly and wisely, it might very well be better, so far as this argument is concerned, to suspend democracy for a while and allow this remarkable person to rule.

Here the replies are obvious. No one is that wise. No one can be trusted with that much power. Given absolute power, people will rule in their own interests, not with the interests of all in mind. These responses have a great deal of force. Indeed, they are arguments that educators might wish to remember when they assert their professional authority against the claims of parents.

The discussion does, however, point out a noteworthy feature of this argument for democracy: It does not seem to justify any inherent right to participate in the decisions of one's government. Rather, it justifies an inherent right to fair treatment and a contingent right to democratic institutions. In this respect, Benn and Peters's argument does not adequately reflect the force of Locke's position, for Locke's basic assumption is not so much the equality of interests as the right of self-determination. The right of self-determination is the primary characteristic of individuals in the state of nature, and this is the right that Locke seeks to preserve by the doctrine of the social contract. The Benn and Peters argument seems to have lost sight of this idea.

We believe that it is an important idea to reaffirm. One of the central characteristics of moral agents is that they are responsible for their choices. Being responsible for oneself is at the heart of the right of self-determination. If we are responsible for ourselves, we must demand the right to make our own decisions. We ought not to submit readily to the authority of others.

This right of self-determination seems to us to be the most fundamental argument for democracy. When a collective decision must be made, democratic institutions give everyone, if not *the* choice, at least a piece of the choice. Participation is a way in which the collective choice becomes linked to the individual's choice. When we participate in making the decision, it becomes our decision, even if we do not agree with it. Democratic institutions, then, can be considered a right in that they show respect for the right of self-determination under conditions of collective choice (for further discussion, see Wolff, 1970).

It is worth noting that insofar as democracy gives expression to a right of self-determination, its justification does not depend on the claim that democratic decisions are always or even usually the best or most competent decisions. People have a right to participate in decisions even if the decisions are made less competently on account of their participation.

These arguments for democracy are not especially comforting to Alex Dumas or the case for professionalism in educational decision making. They seem to affirm a broad right for democratic decision making in education and to affirm it even if democratic choices are not always the most competent choices. There is little in the argument thus far to allow Dumas to assert his professional competence as a reason why he should be allowed to triumph over a legitimately achieved democratic decision.

We will shortly have a few kind words for Alex Dumas. But before we do, let us drive a few more nails into his coffin.

A Democratic View of Bureaucracy

Bureaucracies are not commonly regarded as quintessential democratic institutions. Indeed, the opposite is usually the case. Bureaucracies are seen as highly antidemocratic. They are viewed as institutions that thwart democratic goals and frustrate the will of the people.

Consider two commonplace objections to bureaucracies. The first focuses on their rigidity and complexity. The paradigmatic case of the bureaucratic mind is a person who compels us to fill out a form in triplicate, wait in a dozen lines, and spend days trying to obtain a solution to a seemingly trivial problem only to inform us at the end that our request has been denied on some technicality. Bureaucracies are viewed as organizations that are unresponsive to genuine human needs, make simple things complicated, and bury creativity and care under mountains of paperwork and miles of red tape.

The second objection to bureaucracies is that they ultimately come to serve themselves rather than the purposes they were created to serve. Schools, assuming them to be bureaucracies for the moment, are often accused of conducting their affairs more for the sake of the teachers and administrators than for the sake of the children they are supposed to serve. Governmental bureaucracies are often accused of usurping the role of the legislature in the way they interpret legislation or in the way they create guidelines or rules for applying legislation. Bureaucracies become problematic when they come to have purposes of their own.

We should note two things about these complaints. First, to some extent, they express incompatible expectations. The first complaint sees bureaucracies as too rule-governed and too inflexible in their procedures. The second sees bureaucracies as too flexible and as able to exercise too much judgment in their procedures. We should remember that it is often the point of detailed bureaucratic rules to ensure that bureaucracies conform to legislative intent. Detailed rules and procedures provide a way of making sure that the bureaucracy is doing what it is supposed to do and that it is serving its purposes in a fair and impartial fashion. To allow a bureaucracy to exercise judgment is to grant it the opportunity to serve purposes other than its intended purposes and to deal with people in an arbitrary or capricious fashion. Most of us, we suppose, do not enjoy paying taxes. We may also, from time to time, find IRS regulations rigid and overly complex. We should consider, however, what our experience with the tax system might be if the IRS were free to set our tax burden on some intuitive basis and were not itself bound by a code. Detailed bureaucratic rules may lead to rigidity and stifle creativity, but they also have certain virtues in producing conformity to legislative intent and due process that should not be overlooked.

The second point is that only the second of our two complaints about bureaucracies suggests that they are undemocratic. That bureaucracies are rigid or that they stifle creativity may suggest that they are mixed blessings, but it does not indicate that they are undemocratic. That bureaucracies come to serve their own purposes and that they subvert legislative intent does, however, indicate that they are undemocratic. At least this is the case if one grants the assumption that the acts of a duly constituted legislative body are expressions of democratic choice.

Perhaps, then, we should consider the questions "Why would a democratic society have bureaucracies at all?" and "What kinds of bureaucracies would a democratic society have?"

The answer to the first question reflects the impossibility of having a democratic process to determine each and every choice that society needs to make and the desirability of expertise in implementing decisions. Consider the difficulties that would be encountered if each time a school wished to order a pencil, pay a bill, throw a light switch, put gas in a bus, teach fractions, or do any of the thousands of things schools do each day, an election or a meeting of the school board were required in order to make the decision democratically. Clearly not everything can be decided by a vote.

Or consider the difficulties involved if legislative bodies begin to make decisions that require specialized expertise. School boards ought to make decisions concerning the broad features of a district's budget, but they ought to hire expert accountants to keep their books. Likewise, school boards should make basic decisions on personnel policy, but if their decisions are challenged, they should hire a lawyer to defend themselves in court. Efficiency is not well served when legislative bodies begin to make decisions requiring specialized training or expertise.

What follows? First, it seems clear that any democratic body requires an agency of some sort to implement its decisions. Further, "implement" here must mean more than doing what has been decided. Characteristically, the decisions of a legislative body cannot simply be done without further decisions. A decision to open a door can be done without further decision making. A decision to have a program in computer literacy cannot. Someone must decide what is to count as computer literacy, plan the curriculum, hire the teachers, and coordinate the schedules. One does not just *do* computer literacy as one just opens a door.

Second, some sort of division of labor between the legislative body and the agency that implements its decisions seems required. Often this is expressed as a distinction between making policy and implementing it. It is the responsibility of the school board to form educational policy. It is the responsibility of educators to implement the policy. Needless to say, the distinction between making and implementing policy is not always clear. What seems to be important in this division of labor is the idea that it is the responsibility of the legislative body to determine the *purposes* to be served, or, to put the point in language employed earlier, it is the responsibility of the legislature to express the *preferences* of the community. The heart of the distinction between making and implementing policy is the idea that it is the right of the democratic body to determine the purposes that any implementing agency will serve.

Third, the delegation of the decisions designed to implement policy is not the same thing as the transference of authority to make those decisions. If we are to think of bureaucratic decisions as the exercise of democratic authority, we must also think of those decisions as expressing the authority of the legislature. The authority of a school administrator is not democratic authority except as it expresses the authority of the school board.

We can now ask about the properties an agency or bureaucracy ought to have if it is to be considered an extension of democratic authority. Certainly bureaucracies ought to have some qualities regardless of whether they see themselves as extensions of democratic authority. Decisions should be made competently, fairly, and impartially. Due process must be respected. If bureaucracies are to make decisions, especially complex decisions, in such ways, they are likely to have certain characteristics. They will have an internal division of labor, specialized tasks, and hierarchies of authority, and they will conduct their activities according to rules. These features tend to serve efficiency and due process. What makes bureaucratic authority democratic, however, is subservience to legislative intent.

Subservience to legislative intent means that the cardinal sins of bureaucracies are not incompetence or rigidity; they are independence of purpose and judgment. It is not just acting to serve itself rather than the public that makes a bureaucracy undemocratic. It is the creation of its own set of purposes or its own idea of what counts as serving the public. A bureaucracy that decides that it has a better idea and acts to improve on the purposes of the legislature may act wisely and justly on that account, but it becomes less democratic as well.

Thus in a democratic society, a bureaucracy is not entitled to an opinion of its own. The exercise of independent judgment is not, in this regard, a virtue of bureaucracies in democratic societies. It is, rather, a means of departure from democratically achieved purpose.

It may be worth inquiring about how subservience to legislative intent and reducing the need for independent judgment can be accomplished. One way is to organize work so that decisions are made in a routine and mechanical fashion. If we can take a complex decision, reduce it to a number of simple steps, and embody these steps in clear rules and simple forms, decisions can be made without the need for someone to exercise a complex judgment.

It is perhaps ironic that some of the most lamentable features of bureaucracies may be precisely those that are crucial to ensuring that bureaucracies are subservient to legislative intent. The attention to following rules, filling out forms, and filing reports seems exactly what one would want of an organization that was expected to implement some purpose consistently and impartially without exercising judgment about it or modifying it in any way. This seems to us to have some bearing on the general issue of accountability in education. Although the increased emphasis on testing and reporting both effort and results is often defended as a means to promote efficiency in education (a proposition that seems doubtful to us; see Wise, 1979), such activities may also be a requirement for making schools responsive to democratic authority. One might see the bureaucratization of schools as an attempt to enforce democratic authority against the independent judgment of educational professionals.

Another aspect of the process of transforming decision making into routine and mechanical procedures is that not only does it reduce the need for judgment, but it also reduces the reliance on expertise. If one can succeed in routinizing a decision—in reducing it to a set of rules—the decision can then be made by people who do not understand what is involved in it. They need only understand the rules for its implementation. If the rules are clear, for example, an IRS official can render a competent judgment concerning a tax matter without understanding the point of tax legislation. One can make quite complex decisions without the need of large numbers of people who understand the point of the decisions thoroughly. No one needs to exercise judgment. Expertise in making such decisions becomes a property of the organization as a whole but may not be required of any particular member of it. Such routinization of decisions may not be a virtue for many purposes. Because it does not require understanding of institutional purposes or any particular expertise or judgment on the part of bureaucrats, it may be alienating and miseducative for them. Nevertheless, it may be an important feature in promoting such virtues as consistency in decision making and, most important, in promoting submission to legislative purpose.

Of course, it is not to be expected, even if it were to be desired, that all need for expertise be eliminated from organizations that are expected to implement some legislative purpose. It would be surprising, for example, to find that the Atomic Energy Commission had produced a new form that enabled judgments about questions of nuclear physics to be made by clerks without training in physics simply by checking the appropriate boxes. How are we to think about such "residual" expertise?

So far as preserving legislative intent is concerned, the important thing is that expertise be exercised about means but not ends. If the reliance on experts is to be consistent with democracy, the experts must be bound by democratically achieved purposes. Expertise and judgment should be reserved for decisions about how these purposes should be implemented. Expertise does not offend democracy until it begins to be applied so as to alter the preferences expressed by the democratic process.

Here it might be argued that the chief offense of professional educators such as Alex Dumas is not in believing that they have some expertise about educational methods but in believing that they have some expertise that entitles them to determine what educational goals ought to be achieved. Surely if anything offends the idea that schools should be subject to democratic authority, it is the idea that the views of educators about what is educationally valuable or about what educational goals to pursue have some authority. To think this is to commit the cardinal sin of an agency created to implement some democratically achieved purpose by making an independent judgment about that purpose. *If one believes that educators are entitled to an authoritative say about the goals of education, one must be against democracy.*

Some Arguments against Democracy in Education

If the arguments made on behalf of democratic decision making thus far have had any force, there seems little that can be said for Alex Dumas in this dispute. Is there anything that can be said on his behalf? We wish to approach this question by looking again, and in a different way, at the idea of a profession. Professionals, as we have noted, are commonly held to have certain rights of self-governance. They are entitled to authority over decisions that fall within their professional domains. Why?

First, how are we to distinguish a professional from a technician? A technician, as we shall understand the term, is someone who has a certain expertise about something but whose expertise does not entitle him or her to any say about the purposes to which that expertise is put. An accountant might, for example, be considered a technician. Accountants have expertise that their employers should respect. But their expertise does not give them any special say about the goals of the company they work for. An accountant who works for General Motors has nothing of particular interest to say about the design of cars by virtue of being an accountant. Nor does an accountant who works for a school board have anything special to say about the goals of education. This is not to say that accountants should be subservient to any organizational purpose, no matter how odious, because they have no special competence about that purpose. Being a technician rather than a professional does not excuse one from the normal range of moral duties. Accountants have a duty to keep honest books. But they have no special expertise in organizational purposes.

This suggests that if we are to identify a class of professionals who are to have some rights of self-governance that are strong enough to be asserted against democratic authority, we will have to show that they have some special competence that extends to the purposes of their enterprises. Recall our earlier argument that democratic decision making was most appropriate when making a decision seemed to require the aggregation of preferences and was least appropriate when the matter to be decided depended on criteria that are objective and independent of anyone's preferences. In effect, if Alex Dumas is to carry the day, he will have to show that the school board's attempt to exercise its authority over the purposes of education is a bit like their taking a vote on the location of Rome. Not only that, but he will have to demonstrate that he has some special competence to make such decisions.

To continue this line of argument, then, we understand a professional to be someone who is a rightful member of a community engaged in what we shall call a practice. We understand a practice to involve the following characteristics:

1. A practice presupposes some specialized and organized body of knowledge or skill that is not generally available and requires an extensive period of training for its acquisition.
2. The specialized body of knowledge or skill is embodied in a community that is to some degree self-perpetuating and self-governing. Since this community is the repository of the relevant expertise, it must accept the responsibility for carrying out the functions that depend on this expertise. It must therefore train new members, determine qualifications for membership in the community, and specify the standards that determine competence.
3. The purposes of the practice must be internal to it in two respects. First, they must be essential to its nature such that engaging in the practice apart from those purposes distorts the practice or renders it perverse in some way. Second, the purposes must themselves be the sorts of things that require the expertise of the community to determine or to judge properly. It must take

some training in the practice to understand them fully and to know that they are being accomplished satisfactorily.

We can illustrate what is meant by a practice by showing how these criteria apply to law. The practice of law assumes the possession of a body of specialized knowledge and skill that is acquired during a lengthy training period. Also, this specialized body of knowledge is often treated as the province of a community of experts who perform the functions of teaching, certification, and standard setting. Are the purposes of the law internal to it?

We believe that they are, in several ways. First, we assume that the central purpose of the law is justice. Judges and lawyers exist not simply to serve their clients or to settle disputes but to do so justly. A lawyer or a judge whose practice of law seeks to serve a government or serve a client without serving justice has perverted the enterprise. Justice is internal to the practice of law also in that it requires professional judgment to decide when justice is done. Thus the standards of the field are required to decide whether its purposes are properly served.

It follows from the law being a practice that lawyers are entitled to a certain degree of independence from democratic authority. They are entitled to a degree of self-regulation of their profession. More important, they are entitled to feel aggrieved if their society requires them to practice their profession in a way that does not serve justice. They are entitled to feel aggrieved even if this requirement is arrived at democratically.

Why should democratic authority be inappropriate when applied to a practice? Two kinds of responses are possible. The first is an appeal to efficiency or competence. Democratic bodies should not regulate the activities of a practice, because they cannot do so competently. Not being members of the community of experts, they lack the required knowledge to make competent judgments. The second argument is that in attempting to regulate a practice, a democratic body oversteps the bounds of its role in aggregating preferences and begins to decide democratically matters that have independent truth conditions. It becomes like the class that voted on the location of Rome.

This second argument becomes especially powerful when it applies to the purposes of the practice, for then it tends to exempt not only techniques but also purposes from democratic authority. We should note, however, that it applies only to the things that professionals do that are conceptually part of their practice. It applies to lawyers, for example, in their practice of law. It does not apply, however, to the economics of the professions. Billing may be essential to lawyers practicing law, but it is not part of the law they practice. This argument does not exempt the externalities of a practice from democratic control.

We have now constructed an argument that may give some hope to Alex Dumas in his dispute with Helen Aristeme. Dumas might wish to argue that education, like law, is a practice. It too deals with a specialized body of knowledge, and it too has purposes that are internal to its activity. Recall that Dumas had argued not only that retention was ineffective in teaching reading but also that building students' self-concept was the major goal of his school. In setting this goal, Dumas has claimed to have some expertise about the purposes of schooling. As a professional educator, he is entitled to exercise his judgment in educational matters, and the board has no right to impose its authority in such cases. In suggesting this, he has in effect held that the goals of education are internal to the practice of educating; it is a perversion to attempt to force it to serve other goals. In cases where goals conflict, final choices should be made by professionals. Boards of education should concern themselves with raising money and heating schools and leave the educational decisions to professional educators.

This line raises quite a variety of questions. Is education a practice in the requisite sense? If it is, what kinds of goals are internal to its practice? And how should we understand the limits of democratic authority with respect to education?

Two kinds of arguments might be made to show that education is a practice. Teachers might claim to be subject matter experts, or they might claim to be experts in pedagogy. Let us consider the first claim for a moment.

Teachers might argue that education is a practice because it is an extension of such activities as mathematics, writing, and science, which are practices. The chemistry teacher, for example, is engaged in the practice of chemistry.

What is there to be said for this claim? At least one thing can be said in favor of it. We do think it reasonable to treat the intellectual professions as practices. Math, chemistry, and poetry meet the criteria. Besides being associated with communities of specialized knowledge, they have purposes—truth, rationality, beauty—that are internal to them. It is a perversion of mathematics to practice it without concern for consistency or of poetry to write it without concern for beauty. Having said this, however, it is not clear that this is helpful to teachers' claims to be professionals engaged in a practice. Teachers of chemistry are rarely chemists. Moreover, teaching chemistry is not the same thing as the practice of chemistry. It is not clear that secondary school teachers are either members of the intellectual professions they teach or that they are engaged in the practice of those professions when they teach. It is even less clear when elementary school teachers are considered.

Nevertheless, there is something to be said for the idea that teachers are entitled to a degree of professional autonomy by virtue of their relationship to the intellectual professions. If chemistry teachers are not chemists, they nevertheless represent chemistry to their students. Presumably, they ought to represent not only the facts and theories of chemistry but its point and its values as well. Perhaps a board of education ought not to be able to compel the teaching of the various subject matters in a way that denies their character as part of the pursuit of truth or as part of the quest of human beings to understand and appreciate their world. Perhaps, for example, a board of education ought not to have the authority to demand that poetry be taught as though it had as its central purpose employment in an advertising firm. On the other hand, boards of education seldom seem to perpetuate such perversions of the intellectual professions. Indeed, perhaps the intellectual professions are more threatened by uncomprehending teachers than by benighted school boards. If this argument scores points for teacher autonomy, the points are few. Moreover, the argument is of little help to Dumas since, as an administrator, he is not a subject matter expert. Nor does his dispute with Helen Aristeme turn on a question of subject matter content.

Perhaps teachers and administrators are engaged in a practice in that they are the proprietors of a body of knowledge concerning pedagogy. This seems to be the argument favored by Alex Dumas. He believes that his expertise as an educator rather than as a subject matter specialist entitles him to authority over educational decisions.

We see several notable difficulties with this argument. The first is that it assumes the existence of an organized body of knowledge about pedagogy such that there could be a community of pedagogical experts. As we have noted, it is unclear that such a body of knowledge exists. No doubt there are many sophisticated views on teaching, and no doubt there is much good research about teaching or administration. Educational research may be a practice. On the other hand, it is quite clear that there is no body of agreed knowledge about teaching. The number of things that are both clearly known to be true and clearly relevant to educational practice is, it seems, small. Moreover, it is not even obvious that such knowledge as we have or could have about good teaching is very important for educators to know. A science of pedagogy might turn out to have the same connection to teaching as physics does to riding a bicycle. Physics can explain how it is possible to ride a bicycle and why certain techniques work and others do not. A knowledge of physics, however, is not merely unnecessary in learning to ride a bicycle, it is not even very helpful. Perhaps something like this is what is meant by saying that teaching is an art. Such a view need not require that no science of pedagogy be possible. It may simply indicate that knowing it is not very important to teaching.

All these comments about the state of educational knowledge can be contested. They do, however, suggest that Alex Dumas will have some difficulty in showing that there is a community of experts in which he may claim membership.

Not only must educators produce a body of pedagogical expertise to be expert about, but if they are to claim some say over the goals of education for public schools, they must also show that their expertise includes some special knowledge about what the goals of education ought to be.

Here the difficulty is that we are simply unaware of any argument that could show what is required. If educators are experts about pedagogy, that expertise presumably consists of knowledge of how children learn, how knowledge is best communicated, or how programs are best developed. How such knowledge, assuming that it exists, can be shown to include knowledge about the goals of education is less than obvious to us. We know of no body of knowledge that would justify Dumas's claim that self-concept is more important than reading competence. But such a body of knowledge is precisely what he requires. In fact, the goals of education are not internal to its practice—they are not resident in its body of knowledge. A privileged position concerning the goals of education is rarely claimed by people who research such matters. Thus Dumas has a considerable intellectual task to perform if he wishes to succeed in this line of argument.

We believe that the case for regarding educators as professionals in any sense that is sufficient to allow them the right to resist democratic decision making about education is weak. We must side with the board against Alex Dumas.

The center of our argument is that the determination of the purposes of education—making policy—is a matter for democratic choice because the primary consideration is the preferences of members of the community. Educators have no expertise concerning these preferences that might count against democratic rule. Thus we believe that professional educators have little right to a say about educational policy aside from their status as citizens. Lest we be misunderstood, however, we want to conclude this part of the argument with a few qualifications and caveats.

First, we do believe that insofar as educators can be seen as representing the intellectual professions, they should have the right to present subject matter in a way that fairly represents its character, including such values and purposes as may be internal to the subject matter. At the same time, we do not see that this argument carries much real force, since "subversion of the purposes of an intellectual discipline" is rarely a matter of dispute between teachers and school boards.

Second, our argument should not be taken to indicate that boards of education are unlimited in their power over education. There are some significant limits. Among them are the rights of students and parents. Teachers also have rights, both as citizens and as employees (see Chapter 7). That they are not entitled to extensive authority over educational decisions does not mean that boards may discriminate against them, deny their right of free expression, or pursue unfair or inhumane employment policies.

Finally, and most important, it is crucial to keep clearly in mind that what we are questioning here is the educators' *right* to authority over educational policy. This argument does not touch the issue of the extent to which it is desirable to *delegate* decisions to educators. It is quite possible that decisions will be made more effectively if teachers and administrators participate in them actively. Reasonable judgments about educators' participation in decision making seems to us to involve a variety of factors that vary from district to district. Such things as the current quality of the teaching staff, district size, the history of district practice, and current expectations are all involved.

Thus our argument is not an argument in favor of strict accountability or for bureaucratization of the schools. People who argue (see Wise, 1979) that bureaucratization of education is a major source of inefficiency may well be correct. Our claim is that legitimate authority over education is democratic authority. Whatever else the educator is, he or she is, first of all, a servant of the people.

Questions

1. Earlier we described four attributes of the ideal type bureaucracy and applied one of these (formal rules and procedures) to public schools. What can you learn about public schools from applying the others in a similar fashion? How do your results differ when the four attributes are applied to colleges and universities?

2. Consider a professional occupation with which you are familiar, one not commonly practiced as fee-for-service work (e.g., nursing, engineering, the clergy). Also consider an occupation not commonly thought of as professional (e.g., shoe salesperson, auto mechanic, house painter). How do these occupations differ from teaching in terms of the attributes of a profession?

3. We have claimed that educators have no special expertise about the goals of education. Is this necessarily true? Can you think of any exceptions?

4. Are the issues Alex Dumas has raised issues about the goals of education or about the means for achieving educational goals? What difference might that make?

5. Helen Aristeme apparently believes that the board is entitled to make policy about retention but that Alex Dumas's view on retention is correct. What course of action should she take?

6. We have provided two discussions of what it means to be a professional. How are they different? Are they inconsistent?

7. In your view, to what extent should boards of education involve themselves in the details of implementing policy? Would you consider the matter of retention something that is better delegated to administrators and teachers?

8. Might a board of education that involved itself in the details of running its schools create a poor work climate for its teachers and administrators?

9. Should parents also have a right to a say about whether or not their child is retained?

CHAPTER 7

Unions, Collective Bargaining, and the Control of Schools

Tough Talk in New Golconda

Walt Fletcher broke up. Starting with an explosive, unsuperintendentlike giggle, his laughter turned Homeric as he viewed the shocked faces around the table. This Janet Corps was something else! He was not sure what to make of her assessment of the union's proposals. He would have to think about that, but as the head of New Golconda's public schools, he had never found anything funny about collective bargaining sessions. This year's session might prove to be different. In any case, his concern about selecting this young woman to go up against the redoubtable Sam Weller was proving groundless.

Sam was the union's hired gun, brought in each year when new contracts had to be negotiated. Weller had a well-deserved and formidable reputation, as Fletcher had learned to his sorrow. With years of both public and private-sector union experience under his belt, he was a skilled bargainer. The school districts he had ministered to seemed to line up to empty their treasuries into teachers' pockets. More significantly, those districts had also rushed to turn over important decision-making authority to their staffs. In short, he was a man to be reckoned with.

On its side, the board was represented by Janet Corps, a young lawyer just beginning to develop a reputation as a negotiator. She had been recommended to Fletcher by the superintendent of a neighboring district. "Don't be fooled by her appearance," this colleague had said enigmatically. "That's one tough lady."

The meaning of the remark about Corps's appearance became clear when Fletcher met her. She stood no more than five feet tall, was dressed in a somber gray suit and frilly blouse, and spoke so softly that he had trouble hearing her. But she was bright, articulate, and forceful. She asked the right questions and listened carefully to answers. In less than an hour's time, she had made a powerful impression on the initially skeptical crew of corporate executives and engineers who were New Golconda's board of education. Corps was hired as the district's chief negotiator.

Nevertheless, Fletcher had worried. Whoever represented management this year would have to be tough. The superintendent and his board were committed to implementing a system of ranks for the teaching staff (''associate teacher,'' ''teacher,'' and ''master teacher''), and they knew that the New Golconda Teachers' Association (NGTA), an affiliate of the National Teachers' Association, would fight the idea. It was, the NGTA would say, merely a variant on merit pay. However, the board was prepared to sweeten this bit of medicine by offering its staff a very hefty salary increase. In addition, master teachers would move up several notches on the salary schedule. Indeed, if the plan went through, New Golconda's new instructional experts would be among the highest-paid teachers in the state.

New Golconda could afford to be generous. It was a small district, but it was not poor. Its families of affluent young professionals had few children, but it sheltered those few in large, expensive, and heavily taxed homes. Swimming pools, expansive, well-tended lawns, and BMWs abounded. The town's high-tech industries and its fashionable shopping centers made New Golconda property-rich. No small part of this wealth was diverted to schools. When a vacancy occurred in the district, it sought the experienced, highly educated, and most professionally oriented from among the many applicants. It could afford to pay its educators well, and it did.

In return for its largess, the community also expected teachers to perform, and it wished to reward those who did. The master teacher proposal was a way to do that. The scheme was not simply a ruse for instituting merit pay, however. Not only were the master teachers to be highly paid, but they would be expected to serve as role models and resource persons for younger or less able faculty. A substantial amount of released time would be provided for these purposes. Presumably the quality of teaching and of student learning would be enhanced as a result.

At the first bargaining session, the two sides had outlined their proposals. The NGTA's were relatively routine—a very large salary boost, expanded medical and dental care, increased sick leave and personal time, and a shorter school day were among its wants. Fletcher smiled to himself. Should the board grant everything Weller was asking, the resulting tax increase would certainly provoke howls of outrage from even New Golconda's wealthy residents. Even so, if Weller knew that the district was prepared to offer as much money as it was, Sam would certainly have doubled his demands.

Corps then outlined the board's proposals. She explained the master teacher plan, but she put more emphasis on the substantial pool of money for salary increases included in the package—''a pool that can only be regarded as generous,'' she said. Fletcher watched Weller's eyes when the size of that pool was mentioned. He saw only the briefest flicker of surprise. In authoritative tones, Corps made it clear that the two proposals were intimately related. ''If teacher ranks aren't accepted,'' she said, ''we might be able to give you folks a COLA—a cost of living allowance—but the bulk of these funds will go to hiring new staff to reduce the pupil-teacher ratio further.'' With that thought (sure to sober NGTA bargainers), the session ended, and the two sides retired to crunch the numbers through their respective computer spreadsheets and formulate their counteroffers.

Sam Weller's opening statement at the next session caught the district's negotiating team off guard. Speaking for the NGTA, he accepted the board's proposals. More precisely, he accepted *if*. His stance was as simple in its strategy as it was complex in its details. Directing his remarks to Fletcher, he began by saying the obligatory things about the financial package being too small. No one took that very seriously. Nevertheless, Sam said that his people were willing to tighten their belts and split the difference between their salary demands and the district's offer—assuming, of course, that their other requests concerning sick leave, personal days, and so forth were met.

Then he turned his attention to the critical issue, the master teacher plan, and proposed a simple trade. The NGTA would accept the plan if master teachers could have a modest role in the educational decisions of New Golconda. He suggested that several additional provisions be included in the new contract.

A "school policy cabinet" would be set up in each building. A cabinet would consist of the school's master teachers, the principal, and the building's NGTA representative. The principal would be obligated to consult with this cabinet on matters of policy and on decisions that affected the building as a whole. Similarly, a district-level cabinet would be formed, consisting of a master teacher representing each school (to be elected by the staff of that building), the NGTA president, the superintendent, and two central-office people of the superintendent's choosing. This cabinet would discuss matters of districtwide policy. Weller stressed that at both the school and district levels, a principal or superintendent need not follow the advice of the cabinet—he or she was required only to seek it. "The exact nature of the matters that require consultation will be worked out in subsequent negotiations," Sam said.

Pending those negotiations, building cabinets would have two immediate roles—one involved in hiring new staff and a second concerning teacher evaluation. With regard to the former, whenever a vacancy occurred, the master teachers, the union representative, and the principal in that building would form a committee to prepare a job description for the position. This committee would screen the credentials of applicants and interview those they selected. Following these interviews, the committee would rank (by vote) the three best applicants. These three would then be interviewed by the superintendent, who would select from among them the person to be hired. "This will give a building's staff a voice in teacher selection," Sam said, "without tying your hands, Dr. Fletcher."

With regard to evaluation, associate teachers would be evaluated for promotion and tenure by their senior colleagues. Specifically, master teachers (from schools other than the candidate's) would prepare performance appraisals. These would be submitted to the superintendent, along with those of the principal concerned. Based on these, the superintendent would make a final recommendation to the board. "Of course," Sam said, turning to Fletcher again, "you would be free either to accept or to reject these recommendations."

Weller claimed that his proposals would have substantial benefits for teacher performance and ultimately the district's children. "For the first time," he said, "teachers would have a real voice in important educational decisions. This will certainly improve teacher morale and student learning. The cabinets will give outstanding teachers a way to use their expertise effectively in educational matters; all decisions will be better as a result. Indeed," he said, "it makes no sense to establish ranks among the staff and then not recognize and use the very expertise the ranks represent."

Finally, Weller again emphasized that cabinet recommendations were just that—recommendations. Neither teachers nor the union would be encroaching on board or administrator prerogatives. Principals and the superintendent would be free to ignore a cabinet's vote if they saw fit. "All teachers are asking for is a meaningful voice in the educational decisions that affect them.

"A bright day is about to dawn in New Golconda," Weller said, in conclusion. "Democracy is coming to its schools."

Fletcher ruefully watched some of his own team nodding in agreement. Weller was certainly persuasive. The essense of his argument was that it did not make much sense to create a new rank of "superteacher"—to recognize some of the staff as experts—and then to ignore the views of those very experts on important educational matters.

Janet Corps, however, wasn't impressed. "Listen," she said to Weller, "let's get back to those basics you people are always talking about. What's basic is the law. This state's legislature, in a moment of insanity, decreed that school boards have got to bargain. When the legislature did that, it gave away some of the public's right to control its schools democratically. But that's history now. So we'll bargain—regardless of the merits of negotiating with public employees. But the law's also clear about what is and isn't negotiable. Terms and conditions of work are negotiable. Educational policy is not. Wages, benefits, and establishing new ranks for teachers, we'll talk about. Involving teachers in hiring staff and performance evaluations aren't "terms and conditions," and we're not going to talk about them.

"Furthermore," she went on, "even if we did discuss them, we wouldn't agree to such proposals. No one here is naive enough to think that merely because cabinets' recommendations aren't binding, administrative discretion will be unaffected. It's one thing to solicit informally a staff's opinions before making a decision—every good administrator does that. But it's quite another to give teachers the right to vote on those decisions. Even if a vote's only a recommendation, it'd be difficult for any administrator to overrule his or her own cabinet.

"And having a NGTA rep on every cabinet is ridiculous," she said. "Since the master teachers will certainly be union members anyway, the whole idea amounts to turning over administrative functions to the union. In case you've forgotten, the board is responsible to the public for making educational policy. The union is responsible only to itself. We're not about to turn over public policy decisions to a private-interest group.

"You know, you people are always talking about democracy in schools," the petite Ms. Corps concluded. "But you haven't got a clue what that word means. It sure as hell doesn't mean that teachers get to vote on school policy. So come off it, Weller. Your union's got its collective head up its ass if it thinks we'll agree to this bullshit."

That's when Walt Fletcher broke up. His amusement distracted him briefly from the fact that eventually he would have to decide about these issues.

Introduction

In the "good old days," people didn't talk to teachers that way. Indeed, just a few years ago, the sort of scenario being played out around the bargaining table in New Golconda would have been unthinkable. In those halcyon times, teachers came with hat in hand to their employers once each year, requested a modest increase in salaries, took whatever a beneficent (or not so beneficent) board gave them, and returned to work. When the administration wished to have the opinions of teachers on some policy matter, it asked for them. When it didn't ask, none were offered. Teachers were not so insolent as to demand that their opinions be solicited, much less that they be adopted over a board's objections.

Those days are gone forever. The advent of collective bargaining is one of the most important changes to occur in American school administration in the last two decades. Prior to the early 1960s, the number of school administrators who were required to face a teacher's representative across a bargaining table was minuscule. Now, thousands of superintendents (or their delegates) do so each year. Most often these sessions are relatively straightforward: The items to be discussed are recognized as negotiable by both parties, the differences between teachers and school boards are manageable, and little or no animosity is generated. In other instances, this does not describe the process. It is no longer unusual for teachers to take to the streets to press their demands. On the other hand, school boards currently seem moved to reclaim some of the benefits and authority previously ceded to unions. Regardless of the nature of the disputes, however, collective bargaining has effected a significant shift of power from boards and administrators to teachers. And it has changed irrevocably the lives of school managers, including those who practice in the few remaining states that do not permit any form of bargaining. For this reason, it is important for practitioners and prospective practitioners to understand collective negotiations in education.

Years ago, Samuel Gompers, a great American union leader, was asked by an exasperated manager, "Just what do you people want?" Gompers's reply is classic in its simplicity: "We want more." It is in the nature of collective bargaining for teachers' unions to want more—more money, more authority, more freedom. School administrators must be able to distinguish when more is justified and when it is not.

The Effects of Collective Bargaining

The Rise and Spread of Teachers' Unions

If one had to point to a single event that established collective bargaining as a legitimate process in education, it would have to be the representational strike of New York City's teachers in 1962. That strike established the right of the United Federation of Teachers (UFT) to represent the interests of teachers before the board of education of the nation's largest school system, at a time when the state had not yet adopted statutes that made such representation permissible. Doherty (1980) notes that less than 6,000 (about 15 percent) of the city's teachers actually took part in the strike. To deal with the walkout, a panel of three labor leaders was asked to consider the situation and recommend whether or not bargaining should be allowed. It should surprise no one, Doherty notes dryly, that such a panel would conclude that collective bargaining would be desirable. The board followed this recommendation, an election was held, the UFT won, and a contract was negotiated the following year.

Given the teachers' seemingly weak support for the walkout, Doherty speculates that had the New York City Board of Education held out against the UFT, it might have broken the strike, and the growing enthusiasm for bargaining elsewhere in the state and nation might have abated. Instead, the board's agreement seems to have led legislators in New York and elsewhere to view collective negotiations as inevitable. While this speculation seems doubtful, it is nevertheless the case that within a few years, many jurisdictions had enacted some form of collective bargaining legislation.

From this small beginning, collective negotiations spread rapidly. In 1964 only 19 school districts had formal written agreements with any of their employees. Two years later there were 419; four years afterward, the number stood at 1,531. By 1979 contracts numbered over 16,000, covering about half the nation's school district personnel. If one uses not the presence of a contract but some form of required discussions (so-called meet-and-confer processes), negotiations over conditions of employment now occur in about three-fourths of U.S. districts (Cresswell, 1982).

Part of this rapid growth was surely due to the sometimes acrimonious competition between the two major organizations seeking to represent teachers, the National Education Association (NEA) and the American Federation of Teachers (AFT). Where legislation permits collective representation, the two organizations seek actively to organize school employees, and this competition swells the ranks of both. Though the NEA is much larger, the AFT has shown the greatest growth, particularly in urban districts.

Initially, the NEA claimed to be the "professional association," in contrast to the "trade union" AFT. In particular, the NEA rejected the idea of a strike to enforce teachers' demands. The success of the AFT in representational elections, however, seems to have led the NEA to modify its posture on this and related matters (e.g., the inclusion of supervisors in a bargaining unit), and it has adopted positions closely resembling those held by its competitor. Today, while the AFT is formally a component of the AFL-CIO, it is difficult to argue that it is a union and that the NEA is not. Doherty (1980) suggests that if an organization intends to represent teachers at the bargaining table, it must *act* like a union, whatever its professed status. In any case, though there have been sporadic talks of merger between the two organizations (and abortive attempts actually to do so in New York and Florida), they remain largely separate and compete for teachers' loyalties and dues. In New Golconda, the behavior of the NGTA, an NEA local, would probably be no different were it affiliated with the AFT.

There are other reasons for the rapid growth of teachers' unions (Cresswell, 1982). In part, the expansion was due to the increase in the number of teachers during the 1960s. Further, union growth throughout the public sector during the same period suggests that the climate of public opinion was favorable to the phenomenon. And certainly the rapid swelling of union ranks has been partly a reaction to economic deprivations and the sometimes arbitrary and high-handed actions of administrators and boards of education. In any event, although the growth has now faltered, the competition between the two major unions (and several splinter groups) is likely to foster a continuing, if somewhat slower, increase.

Teacher Militancy

The factors noted account for at least some of the spectacular growth of teachers' unions, but they are not the whole story. In part, this growth is a function of a change in teachers' attitudes toward their employers. The "hat in hand" image of the "dedicated professionals," whose sole concern was the welfare of children, simply no longer describes U.S. teachers. A recognition of their own legitimate interests and a willingness to fight to protect and extend them is now more typical. This attitude is often termed "teacher militancy."

Numerous studies of this militancy have been conducted. Investigators have sought to explain militancy in terms of historical factors, social and demographic characteristics of teachers, organizational attributes of schools, and political perspectives on the distribution of power in education.

Representative of the historical perspective, Urban (1982) demonstrated that the roots of teacher militancy go back to the turn of the century. Like most observers, he found that economic issues have dominated teachers' organizations' activities through the years, though his analysis also pointed up the role of a nascent feminism (e.g., an antagonism to separate—and higher—salary schedules for men and male dominance of teachers' associations). Research on more recent periods has continued to point to "bread and butter" issues as primary determinants of teacher militancy (where militancy is operationally defined as a willingness to strike). However, economic factors are not the only determinants of strike propensity.

In an early demographically oriented study, Cole (1968) suggested that militancy is related to the demography and prior socialization of teachers. For example, he found that teachers from working-class backgrounds were more prone to strike than their middle-class colleagues. Those with "liberal" political beliefs were more supportive of collective action than those with "conservative" ideologies. Men were more likely than women to favor strikes as a legitimate means to resolve disputes. Cole suggested that this gender effect is due to differing reference groups. Male teachers are likely to compare their occupation to those of physicians, lawyers, and business executives, for example, occupations dominated by men. Women, on the other hand, may compare teaching to the traditionally female occupations of secretary, saleswoman, or nurse. In terms of both economics and prestige, teaching suffers by the former comparisons but not by the latter. Hence male teachers feel a greater degree of deprivation, making them more militant.

From an organizational perspective, Corwin (1970) explained teacher militancy as an outcome of the conflict between a strong professional orientation among some teachers and the bureaucratic setting in which they work. He found that the stronger the professional orientation of teachers, the higher the level of militancy. Presumably, the more professionally oriented were particularly sensitive to bureaucratic procedures impinging on their autonomy. While most teachers would go along with a bureaucratized administration and surrender a degree of their autonomy, the more professionally oriented would resist. Sometimes this resistance took the form of active support of unions and their demands. Thus, in contrast to research such as Cole's, which located the ultimate source of militancy in preoccupational socialization, Corwin saw teacher militancy as resulting from the interaction of occupational attitudes and organizational attributes.

Taking a more political perspective, Jessup (1978) extended Corwin's approach by showing that teacher militancy was a function of perceived powerlessness in educational decision making. Sources of powerlessness include not only a perceived lack of autonomy but also dissatisfaction with administrative leadership and with existing educational programs. Among Jessup's teachers, strong union support came from those who thought that a powerful teachers' organization would give them greater control over educational policy. As we shall see, it is certain that unionization has had this effect. It is also interesting to note that Jessup found that both AFT and NEA locals placed greater importance on economic issues than on influencing educational policy, suggesting that both organizations were somewhat out of touch with their membership. (Sam Weller, it should be noted, has adroitly linked welfare and policy issues in New Golconda.)

Such studies as these may illuminate some of the underlying causes of teacher militancy and may even help Walt Fletcher understand better what motivates the New Golconda staff. It may be the case, for example, that the district's attempt to improve the education of its children by deliberately recruiting experienced and highly educated teachers has had the effect of creating a highly professionalized staff. This professionalism, in turn, may have led to a high level of intolerance for even the slightest intrusion on teacher autonomy and a desire for even greater prerogatives, such as the right to recruit and evaluate their junior colleagues. Similarly, a theory of reference groups and relative deprivation would predict that even high-salaried teachers, finding themselves living among the affluent residents of towns like New Golconda, might think themselves underpaid. Teachers who must park their Chevettes among their students' BMWs each day are forcefully reminded of their relative poverty.

Even if such research provides Fletcher with a better understanding of his staff's demands, it can provide little direct guidance as to an appropriate response. It is less than obvious what tack he should take. He must also understand the consequences of collective bargaining in general and of the proposed contract with the NGTA in particular.

Most of the studies concerned with collective bargaining in public education have centered on its economic consequences, particularly whether or not teachers' paychecks have increased as a result of the practice. We will briefly review that research. However, there are strong reasons to suppose that the economic consequences of bargaining have not been reflected in teachers' wallets.

Collective Bargaining and Teachers' Salaries

When collective bargaining appeared on the scene, it was commonly supposed that teachers' salaries would rise dramatically. Two arguments supported that prediction. The most important of these was the absence of ''market effects'' in the public sector. That is, private sector unions are necessarily constrained when making wage demands on employers. If a union wins an excessively large wage increase, the employer has little choice but to pass the costs along to consumers. But a large price increase may cause consumers to seek alternative products. If enough do, the demand for the employer's product declines drastically, and production must be cut. Ultimately, workers may pay for an excessive wage demand with layoffs or even the demise of the firm. Thus private sector unions must be moderate in seeking wage increases for their members.

These constraints, it was believed, would be largely missing in the public sector. Government generally does not "sell" a product for which most consumers can find an alternative. Government has no competitors. Obvious examples are police, fire protection, and national defense; if the price for these services becomes too high, taxpayers cannot easily "take their business elsewhere." While one might argue that public education does have a competitor in the form of private schools, in most communities and for families without substantial incomes that competition is more apparent than real. Thus, the argument went, teachers' unions would be relatively unrestrained in their salary demands. And on the other side, because school boards are spending other people's money and not their own profits, they would be relatively quick to give in to teachers' demands.

A second argument was that teachers' unions were more powerful politically than their private-sector counterparts. They would be able to bring political pressure to bear on school boards to accede to their demands in a manner unavailable to private-sector unions. The UAW, for example, cannot easily mount a political campaign against the board of directors of General Motors. For these two reasons, then, teachers' salaries were expected to rise spectacularly with the advent of unionization.

As so often happens with social theorizing, the facts seem not to fit the theory. There is now near consensus among students of the subject that if teachers' salaries have gone up as a result of unionization, that increase has been modest. Lipsky (1982), after an extensive review of the voluminous literature on the subject, concluded that the paychecks of teachers in unionized districts were roughly 5 percent greater than those of their nonunionized colleagues. (There are dissenting voices to this conclusion, however; see, for example, Baugh & Stone, 1982.) Assuming Lipsky's estimate to be correct, not only is such an increase small, it is well below the effect of unionization on wages in the private sector, where estimates currently are on the order of 20 percent (Lipsky, 1982).

What might account for this finding? A commonly asserted reason is "spillover"; teachers in nonbargaining districts are presumed to benefit from the wage increases won in bargaining districts. It is common practice for a school board to consider the salaries paid by its neighbors when setting the wages of its own staff. To the extent that spillover occurs, any wage gap between bargaining and nonbargaining teachers will be decreased. The 5 percent figure, then, may substantially underrepresent the true effects of collective negotiations.

A second factor that might account for the lack of large salary differences is monopsony (Landon & Baird, 1971). That is, school boards enjoy a measure of power over teachers' salaries not often enjoyed by private-sector employers. Teachers lack alternative work opportunities; they may not easily take their skills to another, more generous employer. The private sector does not hire many teachers, and, under present conditions at least, neither do neighboring school districts. Hence, to some degree teachers have no choice but to accept what is offered them.

Other factors may also operate to constrain the effects of unionization on salaries (Lipsky, 1982). Among these are the fragmented nature of collective bargaining in education. A wage concession won in one district has no *direct* effect on teachers in other districts, unlike the case of industrywide bargaining in, for example, the steel industry. Further, just as teachers may bring political pressure to bear on boards of education to accede to their demands, taxpayers may exercise countervailing pressure in ways that ordinary consumers of private goods may not. Finally, and perhaps most obviously, state legislatures have sharply limited the power of unionized public employees to enforce their demands, usually by denying them the right to strike. In any case and for whatever reason, where states have granted teachers the right to bargain, they apparently have not also granted them the power to empty the public purse, as some people had initially feared.

Having said this, however, there is some evidence that bargaining has had the effect of causing a *redistribution* of money within salary schedules. Kasper (1973) and Thornton (1971), for example, found that collective bargaining resulted in disproportionate increases for experienced teachers and those with advanced degrees. This should hardly surprise us; unions are more likely to represent the interests of their members than their potential members. As the teacher work force ages and gains in experience, we should expect more negotiated benefits to accrue to those at the higher end of the salary schedule.

Finally, a word regarding fringe benefits is in order. If the evidence of bargaining's effect on salaries is relatively clear, it is much less so in regard to "fringes." This is not due to conflicting evidence but to its lack. Yet it seems that unions are nearly as attentive to fringe benefits as they are to salary increments. Since these constitute a very substantial part of the total compensation costs of most school districts, some of the effects of bargaining may be relatively hidden from researchers attending only to salaries.

Fletcher's problem in New Golconda, however, is not to figure out the average effect of bargaining on salaries and fringes. Rather, he must know the effect of each change in the proposed contract on his district's payroll. He must know its specific cost. While there are various ways to think about costs (see Levin, 1983; Haller, 1974), New Golconda's superintendent will certainly want to know the incremental and total cost of accepting Weller's offer to "split the difference."

Estimating the costs of alternative salary proposals can be a complex (and tedious) business. For example, Fletcher will have to know the price of an across-the-board percentage raise for all his staff, as well as the costs of moving alternative numbers of his faculty to higher steps on the salary schedule as a consequence of their becoming master teachers. Further, since the costs of many fringe benefits are directly related to salaries (e.g., the district's contribution to social security and pension funds), the bill for these must be calculated for each alternative considered. Still further, increasing the sick leave and personal days permitted teachers will almost certainly increase their use. The district can expect to spend more for substitutes in the future. These expenditures must also be estimated, as must the increases for expanded medical and dental insurance. Finally, when all the financial implications of each contract provision have been accounted for, they must be totaled and compared to projected district revenues. If the latter are insufficient, either the proposed contract must be reconsidered, taxes must be increased, or both.

Estimating is not complete when the costs for the next fiscal year are determined. Fletcher must also be concerned about the impact of a proposed contract several years into the future. The cost of a provision is usually not simply carried forward into subsequent years. In part, this is due to the effects of compounding on salary and fringe benefits. However, costs are substantially affected by the upward movement of teachers through the salary schedule, which inevitably increases the total impact of adjustments. Further, future costs and revenues can be only imperfectly estimated, since they depend on a number of unknown factors, such as inflation rates and teacher turnover. A good procedure, then, is to make alternative assumptions about such factors and thereby create several estimates of a contract's budgetary effects—a "best case," a "worst case," and a "best guess."

The advent of sophisticated computer spreadsheet programs has taken much of the drudgery out of such calculations. It is now possible to estimate quickly the total and incremental costs of all contract provisions (in addition to expected revenues) well into the future. As a consequence, negotiators are in a position to be vastly more knowledgeable about the financial implications of whatever they agree to. However, the quality of the estimates generated by these computer programs is largely dependent on the assumptions and economic models built into them by their users.

Collective Bargaining and Resource Allocation Decisions

Obviously Fletcher must consider more than the effects of the NGTA's proposals on his district's compensation package. He must also consider their effects on how he allocates resources in other areas of New Golconda's budget. Only recently have researchers begun to turn their attention to such matters. Consequently, the few studies we mention here should be taken as suggestive of the kinds of effects that are plausibly connected to teacher unionization. There is a substantial need for research in this area.

One of the more interesting approaches to examining the effects of teacher bargaining was that of Eberts and Pierce (1982). These investigators theorized that bargaining increases the number of contraints on administrative decisions, causing changes in the ways resources are allocated. They found that the contracts of unionized districts were more likely to reflect the preferences of older and more experienced teachers, as in sick leave and seniority provisions. One consequence of this was that unionized districts experienced less turnover than nonunion districts, reducing the capacity of administrators to affect the character of their teaching forces through recruitment policies. Further, because administrators in nonunion districts tended to fill vacancies with less experienced teachers, total salary costs were lowered and additional funds were made available for other programs. These tendencies were particularly evident in systems experiencing declining enrollments. The net result was a higher expenditure per pupil in unionized school systems.

Eberts and Pierce also analyzed the effects of specific contract provisions. For example, a provision making layoffs difficult or impossible during enrollment declines caused resources to be shifted away from other programs. Further, they found that the more complex the contract (as measured by the sheer number of its provisions), the greater the budget allocations for instructional expenditures, salaries, and teacher benefits, and the lower the allocations to other budget categories. Teachers in districts with the most complex contracts received $1,855 more per year than teachers in districts with the least complex contracts. Finally, they found that contract provisions concerning reductions in force seemed to decrease the quit rate of experienced teachers but to increase it for those with less experience. In sum, collective bargaining gives teachers a voice in administrative decision making. "Voice" is reflected in contract provisions that may place significant constraints on administrative decisions about seemingly unrelated matters.

The constraints of contract provisions on administrative actions are probably not uniform within a district, however. Kerchner (1984) has shown that building principals interpret the same contract clause in various ways. For example, a provision that specified the length of the school day might be strictly enforced at one school and virtually ignored at another. Thus, as Gouldner (1964) pointed out long ago, organizational rules open new avenues for the exercise of administrative discretion even while they close others.

It should also be remembered that elaborate contracts, those with many provisions, constrain the behavior of teachers as well as administrators. In effect, such contracts have the consequence of bureaucratizing the work process in schools. Thus Kerchner (1984) also found that teachers with highly professionalized orientations toward their work tended *not* to protest these constraints (as Corwin's work would predict). Instead, they tended to withdraw into their classrooms and close the door—to "exit" the organization. The implications of such a reaction, were it to be widespread, are potentially significant.

Resource allocation decisions are affected in other ways by collective bargaining. First and most obviously, the time administrators (and sometimes teachers' union leaders) give to the bargaining process may be significant. At present, we have virtually no research on this matter, though it is commonplace to hear superintendents complain about it. Conceived as opportunity costs, time spent in negotiating a contract must be taken from other activities. In money terms, Kerchner (1979) estimated the costs of bargaining for California school districts to be $35 million greater than those generated by meet-and-confer processes. This figure ignores the costs borne by the state and the unions and the value of contributed services of board members and teachers (Lieberman, 1980). Second, there are undoubtedly substantial costs to contract administration. The part of the salary of a personnel director devoting time to administering contractual obligations is an incremental cost of the process. Similarly, the fees paid to hired negotiators such as Weller and Corps must be included, as well as those paid to attorneys for representing the board in grievance and impasse procedures. (It is worth noting that Sarthory, 1971, found that when lawyers such as Corps represent a school district in the bargaining process, negotiations are more likely to end in impasse.) All such monetary and nonmonetary costs must, of course, be balanced against whatever benefits accrue to the district as a consequence of collective bargaining. The point, however, is that resources expended in these ways are necessarily unavailable for other uses. Lieberman (1980), formerly a staunch advocate of teacher unionization, considers that these costs far outweigh the benefits, especially in small districts. In any case, Walt Fletcher must be cognizant of the hidden costs of protracted negotiations and those incurred as a result of administering a complex contract.

More than administrators' allocation decisions may be affected by bargaining; teachers, too, may be affected. Eberts and Pierce (1982) studied the effect of bargaining on the ways in which teachers allocate their time to five activities: instruction, preparation, administrative and clerical duties, parent conferences, and other (usually after-school) activities. Using survey data from a national sample of over 3,000 teachers in 250 districts, they concluded that collective bargaining results in the reduction of instructional time equivalent to one week per year. This is not a trivial amount; it is well within the range where it might have an adverse effect on pupil learning. About half of this "released' time was given to administrative and clerical activities, and the remainder was spread between preparing lessons and parent conferences. It is problematic whether such uses improve the quality of the remaining instructional time enough to offset the decrement.

The established link between instructional time and student achievement should make administrators such as Walt Fletcher cautious in agreeing to any demands that reduce classroom instruction. The NGTA's desire to reduce the length of the school day must be considered carefully. Much depends on the uses to which teachers' free time would be put. Similarly, increasing the number of personal and sick days permitted is tantamount to reducing instructional time (unless substitute teachers are considered qualitatively equivalent to regular teachers). Finally, both the district's and the NGTA's proposal regarding master teachers should be considered in this perspective. The district's proposal assumes that time spent assisting their less able colleagues will more than offset any reductions in learning in the master teachers' classes when those classes are taught by substitutes. On the other hand, the NGTA's counteroffer involves the reallocation of some of these teachers' time to administrative activities—teacher recruitment and evaluation. It is certainly possible that using the time of superior teachers in either of these ways will have a net positive effect on the pupils of New Golconda; however, neither Fletcher nor Weller can know this.

Collective Bargaining as Participation in Decision Making

If the literature on collective bargaining and resource allocation is skimpy, that on collective bargaining and teacher participation in decision making is almost nonexistent. Such research might seem superfluous. It is obvious that negotiating processes must necessarily involve teachers, or at least their representatives. And since participation is commonly held to be a good thing, it follows that bargaining must also be a good thing. Similarly, if bargaining leads to participation, which in turn leads to higher morale and ultimately higher student achievement, it again follows that bargaining is a good thing. This is the argument made by Sam Weller in defense of his version of the master teacher plan. Walt Fletcher and other administrators need to examine these arguments.

We take it as obvious that collective bargaining has increased some teachers' participation in school district decision making. It is not clear, however, that collective bargaining has, overall, had this effect. It may, in fact, have decreased the participation of some. Recall Kerchner's (1984) research, which suggested that some teachers tended to withdraw in the face of elaborate contracts that they felt constrained their actions. For these people, protesting a contractually agreed-upon procedure is to protest the actions of their colleagues. The Wisconsin Supreme Court has actually prohibited a school board from even listening to a dissident teacher speak (at an open school board meeting) on a matter then under negotiation with the teacher's union. The court found that such listening constituted an unfair labor practice (Lieberman, 1980, p. 138).

More important, it also seems obvious that collective negotiation has decreased the participation of the public in educational decisions. We will have more to say about this shortly. For the moment it is enough to note that in most places, citizens are prevented from participating in negotiations, and, indeed, those negotiations are carried out under a cloak of secrecy. Thus, while it is clear that teachers' union leaders participate more frequently in making school district decisions, it is not clear that the overall participation of others has also increased.

But this is not the main thrust of Sam Weller's argument concerning the proposed cabinets. He argues that these cabinets will increase teacher participation, which, in turn, will improve teacher morale and pupil learning. There is a voluminous literature on these subjects, recently summarized by Conway (1984), who concluded that the beliefs that participating in decisions improves teacher satisfaction, that it increases their willingness to accept and implement changes, or that it produces higher-quality teaching are "myths." More specifically, while numerous studies have suggested such linkages, an almost equal number have not. In any case, whatever the relationships among these variables, they are at best very modest. The obvious problem is that these relationships are not straightforward. Participation can vary in degree; it can vary in its content (i.e., the nature of the decisions involved); and it can vary in its stage (i.e., the point at which participation is sought). It seems unlikely that all of New Golconda's master teachers will be equally eager to participate in the district's personnel decisions. Presumably, they will be selected because of their teaching ability, not their desire to serve on school cabinets. It is equally obvious that not all teachers wish to participate in many decisions. There are costs for doing so—in time, in *individual* autonomy, and (potentially) in collegial disfavor (Duke, Showers, & Imber, 1980). This is *not* to argue against involving a teaching staff in educational choices. It is to say that *which teachers* should be involved in *what decisions* and at *what stages* are important considerations if job satisfaction, morale, and teaching quality are to be improved. Certainly Fletcher should not expect that the cabinets Weller has proposed will automatically lead to these benefits.

Collective Bargaining and Educational Achievement

When one turns to the outcomes of schooling, studies of the effects of collective bargaining are few and far between, and their results are difficult to interpret. At present we must rely mainly on whatever inferences can be made from studies that compare unionized and nonunion districts. Such studies are highly problematic. For example, Sherman (1983), in one of the more carefully conducted investigations of this genre, concluded that the presence of a contract (presumably indicating a highly developed bargaining relationship) had a substantial deleterious effect on pupil learning as measured by standardized tests. Pupils in districts with contracts had both lower levels of achievement and greater variation in achievement than did their peers in noncontract districts.

Obviously, contracts per se do not affect pupil achievement. However, contract *provisions*, where such provisions touch on aspects of teaching thought to affect achievement, might. For example, any provision that sets district policy with regard to class size, administrative leadership, site management, staff stability and renewal, parental involvement, and, perhaps most important, learning time has the potential to affect pupil learning. These are all conditions that the effective schools research suggests as having potent effects on student learning, and many contracts contain provisions regarding them. Doherty (1980), for example, speculated that provisions that limit the length of the school day and the school year have a substantial potential for affecting student achievement.

Contract provisions may cut two ways, however. If a contract limits the length of the school year and hence has a deleterious effect on student achievement, it is also possible (perhaps even probable) that the same contract contains a provision setting a maximum class size. Such a provision has the potential for augmenting pupil achievement. The net effect of such contracts may be nil. For this reason alone, it seems likely that research that attempts to link the presence or absence of a union or a contract to pupil learning is likely to miss important consequences. Research needs to be carried out at the level of contract provisions.

One step in this direction was made by Eberts and Stone (1984), who studied mathematics achievement in a national sample of elementary schools. Using production function techniques, they first identified the factors that seemed to affect pupil performance in that subject. They found that the factors having a positive effect were, in order of importance, principal time spent in evaluating math programs, teacher time spent in math instruction, years of administrative experience of principals, teacher preparation time, and teacher experience. Conversely, the factors negatively related to achievement were advanced degrees held by both teachers and administrators and number of administrators per student. Eberts and Stone then compared union and nonunion districts on these factors and concluded that the net effect of unionization was nil—the various effects indeed balanced each other. For example, because of their contracts, teachers in unionized districts apparently spent less time on math instruction, which lowered average achievement, but more time on preparation, which raised it.

Research on the effects of specific contract provisions is just beginning—and is badly needed. Until we have it, administrators such as Fletcher have only their own best judgment to rely on when considering the implications of a provision for pupil achievement. This is not to argue that achievement should be the only criterion for evaluating a union's proposal. Obviously other things, such as equity, must be considered. It is to argue, however, that to ignore the potential effect of a provision on what and how much students learn is to ignore a central objective of schooling. Until such research appears, the best that Fletcher can do is to be aware of the factors demonstrated to influence pupil learning and then to examine each of the NGTA's proposals for its potential effect on those factors.

Collective Bargaining and Educational Policy

Not very long ago, educators were debating whether or not collective bargaining would affect educational policy. Today the debate is more likely to concern how much policy is affected and whether or not those effects are desirable. This may seem surprising. After all, even in states that permit bargaining, negotiations are commonly restricted to "terms and conditions of work"—salary, fringe benefits, and the like. However, what may be considered a condition of work is unclear. State courts are currently in the process of defining the "scope of bargaining"— what may be legitimately bargained and what may not. It is often thought that matters of public policy may not be items of negotiation between unions and school boards. But some people (e.g., Lieberman, 1980) have argued that *any* contract provision is a matter of public policy. Consider salaries. How much teachers are paid is surely a condition of their work. Equally surely, it is a matter of public policy and is, arguably, an inappropriate matter for bargaining. We shall have more to say later regarding the scope of bargaining. For the moment, let us note that research on this matter is scattered and difficult to interpret.

One of the most extensive studies on this topic was carried out by Goldschmidt, Bowers, Riley, and Leland (1983). Taking a very restrictive view of what constituted policy, these researchers nevertheless concluded that traditional matters of educational policy were being bargained in an increasing number of school districts around the country. For example, they found that 48 percent of the contracts they studied contained provisions regarding the curriculum, 64 percent had provisions pertaining to pupil placement, and 96 percent concerned teacher placement. These have traditionally been thought of as matters of board policy. These results suggest that the policy impact of collective bargaining may be considerably greater than has been supposed. Consider the following curriculum provision from a real contract (Mazzarella, 1984):

> *Nothing in this provision shall prohibit the Board from developing innovative programs and schedules in certain schools so long as staff in such a school by secret ballot votes approval of such innovation.*

We take it as self-evident that what is taught in schools is a matter of public policy. Yet this provision gives teachers the power to veto a curricular change made at a school board's instigation. Though this provision strikes us as atypical, some very common provisions (such as those concerning class size, which is certainly a condition of work) are either arguably matters of policy or have obvious and important policy implications.

Perhaps, however, focusing on whether or not a particular provision affects board policy misses the point. Mitchell, Kerchner, Erck, and Pryor (1981), in a perceptive analysis of bargaining practices in eight school districts, concluded that massive changes in American education are occurring as *accidental* by-products of the negotiation process. They argue that substantial revisions of teachers' work have occurred, that basic changes in the mechanisms of control have arisen, and that important modifications in the authority of school principals have taken place, all without deliberate choice.

Concerning the redefinition of teachers' work, Mitchell and his colleagues point to three examples: the separation of regular from "extra" duties, pressures to eliminate or curtail the work of specialist teachers (such as reading specialists), and the creation of a climate encouraging minimal effort during the active stages of bargaining. With regard to the first of these, they suggest that contractual agreement requiring additional pay for extra duties (such as supervising after-school activities) effectively communicates to teachers that they may *choose* to perform these duties or not as they see fit. Because administrators have taken the position that these are traditionally part of a teacher's job, administrators have strenuously resisted paying anything but minimal compensation for their performance. As a result, teachers find compensation to be so small as to make doing these tasks a matter of volunteer work rather than overtime work for pay. In times of budget constraints, in part generated by bargaining itself, these once taken-for-granted aspects of school life may disappear.

Concerning specialist teachers, Mitchell et al. point to the fact that contracts are implicitly written with the typical classroom teacher in mind (though specialists make up about 13 percent of the work force). In part, this results from the difficulty specialists have in generating support for their demands among their union colleagues. Regular teachers tend to see specialists as enjoying protected, less demanding, and less productive jobs. On their part, administrators are also unsupportive of specialists' demands being written into contracts, because to do so makes the bargaining process more difficult and, in the end, more costly. For example, even if administrators privately agree that a group of specialists require additional planning time during the working day, they will resist agreeing to a provision that grants it (in the event that a teachers' union would even put it forward) because they fear that regular teachers would then make the same demand. The net effect of these forces is to cause a decline in specialists' effectiveness and, ultimately, perhaps, in the number of specialists themselves.

Finally, with regard to the minimization of work, the researchers note that during the time when bargaining was going on in the districts they studied, especially if that bargaining was prolonged and contentious, there was a pronounced increase in tensions between administrators and teachers. Communication between the two groups declined, and program planning came to a halt. These effects were observed regardless of (in some cases in addition to) any "job actions" mounted by the union against the districts. For example, "working to rule," a tactic common in private-sector unions, occurred at some of their study sites; teachers refused to take part in any activities or meet any deadlines not specifically covered in their contracts.

Collective bargaining also affected the mechanisms of control exercised by administrators. The existence of grievance procedures, for example, increased the level of formality between principal and teachers and made administrators disinclined to treat teachers differently, even when their professional judgment led them to believe such treatment was justified. Similarly, bargaining over fringe benefits, Mitchell et al. argue, resulted in serious levels of teacher absenteeism. They found that teachers interpreted a contract that permitted ten sick days and three personal days per year as *entitling* them to be away from work thirteen days, rather than as thirteen days' worth of insurance against adversity. As a last example of how bargaining has affected mechanisms of control, they found that almost all contracts devoted considerable space to specifying when and how teacher evaluations would be conducted. Simultaneously, both teachers and administrators lack confidence in the validity of the evaluation procedures themselves. In effect, bargaining required that both sides undergo a process neither believed would lead to valid judgments.

Finally, the writers suggest that the advent of strong teachers' unions has placed principals in a situation where their subordinates may choose between the organization and their union as the legitimate interpreter of educational policies and practices. One outcome of this was that even the best principals could not count on the cooperation of their staffs in the pursuit of district objectives (Mitchell et al., 1981).

Collective Bargaining: Conclusions

What is one to make of all of this for the practice of educational administration? What guidance does the research on collective bargaining provide to administrators such as Walt Fletcher? Unfortunately, only in the area of the effects of bargaining on salaries do we have a reasonably clear understanding of its impact. Yet it is precisely this area that may be of least importance. As soon as one moves beyond salaries to ask how bargaining has affected the ways in which administrators allocate resources, how it may influence the opportunities of teachers and others to participate in educational governance, what its effects on student achievement might be, and whether or not it has affected the policymaking process, one must rely increasingly on tenuous inferences from the available research.

We have tried to draw some of these inferences here, but we freely admit that other readers of the same literature might reach other conclusions. Perhaps the rise of teachers' unions and the legitimation of collective bargaining in many states has had only salutary effects on the profession. Perhaps, as in the case of salaries, its effects have been minimal. Nevertheless, as we understand it, concern is growing among students in the field that the changes it has wrought have been profound, even though they may be inadequately documented at present.

Perhaps Janet Corps's closing sentiments capture these changes as well as any of the more systematic attempts we have reviewed. In the old days, people did not talk to teachers that way.

Collective Bargaining and the Law

Perhaps the most important issue raised by the negotiations in New Golconda is that of the conflict between unionization and democratic values. The belief that schools should be democratically run is widely held by Americans. We have argued for this view in Chapter 6. Yet it seems that there are good reasons to believe that unionization affects the democratic control of schools adversely. Janet Corps has so argued and has declared her intention to resist the erosion of democratic authority in New Golconda.

Note that this is a matter of concern for administrators as well as for school board members. It is not just that superintendents are often called on to negotiate with the union. Perhaps the more important fact is that administrators must execute and implement board decisions. Thus, de facto, limits on the board's right to make policy are also limits on administrative discretion. Sam Weller's proposals to establish policy cabinets and to involve teachers in hiring and promotions erodes board authority. But they also constrain the ability of administrators to make recommendations to the board. Sam Weller's proposals would alter substantially the relationship between administrators and teachers in New Golconda.

We wish to consider the issue of the conflict between democracy and unionization in terms of the legal and moral standards we should use to judge the issue. Legally, what role is permissible for unions in making educational policy? From the perspective of our ideals about democracy, what role for unions in decision making is justifiable? We will first consider these questions as legal issues, then as philosophical ones.

How do these issues appear in the law? Here we want to address three questions:

1. In what ways does the law conceptualize public-sector collective bargaining as different from private-sector bargaining?
2. Are there legal restrictions on the process of collective bargaining in the public sector that are not placed on collective bargaining in the private sector?
3. Would the proposals Sam Weller has made to the New Golconda Board of Education survive legal challenge?

At the center of the legal view of collective bargaining is the concept of sovereignty. Some of the flavor of this doctrine can be gotten from the remarks of Justice Jennings in one of the most notable cases on collective bargaining by teachers, *Norwalk Teachers' Association v. Board of Education:*

> *Under our system, the government is established by and run for all of the people, not for the benefit of any person or group. The profit motive, inherent in the principle of free enterprise, is absent. It should be the aim of every employee of the government to do his or her part to make it function as efficiently as possible. (p. 273)*

Later in the same opinion, Jennings writes:

> *In the American system, sovereignty is inherent in the people. They can delegate it to a government which they create and operate by law. They can give to that government the power and authority to perform certain duties and furnish certain services. The government so created and empowered must employ people to carry on its task. Those people are agents of the government. They exercise some part of the sovereignty entrusted to it. They occupy a status entirely different from those who carry on a private enterprise. They serve the public welfare and not a private purpose. To say that they can strike is the equivalent of saying that they can deny the authority of government and contravene the public welfare. (p. 276)*

The essence of the objection to the right to strike is that it is *inherently* in conflict with democratic authority—it conflicts with, in Jennings's terms, the sovereignty inherent in the people.

Earlier in its history, this notion of sovereignty was expressed in the doctrine of sovereign immunity, which precluded citizens from taking legal action against their own government. Citizens were not entitled to sue a governmental agency, let alone organize for collective bargaining against it, without its permission.

This traditional version of the doctrine has been much eroded, and this erosion is nowhere better exhibited than in collective bargaining. At most, the doctrine can be construed to require a state to enact legislation authorizing the collective bargaining process for public employees (see Alexander, 1985). Most states have done so. Even where teachers have not been awarded the right to organize for collective bargaining, the rights of freedom of assembly can be construed to grant them the privilege to form voluntary associations and to petition their employers.

The law governing collective bargaining is to be found largely in state statutes. These statutes characteristically cover such topics as procedures and regulations for organizing a bargaining unit, the composition of bargaining units, impasse resolution and the right to strike, and the scope of bargaining. Some states have statutes that deal specifically with schools; others deal more generally with collective bargaining in the public sector. They vary greatly and defy summary in a work such as this. So we will focus on two topics: (1) the right to strike and impasse resolution and (2) the scope of collective bargaining. The following Rhode Island statute illustrates a common approach to each area.

It is hereby declared to be the public policy of this state to accord to certified public school teachers the right to organize, to be represented, to negotiate professionally, and to bargain on a collective basis with school committees covering hours, salary, working conditions, and other terms of professional employment, provided, however, that nothing contained in this chapter shall be construed to accord to certified public school teachers the right to strike. (R.I. Gen. Stat. Ann., § 28-9.3-1, 1968 Reenact.)

In most states, the right to strike is denied to public employees and thus to teachers. Several states, however, have expressly permitted such strikes. Some states that prohibit strikes also attach penalties to striking teachers and their unions. New York's Taylor Law, for example, provides for a loss of two days' pay for every day a teacher is on strike and allows for the suspension of some of the union's normal rights. Generally, where strikes are illegal, school districts may get court injunctions against strikes, and unions or union officials who violate such injunctions run the risk of being cited for contempt of court. That strikes are illegal does not, of course, always serve to prevent them. Nor do penalties. Indeed, the existence of penalties may also serve to expand the agenda to be dealt with in order to settle a strike. The union may simply add a no-penalty demand to the list of things to bargain.

Given that public employee strikes are normally illegal, many states provide for other forms of resolving bargaining impasses. Such devices include mediation, arbitration, and fact finding. States sometimes create bureaus to provide such services.

Teachers' unions also may engage in coercive tactics that fall short of striking. For example, they may reduce the services of their teachers to the contractually required minimum (work to rule). A district that has substantially involved its teachers in decision making, particularly if their participation involves the union, will have done a great deal to help make such job actions effective. Should New Golconda agree to the union's demands for teacher participation in the governance of the district, they will have given the teachers considerable leverage.

There are four ways in which the scope of proper subjects for collective bargaining can be determined. First, school boards may be specifically charged, under state law, with certain administrative responsibilities. They may be legally prohibited from delegating these responsibilities. It is unlikely, for example, that a school district would be entitled to delegate hiring and promotion decisions. This is not to say that the board may not solicit recommendations from its administration or teachers or even that it may not routinely accept them. It is to say that they may not transfer ultimate authority over such decisions. Second, revenue limitations may restrict the benefits that can be conferred on teachers. School districts cannot contractually commit themselves to expend resources they do not have. Third, school districts may be prohibited from negotiating some issues, such as retirement benefits or curriculum mandates. Finally, statutes such as that of Rhode Island frequently contain lists of bargainable topics. Rhode Island's statute is, in fact, reasonably typical of the sorts of things contained in such lists. Presumably the point of these lists of negotiable topics is to focus bargaining on economic benefits and working conditions and to steer it away from policy issues.

The similarity among these lists may be misleading, however, for they tend to function differently in different states. New York distinguishes between mandatory and permissible subjects for collective bargaining. Boards *must* bargain about such matters as wages and hours; they *may* bargain about other issues. In other states, items not specifically enumerated in the list of permissible topics are regarded as forbidden. California's statute reads as follows:

> *The scope of representation shall be limited to matters relating to wages, hours of employment, and other terms and conditions of employment. "Terms and conditions of employment" mean health and welfare benefits as defined by Section 53200, leave and transfer policies, safety conditions of employment, class size, procedures to be used for the evaluation of employees, organizational security pursuant to Section 3546, and procedures for processing grievances pursuant to Sections 3548.5, 3548.6, 3548.7, and 3548.8. In addition, the exclusive representative of certificated personnel has the right to consult on the definition of educational objectives, the determination of the content of courses and curriculum, and the selection of textbooks to the extent such matters are within the discretion of the public school employer under the law. All matters not specifically enumerated are reserved to the public school employer and may not be a subject of meeting and negotiating, providing that nothing herein may be construed to limit the right of the public school employer to consult with any employees or employee organization on any matter outside the scope of representation.*

Two caveats are appropriate here. The first is that statutes that attempt to restrict bargaining to wages and working conditions may not be as prohibitive as they initially appear. Certainly an ingenious union can discover devices to expand the concept of working conditions to cover most issues it would like to bargain.

Second, variation in statutes appear not to have made much difference in the range of provisions in collective bargaining agreements. Doherty (1980) summarizes his observations on this topic as follows:

> *Although it would appear that there are substantial differences among the states as to what issues constitute appropriate subject matter, there is considerable similarity in the actual scope of collective bargaining contracts. It may be that in those states that allow for broad latitude of subject matter, the employers have successfully resisted demands they believe to be intrusions into policy matters. It may also be that the unions do not feel keenly enough about many of these issues to push them to impasse. (pp. 529–530)*

Are the proposals that Sam Weller has made permissible topics for negotiation, and if so, could a board of education legally agree to them?

Given the variation in state laws, it is nearly impossible to generalize with any assurance on these questions. Indeed, it is doubtful that they could be answered clearly for many individual states. But several valid generalizations can be made.

First, in states, such as California, that have attempted to limit collective bargaining to a prescribed list of topics, the point of the statutes so far as personnel matters are concerned appears to be to enable negotiation on the due process and procedural aspects of personnel decisions while precluding it on the substance of such decisions. Presumably, they would also preclude negotiations on teacher or union participation in decision making. On the other hand, the California statute does not preclude "consulting" on these forbidden topics. Nor does it clearly preclude a board from voluntarily agreeing to proposals concerning such matters. It does, however, make it clear that a board could not be compelled to negotiate or discuss personnel issues beyond procedural questions.

The second issue concerns the extent to which a board might delegate decision-making power to teachers or to a union over personnel matters. It seems clear that in most states, school boards would find it legally difficult to transfer final authority to teachers, their unions, or anyone else for that matter. What is not clear is whether Sam Weller's proposals amount to such a transfer of authority. Teachers are clearly given a good deal of opportunity to participate in personnel decisions. Moreover, though the board's rights to reject the "advice" of teachers concerning promotions is not waived, it is restricted. Does this amount to an impermissible delegation of board authority?

It is inappropriate for us to speculate on how such provisions would be dealt with in the fifty states. Two observations will have to suffice. First, we believe that the issue of improper delegation of board authority is the central issue in the case both legally and philosophically. Second, stronger provisions (ones that give probationary teachers the due process rights normally reserved to tenured teachers) have been successfully incorporated into some collective bargaining agreements (see Agreement, 1980). Were these provisions adopted, it is not clear that they would be illegal in many states.

In conclusion, we should note that regardless of the legal merits of these proposals, we do not believe that they are acceptable policy. There is much to be said for involving teachers in evaluation and, more generally, in decision making. However, the arguments to this point in this book weigh strongly against either granting the teachers' union control over teacher input into district decision making or transferring effective authority over such decisions to teachers. To do so is to erode democratic control over education.

Teachers' Unions: Questions of Legitimacy and Role

Teachers' unions are widely thought to be good for teachers, but, as we have noted, it is less clear that they are good for the education of children. They are accused of such sins as irrationally inflating the costs of education, protecting incompetent teachers, usurping the prerogatives of school boards and administrators, and setting a bad example for children. They are held to have changed teachers from dedicated professionals trying to maintain professional standards to employees trying to extract the last dollar from the public treasury. They have seduced teachers into such nefarious activities as illegal strikes and work stoppages.

Our case raises some issues that go to the heart of complaints about collective bargaining in education. Janet Corps is concerned that the union will ultimately make teachers less responsible to parents, the community, and the board of education. Her objection to the union seems to go deeper than some of the complaints we noted. She suggests that the union's power over educational policy in New Golconda is illegitimate. It erodes the authority of the community over the education of its children. Indeed, Corps might avail herself of some of the arguments for democratic control of education we made in Chapter 6. If schools ought to be governed democratically, a union's power over decision making is improper, since it will be bought at the expense of democratic control. Sam Weller has proposed some significant types of involvement for the union in decision making in New Golconda. He has argued that the schools will be better run and that teachers will be more effective if they have a role in decision making. Perhaps this is true. But is union participation in district decision making illegitimate and undemocratic?

A second issue is the scope of collective bargaining. If one does not take the extreme position of Janet Corps that collective bargaining is inherently illegitimate, it may nevertheless be argued that it is improper to negotiate certain topics. Unions may, for example, have a legitimate right to bargain about salary or working conditions. But perhaps they should not be entitled to bargain about central matters of educational concern, such as evaluation policy. Evaluation ought to be maintained as a prerogative of the board of education. Sam Weller has proposed some substantial forms of participation for teachers in teacher evaluation and promotion. Arguably, not only should the board not accept his proposals, they should not even be willing to discuss them. To do so is to grant the possibility that it might be permissible for the board to transfer its responsibility to the union. Note that in this case the erosion of board power is also the erosion of administrative discretion. The mechanisms Sam Weller has suggested to enhance teacher participation in decision making work by transferring to teachers some of the usual administrative powers to advise the board. Thus, although the formal authority that is challenged belongs to the board, the real loss of power may be felt most by the district's administrators.

We shall pursue these questions by examining two arguments about teachers' unions that suggest that there may be something illegitimate about them. Neither argument is directly concerned with the effects of teachers' unions on the quality of education, although that is an indirect concern. Instead, they focus on the claim that collective bargaining in education (and in the public sector generally) undermines important values concerning how public institutions should be run.

The first argument holds that collective bargaining by public employees is incompatible with democratic control of public institutions. Collective bargaining results in the negotiation of public policy with a privileged special-interest group. It thus reduces both the ability of the public to participate in what are legitimately public affairs and the power of elected officials to make policy in a democratic way. The second argument holds that collective bargaining in the public sector violates norms of justice in determining employee benefits by granting unions excessive power over boards of education. Unions are able to extract greater benefits than they are fairly entitled to. If potential school administrators understand these arguments, they will be in a position to understand what is really at issue in New Golconda.

Consider first the claim that collective bargaining in the public sector is inconsistent with democracy. Robert Summers (1976) expressed the heart of the argument as follows:

> *Under bargaining laws, some or all of the foregoing public decision-making powers (before then exclusively in public hands) were partially redistributed from the public and public employers to private unions and their members. The statutes legally obligate public employing bodies to share decisional power with entities not subject to the control of or accountable to the public for the positions they take.*
>
> *Thus, the conflict between democratic processes and public employee bargaining is inherent and diminishes democratic decision making, for it requires the sharing of public authority with private bodies (unions). (p. 4)*

This argument involves two assumptions. It assumes that there is a right of democratic control of education. This right is sufficiently strong that if collective bargaining weakens or erodes democratic control, that would be objectionable. It also assumes that collective bargaining in education erodes democratic control. Are there reasons to agree with either of these assumptions?

Both Summers (1976) and Lieberman (1980) treat the first assumption as obvious. They provide only a very sketchy argument for it. That need not concern us here, however, for we have provided an argument in its support in Chapter 6. Let us grant Summers his first premise. The case for democratic control over education is sufficiently strong that good reasons are required to justify any weakening of it. Summers provides several reasons for the second claim. Perhaps, however, the central assumption in both Summers's and Lieberman's second argument is that the conflict between collective bargaining and democracy is inherent. To the extent that a union causes a school district to do something that the elected members of the school board would otherwise not have chosen to do, democracy is frustrated. So conceived, *any* success a union has in securing for its members a benefit that the school board would not have provided voluntarily is an erosion of democracy. Only if it were completely impotent would collective bargaining not erode democracy. Thus the second assumption, that unions erode democratic authority over public policy, requires little real defense. One must only believe that collective bargaining actually makes a difference.

If we grant that Summers has made a prima facie case on behalf of Janet Corps's implied claim that collective bargaining erodes democracy in the governance of educational affairs, we must still ask if there are considerations that might justify such an erosion. We believe that there is a case to be made on the side of collective bargaining.

Consider the following question. Does an individual who is, or who contemplates becoming, a public employee have the right to bargain for his or her services? We believe that the answer has to be yes.

At the heart of the right of an individual to bargain is that person's right to refuse to perform a service or to accept a position unless his or her conditions are met. This is not to say that employers have a duty to grant every demand made by their actual or prospective employees. It is only to say that the right of freedom of choice gives each individual the right to refuse to accept a position or to quit if the conditions of employment are not satisfactory. The employer then has a choice either to meet the individual's demands or to seek another employee.

The process of employees seeking acceptable terms and employers proffering them does not usually take the form of two individuals sitting down together and discussing terms. It works as a market mechanism affecting the cost and quality of labor. Nevertheless, a form of bargaining is going on. The sense of a collection of individuals as to what they will accept and the sense of employers as to what they will offer serves (in conjunction with other factors) to determine the features of the labor market.

Notice two things about this kind of bargaining. First, it seems inconceivable that we should consider it objectionable. To do so would be to give employers the right to compel people to work for them under any and all conditions and at any wage. The common term for such an economic system is slavery.

Second, this form of bargaining goes on in public and private sectors. Hence it is a limitation on democratic power insofar as what a public agency can accomplish is subject to the influence of market forces for labor. If school districts cannot hire a suitable quality of teacher for the wages they are willing to pay, they will be required either to raise their wages or to lower their educational aspirations. It seems implausible to hold that democratic authority is thwarted in some illegitimate fashion by these market forces. To hold such a position is to hold that public employers are entitled to compel individuals to work for them under conditions dictated by some democratic decision-making body. Few people are so enamored of democracy that they will believe that it justifies enslavement by a public agency.

Let us summarize. Individual bargaining or market forces place limits on the scope of democratic authority, just as collective bargaining does. Yet we do not regard individual bargaining as illegitimate for that reason. Indeed, we regard the right of an individual to refuse employment as a highly important right. Why, then, do we find it problematic when collective bargaining is shown to place constraints on democratic authority? An answer to this question must point to some quite fundamental difference between individual and collective bargaining.

Before we ask if there is any such fundamental difference, we need to ask one further question. What is the point of collective bargaining in the first place? Why is the right of the individual to bargain or to refuse employment seen as insufficient to protect the rights or the interests of workers?

One response is that collective bargaining is seen as a remedy to an imbalance of power between the employee and the employer. That is, the power of the individual to bargain with an employer is insufficient to secure a just settlement with the employer. Collective bargaining provides for the equalization of power and promotes the prospects of employer and employee striking a fair bargain.

It follows that if one believes in collective bargaining at all, one must also believe that it is possible for a person to be coerced into accepting employment under conditions that are unfair. And one must believe that the simple fact that an employee has agreed to accept employment is not in itself sufficient to certify the agreed-to conditions as fair. If the power between employer and employee is unequal, it is possible to see individual agreements as exploitative and coercive, despite the fact that the employee has agreed to them.

Nothing about this argument changes because the employer is a public agency. If individuals can be exploited by employers despite the fact that they have accepted the terms of employment, they can be so exploited even if those who employ them are elected officials exercising democratic authority.

What follows from these considerations is that if there are significant differences in collective bargaining in public and private contexts, those differences do not eliminate the question of exploitation. There may be differences in the degree to which public and private employers are inclined or able to exploit their employees, but there is no reason, in principle, why a public employer cannot be an unjust employer. The employee's interest in collective bargaining is the same, regardless of whether the employer is a public or private agency.

We have now shown both that the employee's interests in collective bargaining are the same regardless of whether the employer is a public or a private agency and that individual bargaining erodes democratic authority when an individual bargains with a public agency. We have also shown that despite its effects on democratic power, individual bargaining is a legitimate institution that serves a compelling interest—the liberation of individuals from a form of slavery. Why, then, is collective bargaining illegitimate when it erodes democratic authority? People who wish to object to collective bargaining in the public sector must show that collective bargaining is significantly different from individual bargaining in its effects on democratic authority. They must also show that the risk to democracy run when collective bargaining is permitted outweighs the potential harm to public employees that may result from denying them the right to bargain collectively.

What, then, are the differences between collective bargaining and individual bargaining that makes the former, but not the latter, an unacceptable threat to democracy? Let's consider two possible responses.

One obvious difference is that collective bargaining may be more successful than bargaining by individuals. Collective bargaining alters the relative power between employees and employers. If bargaining per se erodes democratic power, it stands to reason that when the bargaining power of employees is enhanced, the erosion of democracy is also increased. In short, the difference between collective and individual bargaining is one of degree, not of kind. Collective bargaining poses a threat to democratic authority that is the same, in kind, as that posed by individual bargaining. It is simply more likely to be successful.

But this is not the kind of difference between collective bargaining and individual bargaining that seems required by either Robert Summers or by Janet Corps. If bargaining per se is legitimate even though its places constraints on democratic authority, it is difficult to see how it becomes illegitimate merely because it becomes effective. One may wish to argue that the balance of power between employees and employers has been improperly altered; that now employees have an unfair advantage over employers. That may indeed be true, and we shall consider it shortly. But that is a rather different argument. It does not show what Summers claims: that there is an inconsistency between collective bargaining and democracy sufficient to show collective bargaining to be inherently illegitimate. It merely shows that a suitable balance of power has not been struck. Such an argument may indicate that some change in the rules of collective bargaining is required, but it does not show collective bargaining to be the threat to the Republic that Summers claims it is.

A second argument is that collective bargaining and individual bargaining are fundamentally different because they protect rights of radically different sorts and radically different value. The right of an individual to bargain concerning employment is protection against what is tantamount to slavery. In a free society, people must have the right to decline employment if they find the conditions unacceptable. When we balance the right of an individual to bargain with an employer against the erosion of democratic authority that bargaining may cause, we are balancing a fundamental right of individuals against a trivial loss of democratic authority.

The matter is considerably different, however, when we consider collective bargaining. Here, no compelling right of the individual is at stake. The denial of collective bargaining is not tantamount to an affirmation of slavery. The ability of an individual to bargain successfully when he or she cannot bargain collectively may be diminished, but individuals are not compelled to accept employment under conditions unacceptable to themselves. Moreover, the erosion of democratic authority may be more severe under collective bargaining simply because it is more likely to be successful. Thus when we consider collective bargaining in public employment, we are not balancing a trivial loss of democratic authority against slavery; we are balancing a potentially substantial loss of democratic authority against a mere diminution of bargaining power on the part of public employees. The equations seem radically different, and thus a different balance should be struck.

The crux of this argument is the assumption that what is at stake in the denial of collective bargaining to the individual is radically different from what is at stake in the denial of individual bargaining. One might respond to this argument that the right threatened by the denial of collective bargaining and the right threatened by the denial of individual bargaining are qualitatively the same. The difference is merely one of degree. In each case, what is at issue is the right of the individual not to have to work under conditions of unfair coercion. Were individual bargaining to be curtailed, the coercion of the individual would be extreme—it would be virtually equivalent to slavery. But insofar as people must bargain for their services against an employer whose power is substantially disproportionate to their own, they are also subjected to a form of coercion. They can be forced to settle for unfair wages or working conditions. Such coercion is not usually tantamount to slavery, but it is coercion nevertheless. The difference between the denial of individual bargaining and the denial of collective bargaining is thus one of degree. The interests involved in collective and individual bargaining are not qualitatively distinct.

This argument defeats the claim that the conflict between collective bargaining and democracy is a sufficient reason to reject collective bargaining for public employees. We have found that the interests of employees and the effects on democracy in individual and collective bargaining differ in degree, not in kind. These differences are not sufficient to show that the tension between democracy and collective bargaining renders collective bargaining inherently objectionable. Insofar as the strategy of Janet Corps and the New Golconda Board of Education is rooted in the assumption that collective bargaining is inherently illegitimate, we can find no reason to support it. The question to be asked is not whether there is a conflict between democracy and collective bargaining by public employees; there is. The question is how we are to strike a fair balance between the rights of public employees and the demands of democracy. Is the present balance appropriate? Are there things that ought not to be the topic of collective bargaining? This leads us to the second question we posed at the beginning of this discussion: The crucial issues are whether the school district ought to be willing to agree to or even to discuss the kinds of involvement in decision making for teachers that Sam Weller has proposed and whether a strike might be a legitimate strategy for the union to employ to force the board to agree to its proposals.

How, then, are we to think about the issue of whether in public employment, especially in the case of teachers, collective bargaining leads to a proper balance of power between employer and employee? Let us consider two approaches.

One approach might be to attempt to understand what counted as a fair balance of power in terms of the results produced. A fair balance of power is one that produces a just wage and decent working conditions for teachers without excessive erosion of democratic authority. The difficulty with this suggestion is that to apply it, we must know things that are difficult or even impossible to know. For example, what is to count as a just wage for teachers? How shall we decide? Are teachers entitled to more or less than carpenters or bank tellers? And how are we to quantify the actual benefits of teaching in contrast to other professions? Are we to look at annual wages and ignore the fact that teachers do not work for a full year?

A common response to such questions is to try to compare public employees with their counterparts in the private sector. If we wish to know, for example, what it is reasonable for a government to pay an accountant, we should determine the going rate for accountants in the private sphere.

This seems a reasonable approach, but it is difficult to apply to teachers. First, as we have discussed, the private market for teachers may be strongly affected by the public market. They lack the independence this comparison requires. Second, the majority of private schools are associated with religious organizations. They are more likely to be staffed by teachers who see their teaching as part of their religious duty and who are therefore also likely to accept a lower wage.

Perhaps most important, any attempt to determine a just wage by comparing public and private employees assumes that the wages paid in the private sphere are just. All these points would seem to defeat this presumption in the case of private school teachers.

A second approach is to focus on the bargaining process itself. We might assume that collective bargaining in the private sector is known to strike a fair balance between the rights of the employer and those of the employee and ask whether there are any significant differences between the process as it works in the public sector that function to give one party an unfair advantage over the other.

Several factors, some of which we have already discussed, might be held to provide an unfair advantage to the union. First, in the public sector, there is a lack of market constraints on the demands of employees. A union bargaining with a manufacturing company must reckon with the consequences of its demands on the well-being of the employer. It will not benefit from demands that could put the employer at a competitive disadvantage. Excessive wages can result in lost jobs or in the inability of the company to pay those wages.

Teachers' unions, however, run little risk of putting their employers out of business. Public schools do not have to compete for their students in a free market. Nor do they need to worry about pricing themselves out of the market. Thus neither they nor their employees are subject to the discipline of the market.

Second, the people who negotiate with teachers' unions lack the same incentives as corporation executives to resist excessive demands on the part of unions. Board members are characteristically unpaid volunteers who have little personal stake in successfully resisting union demands. Their jobs and livelihoods do not depend on their success. They are not spending their own money, and it is all too easy to view the public treasury as an inexhaustible resource. Nor is the average board member so committed to political advancement that failure to achieve re-election is a notable tragedy. Generally, board members have nothing to lose by yielding to union demands. Finally, they may find that the political pressure that results from failure to achieve a contract exceeds the pressure that arises from raising taxes. The incentives for board members to yield seem great, and the incentives to resist seem small, especially when compared with the incentives in the private sphere.

Third, if one assumes that teachers are willing to strike or to engage in some sort of job action, the coercive effect of such behavior may well exceed that of strikes in the private sphere. Public services are often essential services. Moreover, they are often not available from other sources. If General Motors goes on strike, the public can always buy Fords or Toyotas. If public school teachers go on strike, usually no alternative educational institutions are available. Thus public reaction is likely to be brought to bear in order to settle the strike. The school board member who causes parents to have to contend with their children during normal school hours may be less than popular among his or her neighbors.

Finally, teachers' unions may have disproportionate political power. Their employers can be elected or defeated at the polls. Although unions in the private sphere are just as likely as public employees' unions to attempt to use their political muscle for their own advantage, they do not have the privilege of being able to work for the defeat of their employers if they do not care for their employment policies. The political leverage of public employee unions may therefore be more potent.

There are also factors that distinguish collective bargaining in the public sphere from the private sphere that seem to work against the efficacy of collective bargaining of public employees. One is that, in most states, public employees are forbidden by law from striking. That does not always stop them, but it does increase the personal cost of striking. Moreover, the moral force of the law can be plausibly credited with inhibiting the willingness of some unions to call a strike. For many people, the fact that something is illegal is a reason for not doing it, independent of the penalties the law provides.

The right to strike is central to the theory of collective bargaining. Without the right to withhold services, what has the employee to bargain with? The refusal to perform the job is the employee's basic weapon. Denial of the right to strike is a considerable loss to the power of a union in the process of collective bargaining.

A second limitation (discussed more fully in the legal section of this chapter) is that many states have a statutory limitation on what teachers' unions can bargain about. Often they are limited to bargaining about salary or working conditions and are prohibited from bargaining about matters of educational policy.

This kind of limitation on the scope of collective bargaining for teachers has an important bearing on the argument that collective bargaining for teachers undermines democratic control of education. The center of the public's interest in education is the quality and character of education. It is most important that democratic authority over the purposes and direction of education not be eroded. At the same time, the center of teachers' interest in education is focused on such matters as salary, fringe benefits, and working conditions. It is true that the public has a legitimate interest in having a say about how much tax money goes to pay teachers. It is also true that it is sometimes difficult to separate questions of goals from questions of working conditions. Nevertheless, we believe that statutes that limit the scope of collective bargaining to wages, fringe benefits, and working conditions go a long way toward mitigating the "inherent conflict" between collective bargaining for teachers and democracy.

Given these constraints on union bargaining power, has a fair and equal balance been struck? A great deal more could be said on this issue. We have highlighted only a few of the considerations that might be considered relevant to deciding such questions. Nevertheless, given the factual and ethical arguments we have mentioned, we believe that the present balance struck between unions and school boards is reasonable.

We also believe, however, that schools ought to be governed democratically, and we have argued that there are some significant differences between collective bargaining in the public sector and in the private sector. These factors also need to be taken into account in arriving at a reasonable view of the role of collective bargaining in public education.

Before doing so, one additional caveat is required. In Chapter 6 we discussed the rights and roles teachers and administrators ought to have as professionals. It is sometimes argued that teachers' professional rights are best protected by unions. Given that we have not been overly impressed by the claims of teachers to have a right to make educational decisions by virtue of their status as educational experts, it is perhaps to be expected that we will not be persuaded by such an argument. The role of teacher as a professional and an expert and the role of teacher as union member are certainly different and can occasionally conflict. Unions are not professional societies. They do not exist primarily to promote some set of intellectual or professional goals; rather, they exist to pursue the economic goals of their members. Professional and economic goals can conflict. For example, advancing the professional goals of the teaching profession may well require dismissing its less competent members. Unions, however, are more likely to be attuned to the protection of their members, competent or not. This is not to say that a union must be committed to protecting the job of every teacher, no matter how inept (although they may feel some pressure to do exactly that). It is rather to say that the proper role for a union is to be sure that when a school district wishes to deny continued employment to a current employee, it does so fairly. That is an entirely appropriate role. Nevertheless, it is not a role that is comfortably combined with a pursuit of the professional goals of teachers. The master teachers and the NGTA representative on the evaluation committees proposed by Sam Weller might well find it difficult to reconcile their professional duty to evaluate their colleagues objectively with their loyalty to their union and its duty to protect teachers from negative administrative judgments.

We believe that it is important for school districts not to institutionalize such role conflicts for teachers. An obvious way to do so is to believe that *teachers* ought to participate in decisions regarding educational policy and then to conclude on this basis that the *union* ought to be entitled to govern how teachers are to participate. To invest the union as the voice of the professional judgment of teachers is to invite teachers to use their professional role primarily to pursue their economic goals.

How might these views be applied to the case with which we began? To get a clear idea of some of the implications of these arguments for the case, it will be helpful, first of all, to summarize the arguments of this chapter and Chapter 6 as a set of principles concerning the governance of education and the role of unions in policymaking. We can then apply these principles to questions of evaluation, to some of the particular issues of the case, and to the proper role of administrators in such matters.

Principles
1. The parents and citizens of a district have not only an interest in the education of their children but also a right to participate in a suitably democratic fashion in making educational decisions. Democracy gives expression to the right of a free people to their own view of what is good for themselves.
2. Educational decisions that require a significant degree of expertise are more likely to be made better if they are made by people who possess that expertise.

3. In education, the tension between principle 1 and principle 2 is lessened, if not altogether resolved, by assigning to the school board (or other appropriate democratic body) the right to make policy and to the teaching staff and administrators the duty to implement it.
4. Teachers have legitimate interests in the conditions under which they work, and they have the right to organize to pursue these interests.
5. The tension between principle 1 and principle 4 is lessened, if not altogether resolved, by placing two constraints on the collective bargaining process: (a) Teachers ought not to have the right to strike, and (b) teachers ought not to have the right to bargain about matters of basic educational policy.
6. The role of teachers as educational professionals and the role of teachers as union members are different and potentially at odds. Such decisions as teachers make by virtue of their status as professionals should not be under the control of teachers' unions.

Implications

1. School boards have the right and the duty to make policy about evaluation. It is inappropriate to delegate control over basic policy to the union or to bargain with the union about evaluation policy. Basic policy includes the conception of what is considered good teaching, expectations for teachers' performance, and promotion decisions.
2. Administrators have an obligation to discover and to carry out faithfully their board's intent in such matters. Insofar as they are involved in the process of collective bargaining or in dealing with unions, they should also be expected to defend the interests of the board in these matters.
3. The primary interest of the teachers' union in evaluation is in ensuring that it is done fairly. Thus the union has an important and legitimate role in designing and implementing procedures so far as these procedures are intended to protect the due process rights of teachers.
4. Teachers, as professionals, may also have a valuable contribution to make in evaluation. However, there is a role conflict between the teacher as professional and the teacher as union member. Insofar as teachers are involved in evaluation as professionals, their involvement should not be overseen by the union.

Concerning the particular dispute at New Golconda, these views have some of the following implications. First, such issues as merit pay and master teacher proposals are appropriate matters to negotiate. Pay and the structure of promotions are surely quite central matters in any reasonable notion of the working conditions of teachers. Even if they are also important questions of policy, they touch so fundamentally on the lives of teachers that it is difficult to see how a board would be justified in refusing to negotiate about them. On the other hand, there are several aspects of Sam Weller's counterproposals that we believe the board should resist and, if possible, refuse to discuss. Though we do not object to having master teachers participate in the evaluation of other teachers, we find the proposals for union participation in evaluation, hiring, and promotions entirely inappropriate. Likewise, the effect of the proposed policy committees would surely go beyond advising the board on district policy. They would give the union substantial influence over district decisions. In conjunction, these proposals amount to handing over personnel policy and decision making to the union.

Our objection to these proposals is not primarily motivated by the belief that the union would exercise its power irresponsibly or incompetently. That may or may not be the case. Our real objection is that to give such influence to the teachers' union is to undercut legitimate democratic authority. Teachers' unions represent neither their communities nor teachers qua professionals. They properly represent the interests of teachers as employees. That role does not entitle them to a voice in district policy beyond the range of concerns appropriate to representing teachers as employees.

Postscript: Two Views of Democratic Control

You may feel a certain dissatisfaction with the arguments of this chapter and Chapter 6. It may appear that in the name of democracy we have turned administrators into bureaucrats and teachers into mere functionaries. We have left neither with much right to participate in real decisions, and we have put both in a position of subservience to democratic authority as expressed in school boards and state legislatures. One might wish to ask whatever happened to such virtues as cooperative decision making, dialogue, and the rule of reason. In schools, ought not such virtues to prevail? Consider two arguments for a different view of democracy and educational governance.

First, it has been recently argued that bureaucratization is one of the chief difficulties of contemporary schools and is one of the reasons for their much lamented ineffectiveness (see, for example, Wise, 1979). Sandra Feldman (1984), who, significantly, is a negotiator for the New York City chapter of the UFT, provides a useful summary of this point of view as it applies to teacher participation in decision making.

> *Recent reports on education reform stress that the education of our children would vastly improve if teachers were allowed to participate fully in running schools. John Goodlad summed up the situation aptly in his study of American public schools,* A Place Called School. *"Without doubt, teachers will experience greater work satisfaction when they are viewed by their principals as the professionals they perceive themselves to be." Significantly, Goodlad found that those schools in which teachers felt they had good professional working relationships with their principal and supervisors were also the most successful schools academically. (p. 42)*

This view may well be true. Note that we have appealed largely to arguments concerning who has the right to make decisions. These arguments have not led us to place much decision-making authority in the hands of teachers. It does not follow, however, that teachers might not enjoy their work more and perhaps even perform it better were they given substantial roles to play in decision making.

This position can be justified by appealing to a concept of democracy somewhat different from the one we have developed. This second concept of democracy does not see democracy as a way of making legitimate decisions. Its concerns are not focused on representing the right people or on aggregating the educational preferences of the relevant community. Instead, it sees democracy as a form of collective rationality, a way of institutionalizing intelligence. It sees decisions as emerging from the discussions and debates of members of communities. The authority of these decisions derives primarily from their being the product of a kind of collective thought process. In this view of democracy, it is of fundamental importance that decisions be achieved as the product of a dialogue between the members of a community on how they shall achieve their common goals. The authority that results should be the authority of reason, binding on all because each has come to see that the decision achieved is the right one.

There is much to be said for this idea of how educational decisions should be made. It seems to describe the form of governance that is most appropriate to educational institutions, which, after all, are supposed to be places where reason rules. In such institutions, should not decisions be made by a process of dialogue and reflection among their members?

This view is in many ways ennobling and inspiring. It also strikes us as impossible. If it has application in the modern world, it is very likely only in special communities united by some commonly accepted set of purposes. Schools, we believe, are not such institutions. Before discussing our difficulties with this conception, we shall describe each concept of democracy in more detail, together with the view of administration appropriate to each concept.

View 1: The School as Agent of the Democratic State

In the first view, the central question is that of legitimate authority—the right to make decisions and have them obeyed. Its basic assumption is that the citizens of a state will have different conceptions of their own good and that they have a right to these differing conceptions. The essential problem of justice is to discover a fair set of rules and procedures to regulate the competition between individuals, each of whom is seeking his or her own private good. Authority is legitimated through institutions that fairly attend to the interests of each and give to each an equal right to affect decisions. In representative democracies, giving each person a vote in free elections is supposed to serve these ideals. As we have argued in Chapter 6, one condition of the legitimacy of such authority is that the decisions of duly elected representatives be carried out faithfully by those hired to do so.

A central concern in such societies is power, the ability to secure compliance by others with one's orders or expectations. Obviously, for a government actually to govern, it is not enough for its authority to be legitimate; it must also be obeyed. Governments require the power to force their will on those who would not voluntarily comply with their edicts.

Power is also a concern in the private affairs of such a society. Bargaining, collective or individual, is an attempt to enforce compliance on someone else by threatening to withhold something the other person wants unless compliance is forthcoming. Workers will withhold labor and management wages until the other party agrees to acceptable terms. The process is part of the mechanism whereby people pursue their own good. Justice consists in striking a fair balance of power between parties. The relationship is inherently adversarial.

An administrator who works in institutions governed by such assumptions will be a combination of bureaucrat and broker. In the first case, the administrator will seek to implement, enforce, or transmit decisions made by the proper authority. The administrator's duty is to see to it that the policies decided by the democratic body are faithfully applied. The administrator may also become a broker between groups seeking to impose their will on each other. The public school administrator can often become a mediator of sorts, seeking to establish a reasonable vector between the competing interests of the board and the teachers.

View 2: The School as Democratic Community

In the second view, the central concern is not to legitimate authority but to create ways of decision making that rely on persuasion and dialogue. It tends to assume the existence of a community united by some set of shared values and consisting of individuals willing and able to engage in mutual discussion of how these values are to be pursued. Its emphases are on rationality, cooperation, and collegiality, not on legitimate authority and power. It thus seeks the widest possible participation in decisions by the people within the institution. Ownership of decisions by those who execute them is a central value.

It is not clear that this view requires administrators at all. If it does, the administrator is certainly not a conduit for the authority of some body external to the organization. The administrator is a kind of "first among equals" whose primary responsibility would be to facilitate discussion and to be a channel of communication.

Note the sharp difference between these views, despite the fact that both are articulated as forms of democracy. The administrator who attempts to make a school a democratic community, where decisions are made in a collegial manner, will end up usurping the authority of the board. The administrator who seeks faithfully to implement the will of the board must treat teachers as employees whose first duty is to recognize the authority of their supervisors and serve their community. It does not follow that boards of education may not delegate some decisions to teachers or encourage teachers to offer their opinions on matters of policy. What does follow is that authority is always delegated, and teachers' collegial decisions are always advisory. Collegial discussion may be serious and important, but any sense of genuine autonomy over decisions must be illusory. In view 2, however, these collegial decisions are not advisory. They are the decisions that really matter. And if they matter, the authority of the board cannot.

The view of authority we have developed is essentially that sketched in view 1. The school is seen as the agent of the democratic state. Why not the second view? Is there not much to be said for seeing the school as a democratic self-governing community?

We believe, reluctantly, that there is not. Such communities are based on the assumption of shared goals among community members who work collegially to achieve them. This assumption has not characterized real democratic states since the early Greek city-states—if it indeed characterized them. Perhaps intellectual professions or religious organizations are the closest things we have to such communities today. Modern democratic states are surely not characterized by shared values and common goals. Indeed, they treat their pluralism as a virtue and the privilege of pursuing one's own private values as a civil right. There is a widespread belief that it is both inappropriate and impossible to achieve any rational consensus about values and goals. Rationality is often thought to apply to means, not ends (see MacIntyre, 1981, and Sandel, 1982, for discussion). The task of democratic institutions is not to achieve some collective agreement among the citizens of a democracy about goals but to accept their diversity and to find policies that permit as many people as possible to achieve as many of their own goals as possible.

To treat schools as autonomous democratic communities when they are in fact agents of the democratic state is essentially to claim that teachers have the right to determine what is educationally worthwhile and to impose their sense of educational values on others. To treat education as a self-governing profession is to give educators immunity from the democratic state. It is ultimately to assert that the principle of people's being entitled to their own sense of the good does not apply to schools. The alternative is to insist that schools are first and foremost accountable to the democratic state.

Thus we believe that proposals such as Sam Weller's for management and unions to cooperate and to share decision-making power over schools involve inherent role conflicts for both administrators and teachers. The administrator must strive to be the first among equals facilitating discussion and rational decision making among teachers. But he or she must also be accountable to the democratic state. The union must attempt to represent the economic interests of its members in what is inherently an adversarial relationship. But it must also participate in a collegial arrangement in the pursuit of common goals. These roles are inherently incompatible, and ultimately the logic of accountability to the democratic state must triumph. Such room for teacher participation in decision making as may be desirable will have to be found within its scope.

Questions

1. Should teachers or teachers' unions be able to participate in school district elections? If so, in what ways? Would you favor any legal restrictions on the participation of teachers or teachers' unions in district politics? Might such restrictions be unconstitutional?

2. Should administrators be represented by teachers' unions? What are the advantages and liabilities of such an arrangement?

3. We have claimed that our objections to teachers making policy are rooted in our belief that educational policy should be made democratically. Suppose research showed that

educational policy was generally more sound when made by teachers. Would that be a valid reason for increasing the role of teachers in policymaking?

4. Why do teachers' unions generally object to merit pay and to ranks for teachers?

5. Are there ways in which teacher input into policy decisions can be enhanced without enhancing teacher authority over these decisions? Would this be desirable?

6. Several writers have speculated that collective bargaining has had important effects on teachers' classroom behavior. We have mentioned some of these speculations in this chapter. In your judgment, what is the most likely effect? How would you go about ascertaining whether or not, in fact, that effect occurs?

7. Who should bargain for a board of education? Should outside, "professional" negotiators be employed? Under what conditions? Should school superintendents sit at the bargaining table?

8. There is growing evidence that the United States is about to enter a period of teacher shortage. How might this affect teachers' unions? What would its impact on collective bargaining agreements be?

CHAPTER 8

Teacher Evaluation

A Case of Incompetence?

"You can go to hell," Susan Burnette shouted as she slammed the door on her way out—actions that neatly captured the flavor of their entire meeting. John Stanton sighed and sank back into his chair. He knew that the unpleasantness of the last hour was likely only a mild foretaste of what was to come.

Stanton reviewed the salient facts of the case as he flipped through Burnette's file, which lay open on his desk. She had been hired eight years ago to teach physics and chemistry at Benton High School. Her records showed that she had come well recommended by her professors at the state university. She had done work toward her M.A. during the summers of her first four years at Benton, though there was no indication that she had made any progress on the degree since then. Burnette had been hired by Stanton's predecessor, Bill Hubbard, who was principal of Benton for almost two decades until he died in office three years ago.

Hubbard's evaluations of Burnette—seven in all—were contained in the file. These evaluations, which district policy required principals to conduct twice a year for untenured faculty and annually for permanent staff, covered the three years of Burnette's probationary status and the first year after her tenuring. (There was no evaluation for the following year, probably because Hubbard had been effectively incapacitated by his illness.) These evaluations could be termed "uneven." While Hubbard had commended the teacher for her command of her subject, her generally clear statement of the purpose of each lesson, and her professional cooperation in serving on various school committees, nearly every evaluation contained at least one somewhat ambiguous remark concerning student behavior. For example, on one Hubbard had written, "Some students seemed inattentive"; on another, "Smith kept distracting his classmates"; and on a third, "Talking to the blackboard isn't advisable with these pupils, as control is easily lost." Stanton thought these comments unusual, since the late principal was known for the strict pupil discipline he enforced. It was odd that students would get even slightly out of line in Hubbard's presence. Despite these negative remarks, Hubbard had recommended Burnette for tenure, which the board had granted.

Stanton's first evaluation of the teacher was made three years ago, during his first term as principal. He remembered it vividly. Given Hubbard's evaluations, he had expected a problem or two with classroom control, but he was unprepared for the seeming bedlam that had greeted him when he first entered the chemistry class. Burnette had been carrying out a titration demonstration, but perhaps no more than half the students were attending to it. Several groups of pupils were openly talking among themselves. They were not discussing chemistry projects; they were discussing last night's school dance. One boy was audibly asleep, and two were at the windows watching a girls' gym class playing field hockey. A loud argument between two boys ceased as Stanton entered. While things had improved immediately after his arrival, at no time did Burnette have the attention of her entire class, and there was a noticeable deterioration in discipline as the period wore on. Burnette's occasional attempts to control her pupils seemed to be limited to shouting at someone, "Be quiet and sit down!" Mostly, however, she seemed oblivious to pupil behavior as she doggedly pursued the intricacies of calculating the concentration of solutions, closely attended to by the few students who would watch a wall for an hour if someone in authority told them to do so. As Stanton closed the classroom door behind himself at the end of the observation, the noise level mounted perceptibly, and he distinctly heard vulgarities as the two boys renewed their altercation.

Stanton prepared a brief description of his observation and completed the district's standard teacher evaluation form. This form called for him to comment on the teacher's lesson preparation, attention to individual differences, classroom control, clarity of explanations, pupil motivation, and overall effectiveness and to rate each of these on a five-point scale, where 5 indicated outstanding performance and 3 was "average." Stanton rated Burnette 5, 3, 2, 5, 2, and 3, respectively. In his conference with Burnette following this observation, Stanton had been rather diffident in his criticisms. He was, after all, in his first year as a high school principal and none too sure of himself (he had been principal of a middle school prior to coming to Benton). He suggested to Susan that she needed to develop a variety of techniques for motivating her students and that certain sorts of pupil behavior probably ought not to be countenanced. However, he tempered these criticisms with favorable comments about the clarity of her explanations (even he, an ex–English teacher, had understood the purpose of titration) and the apparent care she had given to her written lesson plan. Despite these remarks, Burnette had bridled a bit at his mildly negative comments, although she had signed the prepared evaluation memorandum (as district policy required) to indicate that she had been apprised of its results without necessarily agreeing with its substance.

During the next two years, Stanton observed Burnette's classroom four times— twice more than was required by district policy—because he was concerned about the teacher's capabilities. During this time he also instituted a process of pupil evaluation of teachers in the school. Because he believed that the judgments of high school students could provide valid additional information on teaching quality, he and a faculty committee had modified a form widely used at the college level for such purposes. This innovation had met with considerable resistance from his staff and the union. But the board of education had been enthusiastic about the idea, and the teachers had finally gone along with it "on a trial basis," for juniors and seniors only, and with the understanding that its primary purpose would be for their own use in improving instruction. Nevertheless, copies of these student evaluations did come to Stanton.

In any case, both Stanton's observations and the students' evaluations were in essential agreement: Burnette had little control over her classes. If anything, matters had gotten worse recently. Once last year he had been called to her class to break up an actual fistfight between two girls. He seldom passed her room without hearing what sounded like pandemonium inside. For a while last year she had sent a virtual parade of students to his office for disciplining, though that seemed to have stopped recently. In his most recent observations he could detect no improvement in her ability to motivate most youngsters.

The problem was not simply one of discipline. Each year the state education department administered standardized tests to all graduating seniors in the state. The results of these tests were routinely sent to each school. Burnette's students were always substantially below the state means in physics and chemistry, and last year this gap had shown an alarming increase. Finally, as if this weren't enough, a wholly new problem had appeared.

After the close of school last year, Stanton had received a letter from a Mr. Raintree, the father of one of Burnette's students. Mr. Raintree claimed that his daughter was convinced that the teacher had been drunk in class on at least three occasions. The evidence for this, the girl asserted, included slurred speech, a violent and unprovoked tantrum, and the strong smell of alcohol on the teacher's breath. Most tellingly, perhaps, the girl claimed that she had actually seen a whiskey bottle in Burnette's desk once, when the teacher had opened a locked drawer to get out her grade book. Mr. Raintree closed by saying that he was not trying to cause trouble, but he did think the principal should be aware of his daughter's belief. In response, Stanton had written that while he doubted the accuracy of the girl's conclusions, he would certainly look into the matter. However, as school was closed, and since both the teacher and the girl were out of town for the summer, the letter had lain unattended to in Burnette's file.

Now Stanton wished that he had pursued the matter more vigorously. During this year he had twice overheard students refer to Burnette as "the boozer." The first time, the students had denied using the term when he questioned them. The second time, however, Stanton had pretended not to hear the remark. Instead, he called one of the students into his office later in the day. The principal knew the pupil, Mark Adams, to be a responsible, mature boy, unlikely to spread false stories. He explained to Mark the gravity of unfounded accusations of this sort against a teacher and said that he intended to get to the bottom of these rumors. Mark said that he could not say that Miss Burnette had ever been drunk in class. However, he did believe that she drank while at work. Further, he said that this was commonly believed by students. Stanton closed the interview by cautioning Mark not to say anything about their discussion until he had had an opportunity to investigate the matter.

The boy's last comment particularly alarmed Stanton. He reflected ruefully that principals were always the last ones to know what went on in their own schools. He did recognize that he had to move quickly on this matter. If it were true, a potentially disastrous situation could arise; chemistry laboratories were not places to leave under the supervision of inebriated teachers. He was unsure, however, exactly what to do. He thought it unlikely that Burnette would admit to drinking on the job if he simply confronted her with the accusation. Instead, he chose to speak confidentially to a few senior teachers who might know something about it.

During the following week, the principal spoke to four teachers, including one, Janet Kramer, whom he knew to be on friendly terms with Burnette. He told them frankly about the rumors circulating among the students and asked them what they could tell him. One had heard nothing and doubted that there was any substance to the story. "You know how kids gossip about teachers' private lives," he had said. Two had admitted hearing the rumors but had no personal evidence on which to judge their truth. The only comment one of these teachers would make was that Burnette seemed to have a problem controlling her classes, a conclusion Stanton had already reached. Janet Kramer, however, was vociferous in her friend's defense. "Sure Susan drinks occasionally. So do I," she said. "We sometimes go out together and have a few beers after work on Friday. There's nothing wrong with that—this isn't the nineteenth century, you know! As for drinking on the job, that's preposterous,'' Kramer asserted. "And anyway," she said, looking Stanton in the eye, "the lack of discipline in this school is enough to drive anyone to drink!"

That was last week. On Monday afternoon, Stanton made an unannounced observation of Burnette's classroom, the first time he had ever done such a thing; it violated an unwritten understanding in the district that observations were to be scheduled in advance. But what was he supposed to do, he thought, administer surprise breath analysis tests to his faculty? Obviously, if the teacher was drinking, she would not do so when she knew he was coming.

Burnette was clearly surprised to see him when he entered the classroom. The observation told him nothing, however, that he did not already know. There were the usual severe problems of inattention, discipline, and poor student motivation. But he could detect no certain signs of alcohol, either in the teacher's actions or on her breath. She became inarticulate a few times, but that could be because she was made nervous by his surprise visit. When he left, he made an appointment with Burnette for the next day.

That night he agonized over his next steps. He was convinced that the teacher was presently incompetent and that she had shown no improvement since his first evaluation of her three years ago. Indeed, he was convinced that she had gotten worse. His own observations and the student ratings supported this conclusion. Burnette seemed to ignore the suggestions he made for improving her teaching. Nevertheless, he considered making an all-out effort in the next year to help Burnette—perhaps calling in some outside consultants to work with her, at the district's expense. But he held no real hope for this strategy. After three years of effort on his part, he was convinced that she was either unable or unwilling to improve her teaching.

More important, he was afraid that this choice could lead to a calamity. If she was drinking on the job, every day that she supervised the chemistry laboratory she was a danger to students. Stanton was acutely aware of his responsibility for their safety. Severe chemical burns, the inhalation of toxic fumes, and explosive fires were distinct possibilities. He also recognized, however, that he had no hard evidence that she drank in school. Could he accuse her of that on the basis of student gossip, a letter from one parent, and some incoherent speech?

He considered the possibility that he simply rest his case on his judgment of her competence as a teacher and recommend that she be dismissed at the end of the year. Her incompetence was sufficient grounds for her dismissal, he reasoned, whether or not she drinks. The problem here, of course, was that Burnette was tenured. Any such attempt was likely to raise a furor. Stanton was unsure of the legal details of dismissing a tenured teacher, but he knew it was difficult to do. Further, the union would almost certainly be out for his hide if he tried to fire her. Suppose he was unsuccessful? Perhaps the worst outcome of an attempt to dismiss Burnette would be to fail. Not only would she continue to teach at Benton, but Stanton's three years of effort to build the confidence and trust of his faculty would go down the drain and almost surely be impossible to restore. His own position at the school would become untenable. It is one thing to be seen as the "bad guy," he thought; it is infinitely worse to be seen as an incompetent bad guy.

He met with Burnette the next morning. He carefully reviewed each of the evaluations of her teaching, including those written by Hubbard. On no evaluation had she received higher than 3 on overall effectiveness, and on several he had rated her

2. He described in detail his judgments about her inability to motivate her students or to control their behavior. He showed her the steady decline in the test performance of her students compared to the statewide averages. He said he was disappointed in her failure to keep up to date in her field by taking college courses. He pointed out that her student evaluations were substantially below those of other teachers in the school. He finished by saying that in his judgment she was incompetent. He did not mention his suspicion that she was an alcoholic. Through all of this Burnette sat in stony silence.

When she spoke at last, Stanton was totally unprepared for the cold fury in her voice. She began by telling him that he was the incompetent, not she. She said that when Hubbard ran the school, discipline was never a problem. Now students treated being sent to the principal's office for disciplining as a joke. She had stopped sending them for precisely that reason; their behavior was worse when they came back to class. Further, he was incompetent to judge her teaching of chemistry and physics. He was, she said, "a junior high school English teacher, and a poor one at that, from all I've heard. You wouldn't know a quark from a quiche. I don't have to submit to evaluations by scientific illiterates. I teach science using discovery methods. That requires that pupils move about and talk. You're so ill-informed about science teaching you didn't even recognize what was going on in my class. And you've got the gall to call me incompetent!"

She went on to say that he was supposed to supervise the faculty but had never done so. Supervision didn't just mean coming into her classroom a few times and writing summary judgments on a stupid form. It meant providing help to a teacher who had difficulties—concrete suggestions that would lead to improvement. "The only help I've gotten from you is a few inane and vacuous comments that I should improve student motivation! In three years, you've never given me a single clear suggestion about how to do that.

"Observations!" she went on. "You sit in the back of my classroom a couple of times each year with your little notebook and totally disrupt my lessons. Your presence would disconcert anyone! Who can teach with a scribbling Buddha back there!" (Stanton was stung by the sarcastic reference to his admittedly rotund physique.) "Yesterday you had the effrontery to show up in my classroom without even telling me you were coming. I'm a professional, and I won't be treated in that way."

Burnette was particularly scathing in her comments on the student evaluations. Since when did high school students have the professional expertise to judge a teacher's ability, she asked. "You foisted this practice on the faculty on the grounds that it would help improve our teaching. Some of us knew damn well what you had in mind! Just this—making comparative judgments among us. Do you call that improving teaching?

"As for the test scores," she said, "half of the students in this school couldn't care less about learning—sex, drugs, and cars are all they have on what passes for their minds. The other half come from homes where a book is a rarity and there is no support for anything intellectual. How the hell am I supposed to teach physics to them? I count it a good year if I get a half dozen of them through chemistry with a modicum of understanding and a howling success if a couple of them catch fire with a love of science—which, incidentally, a few usually do. I'll tell you one thing, Stanton, I'm not going to take this evaluation lying down. We'll see who's incompetent around here!" That's when Burnette told him where to go and stormed out.

Stanton was stunned. Next week he would have to make his yearly personnel recommendations to the superintendent. Burnette's was going to be a problem.

Introduction

In the best of all possible worlds, the confrontation between Stanton and Burnette would never occur. But this is not that world, and such confrontations are frequent enough. In particular, the world of teacher evaluation is something less than perfect. In this chapter we will examine some of the empirical, legal, and ethical issues that arise when school administrators, such as the hapless Stanton, set out to judge the quality of their faculty. We will be concerned with what, in the jargon of education, is termed "summative" rather than "formative" evaluation. That is, we shall be concerned with the process of arriving at defensible judgments about teaching quality for the purpose of making personnel decisions—particularly the decision to dismiss teachers thought to be incompetent. We are only incidentally concerned with arriving at decisions about improving teachers' classroom capabilities.

There have been an almost infinite variety of schemes and criteria for evaluating teachers. At one time or another, frequency of smiling during a lesson, classroom decor, participation in the PTA, and taking courses at summer school—to name only a few—have been used to assess a teacher's competence. Fortunately and unfortunately for the administrator, the validity of most of these schemes is doubtful. It is fortunate because if all were relevant to judging teaching quality, administrators would have little time for anything but gathering data on the multitude of factors thought to indicate teacher effectiveness. It is unfortunate because many of these schemes had the advantage of simplicity. Bulletin boards were either changed regularly or they were not; a teacher either came to PTA meetings or did not. Now, at the end of over half a century of research on teacher evaluation, at least the rough outlines of appropriate evaluation procedures are beginning to emerge. But before we turn to these procedures and the events at Benton High School, it might be useful to get an overview of the *types* of variables that have been involved in judging teacher competence.

Social Science Research on Teacher Evaluation

King (1981) provides such an overview. Five classes of variables can be distinguished, arranged roughly in order of their proximity to being direct measures of the outcomes of instruction:

1. *Product variables:* measures of changes in student behavior, learning, attitudes, and so on
2. *Process variables:* teacher behaviors thought to promote student learning, such as praising students, well-planned lessons, and pupil control
3. *Professional variables:* nonclassroom but professional activities of teachers, such as taking university courses, supervising student clubs, and working on school committees
4. *Presage variables:* characteristics of teachers themselves thought to influence classroom performance, such as personality attributes, level of college achievement, and verbal ability

5. *Personal variables:* nonprofessional activities of teachers, such as church membership, part-time employment, community service, and athletic prowess

Note that as we move from product to personal variables, we get increasingly distant from changes in pupil learning, and the chain of reasoning required to connect a variable to those changes becomes increasingly tenuous. For example, if an administrator considers involvement in community affairs as relevant to an assessment of teachers' competence, the rationale required to justify such a consideration would have to go something like this: Public service activity permits teachers to become more knowledgeable about their communities; this knowledge allows them better to adapt curricular materials to local conditions; materials that reflect local conditions are more relevant to students; and students learn more readily from relevant materials. Embedded in each link of this chain are a number of dubious assumptions. As might be expected, then, with few exceptions (e.g., teacher verbal ability), research has typically failed to validate the variables in classes 3, 4, and 5 as measures of teacher competence. Yet they continue to be used for such purposes. (In the case at hand, Stanton appeared to do so when he noted that Burnette has made no progress toward her degree.) Further, it is the implicit criteria embedded in these last three classes that frequently raise significant legal and ethical issues. For example, when, if ever, is a teacher's out-of-school activity a proper concern of administrators?

Does this indicate that indirect variables—those in classes 3 to 5—should not be considered in teacher evaluations? In recent years there has been a move away from using them. The feeling has been growing that the personal characteristics and out-of-school involvements of teachers are not an administrator's concern. Such a view is mistaken. In some evaluative situations, variables in classes 3 to 5 are all that is available. For example, when hiring a new staff member (certainly an instance of teacher evaluation), an administrator typically has little else on which to discriminate among applicants. College grade point averages and the secondhand impressions of character and personality traits gleaned from letters of recommendation are all that is likely to be at hand. Even though we recognize that research shows that the relation between these qualities and more direct measures of teacher effectiveness is small or even nonexistent, as long as a plausible rationale can be constructed connecting them to teaching effectiveness, their use can be justified. The alternative seems to be flipping a coin. What must be avoided, of course, is consideration of characteristics that are proscribed by law—race and sex, for example.

Susan Burnette, however, is not an applicant for a teaching job. She is an experienced member of Benton's faculty. Are professional, presage, and personal considerations ever appropriate evaluative criteria in such a case? In particular, are they ever appropriately considered in cases of potential dismissal? We think there are two circumstances when they are. First, if these considerations are specified in district policy or contracts, and teachers are informed of their application, they are appropriate. If, for example, a contract specifies that teachers without advanced degrees must work toward earning them or that faculty members are expected to serve on school committees, an administrator is justified in considering compliance in dismissal decisions. It is not required that such behaviors be unambiguously related to teaching effectiveness; it is enough that they be plausibly connected to it. Though research has not been able to demonstrate a causal link (much less a significant correlation) between serving on school committees and being an effective teacher, a credible case can be made that it is. The key element, then, is that these considerations be explicitly stated and that teachers agree to their use in evaluations.

There is at least one other obvious circumstance in which professional, presage, and personal criteria might be appropriately considered in potential dismissal cases, even though they are not specified in district policy and though there is no research establishing their links with classroom effectiveness. This occurs when a teacher's behavior casts serious doubt on his or her personal fitness to teach. A teacher who was unwilling to accede to legitimate requests of a principal, whose behavior precipitated chronic and rancorous conflict with colleagues, or whose private life exhibited deliberate and public flouting of normative or legal standards (e.g., committing a felony) might be dismissed on those grounds. These cases, however, are relatively rare. Failure to meet product or process criteria is much more common and will be our primary concern in this chapter. We turn now to the common procedures for gathering evidence on these criteria.

Criteria derived from product and process variables have played a major role in research on teacher evaluation. The case of Stanton and Burnette illustrates three of the most commonly employed evaluative techniques in education today—and their shortcomings: student achievement, student ratings of instruction, and classroom observations. We will consider each of these.

Student Achievement

The justification for using student performance measures to assess teaching competence rests on the belief that whatever else teaching may be about, one very important objective is helping students to learn. For many years the saying "If students haven't learned, the teacher hasn't taught" was current in educational circles. The aphorism was conceptually confused—both learning and teaching can take place independent of each other. Nevertheless, perhaps most educators would agree that if a substantial proportion of a teacher's pupils consistently fail to learn the prescribed subject matter, that is strong evidence that the teacher is ineffective. The use of student performance measures to evaluate teachers rests on such a belief. In recent years the so-called accountability movement has given further impetus to this practice, often over stiff resistance from organized teachers' groups. The practice of collecting data on student learning for teacher evaluation purposes has been further abetted by the spreading realization that the most common alternative evaluative strategy, classroom observation, has serious deficiencies (as we shall see). When Stanton used the test results of Burnette's students in reaching a judgment that she was incompetent, his behavior was in keeping with this growing practice.

But test scores are not without their own deficiencies as measures of teaching competence. Indeed, Burnette's vociferous objection to being judged on the basis of a statewide test raises one of the most important of these. In essence, Burnette's claim was that the students at Benton High School (and in particular those who take physics and chemistry) are less able academically than the average student who takes these tests. Her pupils will certainly score below the state mean, she argues, regardless of her capabilities as a teacher. She should not be held responsible for their low scores.

This is a serious objection, and if the premise that her pupils are less able is correct, her objection is valid. In its most general form, the argument against using measures of pupil learning as an index of teaching effectiveness is that a multitude of factors affect how well students do on tests. Only one of these is how well they are taught. These other factors fall into three broad categories: pupil attributes, instructional materials, and the classroom setting. With so many factors influencing test scores, it is unfair, the argument goes, to judge a teacher's competence on their basis. We agree. This is not to say, however, that measures of pupil performance should be ignored; it is to say that the limitations on their usefulness should be understood. Let us consider some of the more important of these.

At the outset we wish to note that the nature of the test chosen is terribly important, that what counts as a test should be broadly conceived, and that carefully developed, commercially available, standardized tests are very often *not* appropriate for teacher evaluation purposes. These tests typically have several deficiencies. One of the most important is their lack of curricular validity for any particular classroom. To understand this it is necessary to recognize only that national tests are composed of items designed to tap skills and concepts that the test developers have found to be commonly taught in a nationwide sample of schools. One might say that such tests measure the content of an "average curriculum." It is obvious, then, that any given teacher is unlikely to be using this "average curriculum." If the actual curriculum departs significantly from this mythical average, that teacher's students—and ultimately the teacher—are unjustly penalized.

A related problem with standardized tests as devices for evaluating teachers is the degree to which their contents are amenable to instruction. Even if a test reflects a curriculum accurately, it is quite possible for that curriculum to be relatively impervious to teachers' instructional strategies. At an extreme, consider many of the nationally standardized tests of academic ability or "intelligence" (whatever that elusive quality may be). If we assume that academic ability is primarily an innate characteristic of students, valid test scores would reflect that characteristic. They would be relatively immutable, unaffected by any actions a classroom teacher might take. Obviously tests of academic ability are inappropriate for teacher evaluation purposes. Similarly, tests that reflect the results of years of instruction are inappropriate. The National Merit Scholarship Examination, for example, reflects the results of many years of teaching, both in and out of school. It is unjustified, therefore, to credit a particular teacher (or school) for students' success or failure on this test.

Even standardized achievement tests in particular subjects may be relatively impervious to instruction. Standardized reading tests may serve as examples. Such tests commonly provide measures of reading comprehension and vocabulary. The first of these, measuring the ability to infer meaning from print, is probably less susceptible to teaching than the second, which measures the stock of words students recognize. Learning to comprehend print may be less influenced by teaching than is learning to recognize new words. A similar conclusion seems likely with regard to arithmetic achievement tests: The scores from "mathematical reasoning" subtests are probably more impervious to instruction than are scores from "computation" subtests. Hence it may be unfair to use standardized achievement tests to evaluate teachers' effectiveness.

A second important objection to using student achievement data for evaluating teachers is that students differ widely both within and between classrooms in ways that have a strong effect on what they learn. Some pupils are smarter than others. Indeed, some seem to learn in spite of, not because of, their teachers. Some are more knowledgeable about a subject when they enter a classroom than are others. Much of what they may seem to have learned was already known when the first lesson began. Some work harder than others. But teachers have little control over who enrolls in their classes; hence it would be unfair to penalize a teacher whose students happen to be less talented, less industrious, or less knowledgeable. Burnette makes this point emphatically.

A third class of objections concern the classroom or school itself. Many teachers may have little control over the variety and quality of the instructional materials they use. They may be given relatively large classes and are consequently unable to consider individual pupils' needs adequately. Schools may be noisy, even dangerous places where teaching anything is difficult, if not impossible. It is unreasonable to hold teachers accountable for student learning under such conditions. Burnette's remarks about discipline at Benton High School are in this vein.

These are cogent objections to using pupil performance data as measures of teacher competence. However, they are not decisive. Instead, they suggest criteria that must be considered before such data are used. Satisfying these criteria will go a long way toward meeting these objections and rendering pupil achievement a defensible component of a comprehensive teacher evaluation program. Millman (1981) suggests five considerations for improving the possibility of using student performance measures for assessing teacher effectiveness:

1. *Amenability to instruction.* The indicators chosen must measure skills and cognitions learned from classroom instruction. This criterion requires that each item in a proposed test or item pool be carefully examined. In effect, the question to be asked of each is whether the lessons ordinarily taught in school plausibly lead to pupils' mastering the information the item requires. Tests of general intellectual ability are inappropriate for teacher evaluation purposes.
2. *Content validity.* Even if the information necessary to answer a question correctly is ordinarily taught in schools, it is important to determine if an item reflects the intentions embedded in the curriculum being used. Tests should

measure a course's instructional objectives. Thus national achievement tests should be viewed, at best, as potential item pools from which relevant questions may be drawn. Even teacher-made tests may be biased, since they may oversample easy-to-measure skills and slight more difficult ones. This criterion requires that teachers and administrators agree that each question cover information that they expect pupils to have learned in their classrooms.

3. *Reliability.* Judgments about teaching quality should be based on more than one testing. A single administration can be adversely affected by events peculiar to the time of the test. Several classes and more than one year should be involved. Put another way, the mean of several testings is more reliable than a single one.

4. *Equality.* A test should not unfairly favor one teacher over others. Every teacher should know precisely the knowledge and skills that will be tested prior to the beginning of each school year. This does not mean that teachers must know the specific items to be used. It does require that they know the nature of the information pupils will be expected to master. For example, it is enough that teachers of American government be aware that a test will contain questions on the constitutional limitations on who may serve as president without knowing the specific questions on age or citizenship. Tests may also violate the equality criterion by improper scoring practices. When essay questions are involved, care must be taken to eliminate biased grading. Scoring should involve several readers, a scoring key, and at least two readings by separate markers. The identity of students should be hidden.

5. *Comparability.* To a large extent, measures of something take on meaning only when they are compared to other measures. If a student attains an 80 on some test, is that good? It is if we know that his was the highest grade in the class; it is not if we know that the class average was 91. Similarly, it is important that comparison groups be chosen carefully when using achievement data in teacher evaluations. A teacher should not be disadvantaged because his or her pupils are less able or from homes less supportive of academic achievement when compared to the pupils of other teachers. Ordinarily we use random assignment to ensure that pupils in different classrooms are comparable within a known level of probability. With random assignment, and assuming that the previous criteria are met, if the students in one classroom consistently score well above those in other classrooms, we might be willing to infer that their teacher had been relatively more effective.

It is in the last condition, random assignment to classes, wherein much of the difficulty occurs. We can take steps to ensure that we choose a reliable and valid test, for example, or that all teachers being considered are using the same curriculum, but only rarely can we randomly assign pupils to teachers for the purpose of achieving comparability. This is the technical version of Burnette's complaint about Stanton's use of statewide achievement test results to infer that she is incompetent. Obviously, Stanton had not randomly assigned all of the state's physics and chemistry pupils to their classrooms. Hence he could give no assurance that Burnette's pupils had not scored poorly for reasons other than her teaching ability. Is there any way of dealing with this problem? If the first four criteria for using achievement data are met, is there any procedure for achieving comparability, short of random assignment?

The answer is yes. Such procedures have been available for years. The problem of noncomparable groups is commonly treated using a procedure called analysis of covariance. Essentially, what this technique does is statistically adjust each student's score to remove the effects of other confounding variables (called *covariates*). Suppose an administrator wished to assess the relative teaching ability of a group of high school mathematics teachers. Assume that year-end test results were available for each class and that each of the four criteria for using student achievement data had been met. Assume also, however, that the students in some mathematics classes are, on the average, less talented than students in other classes. Clearly, it would be unfair simply to compare the mean scores of these classes in an attempt to infer which had been taught more effectively. The teachers with the brightest pupils would appear more competent. However, if a measure of academic ability were available for each student, this defect can be ameliorated. With modern computer programs, it is easy to adjust each student's year-end mathematics test score to approximate what that score would have been if all pupils had the same measured academic capacities. Thus the remaining differences in math achievement between classes would presumably not be due to differences in students' intellectual capacities. Further, it would be possible to adjust simultaneously these mathematics scores for other differences among pupils, such as family socioeconomic status. The pupils in different classrooms might be made comparable on several factors that would otherwise confound any interpretation concerning their teachers' competence. Finally, it is also possible to adjust student test scores for classroom differences per se, not simply differences among pupils. Suppose that some mathematics classrooms had many more pupils than others, and the administrator thought that class size might influence teacher effectiveness and consequently pupils' scores. Multiple regression procedures are designed to handle such problems; in effect, the technique could be used to make it as if all classes were of the same size.

There are, then, readily available methods for helping us to deal with the problem of comparability in assessing teacher effectiveness with pupil achievement data. It is important to recognize that these methods are not free from possible bias. For example, all measures are unreliable to some extent, the achievement data as well as the covariates used. Further, it is almost certain that students in different classes will differ on relevant factors other than those taken into account as covariates. The net effect of these biases is to *underadjust* the achievement test scores. As a consequence, teachers with pupils who are handicapped by these unaccounted-for factors and whose pupils thereby achieve at a lower level will appear less able, even though they are as competent as their colleagues. Nevertheless, with careful design, such biases are likely to be small, and it is possible to meet the comparability criterion and thereby use achievement data in the process of teacher evaluation (Millman, 1981).

We have called your attention to Millman's five criteria for deciding whether it would be fair to use pupil achievement as a criterion for evaluating teachers. Consider now John Stanton's use of state achievement test data in arriving at his judgment that Susan Burnette is incompetent.

A potent issue concerning the use of student achievement as a criterion of teacher effectiveness is the political one. Teachers' organizations have been vociferous in their objections to the practice, for many of the same reasons cited by Burnette. These objections may be shortsighted, however. It seems to us that the important question is no longer whether achievement data should be used to assess teacher competence, for it is. The question is how such data should be used. The increasingly widespread practice of statewide achievement testing ensures that pupil performance measures will be available to principals in most schools. The situation at Benton High is now commonplace throughout the country. School administrators—and the lay public—will have readily at hand the information required to make "quick and dirty" comparisons of teachers and schools. Further, principals very often use standardized test results from school testing programs to judge a teacher's effectiveness, regardless of whether those examinations are administered by the state. When Stanton compared the results of Burnette's pupils to those taught by other teachers, he probably was doing no more than what has been common practice among some principals for a long time. What makes Stanton unusual in this regard is not his doing so but his openness in discussing it with Burnette. There is, then, a significant danger to teachers in the current situation. On the one hand, there is a belief among administrators that pupil performance data are relevant to judging teacher competence, the required data are increasingly available, and there is strong public and political support for using these data for just such a purpose. On the other hand, there is the substantial resistance among teachers to even considering student outcomes in evaluations. Caught in these conflicting currents, administrators may be pressed into using test results in a concealed fashion. The possibility exists for a principal to conclude that a teacher is incompetent partly on the basis of a quick, *incorrect* analysis of test data, exactly as Stanton did, and then to present that conclusion as having been arrived at entirely on other grounds, as on the basis of classroom observations. In such a situation, the teacher concerned has no opportunity for self-defense against an unwarranted conclusion on the basis of the relevant evidence. Such a situation is patently unfair. We think it much better to devise an open procedure for using achievement test data fairly, in full recognition of their limitations and with ample provision for teachers to rebut any adverse conclusions reached, than to continue to pretend that pupil performance measures play no role in administrative judgment.

Obviously, in a few brief paragraphs it is not possible to cover adequately all the important issues involved when pupil achievement is being considered as an indicator of teacher competence. We recommend that administrators contemplating such a move begin by reading the relevant research and by consulting with persons with specialized knowledge in research methodology, statistics, and the evaluation of instruction. Any attempt to initiate such a practice will require the cooperation of a district's faculty—cooperation that may not be easily achieved. (One suggestion we might make would be to use pupil achievement measures only for the subset of the staff still in the probationary period and to use it only for making tenure decisions.)

In summary, a few basic ideas should be stressed. First, many persons believe that, in the final analysis, pupil achievement is the most important criterion by which to judge teacher effectiveness. Such a belief is certainly more common among the general public than among professional educators, and it is not without considerable justification. Second, using pupil achievement data is fraught with difficulties. It would rarely be appropriate simply to take a teacher's test results, compare them to a set of norms, and arrive at a defensible judgment regarding competence. Third, it is possible to design a teacher evaluation system that incorporates student achievement data in a responsible manner—one that takes into account likely sources of bias. Designing and implementing such a system requires time, thought, and expertise. Finally, even when such a system is in place, there can be no guarantee that in any given teacher's case, its results will be trustworthy. It follows, then, that pupil achievement information, no matter how carefully collected and analyzed, should not be the only basis on which personnel decisions are made. Other types of information should be considered.

Student Evaluations of Teaching

When Stanton introduced student evaluations at Benton High School, he introduced an innovation that is, curiously, relatively untried in U.S. secondary education. We say "curiously" because it is a widespread practice in American colleges and universities. In effect, high school seniors are judged too immature to have a direct voice in evaluating their teachers. However, three months later, as college freshmen, their opinions may be decisive in such a critical matter as the granting of tenure. We doubt that maturity springs so quickly on most eighteen-year-olds. In any event, bear in mind that nearly all the conclusions we reach in our discussion of student evaluations are derived from research carried out in higher education. That does not make those conclusions inapplicable to primary and secondary schools. However, readers whose major interest is at those levels will need to draw their own inferences about its applicability.

As Aleamoni (1981) points out, several rationales are commonly offered for using student evaluations as one source of information about teaching effectiveness. First, on various important aspects of effective teaching, students are the only or best sources of data. The amount and quality of homework assignments, the adequacy of written comments on essays and term papers, and the willingness of a teacher to provide additional help when it is required, for example, are critical facets of teaching quality not ordinarily accessible to administrators. Second, success in accomplishing many affective objectives may be more easily gauged by pupils themselves; a greater appreciation of music, a heightened interest in mathematics, or an increase in concern for the environment are examples. Third, since teachers are "observed" thousands of times each year by students but only once or twice by administrators, relatively uncommon but decisive behavior or behavior unlikely to be displayed before a school authority is accessible—cruel sarcasm, for example. The case at hand provides another illustration: Burnette's alleged drinking was common knowledge among pupils before Stanton knew of it. Indeed, had he not overhead chance remarks in the hall, or if Mr. Raintree had not written, Stanton might never have become aware of it. Fourth, because students provide a pool of many independent observers, aggregating their observations tends to reduce individual biases, which may go unchecked in an administrator's observations. Fifth, student evaluation forms may provide an important means of communication between pupils and faculty. This may lead to increased student interest and involvement in their own education. Such regular and formal feedback is often lacking. Finally, there are good reasons to believe that this feedback may itself be a very effective sanction. The reactions of students are important to teachers; classroom behavior that students view positively tends to be continued, whereas behavior viewed negatively tends to be discontinued (McKeachie, 1979).

Despite these various rationales for using student opinions for evaluating teaching, faculty members have several reservations about doing so. First, it is said that students cannot make reasonable judgments because they are immature and capricious and lack experience. According to Aleamoni (1981), the evidence from college students supports precisely the opposite conclusion. Student ratings of their instructors are very stable from year to year—interyear correlations range in the mid-80s.

Second, student ratings are said to be little more than a popularity contest— "flashy," joke-riddled classes are preferred over thoughtful, substantive, and carefully developed ones. The evidence, however, indicates that college students, at least, are capable of distinguishing various aspects of an instructor's performance and classroom organization. The captivating speaker might be rated highly for the interest of his lectures, but if his course is poorly organized, reading assignments are not selected carefully, and grading practices are erratic, those aspects of the course will receive below-average marks. Put another way, halo effects are small, and students are capable of reaching relatively independent judgments of various components of a course.

Third, it has been argued that students are unable to provide valid judgments until they have been out of school for a few years. At that point they are able to reflect on their various teachers and to judge the contribution of each to their life. Again, the research does not support this view. Alumni rate their former instructors in much the same way as do those instructors' current students.

A fourth criticism is the technical one of measurement reliability and validity. It is asserted that student questionnaires lack adequate reliability and validity for such an important purpose. There is considerable justification for this complaint. Most locally developed scales are so sadly lacking in these qualities as to be virtually useless for assessing teacher competence; they would lead to capricious judgments. It is virtually impossible for a faculty committee, for example, to produce an instrument of sufficient quality. Simply surveying existing forms and brainstorming some new items is clearly inadequate. However, when professionally developed and carefully tested instruments are considered, the picture changes radically. Aleamoni (1981) reports internal consistency reliability for carefully developed forms to be in the high 80s. Validity is much harder to assess. Most existing scales have demonstrated only content validity—experts agree that the items measure important aspects of teacher competence. Some studies, however, have reported moderate to high correlations between student assessments of instruction and various other forms of assessment—ratings of colleagues, expert judges, and student achievement—suggesting that the instruments are valid. Note that very high correlations would be undesirable. They would indicate that the quality being measured by the student evaluation form was virtually the same quality being measured by the other procedure. If student ratings are to be a worthwhile addition to a teacher evaluation program, they should contribute new information to the judgment process, not simply duplicate existing information.

Fifth, it is held that various extraneous factors affect student ratings, factors over which faculty members have little or no control. Hence these ratings should not be used in evaluating teachers. This argument is precisely the same as the one offered against using pupil achievement measures. Three factors often mentioned as invalidating are class size, status (whether a course is required or elective), and students' expected grades. The evidence is mixed with regard to class size (Aleamoni, 1981). Within normal ranges, say fifteen to forty students, size seems to have relatively little effect. Electivity, on the other hand, seems to have a relatively clear influence on students' ratings; required courses tend to receive lower marks than elective ones. Perhaps the most frequently made claim concerns grades. It is held that students who expect to receive high grades in a course will rate that course more favorably than students who do not. Thus, the argument goes, instructors with high standards are penalized by systems of student evaluation. This claim has been extensively investigated, with somewhat inconclusive results. Aleamoni and Hexner (1980) reported that twenty-two studies they reviewed found no relationship between expected or actual grades and student ratings, while twenty-eight reported positive correlations. In most of the latter instances, however, these relationships were quite weak; the median correlation was .14. In any case, as we shall see, this grade-rating relationship is not a decisive reason to reject the use of student judgments of teaching competence.

There are, then, some good reasons for considering student opinions of their instructors' skills and some good reasons for being cautious when doing so. Collecting student evaluations of teaching competence is an established practice in U.S. higher education. Indeed, at that level they are virtually the only data collected. A priori, we see no compelling reason why it should not be considered in secondary schools as well, though at that level it should not carry the weight given it in colleges and universities. Perhaps the scheme worked out by Stanton and his faculty is appropriate—collecting evaluations from eleventh and twelfth graders.

In any case, when appropriately modified, the criteria proposed by Millman (1981) for the fair use of achievement data can be applied to student evaluations as well. With regard to amenability to instruction, we suggest that rating forms should be especially attentive to aspects of teacher behavior that have been shown to relate to student achievement and are also under the instructor's control. Questions about overall satisfaction with a course are inadequate when used alone. For example, items such as "The instructor pointed out what was important to learn in each class session" and "The instructor indicated when a new topic was being introduced" are substantially correlated with measures of student achievement and are under a teacher's control. (See Tom & Cushman, 1975, for an example of an instrument developed with these criteria in mind.) Such items have a demonstrated validity and offer the important advantage of providing a teacher with low ratings with clear directions for improvement.

With regard to content validity, it is important that items reflect the nature and organization of the course in which they are used. A question regarding homework is likely to be irrelevant to most physical education classes. Hence a single set of items to be used in all courses is likely to be inappropriate. As we shall see, however, comparability is important. Thus separate instruments for each course is not a desirable strategy. A solution to this problem adopted by some colleges seems sensible: An omnibus set of items is developed, some of which are appropriate to all courses, some of which are designed for particular subjects (e.g., mathematics, physical education), and some of which can be chosen by the instructor for his or her own purposes. This procedure allows student rating forms to serve the needs of the institution as well as the teacher concerned.

A third criterion proposed by Millman (1981) for using achievement data concerns reliability. A teacher's evaluation ought not to depend on the results of a single administration of any instrument. We suggest that student evaluations be collected systematically in each course over a period of time. As with achievement test data, the mean of several administrations is a more reliable estimate of performance than is the score from a single administration. Further, the method of administering an instrument can affect its reliability. It is advisable to administer ratings in a formalized manner, using standard directions and providing adequate time to finish. Aleamoni (1981) suggested that questionnaires be given by someone other than the instructor (but not an administrator) or, failing that, that after reading the directions, the instructor leave the room and have a student collect the completed forms.

The fourth criterion concerned equity. The instrument should be fair for all teachers. The strategy of omnibus item pools discussed in connection with validity also helps to meet this criterion. In addition, it is obvious that teachers should know the content of any form to be used. Unlike achievement tests, where specific items need to remain secure, there is no danger of "teaching the test" with pupil evaluations. Indeed, when items consist of teacher behaviors known to promote student learning, teaching to the test is precisely what is desired.

Finally, comparability is essential. Student ratings of instruction can be meaningful only if comparisons may be made across teachers. This is particularly true because these rating instruments have a known positive response bias. That is, on a five-point rating scale, with 3 as neutral or the midpoint, a score of 3 is almost always *below* average. Put another way, without comparative data, virtually all teachers are above-average instructors! Further, as we have noted, some factors are known to affect ratings, notably whether a course is required or elective and students' expected or actual grades. Obviously it would be unfair to compare teachers' ratings without taking these factors into account. As with achievement data, the same procedures (e.g., regression analysis) may be used to adjust ratings for individual or class characteristics that might influence students' judgments. Also as with achievement data, one must remember that these procedures necessarily underadjust; hence student evaluations of teaching should not provide the only criterion for judging a teacher's effectiveness.

Classroom Observation

While soliciting student evaluations of teaching is rare in U.S. high schools and using pupil achievement is controversial, conducting classroom observations to assess teacher quality is widespread. The virtue of this practice is said to be that observing a teacher at work provides insights into critically important matters that are simply not available by any other method. The climate of a classroom, the degree of rapport between teachers and students, the skillful use of questions during a lesson, the quality of the moment-by-moment interactions among participants, and the extent to which classroom control is maintained in a fair and effective manner are just some of the aspects of effective teaching that observation is said to provide. For helping teachers to improve their instructional techniques, it is doubtful that any other single procedure will serve as well.

However, when considered as a technique for summative evaluation of teacher competence, observations have their own peculiar problems—problems that teachers' organizations have regularly pointed out. Notable among these are the problems of reliability and validity. Indeed, some people have concluded that because of these problems, classroom observations by school administrators have little, if any, place in judging teacher competence. McNeil and Popham (1973), for example, argue that "observations are most beneficial for recording and analyzing the teaching act—not judging it. . . . Effective teaching cannot be proven by the presence or absence of *any* instructional variable" (p. 233; emphasis added).

This conclusion is partly a consequence of the observational procedures used by most administrators. However, much of the difficulty derives from the complexity of classroom life itself. There are at least three aspects to this complexity. First, an incredible number of events occur in a classroom. Which of these events is important? To which should the observer attend, and which can safely be ignored? Second, these events are interdependent and related in complicated ways. Teachers do not simply behave; they behave in reaction to students, whose own behavior is in turn a reaction to their instructor and their classmates. And the behavior of both teachers and pupils is influenced by external events over which neither has control or even foreknowledge—visitors (and observers) appear, snow begins to fall, slide projectors break down, fire alarms sound. Finally, the sheer pace of events is often astonishing. Jackson (1968) calculated that an elementary teacher engages in as many as 1,000 interpersonal interactions in a single day—

perhaps 150 per hour. The wealth, complexity, and pace of classroom life, then, make reliable and valid observations difficult.

In response to these difficulties, two general approaches to classroom observation have evolved (Evertson and Holley, 1981). The first seeks to break down the complexity of classroom life into small behavioral units that can be adequately defined and described and can therefore be more reliably observed and coded. (If you are interested in reviewing available observation instruments, consult Simon & Boyer, 1970, and Borich & Madden, 1977.) For example, an often used instrument requires the observer to count the number of times teachers "praise or encourage students," "ask questions," and "give directions" (Flanders, 1970). Put another way, in attempting to increase reliability, many of these observation instruments use "low-inference categories"—categories that require little interpretation or judgment on the part of the observer. As a consequence, some of these systems are quite complex, in order to match the complexity of the events being observed. Coding matrices involving hundreds of cells are quite possible.

If these sophisticated observation procedures provide an increment in reliability, they also provide a corresponding increment in administratively undesirable features. First, many require considerable training for their proper use. Administrators willing to participate in elaborate and lengthy training sessions are, perhaps justifiably, none too plentiful. Further, the typical turnover in an administrative staff would require that this training be relatively continuous and individualized. Second, a much more serious liability concerns these instruments' relations to valued outcomes of instruction. What many of these schemes seem to have gained in improved reliability they have lost in the obvious criterion of validity—pupil learning. Not surprisingly, as the units of (reliably) recorded behavior become smaller, their occurrence seems to bear less and less relation to any measure of pupil achievement. The ratio of "direct" to "indirect" questions, for example (a score yielded by the Flanders, 1970, instrument), has shown inconsistent relations to pupil growth (Rosenshine, 1970). Third, the more refined an observation scheme, the less likely it is to be appropriate to various grade levels and subjects. The direct versus indirect question ratio, to continue the same example, may be more appropriate to an English class than to an auto mechanics shop. Obvious logistic (to say nothing of legal) problems arise when different observational procedures are used by administrators to evaluate different members of their faculty. Finally, the legal status of the findings generated by complex observation schemes is likely to be quite problematic. If a case of contested incompetence were to arrive in a court of law for adjudication, it is unclear what a judge might make of an administrator's claim that the ratio of "direct to indirect questions" in the teacher's classroom was too high.

At the other end of the inference scale are the sorts of observation schemes used in many school systems. Typically these instruments have been locally developed and consist of a few high-inference items—items that require a great deal of judgment of the observer. For example, such an observation form may require an administrator to make judgments of the following order: "Did the lesson appear to be planned and organized appropriately?" "Were instructional methods chosen so as to take individual differences into account?" "Was effective pupil control evidenced?" "Were lesson objectives made clear to all pupils?" Obviously such questions call for a very high level of inference—not to say omniscience—on the part of a school principal.

The problem with these high-inference devices is not simply that they require peculiarly difficult judgments. A major difficulty is their openness to a halo effect. Medley and Mitzel (1963) termed this "the archenemy of objective observation." There is a strong tendency for a judgment about one attribute of a person to be influenced by a judgment already made about another attribute or by a general impression already held of that person. Thus, using the example noted above, if a principal held a favorable impression of a teacher's lesson plans, reactions to that teacher's classroom control are also likely to be favorable. Worse yet, general impressions tend to persist. An unfavorable reaction to one lesson is likely to color the observation of the next. Halo effects, then, present a serious dilemma for administrators using classroom observations to assess teachers' competence. On the one hand, what an administrator sees in each observation will be influenced by judgments made in all of the preceding ones. A spuriously high level of consistency can be reached, and the principal may arrive at a very firm (but quite erroneous) conviction about the teacher's competence. Consider the case of Stanton and Burnette in this regard. The more often Stanton observed her, the more convinced he was that she was incompetent. On the other hand, it would clearly be unreasonable to judge a teacher incompetent on the basis of a single observation.

A second difficulty with these procedures is shared with the low-inference observation schemes discussed earlier. The reactive effect of observers is a matter of concern. It is reasonable to suspect that the mere presence of an observer is sufficient to alter the normal flow of classroom events in such a way as to make an observer's results invalid. Burnette's complaint about the "scribbling Buddha" in the back of her classroom was a reference to this point. One response to this problem has been to increase the frequency of observation; if the principal observes a classroom often enough, presumably, the administrator's presence ceases to be reactive—he or she becomes no more obtrusive than another chair or table. Even if true, however, this strategy exacerbates the problem of halo effects. A third problem of validity plagues many of the locally originated high-inference observation protocols. A great many of these schemes show little, if any, relation with valued outcomes of instruction—pupil learning or satisfaction with school, for example. Administrators' judgments about whether a teacher's lessons were well planned, individual differences taken into account, or lesson objectives made clear are often unrelated to any measure of pupil growth. This deficiency is critical. If administrators' judgments based on observation schemes cannot be related to changes in pupils, firing or retaining teachers on the basis of such schemes can be viewed as capricious. One might as well retain teachers because of their eye color or their taste in music.

We can summarize this discussion of the problems inherent in classroom observations by noting that they derive from defects in what has come to be called the "process-product paradigm" of teacher evaluation (Doyle, 1977). Essentially, that paradigm rests on the plausible view that classroom processes are important determinants of classroom products—that what goes on in schoolrooms makes a difference in pupil learning outcomes. Thus it makes sense to observe classrooms. However, as it is commonly applied by administrators concerned with teacher evaluation, the paradigm often incorporates some less plausible assumptions. First, the phrase "what goes on in classrooms" has tended to be translated into "what the teacher does in classrooms." That is, implicit in many evaluation protocols is the assumption that teacher behavior is, if not the only activity, at least the most important activity to be observed. It is not obvious that this is the case. Pupil behavior, a curriculum's effectiveness, or the availability of various instructional resources may be equally important. However, these aspects of classroom life are commonly ignored in observation schemes. Second, an implicit assumption about the direction of causality is made. For example, greater teacher enthusiasm is presumed to cause greater pupil achievement. However, since most of the research in this area is correlational, causal propositions can be reversed. It is equally possible to argue that teachers become more enthusiastic when dealing with high-achieving pupils. More generally, it may be that pupils cause teacher behavior as much as the reverse. Third, rating schemes used for teacher evaluation tend to focus on frequency of teacher behavior—how often the teacher praises pupils, for example. (The importance of frequency is evident even in protocols that don't require literal counts of various behaviors.) Yet frequency may be much less important than other aspects of what teachers do. The timing of praise may be more important than how often it is dispensed. Rare but salient teacher behavior may be much more critical for pupil learning than easily observed commonplace events. Further, the stability of teacher behavior is often assumed. What an administrator observes during one or two observations per year is assumed to mirror what happens during the hundreds of unobserved hours of classroom time. Finally, the stability (and importance) of the observed teacher behavior is assumed to exist across different groups of pupils, different subject matters, and different grade levels. On a priori and empirical grounds (see, for example, Brophy, 1973; Good & Grouws, 1975; Shavelson & Dempsey-Atwood, 1976), this assumption seems dubious. In any case, it is arguable that stable behavior is an inappropriate focus of teacher observation protocols. Stable behavior may not be nearly as important as a teacher's facility in making moment-by-moment adaptations to changes in classroom conditions.

All of this is not to argue that administrators' judgments based on classroom observations are worthless. It is to say that they should be treated cautiously and their limitations recognized. Substantial research (summarized in Rosenshine, 1976) does suggest that certain teacher behaviors may be important in facilitating pupil growth. These include clarity of instruction, enthusiasm, task orientation (being "businesslike"), using structuring comments, and providing opportunities for pupils to practice what they have learned. Note that these are high-inference items. Indeed, it appears that at the present state of our knowledge, high- rather than low-inference judgments are more likely to have at least moderate correlations with pupil outcomes (Rosenshine & Furst, 1973).

To call attention to these teacher behaviors as being worth observing may seem to do nothing more than to mouth platitudes. Of course teacher enthusiasm is important. However, in this regard, two things are worth remembering. First, many teacher behaviors that have seemed "obviously" important have not shown a consistent relationship to pupil outcomes—teacher warmth, praising students, and encouraging pupil participation in lessons, for example. This is not to say that they are therefore unimportant; it is simply to sound a note of caution in their interpretation. Second, these "obvious" teacher acts are often ignored on many of the observation and evaluation protocols currently used by school administrators.

The foregoing discussion and the events at Benton High School suggest that there are at least five important aspects of implementing good observational systems. Evertson and Holley (1981) have made some helpful suggestions for this. First, a careful choice of instruments is essential. Several published sources are worth consulting (Simon & Boyer, 1970; Stallings, 1977; Kowalski, 1978; Borich & Madden, 1977). However, since these instruments differ considerably in their purposes, complexity, and recording procedures, it is quite likely that modifications will be required to meet local objectives. Consultation with someone who has established expertise is recommended. The choice of what behavior is to be observed, how it is to be recorded, and the nature of the inferences that may appropriately be derived from that record are sufficiently beyond the technical skills of most practitioners that outside help is justified. The state of current knowledge no longer justifies a committee of teachers and administrators sitting down to conjure up a system on their own.

Second, training is essential. Once an instrument has been chosen or developed, training and practice in its use are necessary. Administrators must learn to see what the instrument requires them to see, for, in a fundamental sense, the observer, not the protocol, *is* the instrument. The behavior to be observed must be defined and described, and the many instances of ambiguity that inevitably occur must be clarified. The more abstract the categories, the more training is required. Ultimately, the fairness of the system will depend on the adequacy of this training. A teacher's tenure or retention in a school system ought not to depend on the accident of his or her school assignment or on the training of the administrator who happens to do the observations.

Third, the selection of the frequency, length, and time of observations is important. If results are to be useful, reliable, and valid, administrators must have some assurance that what they observe is reasonably representative of what there is to observe. This problem of representativeness is exacerbated by school district policies or practices that limit observations to one or two a year—a constraint sometimes written into teachers' contracts. Obviously, classroom observation data are very expensive to collect. However, niggardly husbanding of resources (or politically inspired constraints) makes highly suspect any judgments reached by observers. Similarly, the selection of times can be critical. If the purpose of an evaluation is to reach judgments about a teacher's skill, it makes little sense to observe the teacher's class while a test is being given, for example. Finally, in the matter of representativeness, Evertson and Holley (1981) concluded that the presence of an observer in a classroom is not generally so reactive as to invalidate the conclusions reached. Again, multiple observations probably reduce these effects.

Fourth, the known existence of halo effects requires that, at least in problematic cases, more than one observer should be involved. We cannot know the extent to which Stanton's initial observation of Burnette was colored by his reading of his predecessor's evaluations, nor the extent to which his later ones were biased by his earlier visits to her class. More important, neither can Stanton know. Prudence, then, dictates that another evaluator be involved.

Finally, it is almost certainly unreasonable to rely on observations as the sole source of information about teacher effectiveness. Yet this is common practice. Classroom observations are only one of the procedures capable of providing information relevant to judgments of teacher competence. The other sources, notably pupil achievement data and student evaluations, are capable of providing requisite checks on the necessarily fallible judgments of administrative observations.

Professionally competent evaluation procedures, however, are not sufficient. Teacher evaluation takes place in a legal context that bears importantly on practice. We turn to this topic next.

The Law, Teacher Evaluation, and Dismissal

Declining enrollments, school closings, the mounting tendency of women to remain in the teaching profession throughout their childbearing years, and an apparent decrease in teacher job mobility (Mark & Anderson, 1978) are just some of the factors contributing to an increase in the average experience level of the nation's teaching force. Consequently, the emphasis on summative teacher evaluations is very likely to shift from one in which their primary focus has been on probationary teachers—where the award of tenure is a critical decision—to a focus on permanent faculty—where retention or dismissal is a paramount concern. Undoubtedly, the rising emphasis on "accountability" and the public's apparent dissatisfaction with the quality of its schools will contribute to this trend. It is important, therefore, that practicing administrators be especially cognizant of their rights and obligations in evaluating their tenured staff. It is for these reasons, among others, that the case of Susan Burnette is the focus of our attention.

Before turning to the specific legal problems and issues inherent in the evaluation and dismissal of tenured faculty, it is necessary that we state an important caveat, which will apply to the entire discussion. There are substantial differences in the laws pertaining to teacher employment and retention among the fifty states. In addition, within each state, school district policy and teacher contracts differ even more widely, and these may also have the status of law. It is impossible for us to treat all of these variations. Rather, it is our intention to introduce some of the salient general considerations that characterize the legal context of teacher evaluation and dismissal. You will have the responsibility of becoming familiar with the specific rules that govern your own situation.

John Stanton clearly considers Susan Burnette sufficiently inept as a teacher to consider dismissing her. But Burnette is tenured. Precisely what difference does that make?

In most states, awarding a teacher tenure results in a dramatic shift in the teacher's legal status with regard to employment. However, this shift is *not* the granting of a sinecure. Contrary to the widely accepted myth, if incompetent, indolent, or otherwise errant (but tenured) teachers are tolerated in schools, it is not because they must be. Certainly no state law requires it. Hence the administrator's plaint, "There's nothing I can do—he's got tenure," is unjustified. The law is meant to protect tenured teachers from arbitrary or capricious dismissal and from being fired on grounds irrelevant to their work. It does not protect incompetents from losing their jobs. Typically, an administrator faced with an unsatisfactory teacher needs reasoned grounds for dismissal and careful attention to procedure—and perhaps some "guts." Thus this school district has the power to dismiss its science teacher; tenure, in itself, does not protect Burnette.

If the award of tenure did not guarantee Burnette's continued employment, it did cause two fundamental changes in her legal relationship with the school district. First, it created a property interest. That is, her job in Benton High came to be viewed as property in which she has a substantial claim. As property, the full protection of the due process clause of the Fourteenth Amendment comes into play: She cannot be deprived of this property without due process of law. More specifically, she may not be dismissed without demonstration of legitimate cause and without careful adherence to constitutional and statutory procedures, as well as any procedures that may be contained in the local teachers' contract and district policy.

A second fundamental change in Burnette's relation to Benton High regards a presumption of competence. The tenured teacher is presumed to be competent; the award of tenure is itself taken as evidence that this is the case. The burden of proof shifts to the district, which must adduce evidence showing that she is no longer fit to teach. In many states, prior to the award of tenure, it is sufficient for an administrator merely to pronounce a teacher unfit, leaving to the teacher the virtually impossible task of proving otherwise, should he or she wish to contest that judgment. Indeed, in the decision not to renew an untenured teacher's contract, it is often the case that no reason for the nonrenewal need be given. (In practice, the tenured-untenured distinction is not so sharply drawn as this paragraph may seem to imply. Some states do not have tenure laws; instead "continuing contracts" statutes exist, which vary considerably in the degree to which teachers are afforded protection. Similarly, the statutes of some states or local contracts provide probationary teachers with some of the protections enjoyed by their tenured colleagues. Finally, dismissing a probationary teacher *during* a contract, rather than simply not renewing a contract when it expires, is likely to require treatment as a tenure case.) The ideas of due process and the presumption of competence encapsulate two of the fundamental distinctions that characterize the difference between tenured and nontenured teachers in most places.

Legitimate Cause and the Process of Teacher Evaluation

With regard to dismissal, perhaps the first thing to note is the courts' emphasis on legitimate cause; no tenured teacher may be dismissed without showing cause. What counts as legitimate cause, however, varies widely among the states. Some specify rather precisely the reasons that justify dismissal; others are quite vague. Connecticut's statute may be representative:

(b) Beginning with and subsequent to the fourth year of continuous employment of a teacher by a board of education, the contract of employment of a teacher shall be reviewed from year to year, except that it may be terminated at any time for one of the following reasons:
(1) Inefficiency or incompetence;
(2) Insubordination against reasonable rules of the board of education;
(3) Moral misconduct;
(4) Disability, as shown by competent medical evidence;
(5) Elimination of the position;
(6) Other due and sufficient cause.

Pennsylvania lists "immorality, incompetence, intemperance, cruelty, persistent negligence, mental derangement, and persistent and willful violation of the school laws" (Strike & Bull, 1981, p. 323).

Incompetence (or "inefficiency," its legal equivalent) is listed among the permissible reasons for dismissal by most states, and it is the one most obviously relevant to standard teacher evaluation procedures. Hence it is the cause of most interest to us here (although Burnette's alleged alcoholism raises the possible grounds of "moral misconduct" or "intemperance" as well). It is important to note, however, that incompetence is typically left undefined by the states that mention it. Instead, common sense, conventional wisdom, and, most important for us, professional judgment have played a large part in defining its nature. Among the qualities that courts have permitted to count as incompetence are deficiencies in subject matter knowledge, poor teaching methods, disorganized teaching, inability to maintain pupil discipline, excessive force, inability to motivate students, inflexibility, uncooperativeness, permitting student vulgarity, causing low morale, poor communication, poor attitude, violation of rules, mishandling funds, low student achievement, unsatisfactory ratings, poor record keeping, arbitrary grading, and lack of self-control (Strike & Bull, 1981, p. 324).

Such a list is of little help to a practicing administrator. "Poor teaching methods" or "inflexibility" are little more precise than "incompetence." Virtually any action or mental state that can be plausibly related to the quality of a teacher's performance has been treated as evidence of incompetence in some courtroom. Nevertheless, a core of meaning can be extracted from these examples, a core that appears frequently in dismissal cases that reach the courts. Four common elements of incompetence can be discerned: (1) a deficiency in the teacher's own knowledge of the subject taught, (2) an inability to convey that knowledge to students, (3) an incapacity to maintain satisfactory classroom discipline, and (4) irremediable behavior (despite warnings and the provision of assistance intended to promote improvement, no substantial changes in performance occur).

This core of meaning provides guidelines as to the nature of summative teacher evaluations; it suggests the categories of information that should be routinely attended to. Put another way, deficiencies in subject matter knowledge, in the capacity to convey knowledge, in pupil control, and in the power or willingness to improve qualify as legitimate cause for denying reappointment to a tenured teacher. Though a district's evaluation practices may have several purposes, one is almost certainly to ensure that only competent staff are retained. This core of meaning provides important criteria to be considered and the nature of the evidence to be collected in any evaluation system.

Considered in this light, the lacunae in common practices are obvious. Consider the matter of teachers' subject matter knowledge. Administrators, particularly at the secondary school level and above, are typically relatively ignorant of a teacher's subject. It is not implausible to think that Stanton really did not know "a quark from a quiche." Hence he is unfit to comment on Burnette's command of physics and chemistry. In recent years, the development of competency tests in various subjects provides one mechanism for obtaining information relevant to a teacher's knowledge, but use of such tests is still rare. A second procedure has been to seek the judgments of subject matter specialists, most often a teacher's senior colleagues. This strategy has at least three potential liabilities. First, teachers are loath to become involved in summative evaluations of their peers (Lortie, 1975). Second, as we have noted, the aging of the nation's teaching force works against the validity of such judgments. That is, senior colleagues, unless they themselves have invested in retraining, may not be particularly current in their fields. (This can be a defect in procedures that rely on department heads for evaluating subject matter competence.) Finally, in small districts, knowledgeable experts may be unavailable, particularly in advanced elective subjects such as physics and chemistry. Instead of securing assessments from tests or colleagues, common practice has been to rely on the possession of an advanced degree as an index of subject matter knowledge. Perhaps this was at the root of Stanton's concern with Burnette's failure to continue her graduate studies. But in the face of the rapid advances made in some fields and the lack of any substantial relation between teachers' possession of an M.A. and student learning (Coleman, 1966), his use of this index is questionable. Despite these liabilities, there currently appear to be few alternatives to judging subject matter competence than the assessment of senior teachers in the area of specialization and the currency and quality of the teacher's own training. In the former case, it behooves the administrator at least to ensure that the credentials of the senior teacher involved are adequate to support a claim to expertise and that the teacher is willing to render a negative judgment if one is required.

A second lacuna in evaluation practice illuminated by the judicial view of incompetence concerns a teacher's ability to convey knowledge to students. Here the deficiency of observation procedures is obvious. Observations tell an administrator little or nothing about any changes in student knowledge being induced by the observed lesson. Stanton could only infer that students were not learning chemistry in Burnette's classes on the basis of his observation of them. His use of the results of statewide achievement tests is notable in this regard for two reasons. First, such a practice is likely to be a legally permissible (albeit professionally contentious) mechanism for assessing the capacity to convey knowledge, and second, it is seldom used—at least in so open a manner—by practicing administrators. We have already called attention to the technical deficiencies of his procedure. Should the events at Benton High end in a courtroom, those deficiencies will almost certainly come to light.

In contrast to the first two categories of incompetent teaching, maintaining classroom discipline is perhaps most easily and directly assessed by observation. If Stanton found "bedlam" in Burnette's room on his first observation, he had the evidence of his own eyes and ears to rely on in reaching that judgment. It is worth noting that the argument that a principal's presence has a detrimental effect on a teacher's performance cuts two ways. It seems plausible to suppose that having the school principal sitting in the back of a classroom leads to a somewhat higher level of pupil decorum than might ordinarily obtain. Burnette's pupils were probably better behaved when he was in her classroom than when he was not.

Finally, the core of meaning found in the courts' view of incompetence draws our attention to the importance of making as precise as possible any recommendations for improvement that follow an observation and of noting those recommendations in the written record of that observation. Further, it increases the significance of attending to the implementation of those suggestions in subsequent evaluations. Legally contested dismissals for incompetence may hinge on the extent to which a teacher has been informed of the nature of any deficiencies, provided with suggested techniques for correcting them, and then given the time and opportunity necessary to put those suggestions into practice. It is arguable whether Stanton's brief comments to the effect that Burnette "needed to improve student motivation and discipline" are satisfactory.

We can see, then, that case law on teacher dismissal has provided some useful guidelines for appropriate criteria to be considered in teacher evaluation. It suggests that teachers' command of their subjects, pupil learning, classroom discipline, and an opportunity to improve are important facets of any evaluation scheme. This is not to suggest that these are the only criteria that a district may employ in evaluating its staff. Rather, it is to suggest that careful attention to these four will enhance the legal status of any procedure that results in a contested dismissal. We can also see that common practice is deficient on several of these criteria, most particularly, perhaps, the first two. There seems to be relatively little in current practice in the way of systematic attempts to evaluate the state of teachers' knowledge or of pupil achievement. In the former case, the norms and organization of many public schools are not conducive to evaluating subject matter competence. (Indeed, in the case of elementary schools, it is unclear what subject matter would be involved. In contrast, the emphasis on research and publication in many universities provides a relatively direct assessment of competence via the judgments of peers.) In the latter case, the use of pupil achievement data has been strongly resisted by teachers, with some justification, as pungently noted by Susan Burnette. Although we have not analyzed court decisions on these matters, we would not be surprised to find that inadequate pupil discipline figures prominently as a primary ground for dismissal. The folklore among teachers supports this inference—it is often claimed that, above all else, pupil control is "what really counts in getting a good evaluation from administrators." Given the obstacles to securing data relevant to subject matter knowledge and pupil achievement, discipline may have come to assume inordinate importance.

Due Process in Teacher Evaluation

The remarks concerning legitimate cause should not be taken as implying that the substantive judgment of a school administrator about a teacher's competence are likely to come under searching scrutiny in a court. The opposite is the case. When a school board dismisses a teacher because he or she lacks adequate control of pupils, for example, it is unlikely that a judge will question that judgment. Put bluntly, it is not necessary for an administrator to be right. Conversely, a dismissed teacher is unlikely to win reinstatement by arguing that those judgments were erroneous. A federal court commented on this matter as follows:

It is possible that the discretion of a Board may, at times, to those more generously endowed, seem to have been exercised with a lack of wisdom. But the Board's decisions in the exercise of its discretion are not vulnerable to our correction merely if they are "wrong," sustainable if they are "right." . . . Such matters as the competence of teachers and the standards of its measurement are not, without more, matters of constitutional dimensions. They are peculiarly appropriate to state and local administrations. (Scheelhaase v. Woodbury Central Community School District, *pp. 241, 244*)

However, while a court is unlikely to question the substance of an administrator's judgment, it will pay very close attention to the procedures by which that judgment was reached. It will require that school administrators scrupulously follow all legislated and contractual procedures in evaluating one of their staff, and it will further require that these procedures produce evidence that is clearly relevant to a judgment of competence. If stipulated procedures are followed and the evidence gathered is germane to the judgment reached, it is not required that the interpretation of this evidence be unarguably correct. The fact that reasonable people may disagree about its interpretation is not sufficient to overrule a decision. Stanton's conclusion that the noise in Susan Burnette's classroom was a consequence of her lack of control rather than her teaching methods is unlikely to be reversed by a judge.

Nor will a judgment of incompetence be reversed simply because it is based on ad hoc procedures. Neither state statutes nor courts commonly specify the nature of the processes used to evaluate teachers. A district might have very detailed directions as to how such evaluations are to be carried out, or it might have no directions at all. Procedures, if they are specified, are likely to find expression in school district policy or teacher contracts. Where they are specified, however, they must be followed. Although the law is generally silent on the procedures of teacher evaluation, it is rather more voluble on procedures for dismissing tenured teachers for incompetence. Since one purpose of evaluation (albeit not the only one) is to provide evidence should dismissal be required, it is important on these grounds alone that evaluations be designed with the possibility of a contested dismissal in mind.

We have noted the application of the Fourteenth Amendment's due process clause to the dismissal of tenured faculty. The intent of this clause, as applied to the matter at hand, is to prevent a school district from taking arbitrary or capricious action against a member of its faculty. An action is arbitrary when it is taken without reason. Thus due process requires that a teacher's dismissal be predicated on established facts—in particular, facts about the teacher's performance, behavior, or abilities. These are precisely the sorts of facts provided by a well-designed evaluation procedure. Thus one important way in which administrators may protect themselves against a charge of offending due process is to establish such a system. It provides a natural mechanism to meet the nonarbitrariness criterion.

Nor may a school district dismiss a tenured faculty member in a capricious manner. To act capriciously is to act whimsically or unpredictably. This suggests three requirements for a carefully wrought evaluation system (Strike & Bull, 1981). First, any action should be based on clearly formulated and publicly announced policies. This implies that teachers have a right to know prior to their evaluation what criteria and standards are to apply and to know that decisions regarding their continued employment depend on the results of such evaluations. Further, school district policy should specify in as much detail as possible the sorts of evaluation findings that are likely to lead to dismissal. Second, policies should be general in their scope. They should apply equally to all members of a specified class and may not be rigged so as to single out particular individuals for special treatment. All teachers eligible to be evaluated should be assessed. Third, policies must be regularly applied. The consequences of any evaluation should be felt equally by all who are subject to those consequences. The same contract renewal decisions, for example, should be made for all teachers whose evaluations produced similar results. Strike and Bull conclude that an administrator accused in court of arbitrarily dismissing a teacher may establish a "nearly iron-clad rebuttal" if it can be demonstrated that (1) the grounds of termination are written into school policy, (2) all teachers were subjected to a similar evaluation, and (3) other teachers have been dismissed for similarly deficient evaluations.

If Stanton moves to dismiss Burnette on grounds of incompetence, he will be very vulnerable to a charge of capriciousness. Recall that the procedure used in his observations required him to rate teachers on a five-point scale, with 3 indicating average competence. On such scales, which are very commonly used, it is rare for a teacher to receive a 1 ("unsatisfactory"). Indeed, an overall rating of 3 is ordinarily *below* average. Principals are seemingly unwilling to give a low mark to a teacher in a category of judgment, and when they do, there is a strong tendency to compensate by giving an above-average rating in another category. Perhaps this is a consequence of the natural urge to find something nice to say and not to be overly "negative" by rating a teacher unsatisfactory. Explaining such a low rating to the teacher after an observation is, after all, likely to be unpleasant. As we saw, Burnette even became upset at Stanton's mildly negative remarks following his first observation of her class.

This tendency to be positive, to rate unsatisfactory performance as something better, is a serious mistake. Should Burnette's case end up in court, Stanton may have created a serious problem for himself and his school district. We do not know, of course, what all of his ratings are. But if the results of the given one are close to representative, Burnette is satisfactory. The ratings from her first observation have a mean of 3.3—slightly above average. Undoubtedly Burnette's lawyer would be quick to point this out. The lawyer, with complete justice, would argue that she was judged competent by the very person who now claims to have found her incompetent! It is important, then, when an administrator concludes that a teacher's performance, in part or overall, is unsatisfactory, that that judgment be rendered accurately. It is a disservice to the school district (as well as to the teacher) to give inflated ratings in a misguided attempt to avoid unpleasantness. To do so is to risk the justifiable charge of capriciousness.

While prohibitions against arbitrary or capricious dismissal ultimately find their source in the Fourteenth Amendment's due process clause, they find their specific expression in state statutes and teachers' contracts. Though specifics vary from place to place, they commonly include several requirements. First, written charges (e.g., of incompetence) must be filed, usually with the school board or its clerk, during a specified period of time. These charges must follow reasonably closely upon the occurrence of the pertinent events. In the case of evaluations, this might mean sometime during the year following the last unsatisfactory rating. Limits on this period are often specified. Second, if the board moves to dismiss the teacher, detailed charges must be communicated to the accused within a few days. A statement of the teacher's rights must accompany such charges, including the right to a hearing. Third, at the hearing, before an independent panel, the teacher has the rights to defend himself or herself, to testify, to present evidence, to cross-examine witnesses, and to be represented by counsel. Testimony may be under oath, and any transcript of the proceeding is made available to the teacher. Fourth, the written findings of the panel must be forwarded to the teacher, the board of education, and usually the state commissioner of education, and the board is required to act on those findings within a specified time. Finally, the teacher is given the right of appeal—to the state commissioner, the courts, or both. If Stanton recommends Burnette's dismissal, and if she chooses to contest that dismissal, it is likely that procedures similar to these will be available to her.

These common requirements have further implications for practice. Specifically, they imply that evaluations be conducted regularly and that they be formal in nature—a written record must be produced. The written results of an evaluation several years old or unwritten impressions based on current informal assessments provide a less satisfactory evidentiary base than periodic and current formal assessments. Since an important aspect of due process is irremediality, periodic evaluations are able to address the question of whether or not improvement has occurred. Finally, the requirement that teachers be able to respond to alleged deficiencies makes a carefully written statement essential.

Ethical Considerations in Teacher Evaluation

It is not enough that an evaluation system be technically correct—that it be based on the best available procedures for generating reliable and valid information. Nor is it enough that it meet the requirements of the law or that it "stand up in court." Such considerations are important, but they are not the only considerations. An evaluation system should also promote fairness. It is necessary that administrators go beyond the technical requirements of reliable and valid instruments and the intricacies of statutes and contracts. Although the law has a moral point, it is not synonymous with morality. An act can be simultaneously legal and unfair. Perhaps these distinctions can be illustrated by the occasional practice of "eavesdropping" on classrooms via intercom systems. Even if this practice produced technically good information about a teacher's competence, and even if this information were acceptable in a court, most of us would find such covert surveillance unfair.

What is fair? When is an evaluation system fair? We suggest examining three components: equal respect, reasonableness, and effectiveness.

There are two aspects to the notion of equal respect. The first is that human beings—teachers included—are objects of intrinsic worth; they are ends in themselves and are deserving of respect. This requires that evaluation procedures respect the dignity of teachers as human beings. Evaluations that harass or belittle or are gratuitous are precluded.

The second aspect of equal respect is that persons are of *equal* intrinsic value. This does not mean that everyone is entitled to equal treatment; indeed, a major result of teacher evaluation, whether formative or summative, is to produce unequal treatments. However, this aspect of equal respect demands that any decisions made about teachers' competence be made on the basis of relevant criteria applied to everyone in like circumstances. Criteria are relevant when they have a plausible link to some legitimate educational purpose. Irrelevant criteria, such as race or sex, ordinarily have no such link. Thus to use irrelevant criteria in a teacher's evaluation is to exhibit a lack of respect for that teacher. (It is not always easy to decide what is relevant and what is not. Race or sex might be relevant to a decision, for example, if the need to provide a role model were judged important.) Second, the criteria applied in the evaluation of one teacher ought to be applied to all similarly situated teachers. Here, what counts as "similarly situated" may also be difficult to decide. We suspect that "warmth of the pupil-teacher relationship,'' for example, is more appropriate to the evaluation of kindergarten teachers than mathematics teachers. However, when different criteria are applied, this variation should be on educational grounds, publicly arrived at and decided upon before the fact, not after.

Reasonableness is a second component of a fair evaluation system. Its meaning is caught by the due process requirement that decisions not be arbitrary or capricious. Our earlier discussion of this was in the context of the formal due process owed to tenured faculty. Here we suggest that all teachers, probationary or tenured, are owed evaluations that are reasonable—ones that are not arbitrary or capricious but are instead based on the best available evidence, collected in a timely and regular manner and bearing on known criteria. Further, such evidence should be available to the teacher concerned, who should have the opportunity to refute it.

Effectiveness is the final component of a fair evaluation system. The standards of equal respect and reasonableness are primarily intended to protect teachers from unwarranted administrative action. However, there are other parties with an interest in fair evaluation besides teachers and administrators, notably children, parents, and the community that supports the schools. It is possible to design an evaluation system that is so complex, binding on reasonable administrative discretion, or time-consuming that, though eminently fair to the professional staff, it would be quite unfair to these other parties. Procedural rules, therefore, cannot simply address the rights of teachers; they must also consider the rights of these other parties. The point of a good evaluation system, after all, is to ensure that children receive quality instruction.

At first glance it may appear that the standards of equal respect and reasonableness conflict with that of effectiveness. In principle, of course, they do not. Decisions that are based on known and relevant criteria and are nondiscriminatory and reasonable should lead to a more effective teaching staff. Hence one should be suspicious of an administrator who complains that effective teacher evaluations are impossible because of restrictions written into district policy or teachers' contracts.

It is possible that an evaluation system can become inefficient because procedures to enforce fairness are too elaborate. An evaluation system should be ''cost-effective.'' A system should be constructed so as to protect teachers from an actual or likely abuse, not from every imaginable one. In its design, it is unnecessary that administrators be viewed implicitly as malevolent. Moreover, a fair evaluation system should not prevent a negative judgment about a teacher's competence. If a warranted negative judgment is made difficult or impossible, the evaluation system is unfair.

If effectiveness does not conflict with equal respect or reasonableness in principle, in practice it sometimes does. We suspect that this conflict is largely a consequence of the peculiar difficulty of teacher supervision in schools. In few workplaces are the technology of the organization and the competence of its employees so hidden from the people charged with overall responsibility for the organization's performance. For example, contrast the problems of an assembly line supervisor with those of a principal. The former need only "walk the line" to get a continuous and reasonably accurate assessment of employees' competence. The principal strolling his school's corridors, however, is likely to see only closed doors. In schools, work is performed almost in secret.

This secrecy, however, is relative. In another sense, a teacher's performance is an eminently public one. It is typically carried out in front of 20 to 150 persons each day—the teacher's pupils. That students have a much greater opportunity to observe their instructors than do administrators is one of the stronger arguments for incorporating student judgments into evaluation systems, as we have observed. The point here, though, is that as a consequence of this differential opportunity, students—and their parents—are often more quickly aware of a teacher's incompetence or misconduct than are principals. This is why bad news about a staff member often reaches a principal via student gossip or letters from parents. It is why, as Stanton ruefully notes, principals are often the last to know about events occurring in their own schools.

A second structural problem contributes to principals' ignorance of their staffs' performance. There is a norm in public schools (and colleges as well) that administrators should not formally observe classes "too much," particularly those of tenured faculty. Certainly, to sit in on a teacher's lessons once a week for an hour would be viewed by many as an act of hostility. It is doubtful whether many principals would be willing to observe a tenured teacher's classes formally more than once or twice a year, even if they had the time to do so. Thus the physical layout of schools and the informal norm against frequent observation combine to ensure that much of administrators' information (both favorable and unfavorable) about staff performance comes second- or thirdhand. Further, when this information suggests incompetence or malfeasance, the norm against frequent observation tends to preclude direct checking on its accuracy.

As a consequence, the temptation to act unfairly on the grounds of "effectiveness" is perhaps greater in schools than in other places of work. Administrators will often find themselves in possession of hearsay information of a derogatory sort without a normatively acceptable way to assess its truth and thus may be tempted to use such covert surveillance procedures as eavesdropping outside a door or personally delivering routine messages to a classroom. When the third-party information concerns matters of technical competence—teaching techniques—the requirements of equal respect, reasonableness, and, perhaps most especially, effectiveness preclude such evaluation strategies. A principal cannot effectively determine if a teacher is as inept as a parent may claim, for example, by lurking about in the halls or conducting an impromptu poll of a few students. In such instances, fairness demands that the allegation be brought to the teacher's attention and that it be openly investigated with the most appropriate evaluative procedures.

It is sometimes argued, however, that when these third-party allegations concern a matter of outright malfeasance, open investigation not only fails on the criterion of effectiveness but may actually worsen the situation. In the case at hand, for example, some people will assert that if Stanton informs Burnette of the rumors of her drinking and the parent's letter, and if the teacher is in fact drinking on the job, she may not stop doing so but only become more circumspect about it. As a consequence, her present and future students are unfairly endangered. Stanton apparently considered this a possibility, for he chose to make discreet inquiries among other members of the staff and to observe Burnette's classroom unannounced.

A final matter regarding effectiveness as an aspect of fairness in teacher evaluation systems must be mentioned. An effective system of teacher evaluation should rarely require a court of law for settling disputes. That is, an effective system ought to provide numerous opportunities for deficiencies to be corrected, for disputes to be resolved through discussion among the individuals involved, and for those remaining to be mediated by neutral third parties. Only after a succession of increasingly formal procedures for settlement have been exhausted should a dispute reach the courts.

As a summary of the ethical aspects of teacher evaluation, we present what Strike and Bull (1981) term a "bill of rights," which should guide the design of a fair system of teacher evaluation.

Rights of Educational Institutions
1. Educational institutions have the right to exercise supervision and to make personnel decisions intended to improve the quality of the education they provide.
2. Educational institutions have the right to collect information relevant to their supervisory and evaluative roles.
3. Educational institutions have the right to act on such relevant information in the best interest of the students whom they seek to educate.
4. Educational institutions have the right to the cooperation of the teaching staff in implementing and executing a fair and effective system of evaluation.

Rights of Teachers
1. Professional rights
   a. Teachers have a right to reasonable job security.
   b. Teachers have a right to a reasonable degree of professional discretion in the performance of their jobs.
   c. Teachers have a right to reasonable participation in decisions concerning both professional and employment-related aspects of their jobs.
2. Evidential rights
   a. Teachers have the right to have decisions made on the basis of evidence.
   b. Teachers have a right to be evaluated on relevant criteria.
   c. Teachers have the right not to be evaluated on the basis of hearsay, rumor, or unchecked complaints.
3. Procedural rights
   a. Teachers have the right to be evaluated according to general, public, and comprehensive standards.
   b. Teachers have the right to notice concerning when they will be evaluated.
   c. Teachers have the right to know the results of their evaluation.

    d. Teachers have the right to express a reaction to the results of their evaluation in a meaningful way.

    e. Teachers have the right to a statement of the reasons for any action taken in their cases.

    f. Teachers have the right to appeal adverse decisions and to have their views considered by a competent and unbiased authority.

    g. Teachers have the right to orderly and timely evaluation.

4. Other humanitarian and civil rights

    a. Teachers have a right to humane evaluation procedures.

    b. Teachers have the right to have their evaluation kept private and confidential.

    c. Teachers have the right to evaluation procedures which are not needlessly intrusive into their professional activities.

    d. Teachers have the right to have their private lives considered irrelevant to their evaluation.

    e. Teachers have the right to have evaluation not be used coercively to [achieve] aims external to the legitimate purposes of evaluation.

    f. Teachers have the right to nondiscriminatory criteria and procedures.

    g. Teachers have the right not to have evaluation used to [censure] the expression of unpopular views.

    h. Teachers have the right to an overall assessment of their performance that is frank, honest, and consistent.

Principles of Conflict Resolution

1. Remediation is to be preferred, where possible, to disciplinary action or termination.

2. Mediation is to be preferred, where possible, to more litigious forms of conflict resolution.

3. Informal attempts to settle disputes should precede formal ones. (pp. 307–309)

A Comprehensive System of Teacher Evaluation

We have noted that state law typically does not require that schools commit themselves to a clearly specified written system of teacher evaluation. Nevertheless, there are strong reasons for doing so. First, such a commitment is a public statement that an institution intends to respect its teachers as persons by making decisions about them on the basis of relevant performance criteria. Second, it is a statement that it intends those decisions to be reasonable ones, based on carefully gathered information with a bearing on the specified criteria. Third, it is a practical instantiation of the assumption that its faculty is professionally motivated to provide competent service—the assumption that if teachers clearly understand what is expected of them, they will strive to meet those expectations without constant supervision or threats. Finally, a clearly specified system of evaluation has the potential asset of protecting the institution from claims that it has acted illegally in cases of dismissal. We will provide some general guidelines for designing such a system, one that meets the technical, legal, and ethical criteria discussed in this chapter. We shall consider these guidelines under four headings that represent important components of a comprehensive system of teacher evaluation: formal policy, substance, procedures, and participation.

Formal Policy Statements

In keeping with the general moral purpose of meeting due process requirements, it is important that a school district formally state its intention to make performance evaluations a central aspect of its personnel decisions. Several aspects of such a policy bear mentioning. First, and most obvious, the policy must become part of the public record. However, that is not sufficient. A policy that appears in the minutes of a board meeting and ends up in an administrator's files fails to serve its purpose. It must be communicated to the faculty, and its communication should be accompanied by personal discussion with the staff. In the case of a new teacher, an individual meeting with the administrator responsible for evaluating the teacher's performance is required. At this meeting, the exact nature of the policy's implementation at the particular school should be made clear.

Second, the policy should be written with as much precision as possible, given the difficulty of defining good teaching. Vague references to "quality instruction" do not serve the interests of either teachers or the school district. Teachers have an obvious interest in performing well; exhortations to provide quality instruction are not particularly helpful in providing it. Similarly, the district has an interest in ensuring that pupils receive competent instruction. Without further specification, however, it has little to guide it toward making rationally grounded decisions. This is not to suggest that a policy statement be a "laundry list" of behaviorally defined competences. It is doubtful whether such competences define good teaching adequately, and, in any case, teachers are perfectly capable of complying with more generally formulated criteria. It is possible, however, for a district to specify the criteria (e.g., subject matter knowledge) that will go into retention decisions. Further, it is possible and desirable to specify the sorts of information that will be collected to bear on each of the criteria (e.g., continued satisfactory graduate work in the subject specialization and the judgments of senior faculty in the same specialization). Finally, the policy should suggest the kinds of evaluative shortcomings that will lead to dismissal. Again, the purpose of this sort of specification is not to provide an exhaustive formulation of the decision rules that will apply but rather to provide illustrations in sufficient detail to permit teachers to comply with the district's expectations and to permit its administrators to apply the district's criteria conscientiously in making their judgments.

Beyond these general requirements, a policy statement should specify that the evaluation system is to be applied to all personnel. Participation should be mandatory, with no class of teachers excused from systematic evaluation. Further, the policy should specify that similar information will be collected regarding all teachers and commit the district to reaching equivalent decisions on the basis of that information. To excuse a class of instructors (e.g., those who are tenured) violates both the district's obligation to provide quality instruction and the spirit of due process.

The Substance of Evaluation Systems

Information collected in the course of an evaluation should be concerned only with aspects of a teacher's behavior and activities that are directly or indirectly relevant to performing legitimate teaching responsibilities. These responsibilities cannot be construed so narrowly as to preclude teachers from exercising their professional judgment with regard to the methods and materials of instruction. However, within the area of legitimate responsibilities, the administrator must distinguish between information that is relevant and irrelevant to judgments of ability. Here, the core of meaning to the legal notion of competence is useful. At a minimum, competence consists of having an adequate command over the subject for which the teacher is responsible, being able to communicate that information to students, being able to establish an atmosphere in the classroom that is conducive to learning, and being able to recognize and correct previously noted deficiencies. Information that throws light on each of these competences is relevant to teacher evaluation.

Several conclusions follow from this notion of relevance. First, and most obvious, personal characteristics such as sex, race, religion, age, and matters of personal life-style are generally irrelevant to judgments of performance. They are not, however, always and everywhere irrelevant. When they are to be considered, it is incumbent on the administrator to demonstrate a clear and significant link between, say, a teacher's life-style and the teacher's ability to communicate knowledge to students. Put another way, a certain narrow range of information must be considered suspect if used for evaluation purposes.

Beyond this narrow range, however, a variety of types of information can be plausibly supposed to bear on legitimate professional responsibilities. We have suggested several in this chapter. The judgments of colleagues, the perceptions of students, the measured achievement of pupils, and the classroom observations of administrators are all relevant. We do not suggest, however, that evaluation systems be confined to these four. Each educational institution needs to decide the nature of the criteria it will consider in judging teacher performance. When additional criteria are introduced, other kinds of information may be required. For example, if a teacher's capacity to work cooperatively with colleagues or with parents is to be a consideration, assessments of that capacity collected from representatives of those groups would be appropriate. In any case, criteria and the information considered relevant to them should be specified in a district's evaluation policy.

Evaluation Procedures

We have noted that the law of due process applies primarily to a relatively small class of personnel actions, the dismissal of tenured faculty. It does not apply directly to the process of teacher evaluation. Nevertheless, the law's requirements that, for example, notice be given and an opportunity to challenge evidence be provided are a practical illustration of what should constitute fairness in a teacher evaluation procedure. In essence, we have suggested that teachers ought to be able to control their compliance with a district's performance criteria. It is obviously unfair to specify criteria that must be satisfied and then to make their satisfaction difficult or impossible. At a minimum, this means that the criteria for judgment, the standards to be reached, and the information considered relevant should be known to each member of the faculty.

Beyond this minimum, however, control should be extended through two additional measures. First, teachers should be given reasonable advance notice of when routine evaluation information is to be collected. A classroom observation or the administration of a student test, for example, should not come as a surprise. Providing such notice gives the teacher an opportunity to schedule his or her instruction so as to provide the sort of information required. Second, whenever feasible, teachers should have a voice in the scheduling of evaluation activities.

Finally, there are several indirect implications of the due process consideration. First, evaluations should be carried out on a regular basis. The studies cited earlier, which suggest that a large proportion of tenured teachers are not observed for as much as five minutes each year (much less systematically evaluated), are an indictment of current practice. Second, a permanent record of all evaluative information should be maintained in a teacher's personnel file. Third, teachers should have access to this information and have the opportunity to attach explanations, clarifications, or disagreements, which should also become part of the permanent record. Finally, of course, all such material should be kept confidential, and no hearsay evidence should be included. Stanton's retention of Mr. Raintree's letter was improper.

Participation and Mediation

A good evaluation system does more than produce correct decisions. It is also humane, nonalienating, and conducive to the improvement of instruction, and it enhances the opportunity for professional cooperation. With this in mind, we suggest some additional considerations to be taken into account.

It is easy to let the adversarial nature of evaluation—administration versus faculty—dominate teacher assessments. To do so is wrong. Instead, it is important that meaningful teacher participation be incorporated into the design of the system. Such roles go beyond merely participating in its design, however. Provisions that involve teachers in the process of remediation can be incorporated. Every faculty has within it at least a few teachers who are outstanding. It makes sense, then, to create a mechanism to tap this expertise for the benefit of those who might use it. Senior teachers with a history of excellence should be made accessible to beginners and teachers with less notable success. Further, to lessen the contentious nature of evaluation, it is appropriate to involve third parties at very early stages in the process when disagreements have appeared. Initially, senior and respected faculty members might profitably serve as informal mediators in disputes between a teacher and a principal. Often such informal mediation will prevent a dispute from escalating to more formal, costly, and less satisfactory forums. Failing at this level, outside mediation should be available. Often such informal processes will prevent a dispute from turning into a conflict that divides faculty from administration and, regardless of the resolution, leaves a bitter aftermath of ill will in its wake. The dispute between Stanton and Burnette seems headed for just such an outcome.

Questions

1. Can Stanton justifiably consider using test scores in evaluating Burnette? If you answer no, what might he do to use such data in the future?

2. What flaws are detectable in Stanton's use of student evaluations to arrive at his judgment that Burnette is incompetent?

3. Consider Stanton's observations of Burnette. How might these have been improved?

4. An attempt to remove Susan Burnette is likely to involve conflict with the teachers' union and the teachers at Benton. It may cost Stanton greatly in terms of time, stress, and effectiveness. It may cost the district a great deal of money in legal fees. How do you see the costs and benefits of attempting to remove Burnette? Is it worth it? If you decided to attempt to remove her, how might you act to minimize the costs?

5. Is there a viable way to deal with this problem other than to ignore it or to attempt to have Burnette removed?

6. Burnette may have a drinking problem, which could be a danger to herself and her students. Does Stanton have a duty to investigate this? Does the potential danger override Burnette's right to privacy? For example, might Stanton search her desk? Does Stanton have any obligation to help her deal with her problem?

7. Consider the following claim: "An evaluation system that is too zealous in protecting teachers will make it too hard to dismiss an ineffective teacher and will damage the quality of instruction. An evaluation system that grants too much discretion to school administrators will lead to unfair treatment of teachers." Are fairness and effectiveness really at odds? Do you think this chapter strikes a reasonable balance between fairness and effectiveness? What might you wish to change?

8. We have made several suggestions, such as the use of student achievement test scores to evaluate teaching, that teachers' organizations have rigorously resisted in the past. Why are such measures resisted? Do teachers' organizations have a legitimate interest in preventing such evaluation techniques? Might teachers' organizations resist any genuinely effective evaluation measures? If you wished to employ a controversial method, how would you proceed to secure the cooperation of teachers or teachers' organizations?

9. Some people have held that our society is too litigious and that we need more informal ways to settle disputes. Has teacher evaluation become too litigious? Is it possible to settle a dispute informally if everyone understands that informal remarks may become evidence in a legal procedure? Might informal ways of resolving conflicts provide less protection for teachers' rights?

10. Under what conditions, if any, are unannounced investigations properly made into a teacher's conduct?

Conclusion

We conclude with a few thoughts on how we conceptualize the role of an administrator. Our purpose is not to deal with any specific problem or theory but to help you reflect on broad conceptions of the role—to generate a sense of identity as a current or potential administrator. We will also reflect on the view of the administrative role presented in this book.

Consider the ways in which people sometimes think of the administrative role: The administrator is sometimes thought of as an applied social scientist, a kind of social engineer who takes the knowledge produced by social scientists and applies it to the efficient production of educational results. The social sciences give us laws of human behavior. These laws tell us how to arrange conditions so as to generate desired behaviors and to eliminate undesired ones. The administrator is a behavioral engineer.

This model of the administrative role seems to us inadequate, for several reasons. First, it misrepresents the potential of the social and behavioral sciences. Such knowledge of human behavior as we possess often illuminates human behavior and can help us understand our actions and the situations in which we must choose. It can lend wisdom to our choices. It is rare, however, that it allows us to predict human behavior with any confidence, and it is rarer still that it allows us to control what other people do.

Moreover, the kinds of factual knowledge that administrators need to succeed is often quite different from that promised by the behavioral sciences. What is required is more often a sense of how things are done in a given institution and of what people's expectations are than laws of human behavior. The administrator requires an institutional sense.

The main difficulty with this view of the administrative role is that it overlooks the extent to which administration is a moral enterprise. It requires someone who knows what counts as treating human beings fairly and who is willing to do so even when it is personally inconvenient. And it requires someone who can reflect on the meaning of the values that educational institutions are supposed to serve and find ways to achieve these values that are not only effective but are also just and humane. Administration is not just an applied social science, and administrators are not just social technicians. The kinds of knowledge required to be a good administrator go far beyond what the social sciences have to offer. The successful administrator is someone who can bring a variety of knowledge to bear on the solution of human problems, not just scientific knowledge.

A second conception of the administrative role is to see the administrator as a leader. The administrator is someone who is skilled in getting people to work together successfully in achieving the goals of the organization. People who are successful leaders achieve eminence not so much by virtue of the knowledge they possess but by virtue of their personality characteristics and their style. They are leaders, perhaps, because they are dynamic or because they exercise their authority democratically.

It is no doubt true that success as an administrator is connected with personality characteristics and style. Nevertheless, we find this an inadequate view of the administrative role as well. Its first deficiency is that it makes administrative success depend on characteristics that tend to be both intangible and unalterable. One person's dynamic leader is another's tyrant. What one person sees as a democratic style, another will see as the generation of time-wasting committee work. Moreover, insofar as such terms name real characteristics of real people, they are things that seem among the most permanent and least alterable of human traits. The view suggests that administrators are born, not made.

Our basic concern with this view, however, is that it makes the administrative role one of form, not content. Being a successful administrator depends not on the adequacy of one's view, not on the educational policies that one adopts and how reasonable they are, and not on how successful one is in communicating those reasons to others. Success depends on personality and style, or on carefully chosen ways for inducing others to contribute to the organization. It is not what one wants to do and why that is important; it is who one is and how one does things that count. We find such a view offensive. It is incompatible with the values of autonomy, reason, and democracy, which we see as among the central commitments of our society and of our educational system. Of course educational administrators must be leaders, but let them lead by reason and persuasion, not by force of personality.

In the chapter on unionization, we describe the administrator as a combination of bureaucrat and broker. How adequate is this as a conception of the administrative role? The point of that characterization is to note two things about the administrator. First, he or she is the servant of democratic authority. The goals of the schools are legitimately set by the democratic process; the administrator is to implement them faithfully, not subvert them. Second, the administrator often has the responsibility to mediate the struggle between competing interests, to work out a fair result in conflicts between individuals or groups, all of whom seek their own good. Certainly, such things are part of the administrative role.

This view, however, also seems dangerously incomplete. It does not adequately attend to the role of the administrator in building the democratic consensus that he or she must serve. The administrator does have a duty to serve democratically achieved policies, but he or she is also a source of wisdom about what those policies ought to be. The administrator need not, therefore, be a mere link in a chain of command. He or she may also be a facilitator of democratic opinion.

This final role, and our sense of the difficulty with it, raises an issue worthy of more detailed discussion. A central issue emergent in this book is the tension between our insistence that educators engage in moral reflection and think about schooling in terms of its basic purposes and our insistence that they are not fully members of a self-governing profession, that they must be subservient to democratic authority. In one case, we seem to insist that the administrator engage in wide reflection about education and its purposes, and we devote numerous pages communicating some of the things we believe an administrator needs to consider in order to be fair and effective. But we follow this by doubting whether educators are truly professionals and suggest that administrators are accountable to the laypersons who serve on boards of education and other elected bodies. We seek to make the administrator an educated person but burden him or her with a duty to do as told. Similarly, in one breath we seem to view the school as a democratic community governed internally by democratic values shared by administrators, teachers, and students alike. But in the next breath we raise the specter of a chain of command and make everyone in the school accountable to a democratic authority that operates externally to the school. Are these views of the administrative role and, indeed, of education reconcilable?

First of all, we are not the perpetrators of this tension; it is deeply rooted in the American view of politics and decision making. We have merely unearthed and expressed it. Americans seem to believe enthusiastically in the democratic process. We are a representative democracy. Legitimate government is responsive to the will of the people as expressed by their elected representatives. Public employees must therefore be accountable to legislative authority. It is wrong to subvert democratic authority. At the same time, we believe in autonomy, discussion, and participation in decision making, particularly about decisions that affect our lives.

In a small-scale society, these values are easily reconciled. When the people who govern, those whom they govern, and those whom they employ know one another and meet on the street or in the supermarket, there is little tension between internal and external democracy. Accountability and participation need not become incompatible. However, when the scale of a society increases, when the people who govern represent thousands or millions of people and employ hundreds and thousands of public servants, external democracy begins to exclude internal democracy. Accountability precludes participation. The tension in our values becomes apparent, and solutions to the dilemma become important.

Indeed, perhaps one of the saving graces of public schools is that they are among the smallest of public institutions. While it is difficult to think of the New York City School District as a small-scale organization, nevertheless the tradition of local governance in public education serves to give citizens more opportunity to participate directly in the affairs of schools than is possible in most other public agencies. And it creates the potential for contact and dialogue among teachers, administrators, and citizens about matters of educational policy. The potential value of this participation is a powerful argument for local control.

Nevertheless, schools have become large-scale organizations with many of the trappings of bureaucracy. They are often governed from such far away places as Washington and state capitals. In urban areas, even the school board can be a remote legislative body. There is, in fact, a tension between accountability to such governing agencies and democratic participation by teachers and administrators in the governance of the school.

Perhaps the most sensible thing to say about this dilemma is that rather than viewing it as a problem in the argument of this book, one should view it as a central tension in the role of the administrator, one of the basic problems any administrator has to solve. The real question concerns how the school can be a democratic community allowing for the participation of its members in its decision making while still being responsible to the larger democratic community and to its elected representatives.

The core of our response to this dilemma is to view the administrator as more than a link in the chain of command between a board of education and a teaching staff. He or she should also be a channel of communication, a facilitator of dialogue, and a repository of educational wisdom. Nothing in our conception of democracy prevents teachers and administrators from expressing their educational views to both school boards and the public at large. Indeed, who can give better advice? Nor does anything preclude dialogue between educators and the citizens whose children they educate. Our arguments show that educators are not entitled to power over educational decisions against the wishes of the community in which they work. Such arguments do not prohibit educators from participating in the deliberations of their communities concerning education. If the accountability of educators to the electorate is not to exclude them from participation in educational decisions and from a measure of autonomy over their own working lives, such dialogue is essential. The alternative is a struggle between the power of educators and democratic authority.

The administrator can escape the onerous role of broker between competing power centers by valuing and facilitating serious communication between them. In our society, that is not easy, but the alternative is a contradiction between democratic authority and the autonomy of teachers and administrators. Without the sort of dialogue that seeks to generate a community consensus on educational values and programs and builds trust between community and school, teachers and administrators must be either lackeys or usurpers.

We can summarize our view of the role of the educational administrator under two major headings:

1. The educational administrator is someone who brings six kinds of knowledge to the solution of educational problems.
    a. *Social science knowledge.* The administrator is not an engineer. He or she is not someone who is given a goal and applies a formula that tells what to do to achieve it. Rather, social science knowledge provides concepts and suggests possibilities that allow people to reflect and discuss a course of action with intelligence and wisdom.
    b. *Local knowledge.* Social science knowledge must be complemented with a practical knowledge of how things are done and what people expect in the local setting. It is, if you will, a kind of homespun social science, a science that explains how things work in a particular organization and community.

This second sort of knowledge is indispensable to successful administration. And it cannot be gained from a book—this book or any other.

   c. *Legal knowledge.* The administrator need not be a lawyer. However, it is important to understand the legal context of education sufficiently to see what is at stake in a decision and to avoid unnecessary legal problems. Even more important, legal knowledge is essential because the law reflects the moral and political wisdom of Americans. To grasp certain basic legal concepts is also to grasp some of the community's most important moral commitments.

   d. *Moral and ethical concepts.* The administrator must be able to view educational problems using concepts having to do with rights and justice as well as efficiency. Such concepts give insight into what constitutes fair treatment of people.

   e. *Educational goals.* The administrator needs a well-thought-out view of what is educationally worthwhile. Such a view prevents conceptualizing the administrative task primarily in terms of budgets, schedules, and contracts and keeps attention focused on the purpose of education. It also permits effective participation in the public dialogue and political processes that shape educational policy.

   f. *Educational techniques.* If administrators are to function effectively as supervisors of teachers and to lead in the development of educational programs, a knowledge of effective educational practices is required.

2. The administrator is the servant of a democratic society. He or she performs this role in three significant ways:

   a. The administrator must help to articulate and form the community's sense of educational purpose and must generate communication among citizens, teachers, and elected officials in order to make sound educational policies possible. Such policies are reasoned and give to all a sense of participation in their making. At times this may mean that the administrator must help others articulate their views, even when he or she finds those views deficient.

   b. The administrator must faithfully carry out democratically achieved purposes and see to it that they are carried out by others for whom the administrator is responsible. This may, on occasion, require that the professional judgments of a school district's staff be subordinated to the will of the community.

   c. The administrator must help to transmit the values of democracy to staff and students by both precept and example. An absolute desideratum of the latter is the requirement to do justice.

It would be nice to summarize our vision of the role of an educational administrator in a brief and catchy slogan, but we cannot do that in a way that seems adequate. We have, however, constructed a definition of the administrative animal. Its expression is not artful or memorable. But we hope that it makes up for its lack of eloquence and wit with a measure of accuracy and informativeness.

Definition of *Homo administratus normativus:* An educational administrator who shows leadership in seeking just, effective, and reasoned solutions to problems encountered in the process of realizing valued educational objectives—objectives that he or she has helped to articulate and build respect for both within and without the school community and that have been given expression through a legitimate democratic political process.

Bibliography

Abington School District v. Schempp, 374 U.S. 203 (1963).

Agreement between the Board of Education of the City School District of the City of New York and United Federation of Teachers (1980).

Aleamoni, L. M. (1981). Student ratings of instruction. In J. Millman (Ed.), *Handbook of teacher evaluation* (pp. 110–145). Beverly Hills, CA: Sage.

Aleamoni, L. M., & Hexner, P. Z. (1980). A review of the research on student evaluation and a report on the effect of different sets of instructions on student course and instructor evaluation. *Instructional Science, 9,* 67–84.

Alexander, K. (1985). *American public school law.* St. Paul, MN: West.

Allport, G. W. (1954). *The nature of prejudice.* Reading, MA: Addison-Wesley.

Anderson, B., Haller, E. J., & Smorodin, T. (1976). The effects of changing social contexts: A study of students who transferred between schools. *Urban Education, 10,* 333–355.

Anderson, G. J., & Walberg, H. J. (1974). Learning environments. In H. J. Walberg (Ed.), *Evaluating educational performance* (pp. 81–98). Berkeley, CA: McCutchan.

Armor, D. (1972). The evidence on busing. *Public Interest, 28,* 90–126.

Arons, S. (1983). *Compelling belief.* New York: McGraw-Hill.

Averech, H. A., Carroll, S. J., Donaldson, T. S., Kiesling, H. J., & Pincus, J. (1972). *How effective is schooling? A critical review and synthesis of research findings.* Santa Monica, CA: Rand Corporation.

Ayer, A. J. (1935). *Language, truth and logic.* New York: Dover.

Bales, R. F., & Slater, P. (1955). Role differentiations in small decision-making groups. In T. Parsons & R. F. Bales (Eds.), *Family, socialization, and interaction process* (pp. 159–306). New York: Free Press.

Banks, W. (1976). White preference in Blacks: A paradigm in search of a phenomenon. *Psychological Bulletin, 83,* 1179–1186.

Barnard, C. A. (1938). *The functions of the executive.* Cambridge, MA: Harvard University Press.

Bartlett, L. (1979). The Iowa Model policy and rules for the selection of instructional materials. In J. Davis (Ed.), *Dealing with censorship* (pp. 200–214). Urbana, IL: National Council of Teachers of English.

Baugh, W. H., & Stone, J. A. (1982). Teachers, unions, and wages in the 1970s: Unionism now pays. *Industrial and Labor Relations Review, 35,* pp. 368–376.

Becker, H. S. (1963). *Outsiders: Studies in the sociology of deviance.* New York: Free Press.

Beebee v. Hazlitt Public Schools, 239 N.W. 2d 724 (Mich. App. 1976).

Benn, S. I., & Peters, R. S. (1959). *The principles of political thought.* New York: Free Press.

Bentham, J. (1961). The principles of morals and legislation. In J. Bentham & J. S. Mill, *The utilitarians* (pp. 9–398). Garden City, NY: Doubleday.

Bidwell, C. E. (1965). The school as a formal organization. In J. G. March (Ed.), *Handbook of organizations* (pp. 972–1022). Chicago: Rand McNally.

Birenbaum, A., & Lesieur, H. (1982). Social values and expectations. In M. M. Rosenberg, R. A. Stebbins, & A. Turowetz (Eds.), *The sociology of deviance* (pp. 97–122). New York: St. Martin's Press.

Blake, R. R., & Mouton, J. S. (1978). *The managerial grid.* Houston: Gulf.

Blau, P. M., & Scott, W. R. (1962). *Formal organizations: A comparative approach.* San Francisco: Chandler.

Blumberg, A., & Greenfield, W. (1980). *The effective principal: Perspectives in school leadership.* Boston: Allyn & Bacon.

Boocock, S. S. (1980). *Sociology of education.* Boston: Houghton Mifflin.

Borg, W. R. (1980). Time and school learning. In C. Denham & A. Lieberman (Eds.), *Time to learn* (pp. 33–72). Washington, DC: National Institute of Education.

Borich, G. D., & Madden, S. K. (1977). *Evaluating classroom instruction: A sourcebook of instruments.* Reading, MA: Addison-Wesley.

Bossart, S. T., Dwyer, D. C., Rowan, B., & Lee, G. V. (1982). The instructional management role of the principal. *Educational Administration Quarterly, 18*(3), 34–64.

Bowles, S., & Gintis, H. (1976). *Schooling in capitalist America.* New York: Basic Books.

Bradley, L. A., & Bradley, G. W. (1977). The academic achievement of black students in desegregated schools: A critical review. *Review of Educational Research, 47,* 399–449.

Brewer v. School Board of City of Norfolk, Virginia, 456 F.2d 943 (1972).

Bridge, R. G., Judd, C. M., & Moock, P. R. (1979). *The determinants of educational outcomes: The impact of families, peers, teachers, and schools.* Cambridge, MA: Ballinger.

Brodinsky, B. (1982). The new right: The movement and its impact. *Phi Delta Kappan, 64,* 87–93.

Brookover, W. B., Beady, C., Flood, P., Schweitzer, J., & Wisenbaker, J. (1979). *School social systems and student achievement: Schools can make the difference.* New York: Praeger.

Brophy, J. E. (1973). Stability of teacher effectiveness. *American Educational Research Journal, 10,* 245–252.

Brophy, J. E. (1982). *Classroom organization and management.* Berkeley, CA: McCutchan.

Brown v. Board of Education of Topeka, 347 U.S. 483 (1954).

Brown v. Board of Education of Topeka, 349 U.S. 294 (1955).

Brown, A. F. (1967). Reactions to leadership. *Educational Administration Quarterly, 13,* 62–73.

Brundage, E. (Ed.). (1980). *The journalism research fellows report: What makes an effective school?* Washington, DC: George Washington University, Institute for Educational Leadership.

Brunson v. Board of Trustees, 429 F.2d 820 (1970).

Bull, B. L. (1984). Liberty and the new localism: Toward an evaluation of the trade-off between educational equity and local control of schools. *Educational Theory, 34,* 75–94.

Campbell, R. F., Cunningham, L. L., Nystrand, R. O., & Usan, M. D. (1975). *The organization and control of American schools* (3rd ed.). Columbus, OH: Merrill.

Carey, A. (1967). The Hawthorne studies: A radical criticism. *American Sociological Review, 32,* 403–416.

Carlson, R. O. (1964). Environmental constraints and organizational consequences: The public school and its clients. In D. E. Griffiths (Ed.), *Behavioral science and educational administration* (pp. 262–276). Chicago: University of Chicago Press.

Cicirelli, V. (1977). Relationships of socioeconomic status and ethnicity to primary grade children's self-concept. *Psychology in the Schools, 14,* 213–215.

Civil Rights Act of 1964, 28 U.S.C.A. 1447, 42 U.S.C.A. 1971, 1975a–1976d, 2000a–2000h-6.

Clark v. Holmes, 474 F.2d 928 (7th Cir. 1972), cert. denied, 411 U.S. 972 (1973).

Clark, D. L., Lotto, L. S., & McCarthy, M. M. (1980). Factors associated with success in urban elementary schools. *Phi Delta Kappan, 61,* 467–470.

Clear, D. K., & Seager, R. C. (1971). The legitimacy of administrative influence as perceived by selected groups. *Educational Administration Quarterly, 7,* 46–63.

Cohen, M. (1983). Instructional, management, and social conditions in effective schools. In A. Odden & L. D. Webb (Eds.), *School finance and school improvement linkages for the 1980s* (pp. 17–50). Cambridge, MA: Ballinger.

Cohen, M., March, J., & Olsen, J. (1972). A garbage can model of organizational choice. *Administrative Science Quarterly, 17,* 1–25.

Cole, S. (1968). The unionization of teachers: Determinants of rank and file support. *Sociology of Education, 41,* 66–87.

Coleman, J. S. (1961). *The adolescent society.* New York: Free Press.

Coleman, J. S. (1974). *Youth: Transition to adulthood.* Chicago: University of Chicago Press.

Coleman, J. S. (1976). Liberty and equality in school desegregation. *Social Policy, 6*(4), 9–11.

Coleman, J. S., Campbell, E. Q., Hobson, C. J., McPartland, J., Mood, A. M., Weinfeld, F., & York, R. L. (1966). *Equality of educational opportunity.* Washington, DC: U.S. Government Printing Office.

Coleman, J. S., Hoffer, T., & Kilgore, S. (1981). *School and beyond: A national longitudinal study for the 1980's, public and private schools.* Chicago: National Opinion Research Center.

Comer, J. P. (1980). *School power.* New York: Free Press.

Conway, J. A. (1984). The myth, mystery, and mastery of participative decision making in education. *Educational Administration Quarterly, 20*(3), 11–40.

Coopersmith, S. (1975). Self-concept, race and education. In G. Verma and C. Bagley (Eds.), *Race and education across cultures.* London: Heineman.

Corwin, R. G. (1965). Professional persons in public organizations. *Educational Administration Quarterly, 1*(3), 1–22.

Corwin, R. G. (1970). *Militant professionalism: A study of organizational conflict in high schools.* Englewood Cliffs, NJ: Prentice-Hall.

Coser, L. (1956). *The functions of social conflict.* New York: Free Press.

Coser, L. (1967). *Continuities in the study of social conflict.* New York: Free Press.

Coulson, J. E. (1976). *National evaluation of the Emergency School Aid Act (ESAA): Survey of the second year studies.* Santa Moreau, CA: System Development Corporation.

Crain, R. L., & Mahard, R. E. (1981). Minority achievement: Policy implications of research. In W. D. Hawley (Ed.), *Effective school desegregation: Equity, quality, and feasibility* (pp. 55–84). Beverly Hills, CA: Sage.

Crehan, E. P. (1984). *A metanalysis of Fiedler's contingency model of leadership effectiveness.* Unpublished doctoral dissertation, University of British Columbia, Vancouver.

Cresswell, A. M. (1982). Collective negotiations. In H. E. Mitzel (Ed.), *Encyclopedia of Education* (5th ed.), (pp. 296–309). New York: Free Press.

Csikszentmihalyi, M., Larson, R., & Prescott, S. (1977). The ecology of adolescent activity and experience. *Journal of Youth and Adolescence, 6,* 281–294.

Cusick, P. A. (1973). *Inside high school: The student's world.* New York: Holt, Rinehart and Winston.

Daniels, A. F., & Haller, E. J. (1981). Exposure to instruction, surplus time, and student achievement: A local replication of the Harnischfeger and Wiley research. *Educational Administration Quarterly, 17*(1), 48–68.

Davis, S. A., & Haller, E. J. (1981). Tracking, ability, and SES: Further evidence on the revisionist-meritocratic argument. *American Journal of Education, 89,* 283–304.

Deal, T. E., & Celotti, L. D. (1980). How much influence do (and can) educational administrators have on classrooms? *Phi Delta Kappan, 61,* 471–473.

De Fleur, M. L., D'Antonio, W. V., & Nelson, L. D. (1977). *Sociology: Human society.* Glenview, IL: Scott, Foresman.

Doherty, R. (1980). Public education. In G. G. Somers, *Collective bargaining: Contemporary American experience* (pp. 487–552). Madison, WI: Industrial Relations Research Association.

Downs, D., & Rock, P. (1982). *Understanding deviance.* Oxford, England: Clarendon Press.

Doyle, W. E. (1977). Social science evidence in court cases. In R. Rist & R. Anson (Eds.), *Education, social science, and the judicial process* (pp. 10–19). New York: Teachers College Press.

Drowalzky, J. (1981). Tracking and ability grouping in education. *Journal of Law and Education, 10*(1), 43–59.

Duke, D., Showers, B. K., & Imber, M. (1980). Teachers and shared decision making: The costs and benefits of involvement. *Educational Administration Quarterly, 16*(1), 93–106.

Durkheim, E. (1950). *The rules of sociological method* (S. A. Solovoy & J. H. Mueller, Trans.; G. Catlin, Ed.). New York: Free Press. (Originally published in 1895.)

Eberts, R. W., & Pierce, L. C. (1982). *The effects of collective bargaining on public schools in Michigan and New York.* An occasional paper of the University of Oregon, College of Education, Center for Educational Policy and Management.

Eberts, R. W., & Stone, J. (1984). *Unions and public schools: The effect of collective bargaining on American education*. Lexington, MA: Lexington Books.

Edmonds, R. (1979). Some schools work and more can. *Social Policy, 9,* pp. 28–32.

Education for All Handicapped Children's Act of 1975, 20 U.S.C., 1401 (Public Law 94–142).

Educational Research Service. (1978). *Class size: A summary of the research*. Research brief. Arlington, VA: Author.

Educational Research Service. (1983). *Effective schools: A summary of the research*. Arlington, VA: Author.

Elliot, D. S. (1966). Delinquency, school attendance, and dropouts. *Social Problems, 3,* 307–314.

Epps, E. G. (1981). Minority children: Desegregation, self-evaluation and achievement orientation. In W. D. Hawley (Ed.), *Effective school desegregation: Equality, quality and feasibility* (pp. 85–106). Beverly Hills, CA: Sage.

Esposito, D. (1973). Homogeneous and heterogeneous ability groupings: Principal findings and implications for evaluating and designing more effective educational environments. *Review of Educational Research, 43,* 163–179.

Eulau, H., & Prewitt, K. (1973). *Labyrinths of democracy: Adaptations, linkages, representation, and policies in urban politics*. Indianapolis: Bobbs-Merrill.

Everson v. Board of Education of Ewing Township, 330 U.S. 1 (1947).

Evertson, C., & Holley, F. M. (1981). Classroom observation. In J. Millman (Ed.), *Handbook of teacher evaluation* (pp. 90–109). Beverly Hills, CA: Sage.

Farley, R. (1976). Is Coleman right? *Social Policy, 6,* 14–23.

Feldman, S. (1984). Teacher collective bargaining: The critical third decade. *American Education* (Fall), pp. 17–19, 42.

Fiedler, F. E. (1967). *A theory of leadership effectiveness*. New York: McGraw-Hill.

Fiedler, F. E. (1978). The contingency model and the dynamics of the leadership process. In L. Berkowitz (Ed.), *Advances in experimental social psychology* (Vol. 11, pp. 60–112). New York: Academic Press.

Fiedler, F. E., & Chemers, M. M. (1974). *Leadership and effective management*. Glenview, IL.: Scott, Foresman.

Fiedler, F. E., Chemers, M. M., & Mahar, L. (1976). *Improving leadership effectiveness: The leader match concept*. New York: Wiley.

Fisher, R. (1964). Fractionating conflict. In R. Fisher (Ed.), *International conflict and behavioral science: The Craigville papers*. New York: Basic Books.

Flanders, N. A. (1970). *Analyzing teacher behavior*. Reading, MA: Addison-Wesley.

Follett, M. P. (1941). *Dynamic administration: The collected papers of Mary Parker Follett* (H. C. Metcalf & L. Unwick, Eds.). New York: Harper & Row.

Franks, R. H., & Kaul, J. D. (1978). The Hawthorne experiments: First statistical interpretations. *American Sociological Review, 43,* 623–643.

Friday, P. C. (1980). International review of youth crime and delinquency. In G. R. Newman (Ed.), *Crime and deviance: A comparative perspective* (pp. 100–129). Beverly Hills, CA: Sage.

Gallup, G. J. (1984). The 16th annual Gallup poll of the public's attitudes toward the public schools. *Phi Delta Kappan, 66,* 23–38.

Gardner, D. P. (1983). *A nation at risk*. Washington, DC: U.S. Department of Education, National Commission on Excellence in Education.

Geer, B. (1966). Occupational commitment and the teaching profession. *School Review, 74,* 31–47.

Gibbs, J. P. (1975). *Crime, punishment, and deterrence*. New York: Elsevier.

Gilbert, R. M., & Price, A. T. (1981). Is the school day long enough? *Phi Delta Kappan, 63,* 524.

Gittel, M. (1967). *Educating an urban population*. Beverly Hills, CA: Sage.

Glasman, N. S., & Biniaminov, K. (1981). Input-output analyses of schools. *Review of Educational Research, 51,* 509–541.

Glass, G. (1976). Primary, secondary and meta-analysis of research. *Educational Researcher, 5*(10), 3–8.

Glass, G. V., & Smith, M. L. (1978). *Meta-analysis of research on the relationship of class-size and achievement*. San Francisco, CA: Far West Laboratory for Educational Research and Development.

Glatthorn, A. (1979). Censorship and the classroom teacher. In J. E. Davis (Ed.), *Dealing with censorship* (pp. 48-53). Urbana, IL: National Council of Teachers of English.

Goldschmidt, S., Bowers, B., Riley, M., & Leland, S. (1983). *The extent and nature of educational policy bargaining.* Eugene, OR: University of Oregon, Center for Educational Policy and Management.

Goldstein, A. P., Apter, S. J., & Harootonian, B. (1984). *School violence.* Englewood Cliffs, NJ: Prentice-Hall.

Goldstein, A. P., Sprafkin, R. P., Gershaw, N. J., & Klein, P. (1979). *Skill-streaming the adolescent: A structured learning approach to teaching prosocial behavior.* Champaign, IL: Research Press.

Good, T. L., & Grouws, D. A. (1975). Teacher rapport: Some stability data. *Journal of Educational Psychology, 67,* 179-182.

Gordon, C. W. (1957). *The social system of the high school.* Glencoe, IL: Free Press.

Goss v. Lopes, 419 U.S. 565 (1975).

Gouldner, A. W. (1964). *Patterns of industrial bureaucracy.* New York: Free Press.

Gouldner, A. W. (1968). The sociologist as partisan: Sociology and the welfare state. *American Sociologist, 3,* 103-116.

Grant, G. (1982). *Education, character, and American schools: Are effective schools good enough?* Syracuse, NY: Syracuse University Press.

Green v. County School Board of New Kent County, Virginia, 391 U.S. 430 (1968).

Greenfield, W. D. (1982). *Research on public school principals: A review and recommendations.* Washington, DC: National Institute for Education.

Griffin v. County School Board of Prince Edward County, 377 U.S. 218 (1964).

Gross, N., & Herriott, R. E. (1965). *Staff leadership in public schools: A sociological inquiry.* New York: Wiley.

Guthrie, J. W. (1970). A survey of school effectiveness studies. In *Do teachers make a difference?* (pp. 25-51). Washington, DC: U.S. Department of Health, Education, and Welfare, Bureau of Educational Personnel Development, Office of Education.

Hall, R. H. (1968). Professionalization and bureaucratization. *American Sociological Review, 33,* 92-104.

Haller, E. J. (1974). Cost analysis for educational program evaluation. In S. J. Popham (Ed.), *Evaluation in education* (pp. 399-450). Berkeley, CA: McCutchan.

Haller, E. J. (1985). Pupil race and elementary school ability grouping: Are teachers biased against black children? *American Educational Research Journal, 22.*

Haller, E. J., & Davis, S. A. (1980). Does socioeconomic status bias the assignment of elementary school students to reading groups? *American Educational Research Journal, 17,* 409-418.

Halpin, A. W. (1966). *Theory and research in administration.* New York: Macmillan.

Halpin, A. W., & Winer, B. J. (1952). *The leadership behavior of the airplane commander.* Washington, DC: Human Resources Research Laboratories, Department of the Air Force.

Hanson, E. M. (1979). *Educational administration and organizational behavior.* Boston: Allyn & Bacon.

Hanushek, E. (1970). The production of education, teacher quality, and efficiency. In *Do teachers make a difference?* (pp. 79-99). Washington, DC: U.S. Department of Health, Education, and Welfare, Bureau of Educational Personnel Development, Office of Education.

Harrison, M. (1976). Class achievement and the background and behavior of teachers. *Elementary School Journal, 77,* 63-70.

Hauser, R. M., Sewell, W. H., & Alwin, D. F. (1976). High school effects on achievement. In W. H. Sewell, R. M. Hauser, & D. L. Featherman (Eds.), *Schooling and achievement in American society* (pp. 309-341). New York: Academic Press.

Hawley, W. D. (1981). Equity and quality in education: Characteristics of effective desegregated schools. In W. D. Hawley (Ed.), *Effective school desegregation: Equity, quality and feasibility.* Beverly Hills, CA: Sage.

Hawley, W. D. (1983). Achieving quality integrated education--with or without federal help. *Phi Delta Kappan, 64,* 334-338.

Hayek, F. A. (1960). *The constitution of liberty.* Chicago: University of Chicago Press.

Hazard, W. R. (1978). *Education and the law: Cases and materials on public schools* (2nd ed.). New York: Free Press.

Hefley, J. C. (1976). *Textbooks on trial.* Wheaton, IL: Victor Books.

Henderson, V. P., Mieszkowski, P., & Sauvageau, Y. (1978). Peer group effects and educational production functions. *Journal of Public Economics, 10,* 97–106.

Herriot, R. E., & St. John, N. H. (1966). *Social class and the urban school.* New York: Wiley.

Hersey, P., & Blanchard, K. H. (1977). *Management of organizational behavior: Utilizing human resources* (3rd ed.). Englewood Cliffs, NJ: Prentice-Hall.

Hetrick v. Martin, 480 F.2d 705 (6th Cir. 1973).

Heyns, B. (1974). Social selection and stratification within schools. *American Journal of Sociology, 79,* 1434–1451.

Heyns, B. (1978). *Summer learning and the effects of schooling.* New York: Academic Press.

Hills, J. (1975). The preparation of administrators: Some observations from the "firing line." *Educational Administration Quarterly, 11*(3), 1–20.

Hobson v. Hanson, 269 F. Supp. 401 (1967).

Hobson v. Hanson, 327 F. Supp. 844 (D.D.C. 1971).

Hodgson, G. (1975). Do schools make a difference? In D. M. Levine & M. J. Bane (Eds.), *The "inequality" controversy: Schooling and distributive justice* (pp. 22–44). New York: Basic Books.

House, R. J. (1971). A path-goal theory of leadership effectiveness. *Administrative Science Quarterly, 16,* 321–338.

House, R. J., & Baetz, M. L. (1979). Leadership: Some empirical generalizations and new research directions. *Research in Organizational Behavior, 1,* 341–423.

Hoy, W. K., & Miskel, C. G. (1982). *Educational administration: Theory, research, and practice* (2nd ed.). New York: Random House.

Hughes, E. C. (1945). Dilemmas and contradictions of status. *American Journal of Sociology, 50,* 353–359.

Humphreys, L. (1970). *Tearoom trade: Impersonal sex in public places.* Chicago: Aldine.

Hyman, H., & Wright, C. (1979). *Education's lasting influence on values.* Chicago: University of Chicago Press.

Iannaccone, L. (1964). An approach to the informal organization of the school. In D. E. Griffiths (Ed.), *Behavioral science and educational administration* (pp. 223–242). 63rd yearbook of the National Society for the Study of Education, Part 2. Chicago: University of Chicago Press.

Island Trees Union Free School District Board of Education v. Pico, 102 S. Ct. 2799 (1982).

Jackson, P. (1968). *Life in classrooms.* New York: Holt, Rinehart and Winston.

Jackson, P., & Belford, E. (1965). Educational objectives and the joys of teaching. *School Review, 73,* 267–291.

James v. Board of Education of Central District No. 1, 461 F.2d 566 (2d Cir. 1972).

Jencks, C. S. (1972). The quality of the data collected by the *Equality of educational opportunity* survey. In F. Mosteller & D. P. Moynihan (Eds.), *On equality of educational opportunity* (pp. 437–512). New York: Random House.

Jencks, C. S., Smith, M., Acland, H., Bane, M. J., Cohen, D., Gintis, H., Heyns, B., & Michelson, S. (1972). *Inequality: A reassessment of the effect of family and schooling in America.* New York: Harper & Row.

Jessup, D. K. (1978). Teacher unionization: A reassessment of rank and file motivations. *Sociology of Education, 51,* 44–55.

Kant, I. (1956). *Critique of practical reason.* Indianapolis: Bobbs-Merrill.

Karweit, N. (1976). A reanalysis of the effect of quantity of schooling on achievement. *Sociology of Education, 49,* 236–246.

Karweit, N. (1983). *Time on task: A research review* (Rep. No. 332). Baltimore: Johns Hopkins University, Center for Social Organization of Schools.

Kasper, H. (1973). On the effect of collective bargaining on resource allocation in public schools. *Economic and Business Bulletin, 23,* 834–841.

Katz, D. N., & Kahn, R. L. (1978). *The social psychology of organizations* (2nd ed.). New York: Wiley.

Keeler, B. T., & Andrews, J. H. M. (1963). Leader behavior of principals, staff morals, and productivity. *Alberta Journal of Educational Research 9*(3), 179–191.

Kerchner, C. T. (1979). Bargaining costs in public schools: A preliminary assessment. *California Public Employee Relations* (June), 16–25.

Kerchner, C. T. (1984). *Labor policy in school districts: Its diffusion and impact on work structures.* Eugene, OR: University of Oregon, Center for Educational Policy and Management.

Kerr, N. D. (1964). The school board as an agency of legitimation. *Sociology of Education, 38,* 34–59.

Keyes v. School District No. 1, Denver, Colorado, 413 U.S. 189 (1974).

Keyishian v. Board of Regents of the State of New York, 385 U.S. 589 (1974).

King, J. A. (1981). Beyond classroom walls: Indirect measures of teacher competence. In J. Millman (Ed.), *Handbook of teacher evaluation* (pp. 167–179). Beverly Hills, CA: Sage.

Kohlberg, L. (1973). *Collected papers on moral development and moral education.* Cambridge, MA: Harvard University, Center for Moral Education.

Kowalski, J. D. S. (1978). *Evaluating teachers' performance.* Arlington, VA: Educational Research Services.

Kroll, R. A. (1980). A meta analysis of the effects of desegregation on academic achievement. *Urban Review, 12,* 211–224.

Kunz, D., & Hoy, W. K. (1976). Leadership style of principals and the professional zone of acceptance of teachers. *Educational Administration Quarterly, 12*(3), 49–64.

Landon, J. H., & Baird, R. N. (1971). Monopsony in the market for public school teachers. *American Economic Review, 51,* 966–971.

Lasswell, H. (1958). *Politics: Who gets what, when and how.* New York: New American Library (Meridian Books).

Lerner, B. (1982). American education: How are we doing? *Public Interest, 69,* 59–82.

Levi, E. H. (1948). *An introduction to legal reasoning.* Chicago: University of Chicago Press.

Levin, H. M. (1983). *Cost effectiveness: A primer.* Beverly Hills, CA: Sage.

Levine, D. B., & Havighurst, R. J. (1984). *Society and education* (6th ed.). Boston: Allyn & Bacon.

Levittown UFSD v. Nyquist, 57 N.Y. 2d 27 (1982).

Lieberman, M. (1980). *Public sector bargaining.* Lexington, MA: Lexington Books.

Lindblom, C. E. (1968). *The policy-making process.* Englewood Cliffs, NJ: Prentice-Hall.

Lipham, J. A. (1964). Leadership and administration. In D. E. Griffiths (Ed.), *Behavioral science and educational administration* (pp. 119–141). 63rd yearbook of the National Society for the Study of Education, Part 2. Chicago: University of Chicago Press.

Lipham, J. A. (1981). *Effective principal, effective school.* Reston, VA: American Association of Secondary School Principals.

Lipsky, D. B. (1982). The effect of collective bargaining on teacher pay: A review of the evidence. *Educational Administration Quarterly, 18*(1), 14–42.

Locke, J. (1963). *Two treatises of government.* New York: Minton Books.

Lortie, D.C. (1975). *Schoolteacher: A sociological study.* Chicago: University of Chicago Press.

MacIntyre, A. (1981). *After virtue.* Notre Dame, IN: University of Notre Dame Press.

Mailloux v. Kiley, 436 F.2d 565 (1st Cir. 1970).

Mankoff, M. (1971). Societal reaction and career deviance: A critical appraisal. *Sociological Quarterly, 12,* 204–218.

Mark, J. M., & Anderson, B. D. (1978). Teacher survival rates: A current look. *American Educational Research Journal, 15,* 379–384.

Martin, R. C. (1962). *Government and the suburban school.* Syracuse, NY: Syracuse University Press.

Mazzarella, J. A. (1984). The collective bargaining mystery: Some new clues. *R. & D. Perspectives* (Spring). Eugene, OR: University of Oregon, Center for Educational Policy and Management.

McCarty, D. J., & Ramsey, C. E. (1971). *The school managers.* Westport, CT: Greenwood.

McConahay, J. B. (1978). The effects of school desegregation upon students' racial attitudes and behavior: A critical review of the literature and a prolegomenon to future research. *Law and Contemporary Problems, 42*(3), 77–107.

McConahay, J. B. (1981). Reducing racial prejudice in desegregated schools. In W. D. Hawley (Ed.), *Effective school desegregation: Equity, quality, and feasibility* (pp. 35–53). Beverly Hills, CA: Sage.

McKeachie, W. J. (1979). Student ratings of faculty: A reprise. *Academe, 65,* 384–397.

McKissack, I. J. (1973). The peak age of property crimes: Further data. *British Journal of Criminology, 12,* 253–261.

McLean v. Arkansas Board of Education, 529 F. Supp. 1255 (1982).

McNeil, J. D., & Popham, W. J. (1973). The assessment of teacher competence. In R. M. W. Travers (Ed.), *Second handbook of research on teaching* (pp. 218–244). Chicago: Rand McNally.

Medley, D. M., & Mitzel, H. E. (1963). Measuring classroom behavior by systematic observation. In N. L. Gage (Ed.), *Handbook of research on teaching* (pp. 247–328). Chicago: Rand McNally.

Merton, R. K. (1957). *Social theory and social structure.* New York: Free Press.

Meyer v. Nebraska, 262 U.S. 390 (1922).

Meyer, J. W., & Rowan, B. (1978). The structure of educational organizations. In M. Meyer and associates (Eds.), *Environments and organizations* (pp. 78–109). San Francisco: Jossey-Bass.

Mill, J. S. (1956). *On liberty.* Indianapolis: Bobbs-Merrill.

Millman, J. (1981). Student achievement as a measure of teacher competence. In J. Millman (Ed.), *Handbook of teacher evaluation* (pp. 146–166). Beverly Hills, CA: Sage.

Mitchell, D. E., Kerchner, C. T., Erck, W., & Pryor, G. (1981). The impact of collective bargaining on school management and policy. *American Journal of Education, 89,* 147–188.

Monk, D. H. (1981). Toward a multilevel perspective on the allocation of educational resources. *Review of Educational Research, 51,* 215–236.

Moore, G. E. (1959). *Principia ethica.* Cambridge, England: Cambridge University Press.

Moos, R. H. (1979). *Evaluating educational environments.* San Francisco: Jossey-Bass.

Moses v. Washington Parish School Board, 330 F. Supp. 1340 (1971).

Mosteller, F., & Moynihan, D. P. (Eds.). (1972). *On equality of educational opportunity.* New York: Random House.

Moynihan, D. P. (1972). Equalizing education: In whose benefit? *Public Interest, 29* (Fall), 69–89.

Mulkey, Y. J. (1977). *Character education and the teacher.* San Antonio, TX: American Institute for Character Education.

Murnane, R. J. (1975). *The impact of school resources on the learning of inner city children.* Cambridge, MA: Ballinger.

Murnane, R. J. (1983a). How clients' characteristics affect organization performance: Lessons from education. *Journal of Policy Analysis and Management, 2,* 403–417.

Murnane, R. J. (1983b). Quantitative studies of effective schools: What have we learned? In A. Odden & L. D. Webb (Eds.), *School finance and school improvement linkages for the 1980's* (pp. 193–209). Cambridge, MA: Ballinger.

National Education Association. (1984). *NEA 1984–85 handbook.* Washington, DC: Author.

New Jersey v. T.L.O., 45 C.C.H. S. Ct. Bull P. (1985).

New York State Education Department. (1984). *Analysis of school finances: New York State school districts, 1982–83.* Albany, NY: Author.

New York State Education Department, Bureau of School Programs Evaluation. (1972). *Variables related to student performance and resource allocation decisions at the school district level.* Albany, NY: Author.

Norwalk Teachers' Association v. Board of Education, 138 Conn. 269 (1951).

Owens, R. G. (1970). *Organizational behavior in education.* Englewood Cliffs, NJ: Prentice-Hall.

Page, A. L., & Clelland, D. A. (1978). The Kanawha textbook controversy: A study of the politics of lifestyle concern. *Social Forces, 57*(1), 265–281.

Parducci v. Rutland, 316 F. Supp. 352 (N.D. Ala. 1970).

Parfit, D. (1984). *Reasons and persons.* Oxford, England: Clarendon Press.

Park, J. C. (1980). Preachers, politics and public education: A review of right-wing pressures against public schooling in America. *Phi Delta Kappan, 61,* 608–612.

Pascal, A. (1977). *What do we know about school desegregation?* Santa Monica, CA: Rand Corporation.

Patchen, M. (1982). *Black-white contact in schools: Its social and academic effects.* West Lafayette, IN: Purdue University Press.

People v. Overton, 24 N.Y. 2d 522, 249 N.E. 2d 366 (1969).

Peters, R. S. (1970). *Ethics and education.* London: Allen & Unwin.

Peterson, P. E. (1976). *School politics, Chicago style.* Chicago: University of Chicago Press.

Peterson, L. J., Rossmiller, R. A., & Volz, M. M. (1978). *The law and public school operation.* New York: Harper & Row.

Pettigrew, T. F., Smith, M., Useem, E., & Normand, C. (1973). Busing: A review of the evidence. *Public Interest, 30* (Winter), 88–118.

Pickering v. Board of Education, 393 U.S. 563 (1968).

Pierce v. Society of Sisters, 268 U.S. 520 (1925).

Plessy v. Ferguson, 163 U.S. 537 (1886).

President's Commission on Law Enforcement and Administration of Justice. (1967). *The challenge of crime in a free society.* Washington, DC: U.S. Government Printing Office.

Raths, L. E., Harmin, M., & Simon, S. B. (1978). *Values and teaching: Working with values in the classroom* (2nd ed.). Columbus, OH: Merrill.

Rawls, J. (1971). *A theory of justice.* Cambridge, MA: Harvard University Press.

Reddin, W. J. (1970). *Managerial effectiveness.* New York: McGraw-Hill.

Rhode Island General Statutes Annotated, 28-9.3-1 (1968 Reenact.).

Rist, R. C. (1970). Student social class and teacher expectations: The self-fulfilling prophecy in ghetto education. *Harvard Educational Review, 40,* 411–451.

Robbins, J. H. (1975). *A summary of selected major studies which associate input and process variables with various measures of school quality or output.* Unpublished paper, New York State College of Agriculture and Life Sciences, Cornell University, Ithaca, NY.

Robinson v. Cahill, 62 N.J. 473, 303 A. 2d 173 (1973).

Roethlisberger, F. J., & Dickson, W. J. (1939). *Management and the worker.* Cambridge, MA: Harvard University Press.

Rogers, D. (1978). *110 Livingston Street: Politics and bureaucracy in the New York City school system.* New York: Random House.

Rosenberg v. Board of Education of the City of New York, 196 Misc. 542, 92 N.Y.S. 2d 344 (1949).

Rosenshine, B. (1970). Evaluation of classroom instruction. *Review of Educational Research, 40,* 279–300.

Rosenshine, B. (1976). Classroom instruction. In N. L. Gage (Ed.), *The psychology of teaching methods* (pp. 335–371). Chicago: National Society for the Study of Education.

Rosenshine, B. (1979). Content, time, and direct instruction. In P. L. Peterson & H. J. Walberg (Eds.), *Research on teaching: Concepts, findings, and implications.* Berkeley, CA: McCutchan.

Rosenshine, B., & Furst, N. (1973). The use of direct observation to study teaching. In R. M. W. Travers (Ed.), *Second handbook of research in teaching* (pp. 122–183). Chicago: Rand McNally.

Rosenthal, R., & Jacobson, L. (1968). *Pygmalion in the classroom.* New York: Holt, Rinehart and Winston.

Rossell, C. (1975). School desegregation and white flight. *Political Science Quarterly, 90,* 675–695.

Rowan, B., Bossart, S. T., & Dwyer, D. C. (1983). Research on effective schools: A cautionary note. *Educational Researcher, 12*(4), 24–31.

Rutter, M., Maughan, B., Mortemore, P., & Ouston, J. (1979). *Fifteen thousand hours: Secondary schools and their effects on children.* Cambridge, MA: Harvard University Press.

St. John, N. H. (1975). *School desegregation: Outcomes for children.* New York: Wiley.

San Antonio Independent School District v. Rodriguez, 93 S.Ct. 1278 (1973).

Sandel, M. J. (1982). *Liberalism and the bounds of justice.* New York: Cambridge University Press.

Sarthory, J. A. (1971). Structural characteristics and the outcome of collective negotiations. *Educational Administration Quarterly, 7*(3), 78–89.

Scheelhaase v. Woodbury Central Community School District, 488 F.2d 237, 8th Cir. (1973).

Scheirer, M., & Kraut, R. (1979). Increasing educational achievement via self-concept change. *Review of Educational Research, 49,* 131–150.

Schofield, J. W., & Sagar, H. A. (1977). Peer interaction patterns in an integrated middle school. *Sociometry, 40,* 130–138.

Schrieshiem, C. A., & Kerr, S. (1977). Theories and measures of leadership: A critical appraisal of current and future directions. In J. G. Hunt & L. L. Larson (Eds.), *Leadership: The cutting edge* (pp. 9–45). Carbondale, IL: Southern Illinois University Press.

Schur, E. M. (1971). *Labeling deviant behavior.* New York: Harper & Row.

Scott, R. A. (1969). *The making of blind men.* New York: Russell Sage.

Serow, R. (1983). *Schooling and social diversity.* New York: Teachers College Press.

Serrano v. Priest, 487 P. 2d 1241 (Cal. 1971).

Shavelson, R., & Dempsey-Atwood, N. (1976). Generalizability of measures of teaching behavior. *Review of Educational Research, 46,* 553–611.

Sherman, D. R. (1983). *Teachers' unions and the production and distribution of educational outcomes: The case of California.* Unpublished thesis, Cornell University, Ithaca, NY.

Silberman, C. E. (1970). *Crisis in the classroom.* New York: Random House.

Simon, A., & Boyer, E. G. (Eds). (1970). *Mirrors for behavior: An anthology of classroom observation instruments.* Philadelphia: Research for Better Schools.

Simon, H. A. (1957). *Administrative behavior* (2nd ed.). New York: Macmillan.

Singleton v. Jackson Municipal Separate School District, 419 F.2d 1211 (5th Cir. 1978).

Sizemore, B. A. (1972). Is there a case for separate schools? *Phi Delta Kappan, 53,* 281–284.

Skerry, P. (1980). Christian schools versus the I.R.S. *Public Interest, 61* (Fall), 18–41.

Slavin, R. E., & Madden, N. A. (1979). School practices that improve race relations. *American Educational Research Journal, 16,* 169–180.

Small, R. (1979). Censorship and English: Some things we don't seem to think about very often (but should). In J. E. David (Ed.), *Dealing with censorship* (pp. 54–62). Urbana, IL: National Council of Teachers of English.

Smart, J. J. C., & Williams, B. (1973). *Utilitarianism: For and against.* New York: Cambridge University Press.

Snook, I. A. (Ed.). (1972). Concepts of indoctrination. London: Routledge & Kegan Paul.

Spady, W. G. (1973). The impact of school resources on students. In F. N. Kerlinger (Ed.), *Review of research in education* (pp. 135–177). Itasca, IL: Peacock.

Spradly, J. P. (1970). *You owe yourself a drink.* Boston: Little, Brown.

Stallings, J. A. (1977). *Learning to look.* Belmont, CA: Wadsworth.

Stallings, J. A., & Kaskowitz, D. H. (1974). *Follow through classroom observation evaluation 1972–73.* Menlo Park, CA: Stanford Research Institute.

State of New Jersey v. Engerud, 94 N.J. 331, 348, 463 A. 2d 934, 343 (1983).

Stinchcomb, A. L. (1964). *Rebellion in a high school.* Chicago: Quadrangle.

Stogdill, R. M. (1948). Personal factors associated with leadership: A survey of the literature. *Journal of Psychology, 25,* 35–71.

Stogdill, R. M. (1974). *Handbook of leadership: A survey of theory and research.* New York: Free Press.

Strike, K. A. (1982a). *Educational policy and the just society.* Urbana, IL: University of Illinois Press.

Strike, K. A. (1982b). *Liberty and learning.* Oxford, England: Martin Robertson.

Strike, K. A. (1983). Fairness and ability grouping. *Educational Theory, 33,* 125–134.

Strike, K. A., & Bull, B. (1981). Fairness and the legal context of teacher evaluation. In J. Millman (Ed.), *Handbook of teacher evaluation* (pp. 303–343). Beverly Hills, CA: Sage.

Strike, K. A., & Soltis, J. F. (1985). *The ethics of teaching.* New York: Teachers College Press.

Subcommittee to Investigate Juvenile Delinquency. (1975). *Our nation's schools—a report card: "A" in school violence and vandalism.* Washington, DC: U.S. Government Printing Office.

Subcommittee to Investigate Juvenile Delinquency. (1977). *Challenge for the third century: Education in a safe environment—final report on the nature and prevention of school violence and vandalism.* Washington, DC: U.S. Government Printing Office.

Summers, A. A., & Wolfe, B. L. (1977). Do schools make a difference? *American Economic Review, 67,* 639-652.

Summers, R. (1976). *Collective bargaining and public benefit conferral; A jurisprudential critique.* Ithaca, NY: Cornell University, New York State School of Industrial and Labor Relations.

Sutherland, E. H., & Cressey, D. R. (1978). *Criminology.* Philadelphia: Lippincott.

Swann v. Charlotte-Mecklenburg Board of Education, 402 U.S. 1 (1971).

Sweezy v. New Hampshire, 354 U.S. 234 (1957).

Sykes, G. M., & Matza, D. (1957). Techniques of neutralization: A theory of delinquency. *American Sociological Review, 22,* 664-670.

Taylor Law. Public Employees' Fair Employment Act, Article 14 of the Civil Service Law. (1983). New York State Public Employment Relations Board.

Thomas, K. (1976). Conflict and conflict management. In M. D. Dunnette (Ed.), *Handbook of industrial and organizational psychology* (pp. 889-936). Chicago: Rand McNally.

Thornton, R. J. (1971). The effects of collective bargaining on teachers' salaries. *Quarterly Review of Economics and Business, 11*(4), 37-56.

Tinker v. Des Moines, 393 U.S. 509 (1969).

Tom, F. K. T., & Cushman, H. R. (1975). The Cornell diagnostic observation and reporting system for student description of college teaching. *Search, 5*(8), 1-27.

Traub, S. H., & Little, C. B. (1980). *Theories of deviance.* Itasca, IL: Peacock.

Tucker, H. J., & Zeigler, L. H. (1980). *Professionals versus the public: Attitudes, communication, and response in school districts.* New York: Longman.

Urban, W. J. (1982). *Why teachers organized.* Detroit: Wayne State University Press.

Vail v. Board of Education of Portsmouth School District, 354 F. Supp. 592 (C.D.N.H. 1972).

Vance, V. E., & Schlechty, P. C. (1982). The distribution of academic ability in the teaching force: Policy implications. *Phi Delta Kappan, 64,* 22-27.

Vecchio, R. P. (1977). An empirical examination of the validity of Fiedler's model of leadership effectiveness. *Organizational Behavior and Human Performance, 19,* 180-206.

Vroom, V. H., & Yetton, P. W. (1973). *Leadership and decision making.* Pittsburgh: University of Pittsburgh Press.

Waller, W. (1932). *The sociology of teaching.* New York: Wiley.

Walton, R. E. (1969). *Interpersonal peacemaking: Confrontations and third-party consultations.* Reading, MA: Addison-Wesley.

Walton, R. E., & McKersie, R. B. (1965). *A behavioral theory of labor negotiations: An analysis of a social interaction system.* New York: McGraw-Hill.

Weber, M. (1947). *The theory of social and economic organization* (A. M. Henderson & T. Parsons, Trans.; T. Parsons, Ed.). New York: Free Press.

Weick, K. E. (1976). Educational organizations as loosely coupled systems. *Administrative Science Quarterly, 21*(1), 1-19.

Weigel, R. H., Wiser, P. L., & Cook, S. W. (1975). The impact of cooperative learning experiences on cross-ethnic relations and attitudes. *Journal of Social Issues, 31,* 219-244.

Weinberg, M. (1977). *Minority students: A research appraisal.* Washington, DC: National Institute of Education.

Wellisch, J. B., MacQueen, A. H., Carriere, R. A., & Duck, G. A. (1978). School management and organization in successful schools. *Sociology of Education, 51,* 211-226.

Wiley, D. E. (1976). Another hour, another day: Quantity of schooling, a potent path for policy. In W. H. Sewell, R. N. Hauser, & D. L. Featherman (Eds.), *Schooling and achievement in American society* (pp. 225-265). New York: Academic Press.

Williams v. Board of Education of the County of Kanawha, 388 F. Supp. 93 (S.D.W. Va. 1975), aff'd, 530 F.2d 972 (4th Cir. 1976).

Wilson, A. B. (1967). Educational consequences of segregation in a California community. In U.S. Commission on Civil Rights, *Racial isolation in the public schools* (pp. 165-241 of Appendix). Washington, DC: U.S. Government Printing Office.

Wilson, J. Q. (1983). *Thinking about crime* (2nd ed.). New York: Basic Books.

Winkler, D. R. (1975). Educational achievement and school peer group composition. *Journal of Human Resources, 10,* 189–204.

Wise, A. (1979). *Legislated learning.* Berkeley, CA: University of California Press.

Wolff, R. P. (1969). *The ideal of the university.* Boston: Beacon Press.

Wolff, R. P. (1970). *In defense of anarchism.* New York: Harper & Row.

Zeigler, L. H., Kehoe, E., & Reisman, J. (1985). *City managers and school superintendents: Response to community conflict.* New York: Praeger.

Zeigler, L. H., Jennings, M. K., & Peak, G. W. (1974). *Governing American schools.* North Scituate, MA: Duxbury Press.

Zeigler, L. H., Tucker, H. J., & Wilson, L. A. (1976). How school control was wrested from the people. *Phi Delta Kappan, 57,* 534–539.

Author Index

Subject Index